Speculative Light

Speculative Light

The Arts of Beauford Delaney and James Baldwin

EDITED BY
AMY J. ELIAS

DUKE UNIVERSITY PRESS
Durham and London
2025

Printed in the United States of America on acid-free paper ∞
Project Editor: Livia Tenzer
Designed by A. Mattson Gallagher
Typeset in Minion Pro and Cronos Pro
by Westchester Publishing Services

Library of Congress Cataloging-in-Publication Data
Names: Elias, Amy J., [date] editor.
Title: Speculative light : the arts of Beauford Delaney and James Baldwin / edited by Amy J. Elias.
Description: Durham : Duke University Press, 2025. | Includes bibliographical references and index.
Identifiers: LCCN 2024026620 (print)
LCCN 2024026621 (ebook)
ISBN 9781478030058 (paperback)
ISBN 9781478024873 (hardcover)
ISBN 9781478059042 (ebook)
Subjects: LCSH: Delaney, Beauford, 1901–1979. | Baldwin, James, 1924–1987. | Arts, Black. | Aesthetics, Black. | African American gay people—France—Biography. | African American painters—France—Biography. | African American authors—France—Biography. | LCGFT: Biographies.
Classification: LCC NX652.A37 S64 2025 (print) | LCC NX652.A37 (ebook) | DDC 759.4 [B]—dc23/eng/20240919
LC record available at https://lccn.loc.gov/2024026620
LC ebook record available at https://lccn.loc.gov/2024026621

Cover art: Beauford Delaney, *Portrait of James Baldwin* (detail), 1965. Oil on canvas, 25½ × 21¼ in. (64.8 × 54 cm). Chrysler Museum of Art, Norfolk, VA. Museum purchase, 2015.28. © Estate of Beauford Delaney, by permission of Derek L. Spratley, Esquire, Court Appointed Administrator.

This book is dedicated to
Beauford Delaney
and James Baldwin,
and to all who work for justice,
teach wisdom,
and create beauty in our world.

CONTENTS

IV. Continuing Influence

ILLUSTRATIONS

FIGURES

PLATES

ACKNOWLEDGMENTS

Coordinating the various parts of this project has been challenging as well as exciting, and I am extremely grateful to all who worked with me in so many different ways. Most importantly, I would like to thank the contributors to this volume. Their brilliance, generosity, and patience have been exemplary, and I am humbled and grateful to have been able to work with such amazing scholars.

I would like to give heartfelt thanks to Derek Spratley, Esquire, Court Appointed Administrator for the Estate of Beauford Delaney, for his help with image permissions, for setting up an amazing exhibition of never-before-seen work by Beauford Delaney in the University of Tennessee Student Union Gallery during the 2020 Delaney-Baldwin symposium, and for becoming a wonderful community friend during all phases of this project. I would also like to thank those galleries, institutions, and individuals that have provided permission to reproduce Delaney's work, most notably Derek Spratley and the Delaney Estate; the Michael Rosenfeld Gallery in New York; the Knoxville Museum of Art; the Museum of Modern Art; SCAD Museum of Art; the Art Institute of Chicago; the Chrysler Museum of Art; the Tate Museum; the Guggenheim Museum; Clark Atlanta University Art Museum; the Memorial Art Gallery at the University of Rochester; the Terra Foundation for American Art; the Smithsonian American Art Museum; David Leeming; Henry Louis Gates Jr.; Beatrice Cazac; Statens Museum for Kunst Copenhagen; Národní galerie Praha; l'Institut Giacometti; Getty Images; Sandra McPherson; the Robert Mann Gallery; *Playbill* magazine; and the Artists Rights Society.

This collection grew out of a three-day symposium, "In a Speculative Light: The Arts of James Baldwin and Beauford Delaney," funded in part by a 2019 National Endowment for the Humanities (NEH) Connections Grant, which enabled me to bring twenty-six scholars to the University of Tennessee (UT) campus at Knoxville in February 2020 for an extraordinary event linking the university, the public, and scholars of international renown. I am grateful to the NEH for that support. I would also like to acknowledge support for this symposium from units within the University of Tennessee, Knoxville: the Denbo Center for Humanities and the Arts; the Better English Fund of the UT Department of English; the Office of Research, Innovation, and Economic Development; the Frieson Black Cultural Center; the Mildred Haines and William Elijah Morris Lecture Endowment of the College of Arts and Sciences; the UT Office of Diversity and Engagement; and the UT Office of the Vice President for Research, Outreach and Economic Development. The symposium linked the Denbo Center to members of Knoxville's Delaney Project: Gathering Light, who became continuing community partners, and now to the Knoxville Delaney Legacy Project, which is based on university and community partnerships nurtured through the early Delaney Project. I would like to acknowledge and thank everyone for their welcoming hospitality, unflagging energy, and creative, community-oriented souls: Sylvia Peters, chair of the Delaney Project: Gathering Light; the Reverend Reneé Kesler, director of the Beck Cultural Exchange Center and now leading the Delaney Legacy Project; Emily Anderson of Marble City Opera; Brandon Gibson (rest in peace); Warren Dockter, Steve Cotham, and others at the East Tennessee Historical Society; Jack Neely of the Knoxville History Project; Michael and Evelyn Gill; and Alan and Pat Rutenberg. I am honored to know Monique Wells of Les Amis de Beauford Delaney; everyone working on subjects related to Beauford Delaney recognizes her invaluable ongoing work to resurrect, publicize, and archive information about Delaney's art.

The Knoxville Museum of Art (KMA) has also been a key partner, and I would like to thank former KMA director David Butler for his support and friendship as well as for working with me on the extraordinary opening-night symposium keynote and reception with Hilton Als at KMA. I am thrilled that Stephen Escar Smith, dean of libraries at UT, has been able to work with the Delaney Estate, the Beck Cultural Exchange Center, and KMA to acquire the archive of Delaney's personal papers for future public use, and I am grateful for any role that the UT symposium and the efforts of the Denbo Center played in that.

No one deserves more thanks from me than Stephen C. Wicks, Barbara W. and Bernard E. Bernstein Curator at KMA and curator of the extraordinary 2020 KMA exhibition *Beauford Delaney and James Baldwin: Through the Unusual Door*, with which we synced the UT symposium. I have never met a more generous and knowledgeable collaborator than Stephen: he has worked on all phases of this project with me with unflagging goodwill, energy, and preeminent expertise. He has been essential to advising me and my staff on permissions for images reproduced in the present volume, to the point that he could be named artistic consultant for the volume. Furthermore, his willingness to share, absolutely freely, his twenty-year work on Beauford Delaney with others has launched careers (often with little acknowledgment) and will continue to launch publications on Delaney well into the future. I would also like to thank Joan Murray, former staff at the Denbo Center, who worked with me unstintingly to put together the 2020 Baldwin-Delaney symposium. Emily Harrison worked as my graduate research assistant on both the symposium and all phases of the related book project. Thank you, Emily, for always doing exemplary work, meeting deadlines, working extraordinarily well with others, coordinating permissions mailings and documents, and putting up with my constant requests for charts, workflow documents, and editing tasks.

We held the UT symposium a few weeks before the COVID-19 pandemic struck the world and before the United States melted down politically and socially over lockdowns, Black Lives Matter protests, and incendiary political rhetoric from our highest elected public officials. The scholars represented in this volume overcame extraordinary mental and sometimes physical challenges to see this publication through. I thank all of the contributors for their perseverance, generosity, and commitment to this project. I also thank Laura Jaramillo and Livia Tenzer at Duke University Press and especially editor Courtney Berger for her continuing faith in this project, which took longer than it normally would, given the world-historical events in which it incubated. Thank you also to the two anonymous reviewers of the book proposal and manuscript; your suggestions have made the book better.

This book was conceived in a time of plenty but also a time of silenced voices. It was birthed through a scholarly event built on collegiality and care and put together in a time of pandemic and outrage. One can hope that it is read in a time of renewal and freedom. I think Beauford Delaney and James Baldwin would appreciate all of that, and I thank them both, profusely, for what they brought to these historical moments, and after.

INTRODUCTION

Speculative Light

The Arts of Beauford Delaney and James Baldwin

Amy J. Elias

I do know that great art can only be created out of love.

James Baldwin

Delaney's world is less programmatic in its construction and ultimately more about love.

Pamela Wye

The chapters in this volume examine the work of two famous and unique US artists—the painter Beauford Delaney (1901–79) and the author James Baldwin (1924–87). Delaney and Baldwin met in 1940 at Delaney's Greene Street apartment in New York City when Baldwin was a teenager and

Delaney was thirty-nine years old. They were friends, even family, for almost forty years. Very little to date has been published about their relationship, yet in fact the lifelong Delaney-Baldwin friendship was instrumental in shaping how these world-famous artists conceptualized creative life and the form and social meaning of art. Baldwin found in Delaney a father figure, an artistic genius, and model of perseverance as a southern, gay, Black man; he wrote that "Beauford never gave me any lectures, but he didn't have to—he expected me to accept and respect the value placed upon me."[1] In a 1984 interview printed in *Paris Review*, Baldwin notes that Delaney "taught me how to see, and how to trust what I saw."[2] Baldwin's short story collection *Going to Meet the Man* (1965) and his children's book *Little Man, Little Man* are dedicated to Delaney, and Delaney is included in the dedication to *No Name in the Street* (1972). In Delaney's last years in a sanitarium in France, Baldwin was appointed one of his primary trustees and helped see to his needs. A famous picture by Max Petrus taken in 1976, shortly before Delaney's death, shows them standing together in a garden, gently holding hands.[3] Baldwin wrote eloquently of the older painter in his 1985 essay "The Price of the Ticket": "Beauford was the first walking, living proof, for me, that a black man could be an artist. In a warmer time, a less blasphemous place, he would have been recognized as my Master and I as his Pupil. He became, for me, an example of courage and integrity, humility and passion."[4] As the essays in this volume make clear, Delaney educated a young Baldwin about light as both inner illumination and artistic trope: remembering Delaney teaching him about the beauty in ordinary street life, Baldwin wrote, "He is a great painter, among the very greatest."[5]

We know less of Delaney's feelings about Baldwin, but it is clear from his letters and long companionship with the writer that he considered Baldwin to be family. Baldwin's influence on Delaney is asserted by David Leeming, whose personal relationship with both artists and former position as Baldwin's secretary gave him access to their meetings and their correspondence (see his chapter in this collection and his books *James Baldwin: A Biography* [1994] and *Amazing Grace: A Life of Beauford Delaney* [1998]). Delaney, of a generation that felt viscerally the policies of Jim Crow, found in Baldwin a powerful intellectual with a fearless social conscience committed to civil rights causes. He also found a spiritual partner and muse who provided emotional comfort, stability, and creative validation. A now-famous Delaney painting titled *Dark Rapture* (1941; plate 1) is known as the first of many portraits of Baldwin that Delaney would complete during his lifetime. Delaney took Baldwin to galleries and introduced him to friends, and he made the funeral arrangements after the death of Baldwin's father. Encouraged by Baldwin, who left the United States for France in the 1940s, Delaney left in 1953 and likewise settled in Paris. He lived in France until his death in 1979 and there created some of his best work. Delaney lived with Baldwin for a time, traveled to various locations with him over many years (including Istanbul), and kept in touch through correspondence.

Both men devoted their lives to art. Beauford Delaney and James Baldwin admonished everyone to look down from the shop signs dominating the public's gaze and outward from our mental gated communities; they asked us to contemplate a fallen brown leaf on the asphalt city sidewalk and to perceive its actual colors, its simplicity, and its natural truth. Penning essay after essay, page after page, Baldwin felt the urgency of a calling—what for him was an obsession to connect with the Word. And while Baldwin poured forth jeremiads like a holy stream, Delaney painted with equal urgency, equal fervor, "trying to say with my life the unsayable," for "art is the authority to induce what we cannot perceive."[6] In 1963, Delaney wrote to his friend, the author Henry Miller: "I pray for the courage to keep struggling to express in color the substance of what life is directing. The need in the world for beauty, harmony, good confidence, brotherhood, sunlight, music, humanity . . . was never so urgent. The creative life is holy."[7] Like Baldwin, Delaney created art as if his life depended on it, as if the world depended on it.

The profligacy of their efforts is astounding. Both Delaney and Baldwin spent themselves in words and colors, recklessly emptying themselves out into writing and painting and conversation. They broke their bodies and their minds straining toward expression, toward some connection that hovered—pleading, coy, cruel, disdainful, yet sometimes full of perfect love—behind the indices and icons that danced on their pages and canvases. Baldwin asserts in his short essay "The Price May Be Too High" (1969) that the Black artist wants "to reach something of the truth, and to tell it—to use his instrument as truthfully as he knows how,"[8] and much criticism has explored how Baldwin's own identity as a child preacher and son of a preacher affected both his writing style and his view of truth telling.[9] Both men felt art to be an almost religious calling. In the 1930s, while teaching at the Primitive African Art Center in New York, Delaney (along with his younger brother Joseph Delaney and the painters Ellis Wilson and Palmer Hayden) formed a group they called "The Saints."[10] In *Beauford Delaney: A Retrospective* (1978)—the exhibition catalogue for the important Studio Museum in Harlem show meant, in part, to raise money in the last years of the painter's life—Mary Schmidt Campbell writes, "Beauford Delaney. To a small coterie of artists, writers and critics he is 'Amazing and Invariable,' a master colorist, religious in his devotion to his craft. Because of his austere, impoverished life-style, a martyr."[11]

Martyrdom, however, does not come cheap. Moreover, as socially conceived, it participates both in human categories and in a logic of triumphant sacrifice disallowed Black persons by the operations of white supremacy.[12] Martyrdom was, to these two artists, too historically fraught a concept to encompass the figurative, discursive significations of the Black body and voice. As it does in both religious philosophies and Black aesthetics, the liminal logic of paradox and its psychological tensions informed Baldwin's speech and Delaney's brushstrokes. On the one hand, these two artists waged an ideological battle against the atrocities and legacies of US race history; on the other hand, they lived fully in a spiritual artistic life of becoming and connection. (Writes Baldwin, "Memory is a traitor and . . . life does not contain the past tense.")[13] They dedicated themselves to human community in lived time and space while the abrasive everyday, the intelligible and sensible world, buffeted them and rebuked them, relentlessly. Delaney and Baldwin lived in postwar America and France, and as Black, gay expatriates, both knew the duplicity and motivated cruelty of representation. Yet they also devoted their lives to representation, redefined in a pure space of art. To see Black life as something of beauty, if one knew how to look, and to voice its abjection without pronouncing abjection its permanent lot—this was, for both men, to carve out a third way, apart from simulation and co-optation. It was to engage in an act of politicized love.[14] Both grappled with an impossible task: to communicate and connect to truth through disciplinary formations and mediations that are structured to evade, undermine, pollute, and starve truth. If they served as cosmopolitan priests of art like many of the high modernists of their time, they themselves pursued a different heresy, a Gnostic rather than a Romantic one, reaching toward origins obscured under settler colonialism and genocide and errantly exploring the volatile and politicized relation between illusion and enlightenment in the afterlife of slavery.[15]

Baldwin's work was often autobiographical, and we should be curious about how his lifelong friend Delaney figures in his work as an unseen interlocutor, for Baldwin the writer and Delaney the painter cultivated a queer familial relation in both life and art.[16] In short stories such as Baldwin's famous "Sonny's Blues" (1957), for instance (discussed by a number of contributors to the present collection), the logic of the "abstract" musical form of jazz redefines the family relations of Baldwin's characters, just as Delaney's abstract art—particularly his abstract portraits—redefines relations with friends and artistic figures as familial ones.[17] In Baldwin's and Delaney's art as well as in their lives, we see a queered masculinity that creates a nonconsanguineous kindred, a nurturing care.[18] Fred Moten argues in *In the Break: The Aesthetics of the Black Radical Tradition* (2003) that the feminine is the denigrated natal origin of Blackness, and that "the ongoing loss or impossible recovery of the maternal" must occur through voiced significations that elide, blur, evade, and transgress the Word of the Western Father and the historical commodification of Blackness by the capitalist West.[19] Such an insight gives a new valence to biographer Leeming's observation of Baldwin in his last days: "He wanted men to take care of him—not, I was sure, because he disliked or mistrusted women, but because it was important to him that men express the feminine within themselves, that they adopt the kind of tender nurturing usually associated with women. We became 'disciples' of his gospel, 'gentle' men of the 'welcome table.' To put it another way, we ritually experienced the 'stink of love' in Giovanni's room."[20] The radical gesture in Baldwin's work is the countering of white racist formulations of criminalized, violent, hypersexualized Black masculinity with a gesture toward porosity and Black care between men—Sonny and Creole, but also James Baldwin himself and Beauford Delaney.

Delaney was always within Baldwin's kinship circle. If we take seriously Moten's injunction that Blackness "consent not to be a single being," then looking at how Baldwin wanted his circle to "express the feminine within themselves" opens us to a discussion of how the Baldwin-Delaney friendship—and the concentric circles of care in which it lived—offers a vision of Black masculinity and Black arts as multiple but not fungible, as moving beyond the trap of the signifying body to a presence in sound and light on a stage of deterritorialized Being.[21] Not Blackness as a universal, but *this* Blackness—the specific relation between two Black and gay men who conflate aesthetics with relative-ity and care in a specific relation to history—asks us to reflect on art and community in a new way.

In what ways can we analyze not only the blues or jazz aesthetic operating in Delaney's work but also the influence of Baldwin operating there, an enactment of a beauty that is "beautiful because it wasn't hurried and it was no longer a lament"?[22] In what ways can we understand the lifelong interchange between Baldwin and Delaney as creating a dialogic and synesthetic aesthetic that is *both* negation and affirmation—an aesthetic that might be described by the Latin *interesse*, or perhaps by Moten's "form and content of a dialectic of the not-in-between"?[23] How can we begin to understand the Baldwin-Delaney nexus as an imprecise relationality that "interrupts knowledge systems that seek to observe, index, know, and discipline blackness"?[24]

James Baldwin, Beauford Delaney: Scholarship and Sources

James Baldwin is by far the better known of the two friends. Born in Harlem, New York City, to a poor family with a stern preacher father at its head, Baldwin began writing at age thirteen. He left the United States for France when he was twenty-four years old, and in adulthood he adopted three primary locations as "home": New York, Paris, and Istanbul. He would pass away in Saint-Paul-de-Vence, another location he frequented in France. Because Baldwin's career was long and he was a prolific writer, because he was open about his homosexuality in a dangerously repressive time, because he became an icon of the US civil rights movement, and because he knew virtually everyone of consequence in the New Left political arena and the literary, Hollywood film, and theater worlds, the literature about him and his work is robust (and includes his own autobiographical nonfiction essays).

Baldwin's oeuvre is vast and varied—novels, plays, poems, and essays created from the 1940s to the mid-1980s. Today, scholarship about Baldwin is flourishing, with art exhibitions, international conferences, entire journals, and books devoted to his life and work.[25] New access to Baldwin's papers has contributed to the boom. Many of the writer's papers had been sealed by his estate and were purchased and made available to scholars only in 2017, by the New York Public Library's Schomburg Center for Research in Black Culture. Yet the letters have not been published, and correspondence with David Baldwin, Beauford Delaney, Lucien Happersberger, and Mary Painter is closed until 2036, while material related to Baldwin's unfinished manuscript "Remember This House"—the basis for the documentary film *I Am Not Your Negro* (2017), directed by Raoul Peck—is closed until 2026.[26]

Nonetheless, many today—and especially artists and critics working in film, the visual arts, and literary studies—see Baldwin's life and writing as fundamentally important to twenty-first-century Black Lives Matter, LGBTQIA, and other social-justice struggles. Justin Joyce, Dwight McBride, and Douglas Field, the authors of "Baltimore Is Still Burning: The Rising Relevance of James Baldwin" (2015), note, "The ongoing public interest in Baldwin's works, just as the seeming ever-readiness for journalists and pundits alike to call upon his critical voice in moments of tragedy, testifies to our need for an artist whose searing words can so uniquely lay bare the demands of a time, people, or nation."[27] Examples abound. In 2015—amid the years of police shootings of Michael Brown and Walter Scott—digital sound artists Mendi and Keith Obadike created *Blues Speaker [for James Baldwin]*, a twelve-hour work of digital sound shown on the walls of a New School university building and based on Baldwin's short story "Sonny's Blues."[28] Later, Peck's film *I Am Not Your Negro* adapted to the screen Baldwin's notes for an unfinished book centered on Malcolm X, Martin Luther King Jr., and Medgar Evers. But then came report after report of Black deaths at the hands of police and the 2020 riots resulting in part from the death of George Floyd, a forty-six-year-old Black man murdered by a white policeman in Minneapolis, Minnesota; Floyd's death galvanized nations and sparked worldwide Black Lives Matter protests. The world's eyes once again turned to Baldwin's prophetic writings, and during and after the COVID-19 pandemic, his work once again became fundamental to reading groups, course curricula, and TV news.[29] In 2023, in the aftermath of a global pandemic and worldwide protests, Darryl Pinckney introduced a three-film exhibition dedicated to Baldwin, *James Baldwin Abroad*, at Film Forum in New York City.[30] One could cite scores of other examples and specific instances of how Baldwin's work is influencing writers today (e.g., see Shawn Anthony Christian's chapter in this volume). On video sites such as YouTube, a full archive of Baldwin interviews, films, and commentaries is now available, including trailers for Terence Dixon's *Meeting the Man: James Baldwin in Paris* (1970), clips from Sedat Pakay's *James Baldwin: From Another Place* (1973), and recordings of Baldwin's television appearances and lectures. At the time of this writing, a biopic is being discussed based on Leeming's 1994 biography, with Billy Porter playing Baldwin and cowriting the script with Dan McCabe.[31] And even in popular culture Baldwin is ubiquitous. In 2004, the United States Postal Service created a first-class postage stamp dedicated to Baldwin. In the Emmy-winning comedy series *The Marvelous Mrs. Maisel*, we saw a "Shy Baldwin" (a mirror image of the real Baldwin, for this "Baldwin" is a closeted Black man who through the late 1950s and early 1960s entertains white club-goers in segregated hotels at which he himself can't stay); and on social media platforms such as Twitter, Baldwin references abound.[32] Indeed, by 2017, Jennifer Schuessler could note that "James Baldwin died in 1987, but his moment is now. His books are flying off the shelves. . . . Baldwin's prophetic essays on race read like today's news."[33]

There is also a new interest in Baldwin as a cross-disciplinary artist, a writer intimately involved with music, visual arts such as film and photography, and performance. Baldwin's 1964 collaboration with the photographer Richard Avedon, *Nothing Personal*, was reissued in 2017 with an introduction by Hilton Als; it collects Avedon's photographs and presents a four-part essay by Baldwin on love, racism, and social ills. Als himself (see his chapter in this collection) curated the 2019 installation *God Made My Face: A Collective Portrait of James Baldwin* at David Zwirner Gallery in New York City; the installation presented some work by Delaney but also put Baldwin into conversation with filmic artists and painters such as Njideka Akunyili Crosby, Diane Arbus, Avedon, Alvin Baltrop, Marlene Dumas, Ja'Tovia Gary, Glenn Ligon, Alice Neel, Cameron Rowland, Kara Walker, and James Welling.[34] Artists have long referenced Baldwin in their visual work, and one sees Baldwin's long-term influence today in contemporary works such as Glenn Ligon's *Stranger (Full Text) #1* (2020–21), a diptych that measures 10 feet high and 45 feet long (3 × 13.7 m), from his *Stranger* series, which he began in 1997 and features stenciled excerpts from Baldwin's 1953 *Harper's Magazine* essay "Stranger in the Village." One might also cite Don Bachardy's 1964 sketch of Baldwin, Jack Witten's *Black Monolith I, a Tribute to James Baldwin* (1988), or Garrett Rittenberg's *Portrait of James Baldwin* (2018), among the scores of references and influences.[35]

Yet for the most part, while Baldwin's film criticism has been examined, there is a dearth of commentary about Baldwin and painting/sculpture. We do see him discussing African arts in the Center for African Art's 1987 *Perspectives: Angles on African Art*, where ten rather famous people involved in the arts were asked to choose, and give their impressions of, ten African art objects. As Center founder Susan Vogel notes in the exhibition catalogue, which was published the year of Baldwin's death, Baldwin "is clearly drawn to sculptures that have a narrative quality, that show more than one figure, often in interaction—a rare feature in African art."[36] He also struggles to think of the stories or narrative scenes these figures represent ("It's all done in another vocabulary which I am not equipped to try, and I wouldn't even attempt to articulate"), but he often aligns the art objects with a Black diasporic history ("This art speaks directly to me out of my maligned and dishonored past"). What is interesting is Baldwin's voicing (in 1987, eight years after Delaney's death) of a statement about form and content that crosses through his earlier work and aligns him with Delaney's theory of color and the artist's deep connection to the subjects of his work: "The artist's work is his intention. There's this curious dichotomy in the West about form and content. The form *is* the content. I think the work of artists is to be useful . . . to have them on the wall—you walk in and you are among friends."[37]

This was how Delaney's apartments often looked: the poor rooms draped in white sheets and hung with his paintings of friends and beloved locales—rooms known, moreover, as places of unceasing, generous talk and companionship, where "you walk in and you are among friends." Yet while he was internationally recognized as a master painter during his lifetime, Delaney was almost lost to history. Born and taught to draw in Knoxville, Tennessee, he became a central figure in Boston, New York, and Paris high-art circles, exhibiting in Europe and in the United States. He was beloved among writers, painters, and filmmakers; promoted by numerous patrons of the arts (such as American cultural attaché Darthea Speyer); and befriended by notable figures such as Georgia O'Keeffe (who drew charcoal and pastel portraits of Delaney in 1943), Carl Van Vechten (who took portraits of Delaney in 1953), Countee Cullen, Louis Armstrong, Romare Bearden, and, later, Henry Louis Gates Jr. He painted (sometimes from memory) writer Jean Genet, singer Marian Anderson, and the surrealist poet Stanislas Rodanski. By the 1970s, he had seen his work at the Whitney Museum in New York and the Smithsonian's National Portrait Gallery, in *Playboy* magazine, at the National Center of Afro-American Artists in Dorchester, Massachusetts, and at the University of Texas Art Museum, while *Jet* magazine referred to him as the "dean" of African American painters.[38] And, of course, there was the friendship with Baldwin. In a 1976 interview with *Essence*, Baldwin noted that "the most important person in my life [as a writer] was and is a very great but not very well-known Black painter named Botha [*sic*] Delaney."[39] Delaney often was referred to as a figure of inspiration and wisdom; he cultivated an urbane, generous demeanor and a tutelary one with protégés, and his outwardly monastic life and his complete dedication to his painting led many to see him as a wise elder. Moving among luminaries, Delaney nonetheless always lived in extreme poverty and was plagued by mental illness throughout his life, hearing inner voices that mocked and condemned him both for his Blackness and for his homosexuality.

The earliest treatments of Delaney's artistry appeared in publications such as the now famous and much quoted encomium *The Amazing and Invariable Beauford DeLaney*, written by Henry Miller in 1945. Miller and Delaney were lifelong friends. On the occasion of Miller's eightieth birthday in 1971, the Centre Culturel Américain in Paris, affiliated with the University of California, Los Angeles, hosted an exhibition in tribute to the writer, *Les amis parisiens de Henry Miller*, in which Delaney showed his *Portrait de Henry Miller* and six other works, in the company of artists Brassaï, Grégoire

Michonze, and Hans Reichel, as well as a film by Robert Snyder titled *The Henry Miller Odyssey*.[40]

In a 1958 issue of *Preuves*, in one of the very rare instances in which he wrote about his views publicly, Delaney appears as a commentator on "la culture noire" in a forum (in French) organized by Jean-José Marchand and in the company of Ralph Ellison, Davidson Nicol, Gilbert Gratiant, Richard Wright, and Richard Gibson.[41] Later, James Jones and James Baldwin wrote commentaries on Delaney's exhibition at the Galerie Lambert in the Île Saint-Louis. In Delaney's last years, Richard A. Long and others traveled to Paris to rescue more than sixty of his paintings that had been locked in his abandoned apartment by the French government as collateral for delinquent accounts; those paintings formed the basis of the historic exhibition *Beauford Delaney: A Retrospective* held in 1979 at the Studio Museum in Harlem. For the most part, in fact, both during his lifetime and posthumously, essays about Delaney's work appear in catalogues of museum and gallery exhibitions devoted solely or largely to him.[42]

Tragically, Delaney died in 1979, in Paris, in Sainte-Anne Hospital for the Insane, and was buried in something like a pauper's grave outside of the city. Tributes, however, surfaced both toward the end of his life and after his death. For example, writing in 1973, the jazz poet, painter, and trumpeter Ted Joans published an homage to Delaney in *Black World* magazine. In that brief piece, noting that he first became acquainted with Delaney's work through a 1948 article in the short-lived magazine *Our World*, Joans wrote that Delaney and Jacob Lawrence "were the only *consistent* Afroamerican artists on the scene" in the 1940s and that "one has nothing to fear from the paintings of Beauford Delaney but the truth."[43] In December 1976, after visiting Delaney at Saint Anne's, Joans wrote a poem, "In Thursday Sane," in a used copy of Amos Tutuola's *The Palm-Wine Drinkard* (1952); it was found in a used bookstore by poet Sandra McPherson in 1999 and published by her in 2001 (see figures I.1a–c).[44] In the poem, Joans calls "Beaufordelaney" "the best / Oldest modern Black painter / In the West" and expresses regret that Delaney was being held, seemingly wrongfully, in Saint Anne's, "In spite of B.D. not being / Insane / In any way that he should be." As Delaney biographer Leeming later makes clear, however, Delaney suffered immensely from auditory hallucinations and major health problems, had attempted suicide, and by the late 1970s was incapable of living on his own. Leeming records how Baldwin and other friends rallied around Delaney, trying to find a way for the impoverished artist to be safe and have dignity in his last years.

After Delaney's death, his work was too frequently neglected on the international arts scene. Yet a number of exhibitions—often curated by those who knew him—featured his paintings.[45] He had been, and continues to be, championed by the Paul Facchetti Gallery in Paris and by the Michael Rosenfeld Gallery in New York.[46] According to Monique Wells, by 2010 the Michael Rosenfeld Gallery had mounted more than twenty-five exhibitions that included some work by Delaney; the most recent at the time of this writing was *Be Your Wonderful Self: The Portraits of Beauford Delaney*, held in 2022.[47] Central to Delaney scholarship, however, has been Leeming's biography, *Amazing Grace*, published almost twenty years after the artist's death and the first (and for many years the only) book on his life and work. A meticulous work of integrity and sympathy, it has supplied almost all details of Delaney's life to subsequent scholars, given that Delaney's papers were for a long time in disarray and, later, not available to the public. A few more tributes also appeared at this time: in 1999, for example, Delaney's friend the Beat poet Cid Corman published *Tributary: Poems*, a book about Delaney and his work that included fifty short poems and five color plates of the artist's paintings (*The Burning Bush*, 1941; *Self Portrait*, 1944; *Chartres*, 1954; *Untitled, Clamart* 1961; and *Yellow Cypress*, 1972). The poems, dedicated to gallerist Philippe Briet, include references to Henry Miller and to James Baldwin.[48]

For the most part, however, after his death discussion by the general public about Delaney's work was muted. While the Delaney estate has been working diligently for twenty years to collect, curate, store, and sell the work, and while prominent galleries continue to champion it, two projects—one centered in the Paris and one in the United States—helped to garner public attention and generate interest among collectors and auction houses. The first comprises Les Amis de Beauford Delaney and the Wells International Foundation, both led by the American entrepreneur Monique Wells, whose research and writing led to her uncovering the story of Delaney's unmarked grave. In 2009 she founded Les Amis de Beauford Delaney as a French and US nonprofit association that helped launch a Paris exhibition of Delaney's work. The Wells International Foundation announced in 2020 that a full-length documentary film on Delaney, *Beauford Delaney: So Splendid a Journey*, was in preproduction.[49] The second, based in Knoxville, birthplace of Beauford and his brother, the likewise renowned painter Joseph Delaney, is the Delaney Project: Gathering Light, formed as a consortium of business, public, and educational entities working to make Knoxville an international center for Delaney studies.[50] That enterprise is now complemented by the Delaney Legacy Project, following the purchase in 2022 of the Beauford

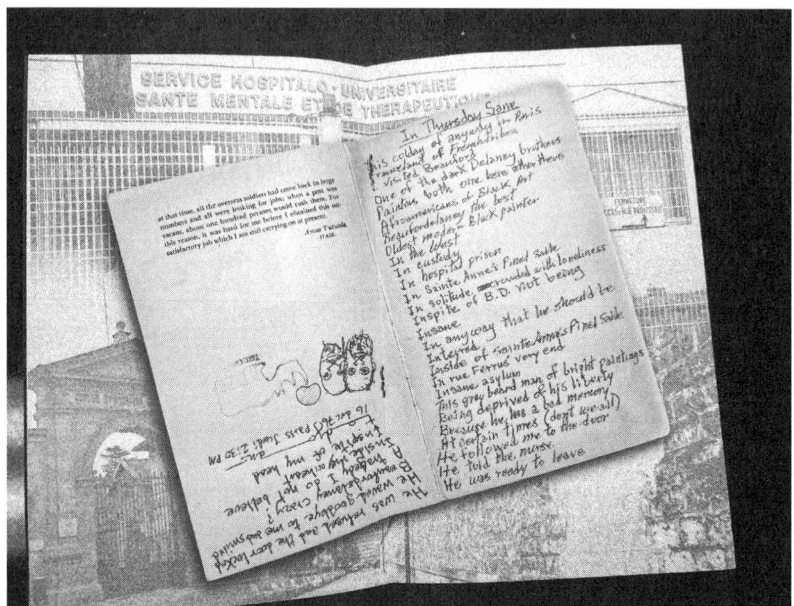
SERVICE HOSPITALO-UNIVERSITAIRE
SANTE MENTALE ET DE THERAPEUTIQUE
at that time, all the overseas soldiers had come back in large numbers and all were looking for jobs; when a post was vacant, about one hundred persons would rush there. For this reason, it was hard for me before I obtained this unsatisfactory job which I am still carrying on at present.
Amos Tutuola
In Thursday Sane
This colday of anyway in Paris
Franceland of Frenchtribes
I visited Beauford
One of the dark Delaney brothers
Painters both one here other there
Afroamericans of Black Art
Beaufordelaney the best
Oldest modern Black painter
In the West
In custody
In hospital prison
In Sainte Anne's Pinel Salle
In solitude, crowded with loneliness
Inspite of B.D. not being
Insane
In anyway that he should be
Interred
Inside of Sainte Anne's Pinel Salle
In rue Ferrus' very end
Insane asylum
This grey beard man of bright paintings
Being deprived of his liberty
Because he has a bad memory
At certain times (don't we all)
He followed me to the door
He told the nurse
He was ready to leave
He was refused and the door locked
He waved goodbye to me and smiled
Paris Jeudi 2:30 PM

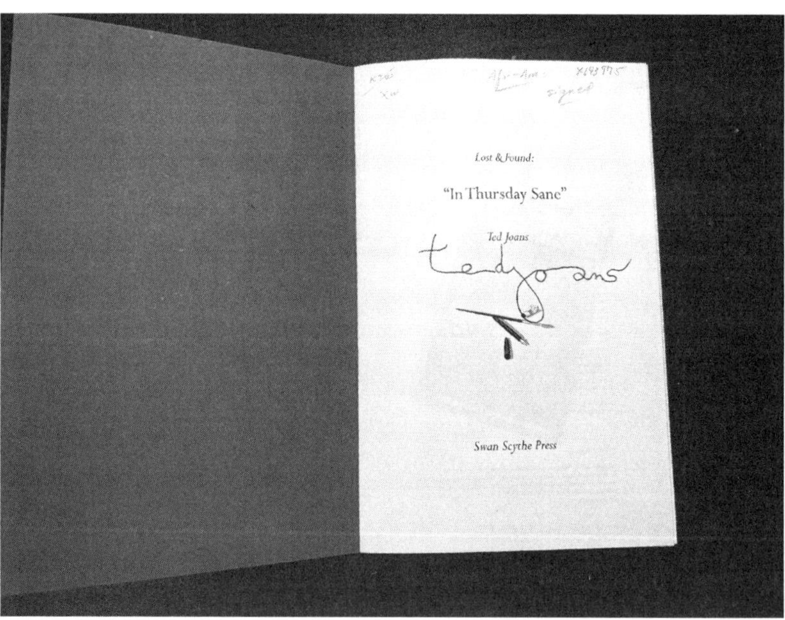
Afro-Am
signed
Lost & Found:
"In Thursday Sane"
Ted Joans
tedjoans
Swan Scythe Press

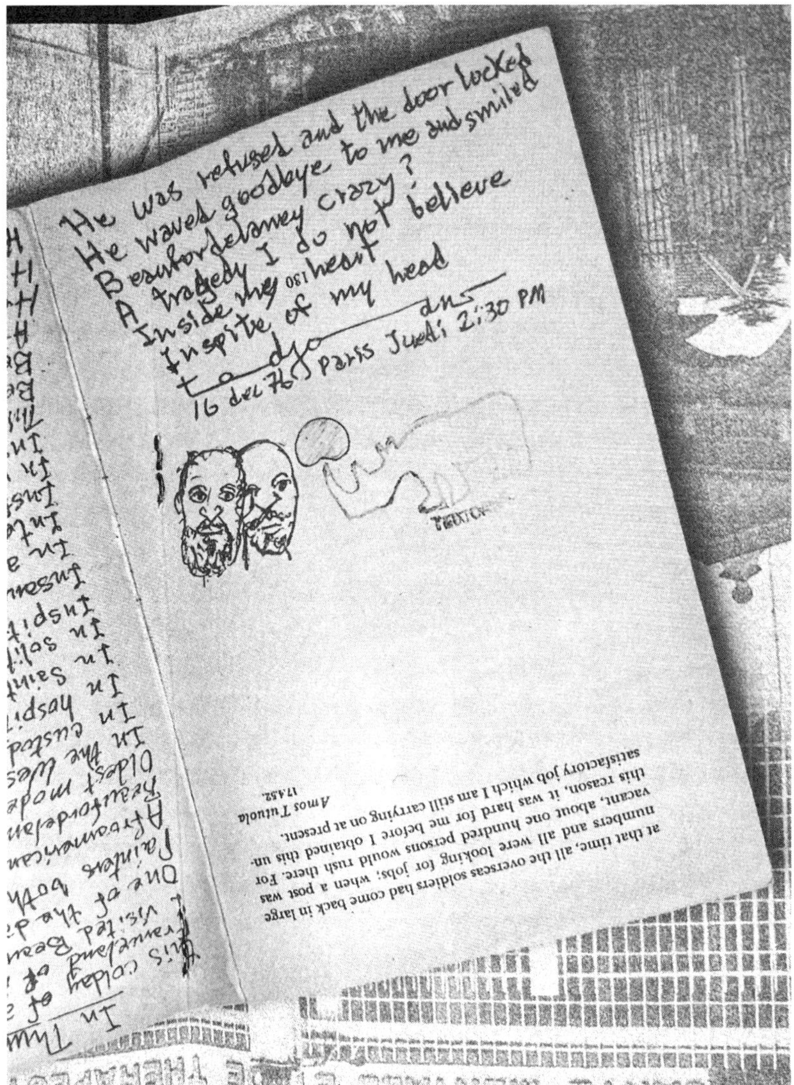

I.1a–c

(*opposite, top*) Ted Joans, "In Thursday Sane," drawing and poem inscribed in Amos Tutuola's *The Palm-Wine Drinkard* (London: Faber and Faber, 1952); background image, asylum in Paris where Beauford Delaney stayed. (*opposite, bottom*) *In Thursday Sane*, edited by Sandra McPherson (Davis, CA: Swan Scythe Press, 2001). Courtesy of Sandra McPherson/Swan Scythe Press. (*above*) Detail of drawing and inscribed poem.

Delaney papers by the University of Tennessee, Knoxville, and by a partnership with Knoxville's Beck Cultural Exchange Center, headed by the Reverend Reneé Kesler. The Beck purchased one of the Delaney family homes, and at the time of this writing is working to create an artist residency, center of excellence, and museum in that space.[51]

By 2015, one could find the kitschy *Beauford Delaney: A Folio of Notecards* through the Michael Rosenfeld Gallery's online gift shop, perhaps signaling that Delaney's art had truly begun to reenter the mainstream.[52] Certainly high-art circles had returned to his work. The US artist Glenn Ligon curated a 2015 exhibition at the Tate Liverpool titled *Glenn Ligon: Encounters and Collisions* that featured two works by Delaney (one a portrait of Baldwin) and put Delaney in the company of the abstract expressionists. The Wells International Foundation helped lay a stone at Delaney's unmarked grave at Thiais Cemetery and placed commemorative markers in Paris, and in 2016, with Columbia Global Centers, it organized the first solo exhibition of Delaney's works in France since a show organized by Darthea Speyer in 1992. In 2019, writer Hilton Als curated an exhibition on Baldwin (*God Made My Face: A Collective Portrait of James Baldwin*) at the David Zwirner Gallery that prominently featured three paintings by Delaney, including *Dark Rapture*, his 1941 portrait of a teenage Baldwin (plate 1).[53] In 2020, the Knoxville Museum of Art held a groundbreaking exhibition of Delaney's work that for the first time put the artist and Baldwin together in a substantial way: *Beauford Delaney and James Baldwin: Through the Unusual Door*. Today, Delaney's paintings hang prominently among modernist and postwar works in New York's Museum of Modern Art, the Smithsonian American Art Museum, and the National Portrait Gallery (notably featuring one of his portraits of Baldwin). However, for a number of reasons—because Delaney's estate has been largely closed to scholars, because Baldwin's correspondence with Delaney is still under a twenty-year seal, and because Delaney's reputation waned after his death—critical writing about the painter is appearing only now, with this renewed interest in his work and with the flourishing of Baldwin studies across disciplines. One might argue that Fred Moten's 2003 treatment of Delaney in his paradigm-shifting book *In the Break* reignited *academic* interest in Delaney's work, and it is encouraging that some of Delaney's papers are now available to scholars at the University of Tennessee. At least one new scholarly biography, based on access to that and other archives, is soon to be published. Today, Delaney's work is just starting to be aligned with discussions of queer art and Black aesthetics and discussed in relation to philosophical writing.[54]

Beauford and Jimmy, Together

It is not a coincidence that Moten begins his chapter on Baldwin in *In the Break* with an anecdote concerning Delaney.[55] In Baldwin's 1985 essay "The Price of the Ticket," he wrote, "If Beauford and Miss [Marian] Anderson were a part of my inheritance, I was a part of their hope," and noted Delaney's "absolute integrity: I saw him shaken many times and I lived to see him broken but I never saw him bow."[56] The two, Baldwin and Delaney, were friends for almost forty years, and their lives and works were incalculably altered by their relationship. Yet there is little published scholarship about the relationship, and to date there is no full-length study about Baldwin and Delaney as artists and friends. In 2004 Rachel Cohen included two chapters about Delaney in her award-winning book *A Chance Meeting*, speculating about Delaney's documented meetings with W. E. B. Du Bois and Baldwin. The Baldwin chapter is a short meditation on the two men that draws heavily from information in the Leeming biographies and Delaney's journal. Cohen saw that the Delaney-Baldwin relationship should be a lens through which we analyze the respective works of these two midcentury artists, yet little work has been done since.[57] *Speculative Light: The Arts of Beauford Delaney and James Baldwin* asserts that the lifelong Delaney-Baldwin friendship was in fact instrumental to the aesthetics of both artists, affecting how they each saw the world and conceptualized the artistic life. This most significant relationship in the lives of these two American artists had a vital impact on their respective work and cultural legacies.

As noted above, many of Baldwin's writings throughout his career contain references to Delaney—for example, in his 1965 essay "On the Painter Beauford Delaney" and in "The Price of the Ticket"—and one sees glimpses of Delaney in photographs of Baldwin and throughout the biographical film about Baldwin *The Price of the Ticket*, which premiered at the Sundance Film Festival in 1990 and has been broadcast in more than forty countries to date.[58] In criticism, however, only Leeming's respective 1990s biographies of the two friends extensively address how their relationship shaped their works and lives.[59] In 2020, Stephen C. Wicks curated the Knoxville Museum of Art's Delaney-Baldwin exhibition *Beauford Delaney and James Baldwin: Through the Unusual Door*, the catalogue for which includes a timeline that presents Delaney and Baldwin's entwined lives.[60] Funded by the Luce Foundation and the National Endowment for the Arts, the exhibition was a groundbreaking intervention in Delaney and Baldwin studies, one that featured more than forty-eight paintings in addition to works on paper, letters and photographs, and audiovisual recordings. The museum is now the holder of more than fifty paintings and works on paper by Delaney and is "a vital resource for the study, preservation, and promotion" of the artist's work.[61] In conjunction with the exhibition, as director of the Denbo Center for Humanities and the Arts at the University of Tennessee, Knoxville (then titled the UT Humanities Center), I ran a public, National Endowment for the Humanities–funded symposium, "In a Speculative Light: The Arts of James Baldwin and Beauford Delaney," that brought twenty-six scholars to Knoxville for presentations that form the basis of the present collection. At the time of this writing, the only published sources that bring Baldwin and Delaney together include Wicks's exhibition catalogue; one chapter in Cohen's *A Chance Meeting*; an article about Baldwin's short story "Sonny's Blues" that reads Delaney rather problematically into one of the key characters; Ligon's comments on his curatorial work for *Glenn Ligon: Encounters and Collisions* and in the exhibition catalogue for the Delaney-Baldwin exhibition in Knoxville; blog entries at Monique Wells's website Les Amis de Beauford Delaney; a one-page discussion in *Soul of a Nation: Art in the Age of Black Power* (2017), the catalogue from the Tate Modern exhibition of the same name that reprints parts of Baldwin's 1964 essay "Introduction to Exhibition of Beauford Delaney" for the Galerie Lambert in Paris; and forward-looking articles by Tyler T. Schmidt and James Smalls. Almost all of the work bringing Baldwin and Delaney together has been published in the past nine years.[62]

The chapters in the present collection underscore how the lifelong Delaney-Baldwin intellectual and familial relationship offers an extremely productive platform on which to construct new theoretical discussions about Black care, love and affect, queer and masculine identity, and synesthetic aesthetics. Both artists were sons of preachers from the American South, were prolific craftsmen who moved through many artistic genres and modes, were influenced by jazz and blues, were obsessed with the connotations of color and light, and were gay expatriates from the United States alienated by homophobia and racism that permeated society and the arts. Yet, though they shared all these commonalities, there are few studies that flesh out and historicize how Baldwin and Delaney's queer familial relation may revise how we understand Black masculinity, queer-of-color cultures, new Black aesthetics, or the development of postwar Black arts. As Delaney comes back onto the arts scene, critical race studies open up new ways to discuss the men's identities and relationships.

For example, both Baldwin and Delaney were deeply moved by jazz and explored synesthetic aesthetics—a concern of much Black aesthetic theory today. As noted in many of the chapters in the present collection, jazz appears throughout Baldwin's writing, as in his most-reprinted short story, "Sonny's Blues," and affected his writing patterns perhaps as much as did sermonic rhythms.[63] Baldwin strove to create words that rose above the marketplace and the colonial decimation of language and communication, phrases that resembled iconic images; Delaney labored to create images that spoke outside of the rules of visual representation, paintings that embodied the *jouissance* of Barthesian writing. Delaney once noted that "the painting has its own speech."[64] Delaney also spoke of "'composing and orchestrating' color" and showed his work in an exhibition called *L'âge du jazz* at the Musée Galliera in Paris in 1967.[65] Delaney illustrated W. C. Handy's *Unsung Americans Sung* (1944), a book of musical scores, poetry, sketches, essays, dramatizations, and assorted historical records that were to be seen as tributes to Black historical figures.[66] (Delaney had also painted Handy's portrait in 1939, and his large *Portrait of Harriet Tubman* [1953] may have followed from his sketch of Tubman in Handy's text.)[67] Moreover, during his lifetime, Delaney painted or sketched portraits and impressions of jazz artists such as Ethel Waters (*Ethel Waters*, 1940), Ella Fitzgerald (*Portrait of Ella Fitzgerald*, 1968; plate 26), and Charlie Parker (*Charlie Parker*, 1969, and *Charlie Parker Yardbird*, 1958; plate 10), as well as jazz clubs and jazz bands (e.g., *Jazz Quartet*, 1946). For Fred Moten, Delaney's Parisian work in fact is always marked by *sound*: his madness emerges as a synesthetic merging of voices in painted sound that manages to be a "surplus of content irreducible to identity." This surplus (the surplus meaning of Blackness itself under colonial domination, of a reference that has been denied through history) is embodied in what Delaney called his "voices" and "forces," an energy that "animates and awaits release from texts and canvases" in the form of a "phonic substance."[68] For Moten, Delaney's paintings strive to represent jazz in its fugitive resistance.

Moten reads Delaney's schizophrenia at least in part as the mark of both a historical legacy and an aesthetic radicalism: Delaney's painting is "driven by a fugitivity," a force and a sound that animates both jazz music and his canvases and lives in the impossible possibility of the voiced object.[69] Made into objects, denied subjectivity, Blackness finds vehicles of (oxymoronic) objectified resistance, giving human *objects* a new form of *agency* that moves not against or in opposition to dominance (as would a subject) but alongside it and within it, redefining and translating it in the manner of grammatical apposition. This is not to render Black arts incomprehensible but rather to resituate them as the ground (rather than the legacy) of the avant-garde.

And in fact, both Delaney and Baldwin moved in modernist circles where formalist aestheticism was proselytized and rewarded—Delaney even more so than Baldwin, as he was the older of the two. They learned from these circles but also interrogated them, understanding that the avant-garde has been coded in art history if not as a whites-only club, then at least as a white creative rebellion with which others might join. In contrast, what Delaney and Baldwin both asserted was that "the avant-garde is a black thing" and "that blackness is an avant-garde thing."[70] For Moten, Delaney's work exemplifies how a Black Parisian cosmopolitanism underlying the European avant-garde is always marked by and speaks to "earlier migrations, arrivals, or rebirths": Delaney moves in "a multiply sited encounter between the European and African diasporas." Delaney's work gestures to how the expatriate avant-garde's move to the capital of the avant-garde, Paris, is always prefigured in early diasporic moves. Moten searches not for an opposition by artists to the colonial demand to move and speak elsewhere but for an "appositional" and "almost hidden" movement or gesture—one that is not the *spoken opposition* to the colonial aesthetic (since speech is already colonized by a colonial language and Blackness historically could not operate as pure opposition to whiteness) but "a gesture, a glance or glancing blow, that is the condition of possibility of a genuine aesthetic representation and analysis—in painting and prose—of that encounter."[71] Moten in fact reads Delaney's impasto technique—the thick layering of paint in his canvases—as a kind of glossolalia (speaking in an unknown language, or "tongues") that also is the layering sound of Black jazz music.

When we look at Baldwin's writing and hear his words in film and recordings, it is clear that this resistance is at the center of his art.[72] With Delaney, things are a bit more complicated. During his lifetime, it was difficult for Delaney to get critics to give his work the attention given to white painters, particularly those working out variations of abstract expressionism. Even Henry Miller's tribute to him privileges discussion of his Buddha-like personality over analysis of his work, as do many reviews of his work, such as the 1962 article in *Preuves* that noted, "His gaze is bright and lively like that of someone who has kept the gift of childhood. . . . Beauford-Delaney is all joy."[73] It is true that Delaney cultivated the image of the affable mentor, cosmopolitan, and bon vivant and depended upon the patronage of many white benefactors. It is also true that he did not engage with the political sphere radically, as did his friend Baldwin. However, the racist constructions of him as primarily a Black body and affable "nature" preclude analyzing the operations of the aesthetic in his art or considering how his work and life constructed an appositional resistance to the dominant political and arts cultures in which he moved. With Moten, we need to resituate Delaney's work—masterfully re-presenting the everyday—in relation to Saidiya Hartman's claim that "defamiliarizing the familiar" manages to "illuminate the terror of the mundane and quotidian rather than exploit the shocking spectacle," and we need to walk with her as she considers "the diffusion of terror and the violence perpetrated under the rubric of pleasure, paternalism and property."[74] There are some rare glimpses at Delaney articulating this apposition: in one of the few published statements that we have by him, he wrote, "For me, black culture today means the combination of spiritual, philosophical and artistic principles traditional to these peoples who, immersed in an atmosphere of tragedy—and in particular deprived of certain rights—have nevertheless retained their dignity, their magnanimity, and their interest in the complex problems of the twentieth century. What is called black culture is in fact an amalgamation of the heritage of these peoples with other cultures in which they were forced to learn."[75] More frequently, Delaney's resistance, anger, and despair were layered into the paintings themselves—his abstractions in particular standing somewhat to the side of both the abstract expressionism sweeping the New York of his time and the dominant trends of the European avant-garde. His abstractions and antirealist portraiture strive to represent the fugitive sound of the Black diasporic resistance through symbolic placement of African or historical references, gestural iconography, and use of color.

One of Delaney's paintings, *Untitled—1969*, strikingly illustrates this, as I have noted elsewhere.[76] *Untitled—1969* is a tempera work in a four-color palette dominated by the yellows and greens that Delaney long associated with light and life. The painting was done on newspaper—specifically, the front page of the May 24–25, 1969, edition of the *International Herald Tribune*, a daily published in Paris for English-speaking readers (figures I.2a–b).[77] This would have included Delaney, who was living in Paris at the time and who never completely mastered French. Delaney painted other works on newspaper and other nontraditional materials, sometimes because he could not afford canvas, but this work seems different. Delaney has folded the page so that the official state news at the top serves as the back of the painting, and

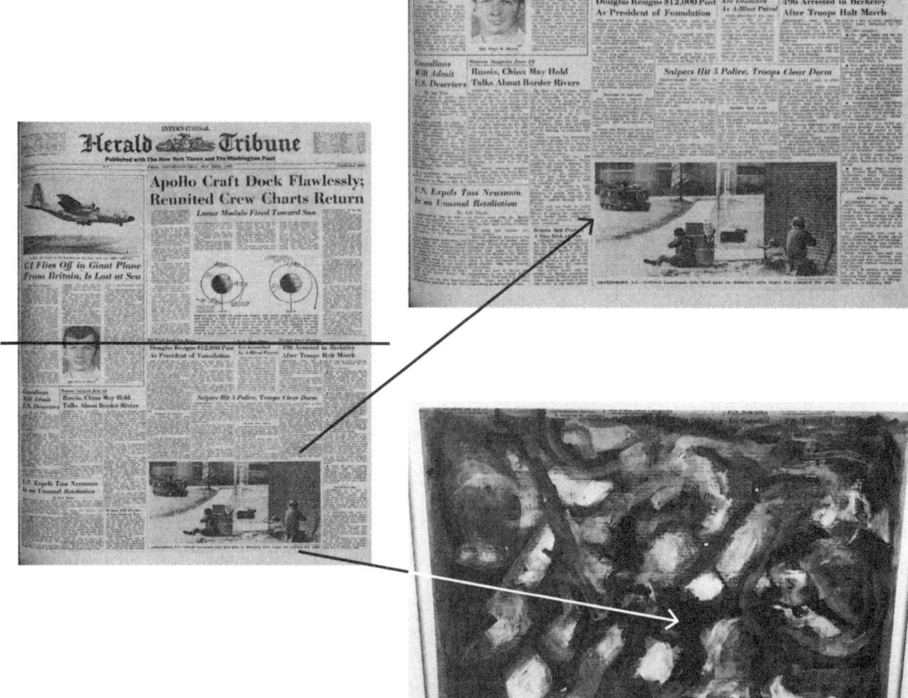

International Herald Tribune
Published with The New York Times and The Washington Post

Apollo Craft Dock Flawlessly; Reunited Crew Charts Return
Lunar Module Fired Toward Sun

GI Flies Off in Giant Plane From Britain, Is Lost at Sea

Douglas Resigns $12,000 Post As President of Foundation

496 Arrested in Berkeley After Troops Halt March

Guardians Will Admit U.S. Deserters

Russia, China May Hold Talks About Border Rivers

Snipers Hit 5 Police, Troops Clear Dorm

U.S. Expels Tass Newsman In an Unusual Retaliation

I.2a–c

(*a and b*) Front page, below-the-fold field, *International Herald Tribune*, May 24–25, 1969. (*c*) Beauford Delaney, *Untitled—1969*, 1969. Tempera on newspaper, 11½ × 16¾ in. (29.2 × 42.5 cm). Estate of Beauford Delaney by permission of Derek L. Spratley, Esquire, Court Appointed Administrator.

the bottom half serves as the top-facing "canvas," over which he paints an abstraction in yellow and greens. What is significant is that the newspaper stories on the bottom half of the page all concern political protests—specifically, the May 15 violence in Berkeley, California, on what became known as "Bloody Thursday," when Ronald Reagan sanctioned police to open fire on a large crowd of unarmed but angry protesters seeking to keep open People's Park community garden, and the 1969 Greensboro Uprising, a student protest following a May 23 assault by police and national guardsmen on students at North Carolina Agricultural and Technical State University, a Black college in Greensboro. As I have previously noted in more detail,

Delaney uses only the bottom half of the paper's front page as his canvas to foreground political stories of people's uprising. In this painting, "Delaney rejects the victimization of Black men, as he scrawls his colors of life over stories of death and violence. . . . He turns language into visual art, overwriting the official voice of public news with color and form."[78]

Art historians and literary critics have repeatedly noted the importance of light effects and light imagery—particularly the color yellow—to Delaney's paintings, referencing Baldwin's now famous anecdote about learning from Delaney the properties of light as a revelation about deep seeing and mindful connection to the quotidian.[79] Delaney painted scores of portraits, for example, that demanded both a representation of a person and a simultaneous expressionistic rendering of that person's inner being (painted in yellow or light colors). Delaney's paintings of African iconography and treatment of civil rights figures such as Rosa Parks use color as discourse, imbuing abstractionist aesthetics with historical reference furtively, fugitively, through a personal symbolism that runs alongside both political representation and abstractionist values (see the color plates in this volume). In the past decade, much has been written about "the everyday," particularly in relation to postwar poetry; less has been written about how "the everyday" itself needs to be intersectionally contextualized and how it may modulate the values of modernist aestheticism in the ways that Delaney and Baldwin demanded.

In *Untitled—1969*, Delaney seems deliberately to choose a type of "canvas" that will make visible political violence related in the mundane, prosaic terms of the everyday, of newspaper reporting. But he then paints over the articles with the colors of life and liberation to create a historical palimpsest, an object worked upon and reused for another purpose. He does so only a week after Baldwin's famous television interview with Dick Cavett, on May 16, 1969, and only a few months after the publication of Baldwin's February 2, 1969, *New York Times* piece, "The Price May Be Too High."[80] Delaney's painting and Baldwin's writing both underscore the plight of the Black artist in a white supremacist world. More needs to be done to show how both of these artists attempted to create a dialogue between art and life, artworks and people, beauty and truth, politics and aesthetics. The present collection is necessary because the lives and arts of these two internationally renowned Black artists embodied new perspectives on the complexity and unique performance of Black aesthetics that we are today just beginning to see critically and to historicize.

Speculative Light: The Arts of Beauford Delaney and James Baldwin

This collection presents original work by twenty internationally acclaimed critics and artists who explore how Baldwin and Delaney together and separately speculate on the present and bet on the future as artists who embrace a reconfigured subjectivity. It asks how they create spaces in their lives and in their artworks that allow thinking anew about Blackness and the social realities in which they move and how they wager and gamble on a different future through their understanding of the power of art. The collection is both extremely focused—on the work and lives of these two artists—and theoretically wide-ranging, for contributors have been asked to address the following questions, which we hope will shape further discussion of these artists' works:

1. *Arts History and Black Aesthetics.* How should we understand the delight in, and despair with, the exploration of light and color in Baldwin's and Delaney's works and lives? What frame is needed to understand their fascination with and withdrawal from pellucidity? Richard J. Powell has written that Delaney's colors have affective charge, indicative of emotional interiority: In what ways might form and affect merge or serve new aesthetic ends in these artists' works?[81] In what ways do expressionism and abstraction contend? How might the works of Baldwin or Delaney be seen to presage new definitions of Black aesthetics, such as new definitions of synesthesia or opacity or contemporary re-visionings of Black abstraction?
2. *Music and Sonic Arts.* How might we reconfigure our understandings of the arts of these two midcentury artists—or the aesthetics of their artistic surround—in relation to the sonic arts, specifically jazz and blues but also other kinds of sonic form? In what ways does "transmedial consonance" resonate through their respective works or shared aesthetics?[82] What roles do the sonic arts play in Black modernism and postwar arts, and how might these resituate Delaney or Baldwin historically, artistically, bodily, politically?
3. *Ethics and Social Values.* How might the friendship between these men be reassessed through the lens of Black care? In what ways do mentorship and love become redefined as an aesthetic relation? How does viewing them through the lens of affect help us to re-historicize Black creativity?

4 *Style and Genre.* What are the contexts and framing discourses that might allow us to reevaluate Baldwin's and Delaney's promiscuous play with genre, style, and form? How might their expatriate wanderings and their generic wanderings demand a new descriptive vocabulary? What are the stakes of their wager on a multiplicity of expression or a polyphony of discourse, or what Fred Moten has called a "categorial blur"?

5 *Gender and Sexuality.* What can queer theory now bring to our understanding of these artists and their productions, and vice versa? On what are they speculating in their cross-generational and improvisational familial/lovers' relation? In their lives and aesthetics, what is the resonance of exile as the basis for creative erotics?[83]

These questions link history and aesthetics through the work and lives of Baldwin and Delaney. But they also provide a link between these midcentury artists and current theoretical conversations. The nineteen chapters in the present volume address different subfields in art and literary studies, not only providing the first critical treatments of Delaney's work in relation to Baldwin's oeuvre but also illustrating how the arts—particularly Black arts—can inform one another while also addressing society in a time of radical change. The chapters are eclectic, following the specializations and interests of Baldwin's and Delaney's contemporary scholarly interlocutors.

The first part of the collection, "Circuits of Selfhood," focuses on biography and redefined subjectivity as shared and contested by Baldwin and Delaney—our understanding of Delaney and Baldwin in the world and how their relation to place and to others informs their respective works. We are honored to include a chapter by David Leeming, employed in his youth as a secretary to Baldwin and later, in his professorial role, as the authorized biographer of Baldwin and author of the only biography to date of Delaney. Leeming's contribution includes some key—and moving—stories drawn from these and other sources that illustrate how intertwined were the lives and worldviews of Baldwin and Delaney, and those artists' lives with his own. Pulitzer Prize–winning author Hilton Als, who hosted the 2019 New York exhibition *God Made My Face: A Collective Portrait of James Baldwin* at the David Zwirner Gallery in New York, contributes a meditation that he read as a keynote speaker at the 2020 Knoxville symposium, provoked by thinking about the Delaney-Baldwin friendship and queer malehood in relation to the artistic life. Ed Pavlić's chapter accounts for Baldwin's experience after leaving Hollywood in 1969, including months when he lived with Delaney in Istanbul and reengaged his private life after a whirlwind decade publicly negotiating American racial politics. Training her eye on a more specific site, Magdalena Zaborowska explores how Baldwin was "fathered" into becoming a revolutionary writer by Delaney, his artistic mentor, as he created a unique literary household in Saint-Paul-de-Vence, France, and composed toward the end of his life the "painterly" works *No Name in the Street* (1972), *The Devil Finds Work* (1976), and *Just above My Head* (1979).

The second part of the collection, "Synesthesia and Arts in Dialogue," presents chapters focused on a synesthetic approach to the arts that allows us to see how Delaney and Baldwin rethought the relations between painting, language, and music. "Synesthetic aesthetics" refers to multisensory experiments whereby one art form provokes insights into, or even is redefined as, another art form—to help audiences "hear" a painting or "see" music, for example, and thus creatively expand their perceptions of both art and the world. But a synesthetic approach also puts arts in dialogue in new ways, forcing us to consider how prose affects visual arts, or how musical rhythms and prose rhythms influence one another. In part 2 of the collection, Fred Moten considers the relationship between Delaney and Baldwin as a rigorous attention to surface, bringing together these artists' use of the colors blue, green, and yellow with the movements of the drummer in blues music. Likewise, Robert G. O'Meally explores how "the blues" is both colorful music and musical color in the two artists' works. D. Quentin Miller, in his chapter, illustrates how Baldwin's short story "Sonny's Blues" is a "visual story" that consistently uses the interplay between light and darkness and shows how the writer's attention to visual aesthetics was catalyzed and refined by Delaney's tutelage in the properties of light, while Walton M. Muyumba asserts a connection between the ubiquitous yellows in Delaney's work and light imagery within Baldwin's film criticism. Part 2 ends with two chapters about James Baldwin's 1976 children's book, *Little Man, Little Man: A Story of Childhood*. Building from his groundbreaking published work, Nicholas Boggs analyzes the collaboration between Baldwin and artist Yoran Cazac, the significance of the book's dedication, and how deeply Delaney's aesthetic vision influenced the final book. Robert Reid-Pharr then examines Cazac's *brulûge* (burning) painting technique and correlates this interest in fire with Delany's interest in light as the act of seeing/not seeing—a trope familiar to African American literature.

The third part, titled "Visibility, Performance, Abstraction," features chapters that focus more on the formal qualities of abstract arts. While abstract art is often taken by the popular imagination as an obfuscation of "realism," these chapters reframe claims in part 2 to explore how abstraction can paradoxically serve as a means toward making the self visible in new ways and toward a performative identity. Contributors play with the multiple connotations of visibility: artistic and creative success within the art world, Black visibility within racist culture, the visibility of politics within an abstract and purely aesthetic art object. Indie A. Choudhury focuses on Delaney's paintings in relation to a performance of Baldwin's play *Blues for Mister Charlie* (1964), demonstrating how performing Blackness configured codes about race and sexuality and enabled seeing Blackness differently. Rachel Cohen considers "visibility" as self-regard and self-reflection: she performs close readings of Delaney's *Self-Portrait* (1944; plate 3) and *Untitled (Village Street Scene)* (plate 6) and the early essays of Baldwin to consider the relationships between city streets and self-regard in these artworks. Monika Gehlawat examines Delaney's daring oscillation between abstract and figurative modes of painting, using the idea of "singularity" to describe a subjective viewpoint in Delaney's figurative paintings that links to a similar viewpoint in Baldwin's confessional testimony. Moving outward from the Delaney-Baldwin pairing, Abbe Schriber argues that for Delaney intimacy was an extension of seeing. She contends that his relationships with Baldwin and other close artist friends, such as Herbert Gentry, are essential to reading Delaney's paintings, where dense chromatic surfaces create an intimacy born not only of multisensory stimuli but also of affiliations and social exchanges embodied in the complexity of color. The last two chapters in part 3 ask us to consider Delaney's painting in relation to modernist aesthetics and the problem of "influence." Levi Prombaum's chapter asks us to consider modern art personas that Delaney cultivates in his portraiture, and he contests recurring claims about Delaney's "unoriginal" use of form. Prombaum asserts that in Delaney's portraits and Baldwin's novels, an aesthetics of "feeling" resounds rather than mimics modernist aesthetics. Stephen C. Wicks in turn posits that the Delaney-Baldwin friendship might recall the relation between Giacometti and James Lord, and might translate into something he calls "the Giacometti effect" in Delaney's painting.

The collection's last part, "Continuing Influence," points to the ways that Delaney and Baldwin's speculative light continues to illuminate the arts today. Tyler T. Schmidt discusses Delaney's *Self-Portrait in a Paris Bath House* (plate 30) as an approach to queer subjectivity influencing artists such as Rotimi Fani-Kayode; he claims that Delaney's self-portrait cites and subverts European modernists' interest in African sculpture by relocating it within the bathhouse, a site where sex is linked to "queer time." In "Complex Visions and Inspired Artists," Shawn Anthony Christian situates Baldwin's "On the Painter Beauford Delaney" as a generative text for exploring and understanding intergenerational artistic inspiration, from Delaney and Baldwin to Jesmyn Ward, Rachael Ghansah, and Kiese Laymon. The last chapter in the collection is a mediation by nationally acclaimed artist Jered Sprecher, who briefly discusses what it means for an artist today to engage with portraiture in the spirit of Delaney, as artists did in the Portrait Project at the Knoxville symposium, and he presents portraits of Fred Moten, David Leeming, Hilton Als, and Sylvia Peters that capture the feeling of Delaney's relational aesthetic.

This volume thus presents numerous points of contact and angles of vision on these artists, ranging from their personal friendship to their artistic values to their situation within culture, past and present. What is emphasized throughout is the importance of an artistic friendship between these

men, reverberating out from shared living space to shared city space to shared historical space. The relationship between Baldwin and Delaney will remain somewhat obscured until all of the archives are made public, but in the meantime, we can see and cogitate upon the familial love and professional respect each gave the other, and how this changes how we understand Blackness, masculinity, sexuality, art history, and the political surround of artistic endeavor, today.

NOTES

Epigraphs: James Baldwin, "On the Painter Beauford Delaney," *Transition* 4, no. 18 (1965): 45; reprinted in "The Anniversary Issue: Selections from *Transition*, 1961–1976," special issue, *Transition*, nos. 75/76 (1997): 88–89; and in *James Baldwin: Collected Essays*, ed. Toni Morrison (New York: Library of America, 1988), 721. Pamela Wye, "Beauford Delaney," *Arts Magazine*, Summer 1991, 71. Wye reviews Philippe Briet's mini-retrospective of Delaney's work, *Beauford Delaney, a Retrospective (50 Years of Light)*. See Philippe Briet, *Beauford Delaney, a Retrospective (50 Years of Light)* (New York: P. Briet, 1991).

1 James Baldwin, "The Price of the Ticket," in *The Price of the Ticket: Collected Nonfiction 1948–1985* (New York: St. Martin's, 1985), xii. Reprinted in, and hereafter cited from, *James Baldwin: Collected Essays*, ed. Toni Morrison (New York: Library of America, 1998), 833.

2 Jordan Elgrably, "James Baldwin: The Art of Fiction No. 78," *Paris Review* 91 (Spring 1984): 54.

3 Information here is from David Leeming, *Amazing Grace: A Life of Beauford Delaney* (New York: Oxford University Press, 1998), particularly pages 194–97. To date there is no archival public record of Baldwin and Delaney being lovers; as far as we know, the two would remain close as mentor/protégé and friends, though Leeming's biographies of Delaney and Baldwin assert that Delaney was in love with Baldwin from the beginning of their acquaintance. See David Leeming, *James Baldwin: A Biography* (New York: Arcade, 1994).

4 Baldwin, "Price of the Ticket," 832.

5 James Baldwin, "On the Painter Beauford Delaney," *Transition* 4, no. 18 (1965): 45. Reprinted in "The Anniversary Issue: Selections from *Transition,* 1961–1976," special issue, *Transition*, nos. 75/76 (1997): 88–89; and in *James Baldwin, Collected Essays*, ed. Toni Morrison (New York: Library of America, 1998), 720–21.

6 Beauford Delaney, letter to Henry Miller from Ibiza, Spain, 1956, quoted in Leeming, *Amazing Grace*, 135; Beauford Delaney, journal entry, quoted in Leeming, *Amazing Grace*, 61.

7 Beauford Delaney, letter to Henry Miller, June 14, 1963, quoted in Patricia Sue Canterbury, "Transatlantic Transformations: Beauford Delaney in Paris," in *Beauford Delaney: From New York to Paris*, ed. Patricia Sue Canterbury (Minneapolis: Minneapolis Institute of Arts, 2004), 61.

8 James Baldwin, "The Price May Be Too High," *New York Times*, February 2, 1969, section D, 9. Much, of course, has been written about Baldwin's construction of a secular New Jerusalem and the religious or Idealistic backgrounds to his expression and ideas; see, as just one example, Christopher Z. Hobson, *James Baldwin and the Heavenly City: Prophecy, Apocalypse, and Doubt* (East Lansing: Michigan State University Press, 2018), https://doi.org/10.14321/j.ctv47wg3r.

9 Douglas Field, "Pentecostalism and All That Jazz: Tracing James Baldwin's Religion," *Literature and Theology* 22, no. 4 (December 2008): 436–57.

10 Leeming, *Amazing Grace*, 41.

11 Mary Schmidt Campbell, foreword to *Beauford Delaney: A Retrospective*, ed. Richard A. Long (New York: Studio Museum in Harlem, 1978), n.p.

12 On the category of "the human," see Sylvia Wynter, "No Humans Involved: An Open Letter to My Colleagues," *Forum NHI* 1, no. 1 (1994): 42–71; Katherine McKittrick, "Unparalleled Catastrophe for Our Species? Or, to Give Humanness a Different Future: Conversations," in *Sylvia*

Wynter: On Being Human as Praxis, ed. Katherine McKittrick (Durham, NC: Duke University Press, 2015), 9–89.

13 Baldwin, "On the Painter Beauford Delaney," 720.

14 See Sean Kim Butorac, "Hannah Arendt, James Baldwin, and the Politics of Love," *Political Research Quarterly* 71, no. 3 (2018): 710–21.

15 On the "afterlife of slavery," see Saidiya Hartman, *Lose Your Mother: A Journey along the Atlantic Slave Route* (New York: Farrar, Straus and Giroux, 2008); on "shoaling" as an interstitial and emerging space of becoming, see Tiffany Lethabo King, *The Black Shoals: Offshore Formations of Black and Native Studies* (Durham, NC: Duke University Press, 2019).

16 Joan Dempsey has argued that the character Sonny in Baldwin's short story "Sonny's Blues" (1957) is Baldwin himself and that the mentor figure Creole is Beauford Delaney; see "Waiting for You: Beauford Delaney as James Baldwin's Inspiration for the Character Creole in 'Sonny's Blues,'" *Obsidian* 12, no.1 (2011): 60–78.

17 In "Baldwin, Bebop, and 'Sonny's Blues,'" in *Understanding Others: Cultural and Cross-Cultural Studies and the Teaching of Literature*, ed. Joseph Trimmer and Tilly Warnock (Urbana, IL: National Council of Teachers of English, 1992), 165–76, Pancho Savery notes that Baldwin merges the language of freedom with the description of the jazz set and alludes to the burgeoning civil rights movement of the time: "Baldwin's concept of family is, therefore, a highly political one, and one that has cultural implications" (173). Tracey Sherard condenses Savery's point to a phrase: "Sonny, through his non-lamenting meta-narrative of jazz, claims for himself and communicates to others . . . the agency some of the more crystallized forms of the blues deny. . . . Baldwin's concept of family is, therefore, a highly political one"; "Sonny's Bebop: Baldwin's 'Blues Text' as Intracultural Critique," *African American Review* 32, no. 4 (1998): 701.

18 On care ethics within contemporary Black aesthetics and Black life, see Christina Sharpe, *In the Wake: On Blackness and Being* (Durham, NC: Duke University Press, 2016).

19 Fred Moten, *In the Break: The Aesthetics of the Black Radical Tradition* (Minneapolis: University of Minnesota Press, 2003), 38.

20 Leeming, *James Baldwin*, 382.

21 On "Black fungibility," see Saidiya Hartman, *Scenes of Subjection: Terror, Slavery, and Self-Making in Nineteenth-Century America* (Oxford: Oxford University Press, 1997). *Consent not to be a single being* is the title of Moten's trilogy *Black and Blur* (2017), *Stolen Life* (2018), and *The Universal Machine* (2018).

22 James Baldwin, "Sonny's Blues," *Partisan Review*, Summer 1957; reprinted in *Going to Meet the Man* (New York: Dial, 1965), 139.

23 Fred Moten, *Black and Blur* (Durham, NC: Duke University Press, 2017), 11, 19.

24 This language is taken from Katherine McKittrick, *Dear Science and Other Stories* (Durham, NC: Duke University Press, 2021).

25 The blossoming of scholarship on Baldwin is exemplified by conferences devoted to his work, such as the International James Baldwin Conference at the American University in Paris, May 26–28, 2016; "'The Evidence of Things Not Seen': Queering Europe with James Baldwin," February 22–23, 2018, Interdisciplinary Center for Gender Studies ICFG, University of Bern; the James Baldwin Conference in Saint-Paul-de-Vence in 2020; the International Conference on James Baldwin at the Centre Universitaire Méditerranéen, Nice, in 2022. The nonprofit organization La Maison Baldwin (https://www.lamaisonbaldwin.org/) holds an annual writers' workshop-conference, with trips to Baldwin sites, and has a popular Facebook page. Important for scholarly work is the open-access journal *James Baldwin Review*, inaugurated in 2015 by Manchester University Press and edited by Douglas Field, Justin A. Joyce, and Dwight A. McBride. For a listing of notable Baldwin scholarship within specific time frames, see the *James Baldwin Review*'s annual "Trends in James Baldwin Criticism."

26 "James Baldwin Papers 1936–1992," New York Public Library Archives and Manuscripts, https://archives.nypl.org/scm/24143#access_use. Baldwin's estate sold the papers to the Schomberg Center in 2017; these include a typescript by Baldwin of unpublished notes on Delaney, according to Jennifer Schuessler, "James Baldwin's Archive, Long Hidden, Comes (Mostly) Into View," *New York Times*, April 12, 2017, https://www.nytimes.com/2017/04/12/arts/james-baldwins-archive-long-hidden-comes-mostly-into-view.html.

27 Justin A. Joyce, Dwight A. McBride, and Douglas Field, "Baltimore Is Still Burning: The Rising Relevance of James Baldwin," *James Baldwin Review* 1, no. 1 (2015): 4, https://www.manchesterhive.com/view/journals/jbr/1/1/jbr.1.issue-1.xml. The authors cite, among other works, D. Quentin Miller's edited volume *Re-Viewing James Baldwin: Things Not Seen* (2000); Herb Boyd's biography *Baldwin's Harlem* (2008); Magdalena Zaborowska's *James Baldwin's Turkish Decade* (2009); Randall Kenan's edited volume of Baldwin's uncollected writings, *The Cross of Redemption* (2010); Cora Kaplan and Bill Schwarz's edited collection *James Baldwin: America and Beyond* (2011); D. Quentin Miller's *A Criminal Power: James Baldwin and the Law* (2012); Matt Brim's *James Baldwin and the Queer Imagination* (2014); Douglas Field's *All Those Strangers: The Art and Lives of James Baldwin* (2015); and Michele Elam's edited collection, *The Cambridge Companion to James Baldwin* (2015).

28 See Julie Beth Napolin, "On *Blues Speaker [for James Baldwin]*: A Conversation with Mendi and Keith Obadike," *Social Text Online*, August 21, 2018, https://socialtextjournal.org/on-blues-speaker-for-james-baldwin-a-conversation-with-mendi-and-keith-obadike/.

29 For Baldwin's relevance during the period 2016 to 2020, see, for example, Jesmyn Ward, *The Fire This Time: A New Generation Speaks about Race* (New York: Scribner's, 2016), the title of which echoes Baldwin's *The Fire Next Time* (1963); Darryl Pinckney's review of Ward, "Catching Up to James Baldwin," *New York Review of Books*, May 25, 2017, https://www.nybooks.com/articles/2017/05/25/catching-up-to-james-baldwin/; and Eddie S. Glaude Jr.'s bestselling *Begin Again: James Baldwin's America and Its Urgent Lessons for Our Own* (New York: Crown, 2020).

30 Darryl Pinckney, Rich Blint, and Brian Meachum introduced *James Baldwin Abroad: A Program of 3 Films*, Film Forum, New York, January 2023, https://filmforum.org/film/james-baldwin-abroad. The films shown were Horace Ové, dir., *Baldwin's Nigger* (1968); Terence Dixon, dir., *Meeting the Man: James Baldwin in Paris* (1970); and Sedat Pakay, dir., *James Baldwin: From Another Place* (1973).

31 Rebecca Rubin, "Billy Porter to Star in James Baldwin Biopic," *Variety*, April 12, 2023, https://variety.com/2023/film/news/billy-porter-james-baldwin-biopic-1235580508/.

32 LeRoy McClain played Shy Baldwin (vocals by Darius de Haas) in *The Marvelous Mrs. Maisel* (2017–23), which was created by Amy Sherman-Palladino for Amazon Prime and won twenty-four Primetime Emmys. For Baldwin on Twitter, see Melanie Walsh, "Tweets of a Native Son: The Quotation and Recirculation of James Baldwin from Black Power to #BlackLivesMatter," *American Quarterly* 70, no. 3 (2018): 531–59.

33 Schuessler, "James Baldwin's Archive."

34 Richard Avedon and James Baldwin, *Nothing Personal* (Los Angeles: Taschen, 2017); *God Made My Face: A Collective Portrait of James Baldwin*, curated by Hilton Als, David Zwirner Gallery, New York, 2019, https://www.davidzwirner.com/exhibitions/god-made-my-face-collective-portrait-james-baldwin.

35 On Glenn Ligon, *Stranger (Full Text) #1* (2020–21), see *Glenn Ligon: First Contact*, Hauser and Wirth, 2021, https://www.hauserwirth.com/hauser-wirth-exhibitions/29232-glenn-ligon-first-contact/. See also Ligon's *Untitled (James Baldwin)* (1990), oil on canvas, 6¼ × 84 in. (15.9 × 213.4 cm), Museum of Fine Arts, Boston, Seth K. Sweetser Fund, 1991.546. For other artworks mentioned, see Don Bachardy, *James Baldwin* (1964), graphite and brush and black on cream wove paper, 30⅛ × 22 1/16 in. (76.5 × 56 cm), Art Institute of Chicago, https://www.artic.edu/artworks/259846/james-baldwin; Jack Witten, *Black Monolith I, a Tribute to James*

Baldwin (1988), Glenstone, Potomac, MD, https://www.glenstone.org/search/black+monolith; and Garrett Rittenberg, *Portrait of James Baldwin* (2018), acrylic on canvas, 27⅞ × 22 in. (70.8 × 55.9 cm), https://onlineonly.christies.com/s/collection-andre-leon-talley-online/garrett-rittenberg-20th-21st-century-183/174291. For discussions of Baldwin and the contemporary arts, see, for instance, Monika Gehlawat, "Strangers in the Village: James Baldwin, Teju Cole, and Glenn Ligon," *James Baldwin Review* 5 (2019): 48–72, https://doi.org/10.7227/JBR.5.4; and Shawn Anthony Christian's chapter in this volume.

36 Susan Vogel, introduction to *Perspectives: Angles on African Art*, ed. Susan Vogel (New York: Center for African Art; Harry N. Abrams, 1987), 12.

37 James Baldwin, "James Baldwin," in Vogel, *Perspectives*, 115.

38 Leeming, *Amazing Grace*, 182.

39 Jewell Handy Gresham, "James Baldwin Comes Home," *Essence*, June 1976; reprinted in *Conversations with James Baldwin*, ed. Fred L. Standley and Louis H. Pratt (Jackson: University Press of Mississippi, 1989), 163.

40 Henry Miller, *The Amazing and Invariable Beauford DeLaney* (New York: Alicat Book Shop, 1945); reprinted in *Remember to Remember* (New York: New Directions, 1947), 15–34; and reprinted in part in Long, *Beauford Delaney: A Retrospective.*

According to the program for the exhibition at the Centre Culturel Américain, the seven paintings by Delaney on display were *Portrait of Jean Genet, Shaman, Portrait of Ambrose, Yellow Abstraction, Madame de Chaillot, Autumn*, and *Portrait of Henry Miller*. See *Henry Miller 80* (Paris: Centre Culturel Américain, 1971). The title page of the program reads: "L'Université de Californie à Los Angeles lui rend en ce moment un tribut officiel auquel assistent nombre de ses amis. Bien d'autres ne peuvent être présents et c'est pour cela que nous avons organisé cette modeste manifestation avec et pour ses amis à Paris. . . . Cette exposition est le témoignage de cette amitié, une salutation à celui qui en retour leur rend hommage" (The University of California at Los Angeles is paying him an official tribute at this moment, which many of his friends are attending. Many others cannot be present and that is why we have organized this modest demonstration with and for his friends in Paris. . . . This exhibition is the testimony of this friendship, a greeting to the one who in return pays them homage). Translation mine.

41 Jean-José Marchand, "Enquête sur la culture noire," *Preuves*, May 1958, 33–44. Delaney's is the shortest of the responses from this eclectic group.

42 See Mary Schmidt Campbell, foreword to Long, *Beauford Delaney: A Retrospective*, n.p. See the bibliography in this volume for a listing of

substantial considerations of Delaney's work that have appeared in exhibition catalogues, such as essays by Maija Brennan, Mary Campbell, Patricia Sue Canterbury, Henry Louis Gates Jr., Ann E. Gibson, David Leeming, Richard A. Long, Michael D. Plante, Richard Powell, Levi Prombaum, Joyce Henri Robinson, Lowery Stokes Sims, Catherine St. John, Stephen C. Wicks, and Yolanda Wood.

43 Ted Joans, "Beauford Delaney," *Black World/Negro Digest* 23, no. 3 (January 1974): 93. This article features a photo of Joans visiting with Delaney.

44 Ted Joans, *In Thursday Sane*, ed. Sandra McPherson (Davis, CA: Swan Scythe Press, 2001).

45 For chronologies of exhibitions of Delaney's work, see *Beauford Delaney: Liquid Light, Paris Abstractions, 1954–1970* (New York: Michael Rosenfeld Gallery, 1999), 51–52; "Beauford Delaney (1901–1979)," in *Stroke! Beauford Delaney, Norman Lewis and Alma Thomas* (New York: Michael Rosenfeld Gallery, 2000), 52; Sylvain Briet, "Chronology of Exhibitions," in *Beauford Delaney: From New York to Paris*, ed. Patricia Sue Canterbury (Minneapolis: Minneapolis Institute of Arts, 2004), 125–31. The Wells International Foundation has also created a timeline to accompany its online exhibition; see Maija Brennan, *Beauford Delaney: A Study in Portraiture*, Wells International Foundation, 2019, https://wellsinternationalfoundation.org/portraiture-exhibition/.

46 Delaney's relationship with the Facchettis began in the fall of 1956, when they included his work in group shows and bought several works; they held a one-man show for him in June 1960 that featured only his abstractions. See the discussion of this show in Leeming, *Amazing Grace*, 142–43; and "Beauford's Solo Show at the Paul Facchetti Gallery," *Les Amis de Beauford Delaney* (blog), May 30, 2015, http://lesamisdebeauforddelaney.blogspot.com/2015/05/beaufords-solo-show-at-paul-facchetti.html.

47 On the Michael Rosenfeld Gallery's support of Delaney's work, see Monique Y. Wells, "Beauford and the Michael Rosenfeld Gallery," *Les Amis de Beauford Delaney* (blog), March 2, 2010, http://lesamisdebeauforddelaney.blogspot.com/2010/03/beauford-and-michael-rosenfeld-gallery.html. For the 2022 exhibition, see the catalogue *Be Your Wonderful Self: The Portraits of Beauford Delaney*, ed. halley k harrisburg and Matthew Newton (West Haven, CT: Michael Rosenfeld Gallery and GHP Media, 2022).

48 Cid Corman, *Tributary: Poems*, ed. Philippe Briet (New York: Edgewise Press, 1999); for references to Miller and Baldwin, see the poem "Pastel," 19.

Philippe Briet opened his eponymous gallery in SoHo, Manhattan, in 1987 and mounted the first Delaney exposition since 1978, titled *Beauford Delaney (1901–1979): From Tennessee to Paris*, in November 1988.

Philippe and his brother Sylvain Briet then organized two further retrospectives: *Beauford Delaney, a Retrospective (50 Years of Light)* (1991) and *Beauford Delaney: The New York Years* (1994). See Monique Y. Wells, "Beauford and the Briet Brothers," *Les Amis de Beauford Delaney* (blog), January 27, 2010, http://lesamisdebeauforddelaney.blogspot.com/2010/01/beauford-and-briet-brothers.html.

49 See Monique Y. Wells, "Welcome," *Les Amis de Beauford Delaney* (blog), December 14, 2009, http://lesamisdebeauforddelaney.blogspot.com/2009/12/welcome.html. The film is to be directed by Zachary James Miller and produced by Monique Y. Wells and Bruce Aitken; see https://zacharyjames9.wixsite.com/website.

50 See The Delaney Project: Gathering Light, https://thedelaneyproject.org/.

51 On plans for the museum, see "The Future Delaney Museum at Beck: Last Remaining Ancestral Home of Beauford Delaney," Beck Cultural Exchange Center, https://www.beckcenter.net/delaney-museum-at-beck.

52 *Beauford Delaney: A Folio of Notecards* (Richmond, VA: Pomegranate Press, 2015).

53 Adrianna Campbell, "Glenn Ligon: Glenn Ligon Speaks about His Curatorial Project 'Encounters and Collisions,'" *Artforum*, June 5, 2015, https://www.artforum.com/interviews/glenn-ligon-speaks-about-his-curatorial-project-encounters-and-collisions-52580; Monique Y. Wells, "Beauford Delaney and Paris: Evolution of an Exhibition," in *Beauford Delaney: Resonance of Form and Vibration of Color* (Paris: Columbia Global Centers, 2016), 42; "Video Explorations of Beauford's Life and Art," *Les Amis de Beauford Delaney* (blog), http://lesamisdebeauforddelaney.blogspot.com; *God Made My Face: A Collective Portrait of James Baldwin*, curated by Hilton Als, David Zwirner Gallery, New York, 2019, https://www.davidzwirner.com/exhibitions/god-made-my-face-collective-portrait-james-baldwin.

54 Moten, *In the Break*. For new approaches to Delaney, see Christopher Capozzola, "Beauford Delaney and the Art of Exile," *Gay and Lesbian Review Worldwide* 10, no. 5 (2003): 10–12; Edward Field, "With Beauford Delaney," *Gay and Lesbian Review Worldwide* 11, no. 3 (2004): 4; Catherine St. John, "Reality and Aesthetics: A Marxist and Crocean Interpretation of the Paintings of Beauford Delaney," *NAAAS Conference Proceedings* (Scarborough, ME: National Association of African American Studies, 2001), 397–414; and Catherine St. John, "A Narrative of Belonging: The Art of Beauford Delaney and Glenn Ligon," in *Proceeding for the School of Visual Arts Eighteenth Annual National Conference on Liberal Arts and the Education of Artists: Art and Story*, ed. Sherry Stone, 43–50, https://www.academia.edu/1411170/INTERPRETATION_NARRATIVE_AND_THE_STUDENTS_SEARCH_FOR_AN_ARTISTS_INTENTIONS.

55 Moten, *In the Break*, 171.

56 Baldwin, "Price of the Ticket," 831, 832.

57 Rachel Cohen, "Beauford Delaney and W. E. B. Du Bois" and "Beauford Delaney and James Baldwin," in *A Chance Meeting: Intertwined Lives of American Writers and Artists, 1854–1967* (New York: Random House, 2004), 182–88, 220–28.

58 *James Baldwin: The Price of the Ticket*, directed by Karen Thorsen, produced by Karen Thorsen and William Miles (DKDmedia, 1989), film, 1 hr. 27 min.

59 Leeming, *Amazing Grace*; and Leeming, *James Baldwin.*

60 Stephen C. Wicks, "Beauford Delaney and James Baldwin: A Selected Timeline," in *Beauford Delaney and James Baldwin: Through the Unusual Door*, ed. Stephen C. Wicks (Knoxville: Knoxville Museum of Art, 2020), xv–xxi. Wicks has also hosted a four-part virtual tour of the exhibition and discussion of the Delaney-Baldwin relationship; videos are available on YouTube and at https://knoxart.org/exhibitions/beauford-delaney-and-james-baldwin-through-the-unusual-door/.

61 David Butler, foreword to Wicks, *Beauford Delaney and James Baldwin*, vii.

62 Wicks, *Beauford Delaney and James Baldwin*; Cohen, "Beauford Delaney and James Baldwin," in *A Chance Meeting*, 220–28; Dempsey, "Waiting for You"; Glenn Ligon, "From Letter to Beauford Delaney," in *Glenn Ligon: Encounters and Collisions, Exhibition Notes*, Nottingham Contemporary, 2015, https://cms.nottinghamcontemporary.org/site/assets/files/1486/exhibition_notes_glenn_ligon__encounters_and_collisions.pdf; "Glenn Ligon to Beauford Delaney: Two Letters," in Wicks, *Beauford Delaney and James Baldwin*, xxiii–xxiv; Monique Y. Wells, "Brief Musings on Beauford and James Baldwin," *Les Amis de Beauford Delaney* (blog), December 1, 2010, http://lesamisdebeauforddelaney.blogspot.com/2010/12/brief-musings-on-beauford-and-james.html; Mark Godfrey and Zoe Whitley, "Beauford Delaney and James Baldwin," in *Soul of a Nation: Art in the Age of Black Power*, ed. Mark Godfrey and Zoe Whitley (London: Tate Publishing, 2017), 116–17; Tyler Schmidt, "Lessons in Light: Beauford Delaney's and James Baldwin's 'Unnameable Objects,'" in *Of Latitudes Unknown: James Baldwin's Radical Imagination*, ed. Alice Mikal Craven (New York: Bloomsbury Academic, 2019), 49–68; James Smalls, "Picturing Jimmy, Picturing Self: James Baldwin, Beauford Delaney, and the Color of Light," in Craven, *Of Latitudes Unknown*, 35–48.

63 The literature discussing Baldwin, jazz, and blues is significant. See discussions and bibliographies in Walton M. Muyumba, *The Shadow and the Act: Black Intellectual Practice, Jazz Improvisation, and Philosophical Pragmatism* (Chicago: University of Chicago Press, 2009); Ed Pavlić, *Who Can Afford to Improvise? James Baldwin and Black Music, the Lyric*

and the Listeners (New York: Fordham University Press, 2015); and the significant work done by Robert G. O'Meally as the founder and director of the Center for Jazz Studies at Columbia University, https://jazz.columbia.edu. One can find extensive programming online related to Baldwin and jazz, often documented on sites such as YouTube.

64 Quoted in Richard A. Long, "Interview with RAL," in Long, *Beauford Delaney: A Retrospective*, n.p.

65 Campbell, foreword to Long, *Beauford Delaney: A Retrospective*, n.p.

66 As noted by Handy in his dedication to W. C. Handy, ed., *Unsung Americans Sung* (New York: American Society of Composers Authors and Publishers, 1944).

67 See Delaney's portrait of Handy in harrisburg and Newton, *Be Your Wonderful Self*. For a discussion of the Tubman portrait in relation to the sketch and the Delaney's probable source for it, see Monique Y. Wells, *Les Amis de Beauford Delaney* (blog), "Les Amis Celebrates Women's History Month, Part 4," http://lesamisdebeauforddelaney.blogspot.com/2021/03/.

68 Moten, *In the Break*, 35.

69 Moten, *In the Break*, 35.

70 Moten, *In the Break*, 32.

71 Moten, *In the Break*, 34.

72 See Monika Gehlawat, "Baldwin and the Role of the Citizen Artist," *James Baldwin Review* 8, no. 1 (2022), https://doi.org/10.7227/JBR.8.6.

73 Jean Grenier, "Beauford Delaney," *Preuves*, June 1962, 75–76. The full passage reads:

> Et son regard est lumineux et vif comme celui de quelqu'un qui a gardé le don de l'enfance. On sent que s'il vous connaissait mieux il aimerait à jouer avec vous, sans arrière-pensée, pour s'amuser, pour vous amuser. Il se retient parce que vous venez de lui être présenté, mais sa mimique est expressive, ses veux pétillent de malice, il vous fait des signes d'intelligence. Comme vous vous sentez âgé à côté de lui, quel soit votre âge! La croyance, l'espérance, l'amour paraissent naturels et faciles auprès de lui. Je n'oublie pas que son père était pasteur dans cette région du Sud-Tennessee où il est né. . . . Beauford-Delaney est tout allégresse. . . . Beauford-Delaney est du côté de la vie dansante et chantante.

> His gaze is bright and lively like that of someone who has kept the gift of childhood. We feel that if he knew you better he would like to play with you, without delay, just for fun, to have fun. He restrains himself because you have just been introduced to him, but his mimicry is

expressive, his eyes sparkle with mischief, he makes signs of intelligence. How old you feel next to him, whatever your age! Belief, hope, love seem natural and easy to him. I don't forget that his father was a pastor in that part of South Tennessee where he was born. . . . Beauford-Delaney is all joy. . . . Beauford-Delaney is on the side of the dancing and singing life. (Translation mine.)

74 Saidiya Hartman, *Scenes of Subjection: Terror, Slavery, and Self-Making in Nineteenth-Century America* (Oxford: Oxford University Press, 1997), 4; quoted in Moten, *In the Break*, 4–5.

75 Beauford Delaney, "Les valeurs humaines amalgament tout l'heritage du passe" (Human values amalgamate all the heritage of the past), answer to question no. 1, within set of interviews by Jean-José Marchand, "Enquête sur la culture noire," *Preuves*, May 1958, 44 (translation mine). The original text reads: "Pour moi, la culture noire signifie aujourd'hui la combinaison des principes spirituels, philosophiques et artistiques traditionnnels a ces peuples qui, plonges dans une atmosphere de tragedie—et en particulier prives de certains droits—ont neanmoins garde leur dignite, leur magnanimite et leur interet pour les problemes complexes du xx siecle. Ce qu'on appelle culture noire est en fait un amalgame de l'heritage de ces peuples avec d'autres cultures auxquelles ils furent contraints de s'initier."

76 Amy J. Elias, "Inappropriate Edges: Beauford Delaney's *Untitled-1969*," *ASAP/J*, May 22, 2023, https://asapjournal.com/hard-soft-lost-the-edges-of-contemporary-culture-inappropriate-edges-beauford-delaneys-untitled-1969-amy-j-elias/.

77 *International Herald Tribune*, May 24–25, 1969, 1.

78 Elias, "Inappropriate Edges."

79 See Richard J. Powell, "The Color of Ecstasy," in *Beauford Delaney: The Color Yellow* (Atlanta: High Museum of Art, 2002), 13–31; see also Baldwin, "On the Painter Beauford Delaney."

80 On the interview with Cavett, see, for instance, Jamill W. Drake, "James Baldwin: Witnessing in Dark Times," *Marginalia*, September 24, 2021, https://themarginaliareview.com/james-baldwin-witnessing-in-dark-times/.

81 See Powell, "Color of Ecstasy."

82 *Transmedial consonance* is term used by Brent Hayes Edwards in *Epistrophies: Jazz and the Literary Imagination* (Cambridge, MA: Harvard University Press, 2017), 7.

83 For the term *creative erotics*, see Magdalena J. Zaborowska, *James Baldwin's Turkish Decade: Erotics of Exile* (Durham, NC: Duke University Press, 2009).

PART I

Circuits of Selfhood

ONE

Jimmy and Beauford

The Bond of the Unusual Door

David Leeming

It was a miserable rainy day in the early winter of 1940. With some hesitation, a sixteen-year-old boy approached a dilapidated building on Greene Street in Manhattan's Greenwich Village. The boy was a senior in high school, uptown in the Bronx, and he was an apprentice preacher at a Pentecostal church in Harlem. He was downtown because he had a part-time job cleaning floors at a shop on Canal Street. The boy was on one of those end-of-the-road missions made in desperation. Depression was overwhelming him. A friend at school had told him about an eccentric painter he had met one Saturday in the Village. The painter was poor but recognized as a serious artist; he was probably queer, but he was a wonderful talker and he loved giving advice. And like the troubled boy, he was African American and—already a symbol and an anomaly—a Black artist living downtown.

And so the boy found his way to the Greene Street door and knocked. The door opened, and the boy, as he would later relate, was confronted by a "short, round, brown man" who "when he had completed his instant X-ray of my brain, lungs, liver, heart, bowels, and spinal column" said simply, "'Come in,' and opened the door."[1]

The boy, of course, was James Baldwin; the painter, Beauford Delaney. Baldwin had come to the right door, and "not a moment too soon." It was the "unusual door" of an old gospel song. By passing through, young Jimmy found a way to a new life, a life marked by an unbreakable bond with Beauford and Beauford's teachings. The "Bond of the Unusual Door" he called it, a bond that would in great part affect the lives of both men.

As a biographer of both Baldwin and Delaney, it was important for me to learn more about the situations and personalities of these two individuals before young Jimmy passed through that door. During the years in which I worked for him and sometimes shared a house with him, Baldwin naturally revealed a lot about himself and his early life to me. And, of course, there were autobiographical essays, such as those contained in *Notes of a Native Son* (1955) and *The Fire Next Time* (1963). But I found that a particularly unguarded vision of the boy at the unusual door eventually emerged in characters developed in early fictional works—especially the novel *Go Tell It on the Mountain* (1953) and the play *The Amen Corner* (1954). The conflicts Baldwin faced and reasons for his depression are all there in *Mountain*, where young John Grimes embodies the situation of young Jimmy Baldwin. In the novel, John, in early adolescence, is saved in his Pentecostal church. During the year of his salvation, he has sexual feelings and experiences that seem to be incompatible with his new religious status. In fictional life and in real life, John and Jimmy were frightened by their sexual awakenings. In both cases there was an unsympathetic, angry, and suspicious stepfather unable to support his family in a racist society. From the beginning of John's salvation and Jimmy Baldwin's role as an apprentice preacher, there was a sense that the church might be a repressive dead end. Both boys are driven by a longing for something new, for a way out of a racial, religious, and family situation that was a de facto prison. In *Go Tell It on the Mountain*, John regularly climbs a hill in Central Park facing midtown Manhattan, a hill from which he expresses that longing: "He felt like a long-awaited conqueror at whose feet flowers would be strewn, and before whom multitudes cried, Hosanna! He would be, of all, the mightiest, the most beloved, the Lord's anointed; and he would live in this shining city which his ancestors had seen with longing from far away."[2] Young James Baldwin climbed that same hill and was driven by the same longing.

In *The Amen Corner*, the longing, further developed, would be expressed by David, the son of a preacher mother and a father broken by racism and poverty. David is his mother's church musician, but he comes to believe that his music belongs elsewhere, that it must not be imprisoned by his mother's religion or his father's victimhood and failures. Announcing his departure, David says to his mother:

> If I stayed here—I'd end up worse than Daddy—because I wouldn't be doing what I know I got to do—I got to do! I've seen your life—and now I see Daddy—and I love you. . . . But I've got my work to do, something's happening in the world out there, I got to go! I know you don't think I know what's happening, but I'm beginning to see—something.
>
> Every time I play, every time I listen, I see Daddy's face and yours, and so many faces—who's going to speak for all that, Mama? Who's going to speak for all of us? I can't stay home. Maybe I can say something—one day—maybe I can say something in music that's never been said before.[3]

This speech is, of course, a projection of James Baldwin's decision to leave the church and home—to risk entering the city that both he and John Grimes had looked down upon from the hill in Central Park.

As it turned out, the door to the city was at 181 Greene Street. The man on the other side of the door was a man Henry Miller once called "the amazing and invariable Beauford DeLaney."[4] When young Jimmy walked through the door into Beauford's life he walked into a world of poverty and ample reason for despair, a world on the surface not all that unlike his own life at home. But Beauford's world was somehow different. It was a world in which poverty and despair were transformed into beauty.

To Jimmy, Beauford's Buddha-like face radiated whatever it was that David in *The Amen Corner* saw as the message his music might send; it conveyed the hopes experienced by Jimmy and John on the Central Park "mountain." With its cot, potbellied stove, and easel, Beauford's apartment was even colder and barer than the Baldwin family apartment uptown, but Jimmy was immediately aware of and amazed by the paintings that were everywhere in the room. They spoke of Beauford's condition and of what art could make of that condition. In his chapbook on Delaney, Henry Miller put into words what he imagined the message of the paintings to be: "Here I sit in Greene Street, said the canvases, and I am invisible to all but the eye of God. I am the spirit of hunger for all that has been denied me, one with the street, one with the cold, dead walls. But I am not dead, neither am I cold, nor yet invisible." And imagining Beauford's voice, Miller continues, "I sit here in Greene Street and I paint what I am, my mysterious mixed bloods, my inscrutable mixed hungers, my elegant and most aristocratic solitudes. . . . Here there are no sun, moon or stars, no warmth, no light, no companionship. But in me, the amazing and invariable Beauford DeLaney, are all the lights, all the stars, all the constellations, all the angels for companions. I am Greene Street as it looks from the angle of eternity."[5]

One of the first things Beauford did after he made Jimmy some tea on that first day was to put a record on his old gramophone. He was to do this often when Jimmy visited. There was classical music and especially blues songs by Bessie Smith and Ethel Waters as well as jazz by Dizzy Gillespie, Fats Waller, and others. Beauford sensed Jimmy's negative reaction to much of the music. For the young Pentecostal preacher, even if a doubting one, blues and jazz were sinful, associated with smoky clubs, booze, and sex. Beauford talked to the boy about the sacredness of nonreligious music. He, like Jimmy, was a preacher's son, and he talked about how Fats Waller and Bessie Smith, just as much as the composers and performers of gospel, used their music to bare their pain and their souls to the world, to celebrate who and what they were. Beauford reconciled for his pupil the music of the Harlem streets and clubs with the music of the Harlem churches—and, by extension, the boy's sexual awakening with his artistic awakening. This was a lesson of great importance to the later writer of "Sonny's Blues" (1957), *The Amen Corner*, and *Just above My Head* (1979).

From that day in 1940, James Baldwin's and Beauford Delaney's lives were bonded. Years later Baldwin would say of Beauford that he was "my primary witness." When Jimmy's stepfather died, Beauford found money to help the family bury him. Beauford found Jimmy a better job, working as a dishwasher and waiter at Connie Williams's Calypso Café, where after closing they would join Connie to share troubles, sing old songs, and enjoy a drink or two—the former boy preacher having widened his horizons on the question of sin. But most of all, between 1940 and 1948, when Baldwin left for Paris, Beauford helped his protégé to see as a creative artist rather than as a preacher—that is, to be a different kind of witness for the world. As Baldwin would put it later, "The reality of his seeing caused me to begin to see."[6] The gramophone was only one of Beauford's teaching tools. He took Jimmy to concerts and introduced him to many of his friends in the jazz world. And he taught Jimmy a blues lesson—to see beauty even in the metaphorical or literal gutter. Jimmy loved telling what he called Beauford's "gutter lesson." One rainy day as they were walking through Greenwich Village, Beauford pointed down at the gutter that they were just crossing. "Look at that," he said, stopping as if at an amazing sight. Jimmy was confused. "It's just a gutter full of oil and trash," he said. "Look again," Beauford said. "Look how the oil on the surface of the water changes the buildings reflected in the water." Some forty-three years later Baldwin, pacing one afternoon in his study in Saint-Paul-de-Vence, talked about that incident and what he saw as the real meaning of Beauford's teaching. It was not simply a question of close observation. It also had to do with a willingness to face and see through ugliness in order to find what the artist has to find. Sometimes finding whatever that is means confronting one's own fears and acknowledging that what you cannot see "says something about you."[7]

The lifelong relationship between Beauford and Jimmy was complex. Beauford was in love with Jimmy; Jimmy loved Beauford but was not "in love" with him. Furthermore, Beauford required permanence—a place to live and paint. Jimmy never completely lost his peripatetic preacher identity. From the 1940s on, he would spend his life moving from place to place—writing and always searching for a new venue for the preaching of his own gospel. The complexity of the bond of the unusual door is reflected in the 1941 painting to which Beauford gave the title *Dark Rapture* (plate 1). It is possible that he was thinking of the 1931 documentary of that name about explorations of the Belgian Congo. In the case of the painting, however, the subject was almost certainly young James Baldwin. Beauford was modest about nudity and almost never painted nude portraits. Yet, here was a sixteen-year-old sitting on a cot (presumably Beauford's cot) surrounded by exotic plants and trees and identified simply as "dark rapture." An inscription on the painting indicates that Beauford gave this painting to a close friend of Baldwin's—probably a lover. This probably says as much about Beauford as does the painting itself. The painting is clearly an act of love, like nothing he had painted before or would ever paint again. Yet the gift, the bestowal of the painting, suggests Delaney's recognition that dark rapture, represented by young Jimmy, was not to be his, but someone else's.

In 1948 Baldwin left for Paris, and Beauford was devastated. For several years he told friends he hoped to visit Paris to see Jimmy. In 1953 the visit became possible. So began the second stage of the bond of the unusual door.

Much had changed since the days when Jimmy and Beauford spent time together in Greenwich Village. Beauford had established a secure reputation as an abstract painter in New York, but he was beginning to be plagued by the inner voices that periodically jeered at him for being queer and Black. As for Baldwin, he was now the author of *Go Tell It on the Mountain* and many of the great essays found in *Notes of a Native Son* (1955), and he was working on *The Amen Corner* and *Giovanni's Room* (1956). But he too was plagued by bouts of depression, and he was increasingly focused on the racial situation at home in the United States.

And yet Baldwin described his 1953 meeting with Beauford on the painter's first day in Paris as a joyous one. He was sitting with a friend at Café Flore when he saw a familiar shape in the street between the Flore and the Brasserie Lipp. Baldwin rushed out of the Flore shouting Beauford's name, and they met in the middle of the street in an ecstatic embrace, horns honking all around them.

Beauford had intended to visit Paris briefly, but in the twenty-five years between 1953 and his death, he returned to the States only once, in 1969 for a short Christmas visit to his Knoxville family. In the 1950s and 1960s Baldwin moved back and forth between Paris and the United States as he became increasingly involved with the civil rights movement. Jimmy and other friends helped Beauford move to the suburban commune of Clamart, and when he was in Paris Baldwin usually stayed with Beauford there. They spent time together in clubs, often with Jimmy's lover, Lucien, and sometimes crossed paths with Richard Wright and his circle at Café Tournon.

Beauford was falling in love with Paris, and he continued to be in love with Jimmy. The two old friends would sit for hours in the house in Clamart, drinking and talking in front of a window that looked through the branches of a tree at a garden behind the house. Baldwin said how much he loved sitting with Beauford in front of that window: it "was a kind of universe, moaning and wailing when it rained, black and bitter when it thundered, hesitant and delicate with the first light of morning, and as blue as the blues when the last light of the sun departed."[8] Jimmy said that it was in front of that window that he really began to understand the centrality of light in Beauford's paintings. Baldwin saw that light as a religious light—a light that "held the power to illuminate, even to redeem and reconcile and heal."[9]

But during the Clamart years Beauford's old role as Jimmy's mentor had changed. It was Beauford now who depended on his young friend for guidance and support, especially as his mental state became more tenuous. Beauford discussed his inner life with Baldwin as he did with few, if any, others. In one letter he writes, "Have been working and living with the many people who make up Beauford and trying to merge them into some sort of composition and a workable form of painting. There is a great chamber in my house which has been vacant for a long time. I don't think I have ever spoken of it—pretend you did not hear . . . —this can often account for a great many odd placements of [mental] furniture."[10]

My own connection to Baldwin and Delaney began in December 1961, when Baldwin flew to Istanbul to visit a friend. It happened that I was there at the time, teaching. I met Baldwin at a party, and so began the biography I did not yet know I was preparing to write. Jimmy had received a letter from Beauford describing his attempted suicide in Greece. Over the years the voices had become more demanding—suggesting that Beauford was a useless freak and that he might as well end it all. Jimmy decided he had better return to Paris to spend Christmas with his old friend. Later he would write to another friend about Beauford's inner world as he saw it. He wondered whether Beauford's growing up in the South had made him too accommodating to the white world in which he lived and on which he depended for the acceptance of his paintings. Baldwin wrote that inside "this despised black man . . . was a secret power" that if he chose to "unleash" it would "humble" his enemies—including the terrifying voices that tortured him.[11] In Baldwin's introduction to the catalogue for a 1964 Galerie Lambert retrospective of Delaney's work, he spoke of his old mentor as his "spiritual father." It was Beauford who taught him to confront reality. But it was also Beauford who taught him that art can only be born of love, and that "no greater lover had ever held a brush." True, Beauford's life was sad—even tragic—but his art was a blues song that redeemed everything.[12]

In the summer of 1966, I found myself at Beauford Delaney's unusual door. I had been working for Baldwin in Istanbul, where he had escaped to write a novel. I had gone to the States on business for him, and on the way back I had arranged to buy a car in Paris. Jimmy asked me to pick up Beauford there and to bring him to Istanbul. I had never met Beauford, and I asked Jimmy what he was like. Jimmy smiled and said, "Well, he's a cross between Brer Rabbit and Saint Francis of Assisi; that's all you need to know. Just don't lose him." And so I found my way to Beauford's building in Montparnasse and climbed the stairs to his door. A note on the door said, "Welcome David." Jimmy must have told him I was coming. I knocked, and a warm, melodious voice said, "Come in."

When I opened the door, I knew immediately that I had entered what for me was a new world. White sheets hung on all the furniture and walls. The owner of the voice was dressed all in white, and the sun streaming through a garret window highlighted a round brown face that seemed to float in all the whiteness. As if to confirm my having passed through the unusual door, the face said, "Won't you lie down?" Beauford then pointed to two cots along the far wall and we both lay down—head to head. We stayed there on those beds for three days and nights except for the occasional visit to the latrine in the hall outside and the odd can of tuna fish under the window. And we talked, when we weren't sleeping. We talked about everything: Beauford's life, my life, Jimmy's life. Without knowing it, I was participating in a major interview for a biography—really two biographies—that I still didn't know I was writing. On the third morning Beauford suddenly announced, "We can go to Jimmy now."

The drive to Istanbul through Yugoslavia was a continuation of life behind the unusual door. Jimmy had said nothing about Beauford's mental condition, nothing about his attempted suicide or his occasional hallucinations—the voices that hounded him. He did not warn me that Beauford might try to jump out of our fast-moving car, which he did. He *had* warned me not to lose him. I understood what Jimmy meant by that when I did, in fact, lose him. One night we were assigned cots next to each other in a transit hotel for people passing through the Iron Curtain. Waking up late at night, I saw that Beauford was not in his cot. Eventually I found him in the village, arguing with a group of drunken men, and, with difficulty, convinced him to come back to bed. Realizing there was only one way of getting some much-needed sleep and not losing him again, I got into bed with him, and we slept together that night and several nights after that in each other's arms. It was not an experience of sexual passion, but sleeping like that with Beauford was the culmination of a lesson I think James Baldwin meant me to learn when he sent me to bring Beauford Delaney to Istanbul. He knew that I and the world I represented needed to hear the voices that Beauford heard—the voices that harangued and threatened him. These were voices that every Black man heard in one way or another, but for Beauford they took personal form in his hallucinations and sometimes drove him literally mad, even almost to his death.

In Istanbul we all shared a house, and eventually Beauford flew back to Paris. There he continued painting until the voices got the best of him. Baldwin had rented and then bought a house in Saint-Paul-de-Vence in the south of France at the end of the 1960s. Whenever messages came that Beauford was not doing well, he brought him to Saint-Paul for extended stays.

He also took him back to Istanbul. At one point they lived in a little garden house along the Bosphorus, and Jimmy joked that they were like Candide and Dr. Pangloss, who ended up in a similar place in Voltaire's *Candide.*

Beauford's condition worsened in the late 1960s and 1970s. He struggled hard, using paint and canvas to hold off the relentless voices. In the 1964 introduction to the Galerie Lambert show, Baldwin had written, "The darkness of Beauford's beginnings, in Tennessee, many years ago, was a black-blue midnight indeed, opaque and full of sorrow. And I do not know, nor will any of us ever really know, what kind of strength it was that enabled him to make so dogged and splendid a journey."[13] But in 1967 and 1970, Delaney painted a series on Rosa Parks that reprises the early Greenwich Village paintings of his African American heroes, such as Marian Anderson and Ethel Waters. In one painting, Parks sits alone on a bench (plate 24), while in another, she shares the bench with a white woman and her baby (plate 28). Perhaps this was Beauford's version of the possibility of civil rights. His great yellow abstractions were a celebration of the light that allowed him to go on living. Indeed, in the catalogue of a 1973 retrospective organized by friends of Beauford, including Baldwin, and gallery owner Dorthea Speyer, Beauford's old New York associates Georgia O'Keeffe and Henry Miller wrote of the painter's uniqueness. And Baldwin wrote, "When we are at a Delaney painting, we are in the light."[14]

In 1975 Beauford's condition became such that a trusteeship of several friends, including Baldwin, agreed to his being committed to Sainte Anne's Hospital in Paris. Baldwin visited him there several times. On March 26, 1979, Jimmy received news of Beauford's death. Suffering from flu and depression, he remained in Saint-Paul with the pain of Beauford's passing "bottled up inside." For the rest of his life, Baldwin felt shame at not having attended Beauford's funeral in Paris. This was his "worst moment," and he later admitted that he had acted like a spoiled child, somehow angry at his spiritual father for dying without his permission.[15]

At the end of his own life, Baldwin was working on several projects, including a novel about Beauford. During his final days, I took turns with his brother David sitting up with Jimmy at night. Somehow, some twenty years after my three days and nights in Beauford's Montparnasse studio, I was privileged to be allowed back through the unusual door. Occasionally Jimmy's voice would penetrate the darkness, and I would answer. Much of our conversation was about Beauford. Jimmy's voice was often an angry voice. At his funeral Amiri Baraka called him "God's black revolutionary mouth." But it was a mouth and a voice tempered and made more powerful by the love and light of Beauford Delaney's constant presence—by the bond of the unusual door.

NOTES

1 James Baldwin, "The Price of the Ticket," in *The Price of the Ticket* (New York: St Martin's, 1985), ix–x; reprinted in *James Baldwin: Collected Essays*, ed. Toni Morrison (New York: Library of America, 1998), 830.

2 James Baldwin, *Go Tell It on the Mountain* (New York: Dial, 1953), 33.

3 James Baldwin, *The Amen Corner* (New York: Dial, 1954), act 3; see the discussion of this scene in David Leeming, *James Baldwin: A Biography* (New York: Arcade, 1994), 108–9.

4 The phrase is the title of Miller's chapbook *The Amazing and Invariable Beauford DeLaney* (New York: Alicat Bookshop, 1945).

5 Miller, *Amazing and Invariable Beauford DeLaney*, reprinted in *Remember to Remember* (New York: New Directions, 1947), 17–18.

6 James Baldwin, "On the Painter Beauford Delaney," *Transition* 4, no. 18 (1965): 45; reprinted in Morrison, *James Baldwin*, 720.

7 Baldwin recalled this incident in 1984 in a *Paris Review* interview with Jordan Elgrably, "James Baldwin: The Art of Fiction No. 78," *Paris Review*, no. 91 (Spring 1984), https://www.theparisreview.org/interviews/2994/the-art-of-fiction-no-78-james-baldwin. For a discussion of this anecdote and its importance to Baldwin, see Leeming, *James Baldwin: A Biography*, 33–35.

8 Quoted in David Leeming, *Amazing Grace: A Life of Beauford Delaney* (New York: Oxford University Press, 1998), 129. This appeared originally in James Baldwin, "Introduction to Exhibition of Beauford Delaney Opening December 4, 1964 at the Galerie Lambert," in *Tableaux de Beauford-Delaney*, exh. cat. (Paris: Galerie Lambert, 1964). This short essay was revised by Baldwin as "On the Painter Beauford Delaney"; see note 6 above.

9 Quoted in Leeming, *Amazing Grace*, 129, from "Introduction to Exhibition of Beauford Delany Opening December 4, 1964 at the Galerie Lambert."

10 Beauford Delaney, letter to James Baldwin, September 17, 1954; James Baldwin Papers, Sc MG 936, Schomburg Center for Research in Black Culture, Manuscripts, Archives and Rare Books Division, New York Public Library.

11 James Baldwin, letter to Mary Painter, undated. Mary Garin-Painter Papers, in the Walter O. Evans Collection of James Baldwin, James Weldon Johnson Collection, Yale Collection of American Literature, Beinecke Rare Book and Manuscript Library, New Haven, CT.

12 Baldwin, "Introduction to Exhibition of Beauford Delaney," n.p.

13 Baldwin, "Introduction to Exhibition of Beauford Delaney," n.p.

14 Quoted in Leeming, *Amazing Grace*, 187, from the catalogue *Beauford Delaney* (Paris: Darthea Speyer Galerie, 1973); see Special Collections Online, University of Tennessee, Knoxville, Libraries, https://scout.lib.utk.edu/repositories/2/archival_objects/272045.

15 James Baldwin, interview with author, 1982.

TWO

The Mentor

James Baldwin, Beauford Delaney, and the Habit of Doing

Hilton Als

I think it's important to remember how you feel when you are alone as yourself. I don't mean that person who is part of the modern condition, alone with his or her or their own thoughts, but the artist-alone: that person whose deepest preoccupations, or should I say engagements, are with those twilight hours of the mind when the body doesn't exist, and the scars that the family inflicts on one's difference are not the point of the day—to avoid or put makeup on, to drink away or excuse. I mean the person who is alone with his queerness and how that influences one's great hope that one will not eventually be alone with it. Imagine what it must have seemed like to Beauford when Emile Capouya, that literary butch trade and, it seems, a friend to everyone, telephoned and said, "I have this friend . . . ," and imagine, on hearing the word *friend*, Beauford saying, "Yes, have him come on over," then putting his phone down and wondering what Emile's friend might be—what he might think of this man from Tennessee living in this strange world of downtown Manhattan, painting more or less in obscurity—and wondering if this friend of Emile's might be his friend, too? Was he queer? Emile did not say, and, in any case, in those days one did not say. And, in any case, what if he was? Beauford had been hurt by any number of men physically and emotionally because of his queerness, and, in any case, it was something he learned to hide from the world—the large flower of himself. Or hide under paint. What did his face reveal about his journey from the South to New York to be an artist? Sometimes his mind did not see his face quite right. His mind veered off in other directions that didn't appear quite real to the world. Sometimes there were voices, other times there were colors, and sometimes his mind told him to do strange things, like walking. He walked all over the city trying to find his face. He couldn't find it in mirrors, when he could look in mirrors, because when the world tells you you have no value or the wrong currency as yourself, you do not look into mirrors.

But now, on the day Emile called him, he was relatively calm. He could smell the paint and see his home for what it was—paint, a home—instead of something fantastical that might gobble him up whole. How many hours did he spend street-haunting in New York, in the night glare of those downtown Manhattan streets where sometimes one saw a sailor, but rarely family? Family you found in artist colonies, where sometimes there were artists like Georgia O'Keeffe and Elizabeth Bishop, who became friends. But what could offset one's queer loneliness? To find someone like "oneself"? And what did that mean? One's self? Who was that self? Experience told him that it was someone who was despised, and so, sometimes, you put a little booze over that fact, or pretended that being alone was better than feeling the misfortune of love.

And yet there were its joys, too. Someone who picked a flower and handed it to you on the street for a penny, or the deep blackness to be found in a curb at night. Love. Imagine that. Imagine it keeping you safe and warm somewhere listening to Mabel Mercer records, Mabel on Cole Porter, or Bessie on the road, suitcase in hand, or better yet, imagine walking in front of someone with suitcase in hand, looking for a room for love in a world that said that everywhere there was no rest to be had because of what you looked like, and to that world that meant what you smelled like, and how could those sheets ironed and bleached to perfection contain your act of love? Where he came from—what Flannery O'Connor called the Christ-haunted South, a segregated world—love was not even a possibility. It was all wrong, your eyes resting on a boy's chin, and in the humid summers, boys at the Tennessee River, unmindful of your loneliness as they ducked and dove in the muddy river that had swallowed its share of death, too.

But he was in New York now, and Emile had just called, and he tried to stay focused on the paint. Because he had a tendency to get excited when there was the possibility of friendship. Friendship protected you from your own mind, sometimes. The mind that heard things. The same mind that longed for friendship and made images born out of loneliness, and memory. In his paintings there was the memory of home mixed in with Black families he observed in New Jersey, but the thing he didn't know how to paint, except sometimes when a sailor would sit for him, was longing. He felt it all the time, but he didn't know how to paint it, to put it on the canvas the way that Toulouse-Lautrec, for instance, with his dramatically crippled and shortened legs, put his longing to have a stronger, straighter, more acceptable form on canvas when he painted those beautiful dancers at the Moulin Rouge. In that work and so many other paintings there was longing, close up and far away, and how do you paint that? Perhaps if he had a friend he would long for them in the best possible way, and he could paint that for history's sake, and as he put the finishing touches on one work the doorbell rang and there was Emile's friend. Skinny and bug-eyed, and he had a face, and the boy smiled that he was a boy, but a smart kid capable of assessing the situation—seeing loneliness in others and articulating it, because he had the words Beauford didn't have. That was clear from the first. Through that gap between his front teeth, words hissed out and in like breath and as simply and complicatedly as him saying: Hi, I'm Emile's friend. Are you the artist? By saying so, this kid—Jimmy was his name—said that he was an artist, and that he was there to learn from him, and Delaney could feel, as the boy agreed to sit for him on their first date, as it were, and he began to paint him leaving the genitals out—he could not face that, to face that would be to face what he wanted. What a strange, strong child this was, dying to be seen; later he learned that his father had said he was ugly, another example of male foolishness and the wounding impulse. But in a forest, a riot of color and density of so-called exotica, a kind of Henri Rousseau in a gay ghetto setting, and he wondered and wanted so much as he painted and the boy did not turn away from him (see plate 1). Could this be the end of loneliness for them both, this sitting? Could they fold racism and hurt into one another's skin and in doing so find not so much freedom but a lessening of their burden, a relative lightness that allowed them to be spirits resting at last, resting and dancing and seeing the world in one another in a universe that, when it saw them coming, for the most part looked away?

THREE

"You Pay for Your Life with Your Life"

James Baldwin's Search for Jimmy Baldwin, 1969–1972

Ed Pavlić

Years ago I did research for a book about James Baldwin to be titled "No Time to Rest." My reading centered on unpublished letters that Baldwin had written to his brother David over the course of thirty-three years. Reading the version of Baldwin's life and work as he told it to the person closest to him in the world, it came to me that this writer, who was both timeless and intensely historically engaged, lived out four roles: (1) "James Baldwin," the illustrious public writer, civil rights icon, and "spokesman for the Negro"; (2) "Jimmy Baldwin," the friend and lover, expansive partier, raconteur, and friend to the people of the night, among others; (3) "Jamie Baldwin," the brother and son and uncle; and (4) the ever-emerging writer who worked, often alone with a typewriter, as if he had a name nobody knew, no name in the street, no name at all. This chapter concerns mainly the second of these interlocked personae, "Jimmy Baldwin," in an era that was pivotal and perilous for them all.

As his Hollywood project, a screenplay telling the story of Malcolm X, fell apart in 1969 (as so many things did in late-1960s America), an all-but-burnt-out James Baldwin intuited that it was time to step away from his direct engagement with American politics and culture. He decided to gather up whatever pieces of Jimmy Baldwin's life could be found and walk off the stage. Jamie Baldwin told his brother David that he thought it must be said he'd done his best, but he'd done all he could. He also told him that his personal life was crushed at the bottom of a suitcase he didn't have the heart to unpack. Leaving Los Angeles, Baldwin touched down in Paris for five days; he picked up his young lover, Alain, and his oldest mentor, Beauford Delaney. The three stopped in Athens on their way to Istanbul, a place where Baldwin meant to unpack his suitcases and reconstruct a private life. This was the crucial dimension of experience—one that existed only between, and at times among, people—that he'd described to David much earlier, in 1959, when he had "no time to rest." A decade later, it wasn't rest Baldwin needed. Instead, he sought a renewed sense of mutuality, a kind of intimate pressure system in which he hoped to regain, or maybe build anew, his sense of who *he* was, what was what, and why it mattered. This realm of mutual intimacy was *Jimmy* Baldwin's world. So it was that he'd go to Istanbul, along with Alain and Beauford, in search of Jimmy Baldwin.

I know about these dynamics mostly from *Jamie* Baldwin's letters to his brother, letters shared with me by their sister. Baldwin's first post-Hollywood note to David was postmarked July 14, 1969. He wrote it on the flight to Europe, saying he was aloft in one way and afloat in another and on the way to Istanbul to live with Beauford and Alain. In *Talking at the Gates: A Life of James Baldwin* (1991), James Campbell lists the following entry from Baldwin's FBI file: "Advised . . . James Baldwin arrived in Istanbul, Turkey, from Athens, Greece, via Air France on July 13, 1969."[1] Walking off the historical stage wouldn't be as easy as getting on a plane. Up to a point, however, it worked.

Baldwin began to realize that locating Jimmy would involve more than eluding television cameras, evading podiums, and enduring political surveillance. He'd have to contend with what his work with the freedom movement and its aftermath had put him through, as it had so many others. He also would have to learn to cope with the warping power of celebrity in his life. There were no easy exits from the public visibility and race politics in which he had immersed himself. He carried their harrowing residues in his body and mind. The velocity and intensity of the public work had changed the chemistry of his multiple selves, skewing their relationships to each other and the world. It wasn't an ordeal he could have survived much longer, but it had been a very *real* experience. Many other people hadn't survived at all; many others, he was quite certain, wouldn't ever recover. Imperceptibly, and in ways he'd need to discover, his experience had established terms he'd need to chart and confront as he sought to change his life into something he *could* continue living. Yet rather than a "return" to Jimmy's world as it had been before the dawn of his politicized fame in 1963, the years between 1969 and 1972 were a period of reassessment and realignment. There was no going back, not for America and certainly not for him. Relationships at every level would never be as they had been.

During the previous years, Baldwin hadn't paid much attention to any of that. He'd had neither the time nor the perspective to do so. Now he knew his first task was to explore how the texture of Jimmy's world—both his interior and his social worlds—had been altered by fame, notoriety and, quite literally, political terror. Baldwin declared in 1969, "I know how you watch, as you grow older, literally, this is not a figure of speech; the corpses of your brothers and your sisters pile up around you."[2] At that point, in his mind, America had killed three of his famous friends, Medgar Evers, Malcolm X, and Martin Luther King Jr. It had also taken John and Robert Kennedy, no friends of Baldwin, to be sure, but deaths he associated with their reluctant embrace of certain aspects of the civil rights movement. All of these corpses and so many others devastated Baldwin's hopes for a broadened democracy based on racial justice and brought about by interracial coalitions such he'd envisioned in the early 1960s.

Just as his relationship to longtime friends had been warped by the intensity of his life in the public eye and political crosshairs, his encounters with new people would be shaped by his compelling but uncomfortable celebrity. James Baldwin's "business" partners would be swept up by Jimmy's charismatic power. New personal acquaintances of Jimmy's would be seduced by James's fame. Baldwin knew, in a way, that whether others would admit it or not, the things that had happened to him *had* happened to everyone. Yet at times, without knowing it, he'd judge artistic peers in relation to what he'd put himself through, the dues he had paid, and where the experience had landed him.

But all that was too abstract to deal with; it was time to refocus on people close at hand and reach outward from there. On February 17, 1970, Baldwin wrote David from Istanbul and described the warped perceptions that were bending him and his world out of shape. It worked both ways: he had trouble gauging the presence of his friends and people he met, and they had trouble gauging him. Nobody, it seemed, was exactly who, what, or where they appeared to be. He could feel a new kind of labor that just talking with people seemed to demand. People, he told David, always wanted to tell him their troubles, as if he had none of his own. He felt that he'd become a kind of symbol, even a drug, for people, especially those he met for the first time. People arrived into his company to deliver their despair, in elaborate and dramatic detail. Some unstated and mysterious power they'd invested in Baldwin catalyzed their catharsis. Yet he wrote that as they spoke, he felt that he knew most of their stories better than they did, even before they told them. It seemed that if he didn't sit there motionless, he'd spill their life stories all over the floor and make a mess. Moreover, he doubted that the version of the story these people unveiled could do anything for them, and he was unsure of his own ability to help them, since he hadn't saved himself.

Having put his life on pause from 1963 to 1969 in order to engage the political movements and public trials of the outside world, Baldwin regarded people he met and some he'd long known as excessively self-involved. Obsessed with themselves, he thought, they hadn't learned very much. He confided to his brother in letters how people wanted to be taken care of, healed, heard, even hurt. *Jimmy* felt himself cast in roles that enlisted *James* in support of people's illusions. He noted in these letters that his thoughts were of disengagement: these were things people mostly had to do for themselves. They were certainly nothing a comment from a famous stranger could make go away.

His old friend and future biographer James Weathersby was one such person. Two weeks after arriving in Istanbul, Baldwin told David that he would no longer write to Weathersby: all his letters did was provoke fear and resentment. As this incident illustrated, in some inexplicable way Baldwin felt distant from exactly the people to whom he was supposed to be closest. He felt this way, for instance, about agent and film producer Gene Lerner. In February 1970, Baldwin told his brother that Lerner had taken it upon himself to sever all of his professional ties in hopes of taking on Baldwin as his only and exclusive client. Playing down his role, Baldwin claimed that all he was trying to do was be Lerner's friend. He'd been unaware of how the weight of his fame and power, real and perceived, twisted and amplified Jimmy Baldwin's dilemmas in dealing with his personal world.

Thus Jimmy Baldwin felt himself cast in new roles by old friends and peers such as Lerner and Weathersby. The novelist James Jones was another. *From Here to Eternity*, the novel (1951) and the movie (1953), had made Jones famous. Part of the tension between Baldwin and Jones arose precisely from their clashing versions of what to do with success. In February 1970, Baldwin told David that he'd had an awful fight with Jones. Jones accused Baldwin of going back on promises he'd made to Beauford Delaney. Baldwin thought his relationship to Beauford was none of Jones's business. For Baldwin, the real issue was how Jones's wife had used their money to manipulate her husband, with Jones's 1967 novel, *Go to the Widow-Maker*, as evidence. What the incident actually showed, however, was that, having lived so much of his time, by then, exposed to political and personal risks at seemingly every level of life, Jimmy Baldwin had little patience with people, even successful artists such as Jones, who had used their success to insulate themselves from the dangers of the world but thereby lost the living textures of their lives. Putting his finger on the threat he represented to Jones's life, one that had nothing to do with Beauford Delaney, Baldwin told David that what made it all so fucking sad was that James Jones was the last person in Paris who didn't know about his own mad crush on Baldwin.

Baldwin was surprised by his power to warp and disturb, even absorb, people he met. And he knew he'd been warped as well. The result was an isolation that enveloped him in new ways. Baldwin knew the effect was partly of his doing. But he couldn't measure it. Fame, for the famous as well as for those who look on, is an *act*. But he knew the act was also real. One must understand fame, he decided, so as to *act* it and not be *acted upon* by it. Boiling the many-leveled dynamic down to an image that either balanced the books or scripted the end, or both, he concluded to David that at a certain point, one paid for one's life with one's life.

Baldwin's relationship with Alain, his lover in Istanbul, allowed him to gauge the distortions and refractions in other people's eyes caused by his fame. That love also helped him to assess how his own point of view had changed while his attention to himself was obscured by the historical spotlight he'd worked in at least from 1963 to the summer of 1969. The time he spent with Alain in Istanbul was the longest, most continuous domestic relationship he'd ever had. Early in his return to Jimmy's world, he wrote to David from Istanbul about the second sight provided by his connection to Alain. The two made their way through abrupt ups and downs. Alain was far more domestic than Jimmy and felt that it was his job to protect him. If anything happened, Alain was fond of saying, what would he tell Jimmy's family? Alain had such control over the home that Jimmy told David, with much irritation, that he'd almost forgotten how to cook. But the hardest thing for Jimmy was to read things about himself, and even about others, as reflected in the eyes of someone who really loved him. He found himself disturbed by how Alain's disdain for people they hung out with revealed something about how those same people felt about Jimmy. He'd always avoided seeing this in people. Now, via these mutual mirrors on his private world, he began to see people as Alain saw them.

Beauford Delaney stayed with Jimmy and Alain for a few weeks. He soaked up the Istanbul summer sun, painted daily, and even gave Alain painting lessons. On July 27, Jimmy wrote to David saying that Beauford considered Alain a very talented student. Baldwin entertained the role of teacher, agreeing that he, now together with Beauford, was giving the young man his first actual education. Baldwin confessed that he realized that this role would teach him plenty about himself as well. By early August, Beauford had left and Jimmy wondered about Alain, his young student-lover, who Baldwin knew was being flung into vast new life lessons. He told David that the results could be creative or destructive for Alain. With a kind of grim wonder, he told his brother that no matter what happened to Alain, Jimmy wouldn't be broken.

James's time in the crosshairs of history had smelted some new steel in Jimmy. In ways very unlike in previous decades, Baldwin felt he could no longer be personally broken. He said that if lovers could know this about each other, a new kind of mutually creative relationship became possible—and that this was the whole point. He'd traveled a long and torturous journey to get to this point. Alain had yet to make such a trip. He ended the letter with a four-line poem in end rhymes about bristling pain that can't be explained.

Assessing his new position, Baldwin drew directly on the social and intimate energies circulating in Jimmy's world. He wrote often about how the pressures of love, its crests and craters, reveal things to lovers about themselves and each other, as well as things about the *world*, that couldn't be revealed in any other way. He wrote to David that he was learning how everything was personal yet also beyond personal. He was beginning to understand how he existed for other people as a possession, not a person—perhaps a puzzle to be solved. Baldwin wondered how he'd avoided doing this same thing to other people. He was coming to understand how one learns certain things about oneself *only* from others, with love, and that the lesson never ends. Now, in middle age, he felt that he was just beginning to recognize himself. And it was in Alain's arms and in Alain's eyes that he was learning the most.

In Istanbul, Baldwin reacquainted himself with the intimate textures of Jimmy's life that were unavailable to James, who faced the glare of history. Triangulating the lovers' views of each other and their witness to the gaze of others upon them, Jimmy measured his relationship to the world in a way that James's public and political pulpits couldn't manage. As a result, he could assess the relationship between his private and public lives and at times even honor the distance between the two.

Jimmy wrote to David from Istanbul about one such occasion, which occurred on September 10, 1969. He'd been to the bank and to the store to buy whiskey—Ken Keith (who was then head of the United States Information Service in Istanbul) and possibly his mother Gertrude were coming to Jimmy's place that evening. Baldwin told David that as he ran other errands, an elderly Turkish man had stopped him in a bookstore and asked him, in French, where he was from. Jimmy told the man he was from New York, and the man recognized him. The man then told everyone in the store that Baldwin was a great writer who was fighting for Turkey, for everyone. Everyone in the store stared and smiled. Then this man translated what he'd told the others into French for him. Baldwin told his brother that, previously in his life, he'd have been embarrassed and disturbed by such a display. But something new had allowed him to accept it. Somehow, in this new phase of his life, at least in Turkey, the famous man and the private person could coexist. Jimmy told the man he was honored. He told David that he felt that maybe, no matter how different they were, one part of himself could now honor the other.

The scene in the bookstore suggested to Jimmy that the public and private dimensions of his experience didn't have to be at such dreadful odds. Somewhat angular mutual needs, even disparate and distant ones, could coexist. James Baldwin's fame didn't have to bring chaos and terror into Jimmy's life. If his different selves could see and know each other, and if he could come to terms with the distinctions as well as the overlaps, maybe he could go on. The only way to keep *James* human, Baldwin was coming to believe, would be to keep him attached to *Jimmy* in a way that was at once personal and beyond personal. Musing on the scene in the store, he told his brother that, while walking home from the encounter, he felt anew his intelligence, his drive, and his anger. He said he could see the monstrous danger the combination might have become. But, he thought, because of how he'd learned about suffering first—his and other people's—a powerful empathy shaped his response to experience at all levels. He knew his angry empathy bore costs, but he also knew it was fundamental.

On October 29, 1969, Baldwin wrote to David that he'd stripped his life down almost exclusively to Jimmy's personal and intimate world. The letter makes clear the importance of David to this world, but it also makes clear how the intensity of Baldwin's life with Alain—and the domestic tension that now characterized it—helped him measure both his place and his weight in the larger social world and the weight of that world in himself. He now marveled at the power his name carried and understood its danger: how other people might react to that power while the famous person notices nothing and simply rides the obsessions that made him famous in the first place. Somehow the famous person slips into a habit of treating people like a public, a single person as a crowd. In *No Name in the Street* (1972), for instance, Baldwin described his impression of himself visiting the home of his old friend Arthur Moore in the spring of 1968, while he felt "millions of people staring at us both."[3] He realized how strange it was that he'd slipped into the mask of a famous man while Moore and his family had become part of a faceless crowd. It was as if they were all there in the room but still couldn't find each other. At the time, no one understood the dynamic and its disastrous results. In Istanbul, from the summer of 1969 into the spring of 1970, Baldwin began to discover and measure this new terrain of experience.

There seemed to be no exit. Jimmy would have to learn to coexist with James Baldwin and his world. That was the bridge to other people, who offered the only viable reflection of one's self in the world. Mirrors be damned; they lied almost as much as cameras. In Istanbul, the pressures of his life with Alain brought this social dynamic into view in a way that he began to understand and that caused Baldwin to reassess the power of fame and of intimacy. He wrote to David that while he loved Alain very much, being loved in return was new to him. Love was about living life, an otherwise ordinary life that was now alert to the possibility that a connection between lovers' bodies could bring something into being, even if only for a moment. Love made possible a transformative alchemy, something unique to the two lovers but also involving many things that were quite beyond them. All this could arise out of the complex chemistry of desire. In a letter sent on October 29, 1969, Baldwin told David that love's possibility, as he learned about it with Alain, was a fully embodied experience, depending on the taste of salt on the skin, the texture of bodies, and the odor of sweat in the room. The powerfully particular and embodied reality of intimacy that love made possible also, he wrote, explained the terror of lovers. After they'd experienced each other—and therefore themselves and the world—to that degree, how could they ever live, alone, without it, or at a distance?

This was sexual; it was also political. As Baldwin worked through these tensions and needs, he reframed the structure of what he called "confessions." Confession, as Baldwin conceived it, had everything to do with how personal and private levels of experience related to social and political ones. Describing those levels to David in his letter of October 29, he said that Alain thought of Jimmy as his grandmother, a woman who'd raised him and whom he had cared for in her old age. In turn, Baldwin told David, in Alain he saw all the kids in the streets that needed to be saved and that—as it felt to him—he'd abandoned. With their intimate life blessed and burdened in these ways, they'd changed each other. This made them responsible to and for each other. *That* was love. Any other details of identity were trivial. The enormous need that allows no time to rest can—indeed, must—be mutually but never identically felt; that accounts for some of the tension as history becomes a living presence in our personal and sexual lives.

Baldwin knew that after their extended time living more or less together, Alain would have to move into his own life, just as Jimmy would have to move on. This would entail Baldwin's turn to *No Name in the Street*. In this book, as he'd written to his brother and sister from California in March 1968, he'd attempt to write like Aretha Franklin sang and to address the person and the people, the intimate and the historical, at the same time. On February 27, 1970, he wrote to David that the play he was directing, *Fortune and Men's Eyes*, was a smash hit in Istanbul and that his novel *Another Country* (1962) had just been published in a Turkish translation.[4] Also, the United States Information Service had created a furor by banning his most recent novel, *Tell Me How Long the Train's Been Gone* (1968). The result was that he was now as famous in Istanbul as he was in New York or Paris.

In spring of 1970, Jimmy launched Alain into his life and finished directing the "play of the year" in Istanbul. Dealing with an illness that would prove to be hepatitis, he tried—and largely failed—to get to work on *No Name in the Street*. Baldwin would leave Istanbul in the summer, after filming the short film *James Baldwin: From Another Place* with Sadat Pakay. By the end of 1970, he'd land in Saint-Paul-de-Vence, France, where, during the next few years, and after many delays, he'd finish *No Name in the Street* and much of *If Beale Street Could Talk* (1974).

On December 7, 1970, Jimmy wrote to David from l'Hôtel le Hameau in Saint-Paul-de-Vence, announcing his arrival in the town where eventually he would establish a sense of home unlike any he'd ever had. Crucially, it was a place where the writer could reawaken. He joked to his brother that he felt like a novice monk who'd landed, again, at an unlikely and secluded perch. He was okay, but work on the first chapter of *No Name in the Street* came very slowly, like drops of blood. He said he knew the struggle all too well. Books were like lovers who tease and taunt and then pretend to be only ticklish when you grab hold of them. Then, in order to avoid violence, you make love with the work. In this drama, he told David, men and women were the same; the details of gender didn't matter. But, he said, if you want to court real serious trouble in the heat of the night, try writing a book.

Baldwin had written to David that Jimmy's point of view on the world, the one he'd reconnected with through his time with Alain, joined his personal life to his social and historical experiences. As he'd been doing increasingly, in Pakay's film Baldwin referred to himself as a poet. In his 1973 interview with the *Black Scholar*, he would explain what he meant by *poet*:

> When I say poet, it's an arbitrary word. It's a word I use because I don't like the word artist. . . . I'm not talking about literature at all. I'm talking about the recreation of experience, you know, the way it comes back. Billie Holiday was a poet. She gave you back your experience. She refined it, and you recognized it for the first time because she was in and out of it and she made it possible for you to bear it. And if you could bear it, then you could begin to change it. That's what a poet does. I'm not talking about books. I'm talking about a certain kind of passion, a certain kind of energy which people produce.[5]

In Saint-Paul-de-Vence, Baldwin continued to search for how to merge the personal and historical point of view he'd need to write *No Name in the Street*, "if [he] could bear it." He had heard clues to this method in Aretha Franklin's album *Aretha Arrives* (1967). In his first letter to David from Saint-Paul, in the midst of finding his position "in and out of it," he told David that he was mostly interested in completing a journey that had begun when he'd first gone to the American South to tour sites of the freedom movement way back in September 1957. In an undated letter from early spring 1971, Baldwin reports having moved from l'Hôtel le Hameau into an apartment in the house he'd eventually buy. The hotel had been fine for convalescing while he was sick, but it had been past time to leave. In addition, the hotel bills were staggering. He told David that the time for sickness and healing was over, unless he wanted to be sick. He didn't. And the hard work was just beginning.

Baldwin's biographers have stressed the conservative culture of Saint-Paul-de-Vence, while noting that, with time, Jimmy's gracious manners eventually won over the hesitant residents. This was likely true, at least in the daytime. His immediate comments in letters to David offer a slightly different impression. He said that leaving the hotel had left him open to a community of wannabe painters, all of whom now wanted to paint him. Or so they said. Jimmy told his brother that it seemed to him that these painters favored working late at night, alone with him, and preferred their subject minus his "jock-strap." He paused to wonder if that was fair. But he let the characterization stand. "James" had followed "Jimmy" even to that place. He told David that things could get weird, which probably meant that they already had. As he'd done for years, he fantasized that heterosexual monogamy might still be possible and might stabilize his private life so he could work. By the early 1970s, the implausibility of these fantasies was apparent in a way that both Jimmy and David recognized.

After *No Name in the Street* was published and had reaped what Baldwin felt was willful abuse from reviewers, Jimmy had a new vantage point on the way James Baldwin had been positioned by both the mainstream and radical tastemakers of American culture. Baldwin was battling his publisher, Dial Press, over contracts that didn't pay him enough. He wanted to buy the house he was renting, and he needed cash. He was thinking about new fantasies of various kinds. Yet what also occurred to him was a letter he'd written to David many years before, on December 17, 1959, saying that the basis for the mutual need between people was that, in the end, no one knew very much about their own lives. Facts that stood independent of people weren't really the point. He said life was about ceasing to dream false dreams and learning to dream truthful ones. This was necessary because the most serious fact of life was that we can never know it. We must, he thought, therefore trust it. That meant trusting each other, or at least trusting something *in* each other.

Recasting that idea, on June 24, 1972, Jimmy wrote to David that fantasies were dangerous necessities. Fame had taught him how it was to be the object of people's fantasies. This had taken him a long time to learn, because he'd become famous by living very close to his own fantasies. One can't give up on one's fantasies, he thought, but it was crucial not to surrender to them, either. A person, and an artist like himself, he'd found, must live extremely close to their fantasies in order to stay within reach of the truth contained in them. This was a truth about things far beyond himself. The key was to *use* one's fantasies and not to *be used* by them.

Through the lens of *No Name in the Street*, Baldwin could see historical flames looming, flames fueled by fantasies: white people's and Black people's fantasies about themselves and each other. White people, having had the choice and power to call themselves anything they wanted, had chosen (and chose anew every day) to consider themselves "white," mystically entitled to happy, clean, and safe lives. That impossible and disastrous social and personal formula would now, as Baldwin saw it, meet up with Black people's fantasies, which were collecting a new and crucial kind of power to name themselves, a power Black people had never before had. He didn't know what would happen, but if the dangers of his own fantasies were any guide, the prospect was terrifying.

Some of Jimmy's fantasies were quite mundane, even mechanical; some more dangerous than others. Baldwin was even mad enough, for a little while, to attempt to learn to drive. He told David he was only learning to drive to prove that he could and to pick him up from the airport in Nice. Then, he told his brother, he'd go back to driving his typewriter. By the summer of 1972, again, Jimmy's point of view sat elbow to elbow with the unnamed writer at work. He told David he was working harder than he'd ever worked. He was lonely, which he knew would always be the case. And he was alone, which he knew was only temporary. He signed off the letter like he'd ended his first novel, quoting Mahalia Jackson. He was, as the song goes, glory hallelujah, on his way.

NOTES

1 James Campbell, *Talking at the Gates: A Life of James Baldwin* (Berkeley: University of California Press, 1991), 232.

2 Michael David Murphy, "'Baldwin's Nigger'—Transcription of James Baldwin in London, 1968," *Medium*, December 7, 2019, https://whileseated.medium.com/baldwins-nigger-transcription-of-james-baldwin-in-london-1968-358f27723506. This source is a transcription of the film *Baldwin's Nigger*, directed by Horace Ové, a 1969 documentary of a lecture by Baldwin at the West Indian Student Centre, London, accompanied by Dick Gregory. On the film, see Inge Blackman, "Baldwin's Nigger, 1969," *BFI Screenonline*, http://www.screenonline.org.uk/film/id/480522/index.html.

3 James Baldwin, *No Name in the Street* (New York: Dial, 1972), reprinted in *James Baldwin: Collected Essays*, ed. Toni Morrison (New York: Library of America, 1998), 364.

4 *Fortune and Men's Eyes* (1967), by John Herbert, is set in prison and explores themes of homosexuality.

5 James Baldwin, "*The Black Scholar* Interviews James Baldwin," in *Conversations with James Baldwin*, ed. Fred L. Standley and Louis Pratt (Jackson: University Press of Mississippi, 1989), 155.

FOUR

Beauford Delaney's Black Queer Fatherhood

Magdalena J. Zaborowska

When James Baldwin first met Beauford Delaney in the older artist's Greenwich Village studio in 1941, he was struck by his powers of seeing: "A short, round brown man . . . looked at me. He had the *most extraordinary eyes* I'd ever seen." Recalling their meeting in his 1985 essay "The Price of the Ticket," Baldwin also mentioned his high school friend Emile Capouya, who introduced him to Delaney, and concluded, "My running buddy had *sent me to the right one, and not a moment too soon.*"[1] Having recently quit preaching in his family's Pentecostal church in Harlem, Baldwin desperately needed an alternative father figure to guide him into the world of the arts and intellectual pursuits that, as an aspiring writer with no college degree, he was determined to enter. In an extraordinary turn of fortune, Delaney became such a guide and surrogate parent. Like Baldwin, Delaney was gay and Black and son of a preacher. He taught his young apprentice how to see himself beyond the destructive vision instilled by his stepfather, the Reverend David Baldwin.

Delaney's spiritual and artistic fatherhood of Baldwin would help the writer achieve a complex and unique literary aesthetic—one inflected by Delaney's idiosyncratic paintings and honed over decades of a familial relationship that included periods of cohabitation in France and Turkey.[2] Rejected by his Harlem stepparent, a physically and verbally abusive fundamentalist Christian, teenage Baldwin seemed caught between two irreconcilable Black father figures: a heteropatriarchal religious one who despised him as a "bastard" and a queer bohemian one who loved and nurtured him and his authorial aspirations. Neither was related to him by blood; both suffered from mental illness and had deep impact on his authorship and life. After David Baldwin's death in 1943, Delaney remained a central influence on Baldwin, until the painter's passing in 1979.

Rather than seeing Baldwin as torn between chronologically distant father figures presiding over discreet phases of his authorial life, I propose that we understand their presence as a persistent, achronological circulation throughout his literary works—intertwined, omnipresent, and in constant tension within the universe of his literary imagination. A triangular tableau of these two fathers together with Baldwin represents key homosocial, familial relationships that inflected his works and life and compels new readings of his oeuvre today. In Baldwin's later books—*No Name in the Street* (1972), *If Beale Street Could Talk* (1974), and *Just above My Head* (1979)—and especially in the essays "Me and My House" (1955), "Here Be Dragons" (1985), and "To Crush the Serpent" (1987), his focus on sexuality, gender, and race reaches far beyond concerns with mid-twentieth-century US masculinity and African American manhood, feeding into a larger humanistic project he first envisaged under Delaney's tutelage.

In what follows, I outline Baldwin's relationship with the Reverend David Baldwin and read achronologically the late essay "Here Be Dragons," in which the bastard son confronts most openly this first paternal relationship. Offering also an achronological reading of the earlier "Me and My House" (subsequently retitled "Notes of a Native Son") alongside several portraits of Baldwin by Delaney, I show how, thanks to Delaney's influence, Baldwin's art evolved in opposition to his stepfather's negation of his identity as a Black queer writer. From the first portrait of "the Prince" (as Delaney called him), *Dark Rapture* (1941; plate 1), which captures the psychic toll exacted by the youth's Harlem preacher father, through *Portrait of James Baldwin*

(1971; plate 31), Delaney's canvases provide a powerful visual context for Baldwin's evolution as a writer and thinker.[3]

As a Black, queer father, Delaney helped Baldwin become a critic and theorist of identity who forged a powerful, nonessentialist (and nonessentializing) form of Black queer literary aesthetics indebted to his painterly and paternal influences alike. By the time "Me and My House" was published in 1955—or a decade and a half after being adopted as Delaney's spiritual son—Baldwin had not only recast his relationship with the Reverend David Baldwin but also developed firm foundations for a revolutionary literary aesthetic that I term "Black queer humanism." This aesthetic blossomed decades later, in the still underappreciated works Baldwin wrote in his beloved house in Saint-Paul-de-Vence, France, and is a vital part of his legacy.

Rupturing Negation

Delaney's *Dark Rapture* (plate 1) is unique among his portraits of James Baldwin. Unlike later works, it focuses not on the writer's expressive face but on the teenage boy's nude, slightly averted body. Young Baldwin's features seem undefined. Delaney lets us look at his model, but it is unclear whether Baldwin is looking at us or turns his gaze away in shy vulnerability. Darkly luminous, his exposed body is splendid and self-contained. Speckled with colors reflecting the background that is part summer landscape, with trees and a fountain, part brightly striped sofa, this is the body of a young man the painter loved and cherished. His later portraits will focus on the face and the eyes of the man who will gradually emerge from this undefinable figure. The teen's face here is a blur of lines shot through with the bright sunshine framing it; floating on top of the erect body, his head is a vessel filled with light of possibility.

What this first painting registers most importantly, though, is how Baldwin has been made vulnerable at this early point in his life, how he has been taught to withdraw from being a strong, fully outlined, directly self-defined person who can look squarely back at the world. His body's position communicates indecisiveness and slight physical discomfort: he is sitting with his right leg bent at the knee and crossed under the left leg, whose foot is firmly planted on the floor and whose calf seems flexed. Should he sit back fully cross-legged or get up and leave? Should he recline comfortably, exposing his groin to view, or should he spring up, covering himself in shame? The positions of his arms amplify the impression, for the right hand is hidden behind the bent knee with elbow slightly curved, while his left palm is strongly planted in front, ready to push at the seat and get up. Delaney's brush captures the tension between vulnerability and shame, pride and sinewy strength. Baldwin is rendered motionless yet dynamic, sparkling with light and energy, yet afraid and uncertain. The Prince, in Delaney's eye, is both a wounded child and an erotically charged demigod, at whose feet he positions the overawed beholder's gaze.

What Delaney seems to have captured here is the painful impact of Baldwin's homophobic and violent stepfather, whose last name the stepson inherited upon his mother's marriage, when he was a young child. While that father figure, or simply "my father," as Baldwin recognizes the Reverend in "Me and My House," is mentioned in passing by scholars and biographers, Baldwin's works recall traumatic details of that relationship that affect how we view his portraits by Delaney.[4] For example, a memory of a beating disrupts the 1985 essay "Freaks and the American Ideal of Manhood," first published in *Playboy*, and later retitled "Here Be Dragons": "Once, my father gave me a dime . . . to go to the store for kerosene for the stove, and I fell on the icy streets and dropped the dime and lost it. My father beat me with an iron cord from the kitchen to the back room and back again, until I lay, half-conscious, on my belly on the floor."[5]

The father is the punisher and absolute ruler of the family and also an extension of the larger heteropatriarchal power that the state holds over children. As Baldwin asserted, "The American idea of masculinity: There are few things under heaven more difficult to understand or, when I was younger, to forgive."[6] In a 1969 interview he described David Baldwin as "righteous in the pulpit and a monster in the house. . . . And it wasn't so much a matter of punishment with him: *he was trying to kill us*. I've hated a few people, but *actually I've hated only one person, and that was my father*. . . . I was not his son. I was a bastard."[7] These beatings imprinted Baldwin with a profound fear of his father and contributed to his lifelong rejection of violence. The Reverend Baldwin also denigrated as ungodly all that his stepson loved and used to escape poverty and abuse at home: books, writing, theater, film, and nonreligious music. At nineteen, James Baldwin left this brutal home to live in Greenwich Village.

That same year, 1943, following a hospitalization for mental illness, David Baldwin passed on, leaving his stepson in charge of their large family. Baldwin had to abandon college aspirations and worked as a laborer for five long years, including alongside racist coworkers transplanted from Georgia. In 1948 he received a fellowship, left its larger part with his mother, and departed for Paris. That bold move was possible because, at sixteen, he had found the courage to pursue his own vocation as an artist, having beheld himself through Beauford Delaney's loving eyes as the "Prince of Dark Rapture," as we could retitle that first portrait from 1941.

Affirming Light

In another work featuring his protégé, *Portrait of James Baldwin* (1944; plate 2), Delaney revises what he saw in Baldwin at age sixteen—the potential but also the repression of an inner light first caught in *Dark Rapture*. These two depictions of Baldwin's body mark important stages in his life that were instrumental to honing his craft as a writer. In the 1944 pastel on paper, the inner light fights its way through the dark blues that encircle the writer's face, shown from the neck up. The face is surrounded by a halo-like silhouette of white, edged with a blue that is streaked here and there with pale orange that shimmers at the edges and corners. Baldwin's expressive eyes, flecked with sunlight, are boring into us, his full lips are half smiling, and the slight asymmetries of his ears, cheeks, chin, and nose are brimming with rich hues of sunshine reflected in water—yellow, red, orange, pinkish gray, purple, green, and brown. He is the Prince, fully and unequivocally. His face, so tentative in *Dark Rapture*, now blossoms into the fullness of keen intelligence and enlightened presence: the "Blue Prince."

In Delaney's later portraits, in black and yellow, in blue and green, indigo, white, and lime, Baldwin's facial features are clear. His eyes stare at us or into space; he is portrayed head-on as a witness and an unwavering interlocutor. This is especially so in the series included in *Beauford Delaney and James Baldwin: Through the Unusual Door*, the groundbreaking 2020 exhibit at the Knoxville Museum of Art: *Portrait of James Baldwin* (1965; plate 16), *James Baldwin* (1966; plate 17), and *Portrait of James Baldwin* (1971; plate 31). These three paintings capture Baldwin's eyes and penetrating gaze almost insistently—even the rather sketch-like yellow-and-black portrait from 1966, which appears almost monochromatic, with its stunning, intensely golden saturation. Thanks to that saturation, the thick, curly black lines outlining the body coalesce brilliantly in the writer's face and eyes, which bore into ours, witnessing us as much as we do the portrait.

Unlike these later works, the portrait *James Baldwin* (plate 5), which I date to 1957 (others place it in about 1945–50), seems an echo and radical reworking of *Dark Rapture* that captures another important moment in the writer's life. In this portrait, the young man's whole body can be seen, seated, even enthroned, with arms relaxing on invisible rests, broad shoulders clad in a blue top that is fluid like water, and strong legs in crimson-and-gold pants crossed at the knee. Here, Baldwin is almost levitating, as if he might be floating both backward and toward us through a tunnel of colorful lines and shapes framing his figure. Delaney's composition pulls together the competing abstract lines and geometric shapes of the pastel background to where Baldwin's abdomen, hips, and crossed legs suggest a center of gravity and a perspectival point. Echoing the coloring of the 1944 pastel *Portrait of James Baldwin* ("Blue Prince"; plate 2), this painting again shows us a Baldwin adored. Yet that is not all we can see.

By 1957, Baldwin's first two novels, a play, and a first essay collection had been published. He was "out" as a man who loved other men in the wake of his controversial second novel, the homosexual romance *Giovanni's Room* (1956). He boldly examined his relationship with his stepfather in "Me and My House," which appeared in *Harper's Magazine* (1955). He returned from France and began travels in the American South and work in support of the civil rights movement. He had *arrived*, in every sense of the word, as a writer, intellectual, and charismatic speaker. In this context, Delaney's adoring portrait of the seated Baldwin embodies a dynamism that suggests that its subject's journey is ongoing. Baldwin's eyes are not as prominent and focused as in the other portraits; he's likely looking more inward than at us. His eyes seem bloodshot; his hair is red, flaming at the top and streaked with white. A slightly greenish hue in his cheeks gives him a haggard look. This is the man who will soon leave the United States again, this time for Turkey, to write *The Fire Next Time* (1963) and *Blues for Mister Charlie* (1964). Up close, Delaney's Prince (take 2) is not as regal and powerful as he may have seemed. The propulsive movements of his levitating body may not be entirely comfortable, seated as if he is making music at a piano that is invisible to and unheard by the rest of us; his slightly ajar lips are blood-red on top and drained-white on the bottom.

Delaney's seductive, sophisticated visual trickery makes me think about brushstrokes as syntax and plot, as literary, textured, and textual. This painting reads like Baldwin's "Me and My House." The first two paragraphs of the essay sketch out Baldwin's life as entangled with his neighborhood, city, and country. The text moves back and forth through space, time, and history; it fuses colors, sounds, and textures. As the family are driving the father's body to the graveyard the day after the Harlem riots of 1943, "through a wilderness of smashed plate glass," the son notes "God Himself" having devised "the most sustained and brutally dissonant of codas" to David Baldwin's life. That Old Testament father and God are still firmly in the son's head, pounding out a guilty message on the day of his nineteenth birthday: "That the violence which rose all about us as my father left the world had been devised as a corrective for the pride of his eldest son."[8] The death is also the beginning of a new intellectual journey, as Baldwin begins to "wonder about . . . [his father's] life and also, in a new way, to be apprehensive of . . . [his] own." That journey and the artistic apprenticeship with Delaney take a dozen years before culminating in this masterful essay.

Like Baldwin's text, Delaney's portrait of 1957 reflects, refracts, and indeed moves with its subject's authorial powers, revealing his fears and traumatic memories. Baldwin looks as if his veins are indeed "pumped full of poison," as if he were deathly ill with effects of racism that killed his father, that "dread, chronic disease, the unfailing symptoms of which are a kind of blind fever, a pounding in the skull, and fire in the bowels."[9] Delaney's painterly advice to his protégé, "Don't describe it, show it," inflects the essay's economic style, while his colors and composition imprint its imagery. Like Baldwin's writing, Delaney's painting reveals its subject's and the portraitist's personal pain; they're father and son in that canvas.

Baldwin wrote in a 1963 letter to Harry Belafonte that he "always considered [Delaney] to be my spiritual father" and that it was "impossible, probably, to describe his work. There is something in it of Cezanne and Van Gogh, and it owes a great deal to the blues." His own writing from that time, and the works that followed, could be described by the next sentence from that letter: "But this is only to suggest, and very weakly, that he brings great light out of the terrible darkness of his journey, and makes his journey, and his endeavors, and his triumph, ours."[10] Learning from the literary son, the spiritual father makes us see, through his canvases, a familial story. Yet in the son's body painted by Delaney, and in the essays that Baldwin wrote, the Reverend Baldwin is still very much part of the family tableau.

Embracing Conundrums

Sixteen years after the 1957 portrait of Baldwin was unveiled, Sedat Pakay filmed Baldwin in Istanbul. In his black-and-white art film *James Baldwin: From Another Place* (1973), Baldwin appears as a complex subject, a visual contradiction. We open to a view of a still, black body entangled in white sheets. We want to gasp, but he stirs and gets out of bed. Clad only in white briefs, he stops at the window, pulls the curtains open, then puts on a bathrobe and sits back on the bed, hunched, lighting up and inhaling a cigarette. In the long shot accompanied by an asynchronous gravel-voiced soundtrack, he looks at the camera, his head cocked slightly. If you let it, his gaze will pull you into the frame: into the room, the bed, into his head and slight body, whose unease registers in the black-and-white film much as it does in Delaney's portraits.

Pakay's film shows us the middle-aged Baldwin through the eyes of the young Turkish artist captivated by the Black American writer's beauty. (Pakay also sought Baldwin's help with a student visa, so as to study with Walker Evans at Yale University.) Pakay's framing helps us trace the vast change the writer had undergone, from the teen model that Delaney painted in 1941, through the successful yet tormented young man he captured in 1957, to the internationally famous African American intellectual and a mentor-model to Pakay in 1970. In the film, Baldwin's initial gaze at the camera communicates maturity and weariness; other scenes reveal him smartly dressed, walking through crowds, feeding pigeons, browsing through a bookstall, and colliding with Turkish passersby. Pakay's direction and Cengiz Tacer's camera embrace the whole man and his body unflinchingly, including the seminude bedroom shot of his morning hard-on. The film mixes close-ups of his face and full-body shots, from a private smile Baldwin flashes on the balcony of his apartment to a tongue-in-cheek scene at the end, where he sits sipping tea, flanked by two stone-faced tuxedo-clad waiters, with a ring of mute onlookers slowly revealed in a slow pan. The voice-over, featuring Baldwin's smoky voice spliced from a previously recorded interview, amplifies Pakay's vision of the artist as subject of a hybrid, asynchronous filmic portraiture.[11]

In Pakay's film, too, we see evidence that Baldwin continuously circled from one father figure to another in his literary imagination. His dueling fathers—the Reverend and the Black queer painter—begin as oppositional figures, but as his craft matures, they change location in his narrative imaginary in relation to each other. We can see Baldwin wrestling with both in a scene in Pakay's film where he discusses his sexuality. Seated at his writing desk, his face filling the screen, he explains his position as a Black, gay man: "I was very quickly in a kind of . . . space, where I had to deal with my life as though I had no father, I had no mother . . . as though I somehow arrived, with no antecedents." The pain of having been rejected by his homophobic stepfather is somewhat obscured by the sophisticated storytelling style he developed after being accepted and loved by his adopted spiritual father. But the preceding frames of his restless hands, face, and eyes reveal someone who, while a master storyteller, is also a tormented man, much as he appears in Delaney's portraits. Baldwin cautions that things are never what they seem: "The life that I actually live . . . is very different from the lives that people imagine." How to read him beyond appearance and the illusion of what and who we would like him to be?

Baldwin's marvelous yet underappreciated last novel, *Just above My Head*, is filled with scenes that allude to this tension between paternal inheritances. The sprawling narrative showcases the painterly craft he learned from Delaney and mobilizes the pain and trauma of his personal and public life at the time. For example, Hall Montana's first impressions of New York City upon his return from a tour of duty in Korea voice this contradiction of belonging through a street tableau we witness through his eyes:

> I had not seen these streets in so long, and I had seen so many other things, that they hit me like a hammer. People adjust to the scale of things around them—cottages, streams, bridges, wells, narrow winding roads—and now I was in a howling wilderness, where everything was out of scale. . . . I had not heard this noise in so long—incessant, meaningless, reducing everyone to a reflex, just as the towering walls of the buildings forced everyone to look down, into the dog shit at their feet. No one ever looked up . . . except to watch some maddened creature leap from the walls, or to calculate their own leap—yet people lived here, and so had I. . . . I was repelled, but fascinated: embittered, but home.[12]

Recalling the urban nightlife scenes of Delaney's paintings, such as *Untitled (Village Street Scene)* (1948; plate 6) or *Untitled (Jazz Club)* (ca. 1950), Montana's "home" is an assault of colors and a cacophony of sound, a canvas filled with stories and movement.[13] Like Delaney's 1941 and 1957 seated portraits of Baldwin, this description registers traumatic memories hitting a body "like a hammer." The people whom Montana is thinking about are not the city dwellers around him, but Koreans and US soldiers he saw killing one another in his past. The past will not let him go; the figures now fill him with unspeakable images that his eyes cannot unsee. He cannot or will not describe them, yet these horrific images burst through the city scene as he takes it in all around him. The sensation is the blow; the text *shows* it.

The narrator of this paragraph is a hybrid of Montana (first person) and the marvelous limited third person that Baldwin adapted from Henry James and, with Delaney's help, transformed into a visionary literary voice. This scene is written as a painting; its intensity is akin to that in Delaney's portraits, where Baldwin stares directly at the viewer, and to that in Pakay's film, where his gaze first bores into us and then evades us while he instructs us to distrust what we see, hear, and know. We feel the power of Baldwin's literary imagination just like Montana feels that hammer blow hitting him once he is, unsafely, back home.

With his two fathers entwined like a Black, gendered cypher at the center of his life and literary project, Baldwin embarked on rewriting, indeed revolutionizing, twentieth-century American national identity by means of what I term his Black queer humanism. Out of pain and trauma, while escaping his violent childhood and learning about beauty, light, and love from Delaney, he crafted a philosophy that arose from the alternative families and households he forged in Turkey and France.[14] Like Delaney with paint and canvas, Baldwin created with pen and paper an imaginary that was visionary and tactile, sensory and metaphorical, and that we can put to good use in our own troubled moment.

NOTES

1 James Baldwin, "The Price of the Ticket," in *The Price of the Ticket: Collected Nonfiction, 1948–1985* (New York: St. Martin's, 1985), x, emphasis added.

2 This chapter glimpses a more capacious rendering of this theme in my forthcoming book, *James Baldwin: The Life Album* (New Haven, CT: Yale University Press, 2025).

3 These portraits are included in Stephen C. Wicks, ed., *Beauford Delaney and James Baldwin: Through the Unusual Door* (Knoxville: University of Tennessee Press, 2020).

4 Beatings and verbal abuse appear in Baldwin's *Go Tell It on the Mountain*; *Another Country*; *Blues for Mister Charlie*; *Going to Meet the Man*; *Tell Me How Long the Train's Been Gone*; and *Just above My Head*, as well as in several essays and short stories.

5 James Baldwin, "Here Be Dragons," in *Price of the Ticket*, 685; first published as "Freaks and the American Ideal of Manhood," *Playboy*, January 1985.

6 Baldwin, "Here Be Dragons," 683.

7 Eve Auchincloss and Nancy Lynch, "Disturber of the Peace—An Interview with James Baldwin," in *Conversations with James Baldwin*, ed. Fred R. Standley and Louis H. Pratt (Jackson: University Press of Mississippi, 1989), 78, 77, emphasis added.

8 James Baldwin, "Me and My House," *Harper's Magazine*, November 1955, 54.

9 Baldwin, "Me and My House," 56.

10 James Baldwin, letter to Harry Belafonte, May 30, 1963, Baldwin Papers (Correspondence), Schomburg Center for Research in Black Culture, New York Public Library, New York.

11 Delaney made pencil and pen sketches of Baldwin's face when they were living in Turkey, such as the blue-ink sketch of Baldwin, circa 1966, now owned by the Knoxville Museum of Art (plate 20); see Wicks, *Beauford Delaney and James Baldwin*, 79. Pakay may have seen these drawings. Pakay also took hundreds of photographs of Baldwin. See Magdalena J. Zaborowska and David Leeming, "Remembering Sedat Pakay 1945–2016," *James Baldwin Review* 3 (2017): 173–85.

12 James Baldwin, *Just above My Head* (New York: Dial, 1979), 288–89.

13 Beauford Delaney, *Untitled (Jazz Club)*, ca. 1950, oil on canvas, 28 × 36 in., Estate of Beauford Delaney; https://www.wikiart.org/en/beauford-delaney/untitled-jazz-club-1950. See also David Leeming, *Amazing Grace: A Life of Beauford Delaney* (New York: Oxford University Press, 1998), 104.

14 See Magdalena J. Zaborowska, *Me and My House: James Baldwin's Last Decade in France* (Durham, NC: Duke University Press, 2018); and Magdalena J. Zaborowska, *James Baldwin's Turkish Decade: Erotics of Exile* (Durham, NC: Duke University Press, 2009).

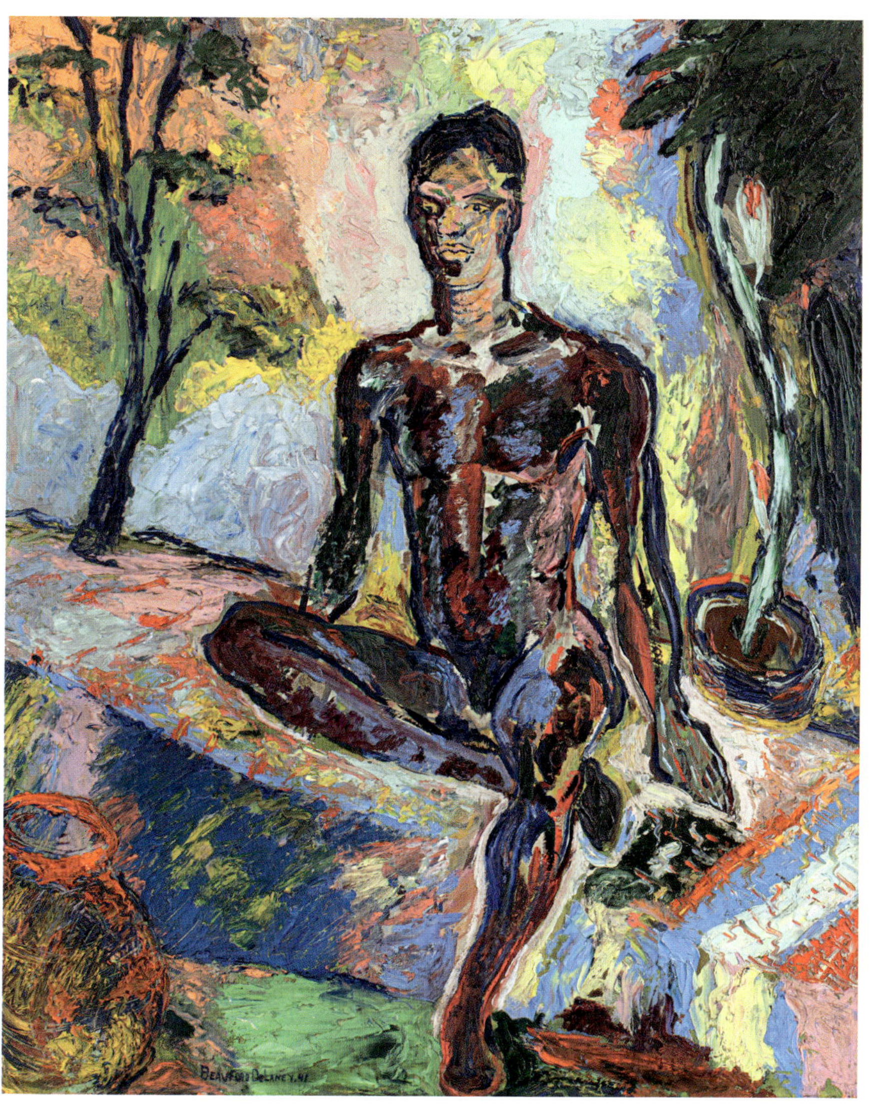

1

Beauford Delaney, *Dark Rapture (James Baldwin)*, 1941. Oil on Masonite, 34 × 28 in. (86.4 × 71.1 cm), signed. Collection of halley k harrisburg and Michael Rosenfeld, New York.

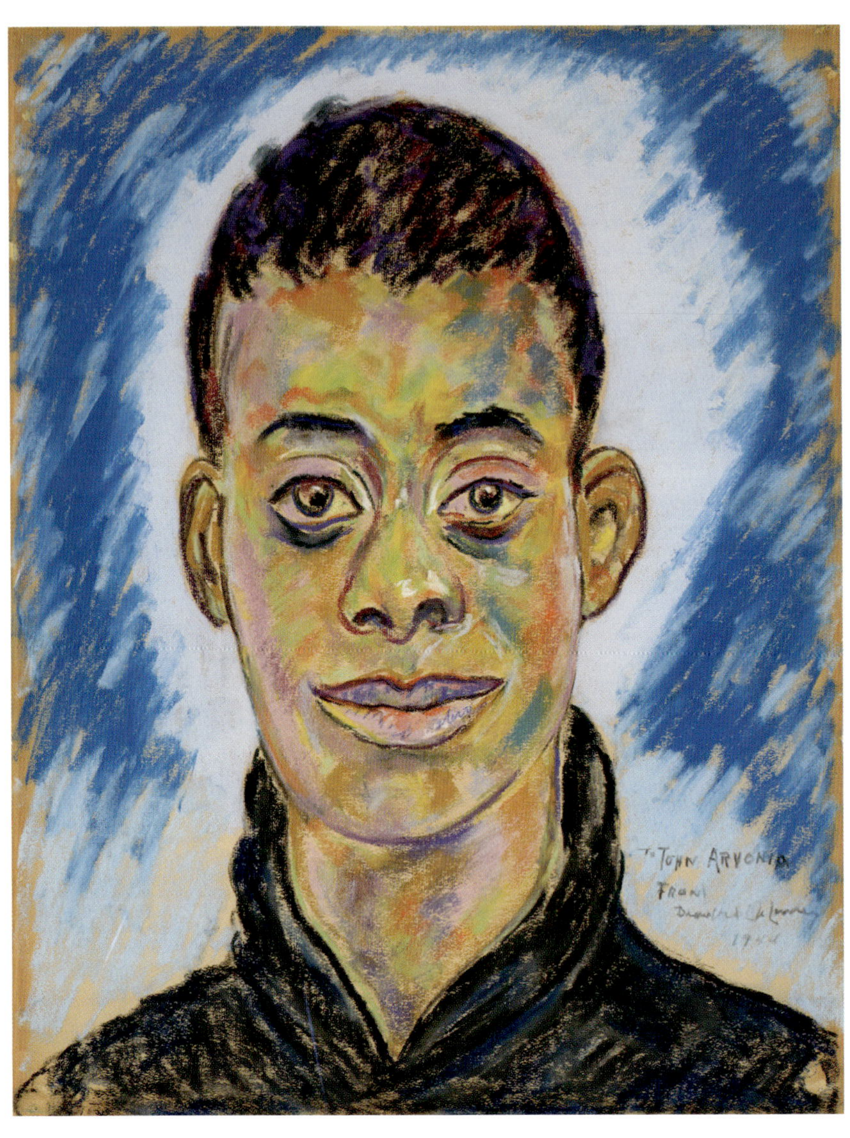

2

Beauford Delaney, *Portrait of James Baldwin*, 1944. Pastel on paper, 24 × 18¾ in. (61 × 47.6 cm). Knoxville Museum of Art. Photograph: Bruce Cole.

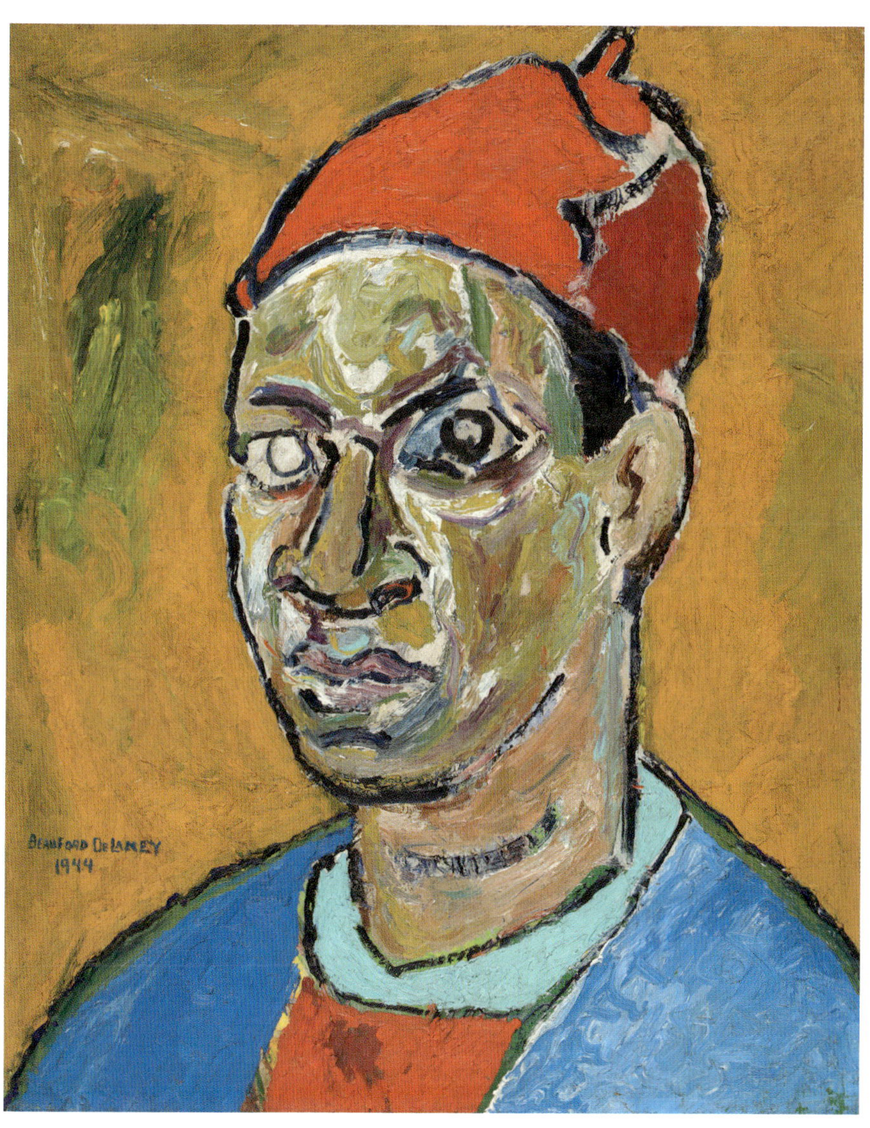

3

Beauford Delaney, *Self-Portrait*, 1944. Oil on canvas, 27 × 22½ in. (68.6 × 57.2 cm). Art Institute of Chicago. Photograph: Art Institute of Chicago/Art Resource, NY.

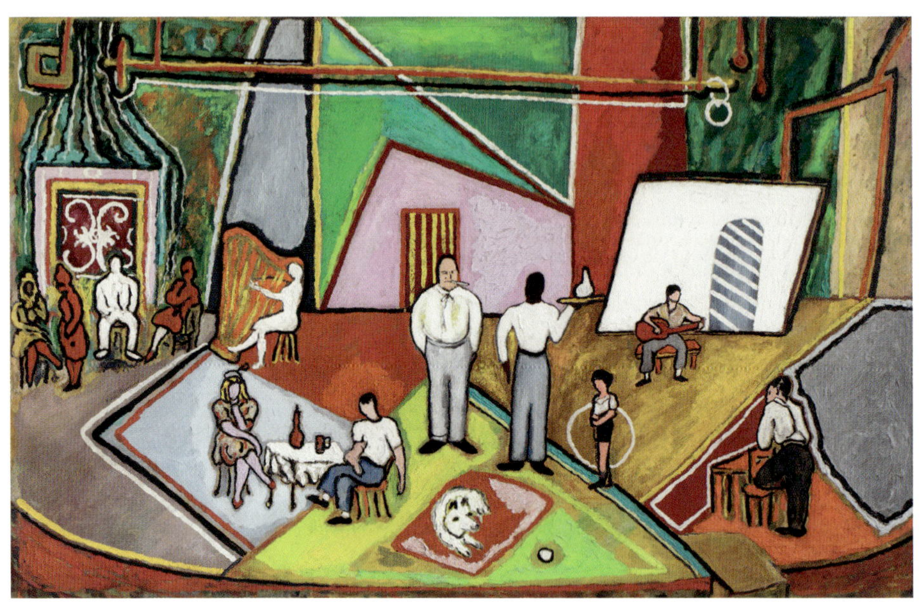

4

Beauford Delaney, *The Time of Your Life*, 1945. Oil on board, 33¾ × 53½ in. (85.7 × 135.9 cm), signed. Private collection.

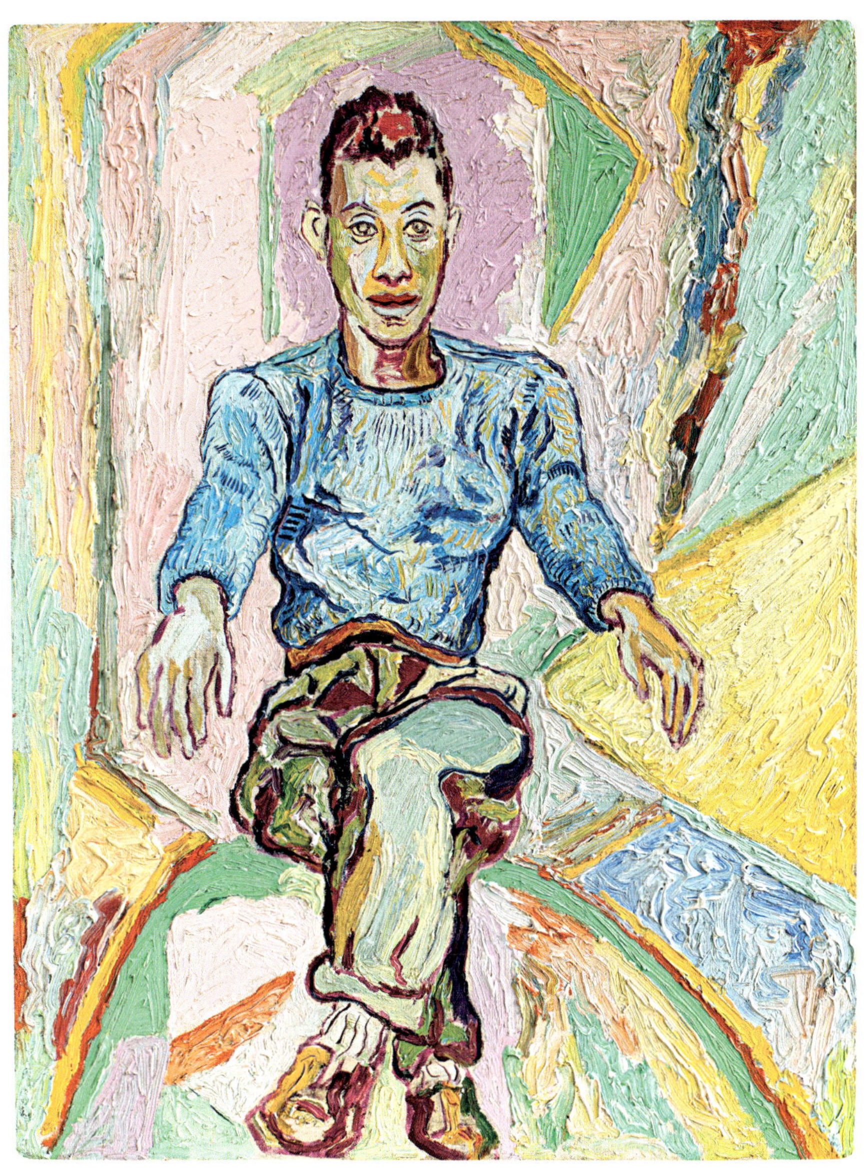

5
Beauford Delaney, *James Baldwin*, ca. 1945–50. Oil on canvasboard, 24 × 18 in. (61 × 45.7 cm). Collection of halley k harrisburg and Michael Rosenfeld, New York.

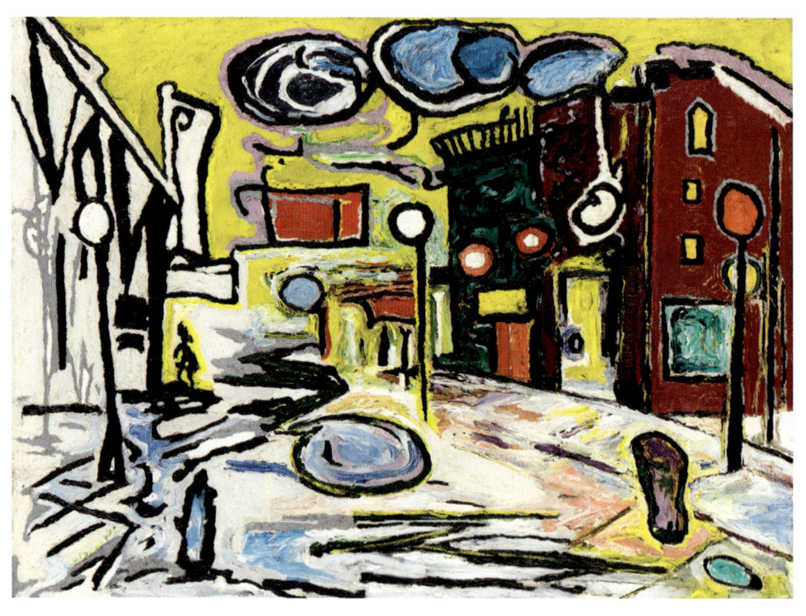

6

Beauford Delaney, *Untitled (Village Street Scene)*, 1948. Oil on canvas, 29 × 40 in. (73.7 × 101.6 cm). Terra Foundation for American Art, Chicago. Photograph © Terra Foundation for American Art, Chicago.

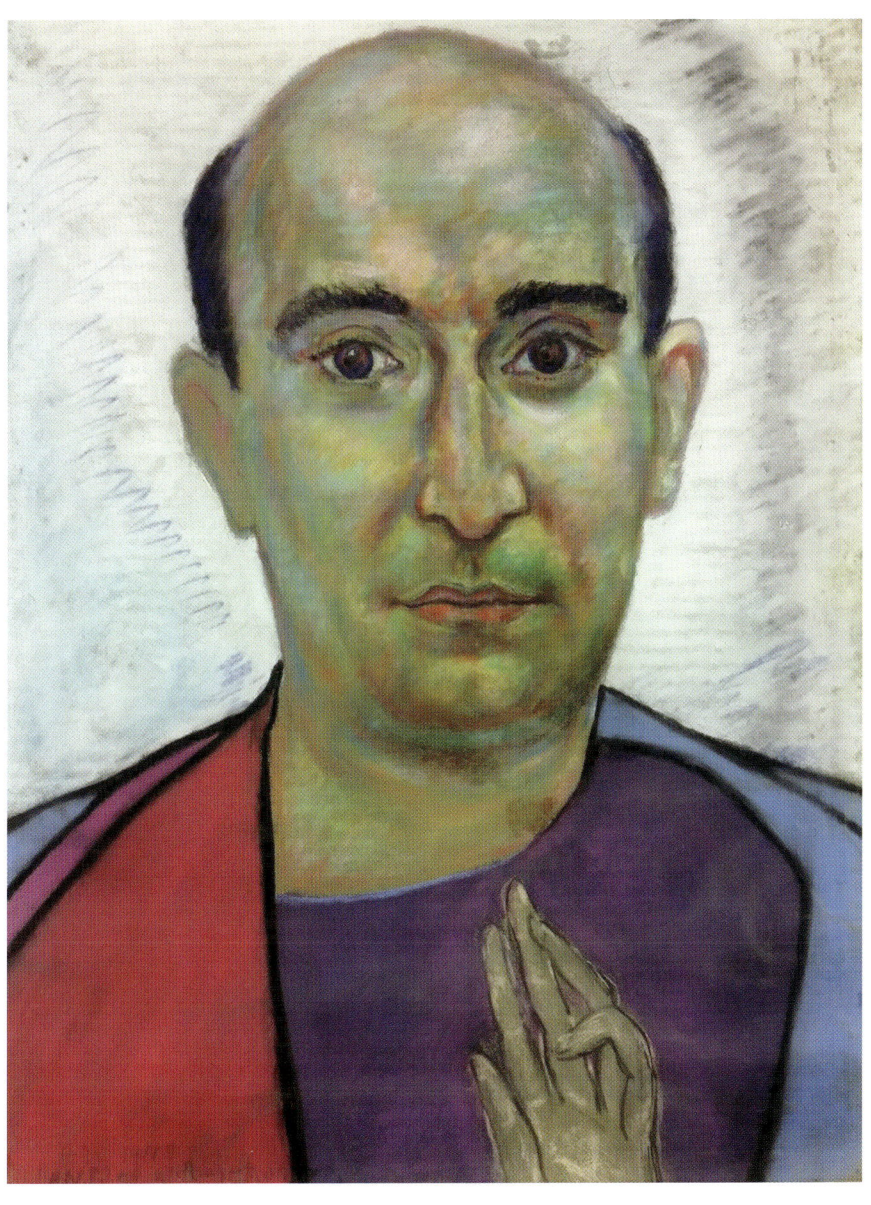

7

Beauford Delaney, *Dante Pavone as Christ*, 1948. Pastel on paper, 23 × 19¾ in. (58.4 × 50.2 cm). Knoxville Museum of Art.

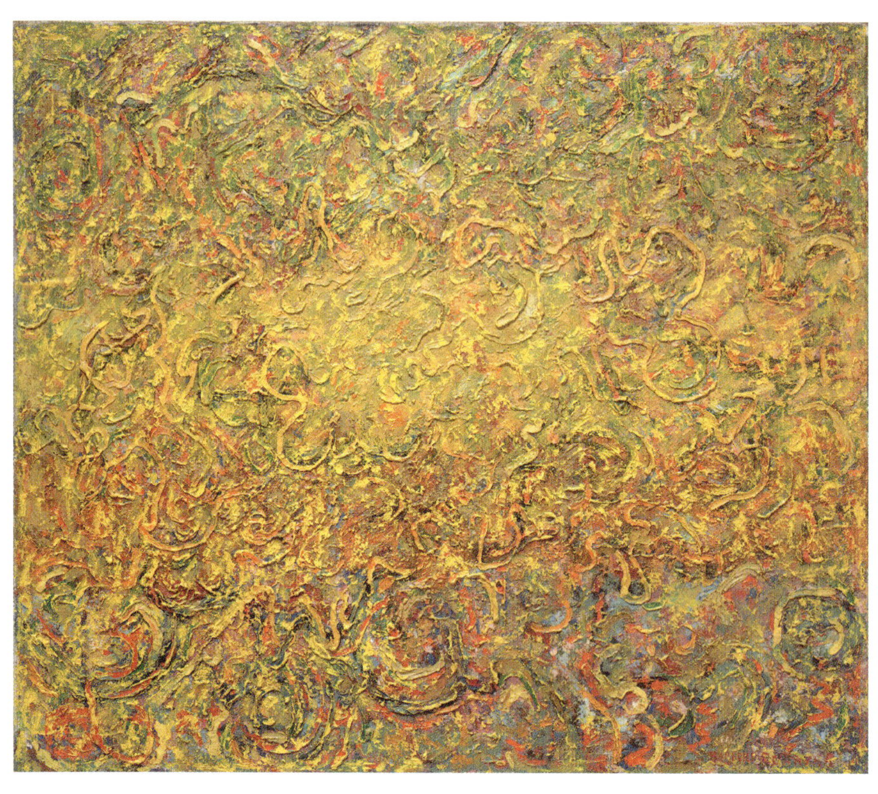

8

Beauford Delaney, *Composition 16*, 1954–56. Oil on canvas, 31½ × 37 in. (80 × 94 cm). Museum of Modern Art, New York. Photograph: Digital Image © The Museum of Modern Art/Licensed by SCALA/Art Resource, NY.

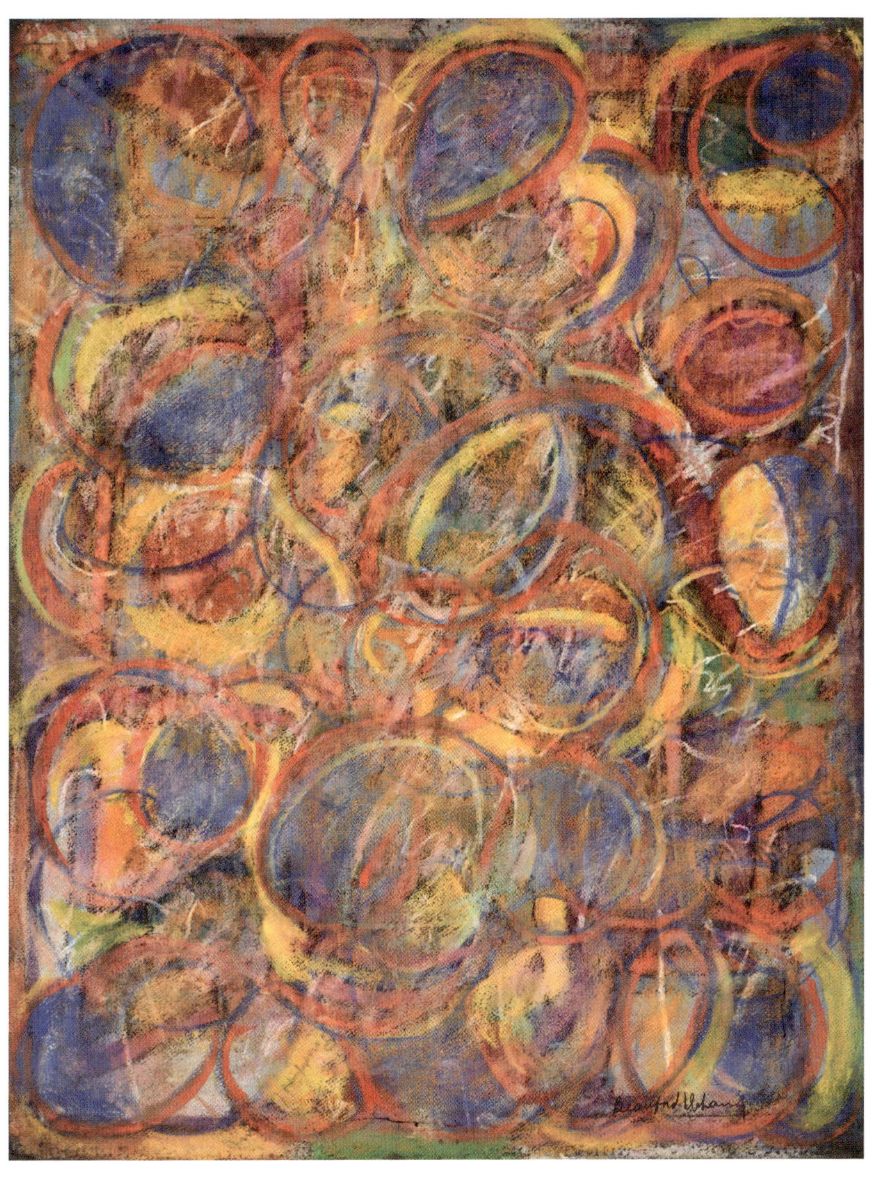

9

Beauford Delaney, *Untitled (Abstract Circles)*, ca. 1956.
Pastel and mixed media on paper, 25¼ × 19½ in. (64.1 × 49.5 cm).
Knoxville Museum of Art.

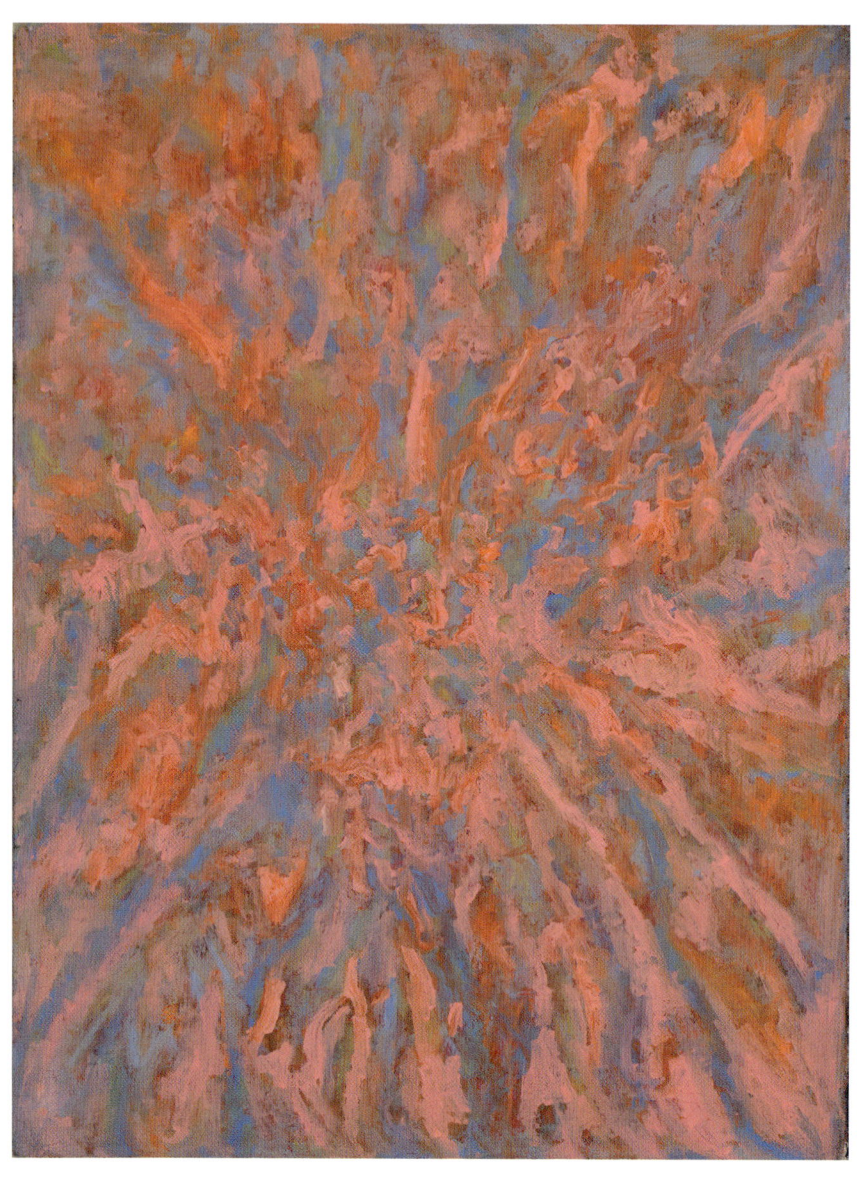

10

Beauford Delaney, *Charlie Parker Yardbird*, 1958. Oil on canvas, 39½ × 29½ in. (100.3 × 74.9 cm). Smithsonian American Art Museum. Photograph: Gene Young.

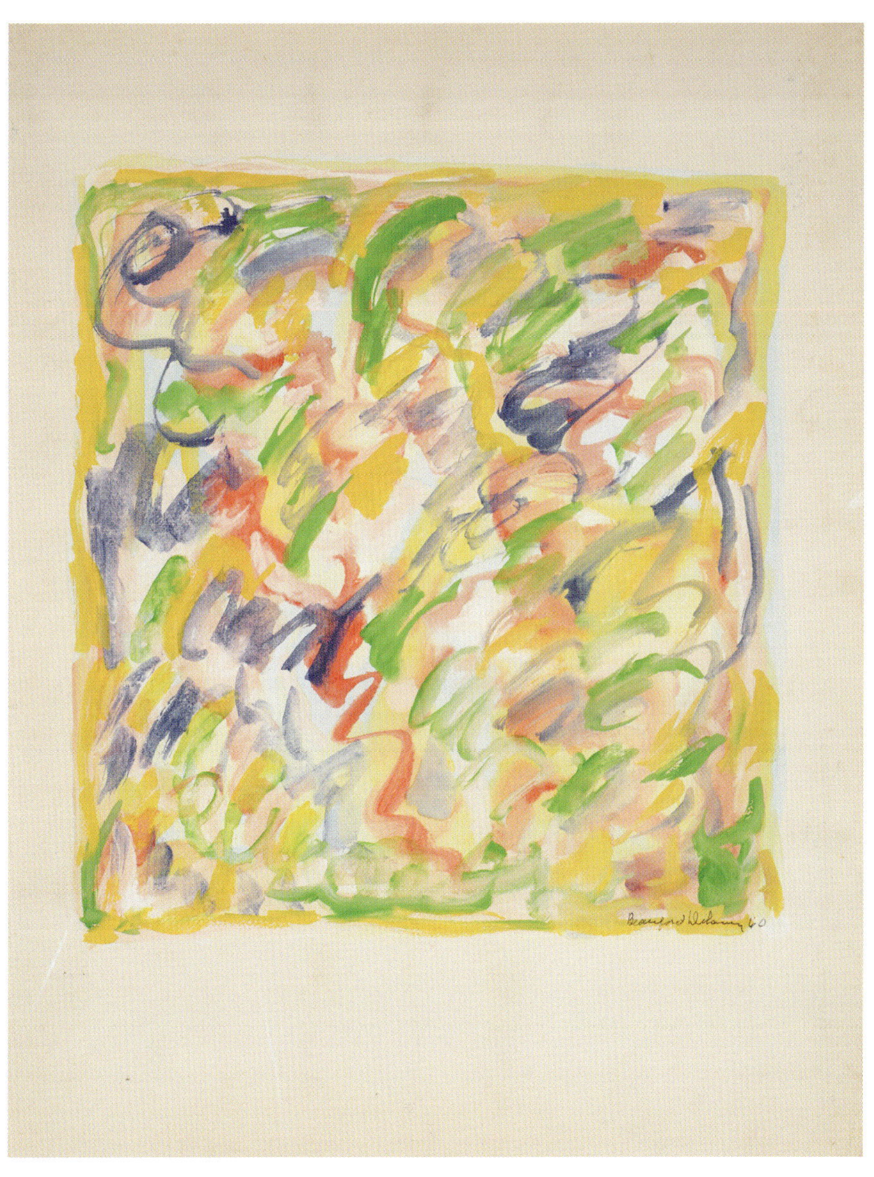

11

Beauford Delaney, *Untitled*, 1960. Watercolor on paper, 26 × 19¾ in. (66 × 50.2 cm). Knoxville Museum of Art. Photograph: Bruce Cole.

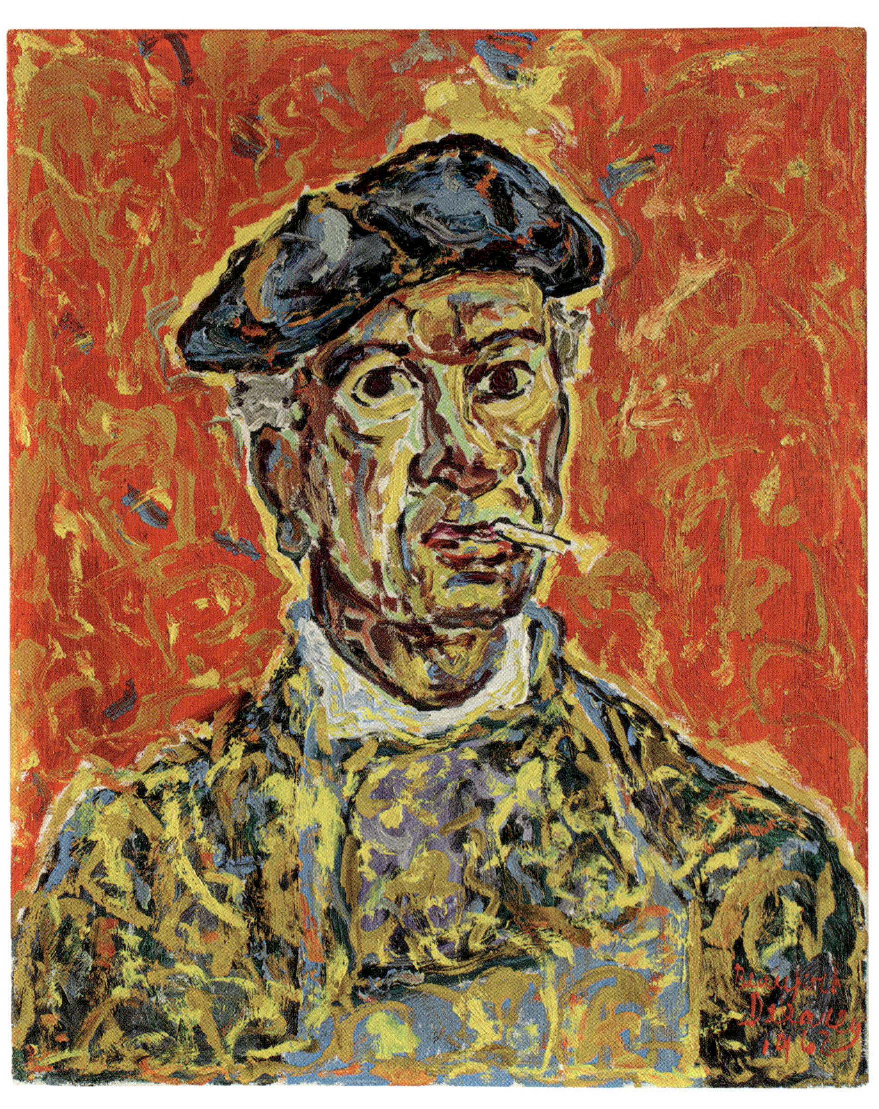

12

Beauford Delaney, *Self-Portrait*, 1962. Oil on canvas, 25½ × 21¼ in. (64.8 × 54 cm), signed. Collection of halley k harrisburg and Michael Rosenfeld, New York.

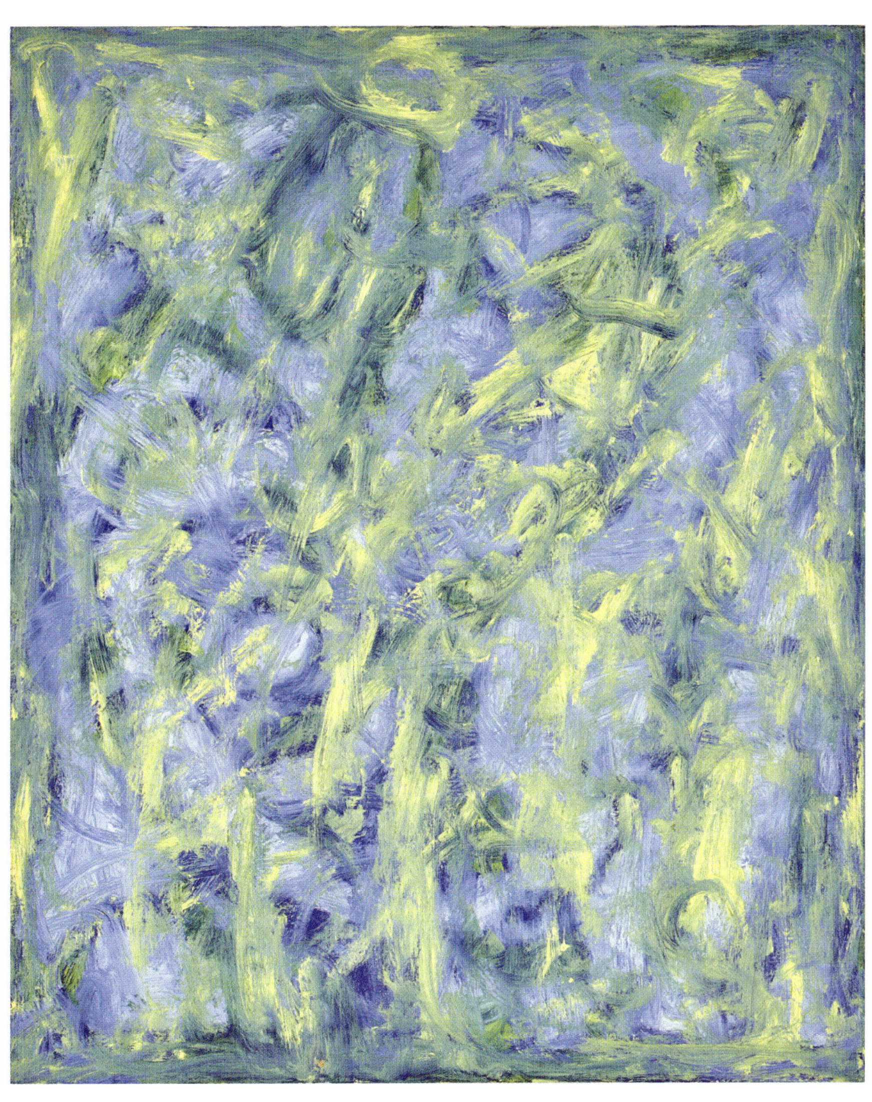

13

Beauford Delaney, *Blue-Light Abstraction*, ca. 1962. Oil on canvas, 25¾ × 21½ in. (65.4 × 54.6 cm). Knoxville Museum of Art. Photograph: Bruce Cole.

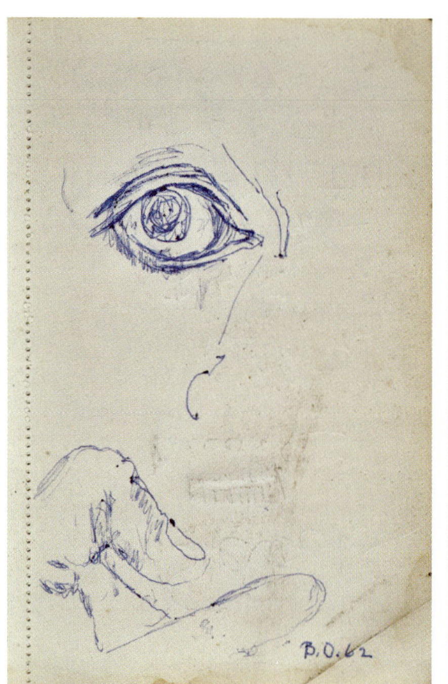

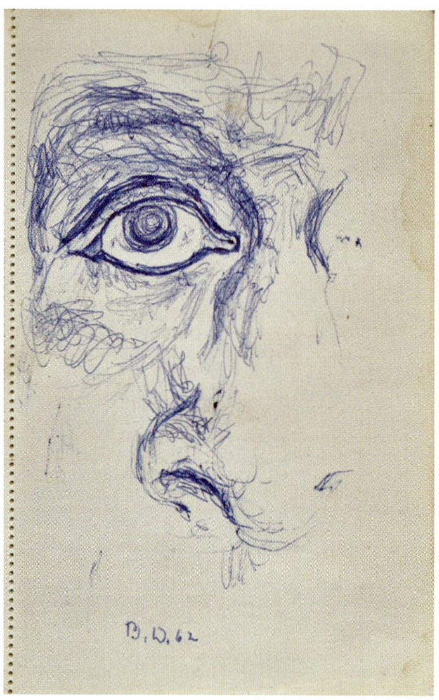

14a–b

Beauford Delaney, Sketchbook (self-portrait eye studies), 1962.
Ink on paper, 6 × 4 in. (15.2 × 10.2 cm) each.
Knoxville Museum of Art.

15

Beauford Delaney, *Moving Sunlight*, 1965. Oil on canvas, 25¾ × 21½ in. (65.4 × 54.6 cm). Knoxville Museum of Art. Photograph: Bruce Cole.

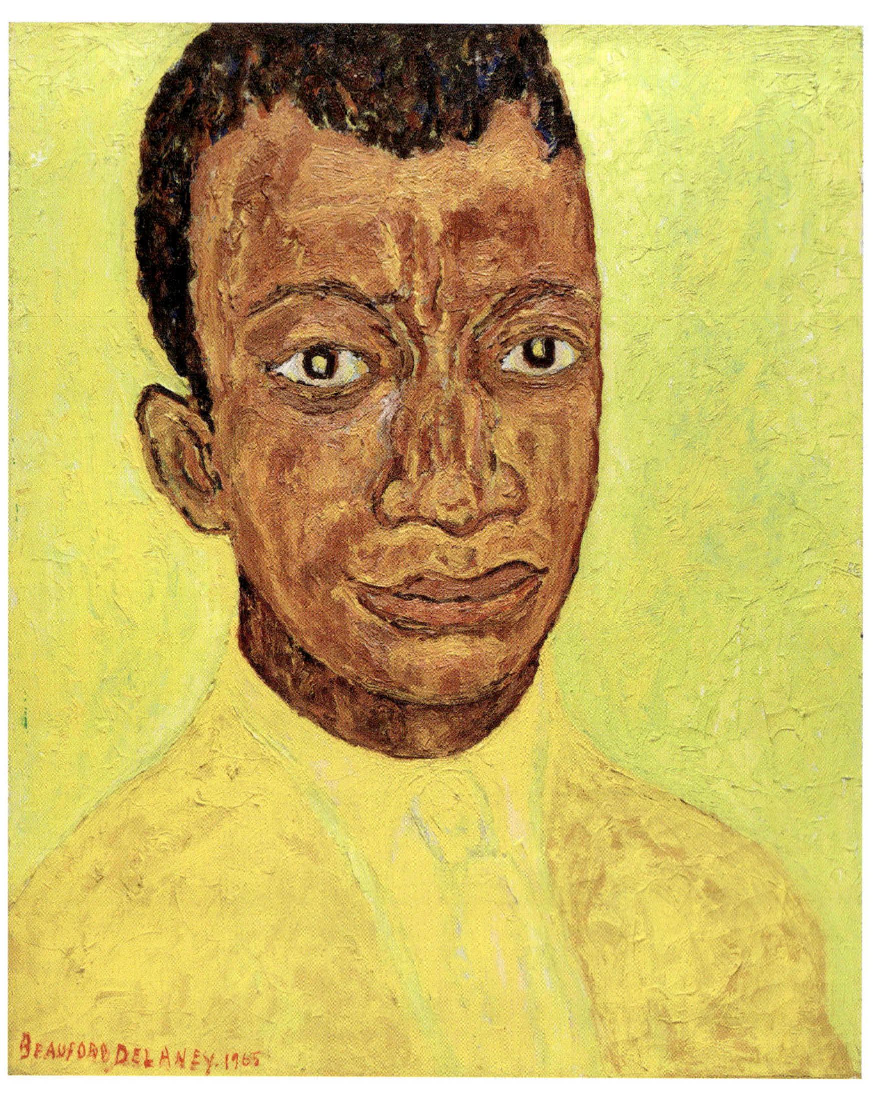

16

Beauford Delaney, *Portrait of James Baldwin*, 1965. Oil on canvas, 25½ × 21¼ in. (64.8 × 54 cm). Chrysler Museum of Art, Norfolk, Virginia.

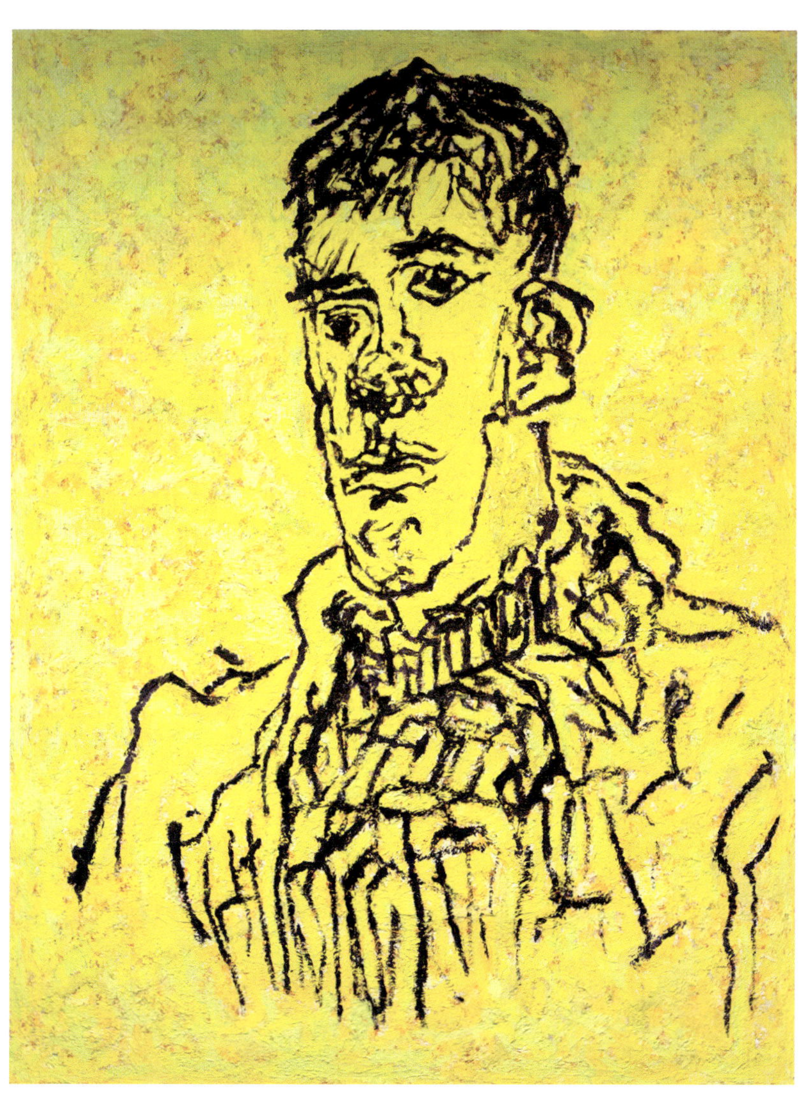

17

Beauford Delaney, *James Baldwin*, 1966. Oil on canvas, 45¼ × 35½ in. (114.9 × 90.2 cm). Collection of Henry Louis Gates Jr.

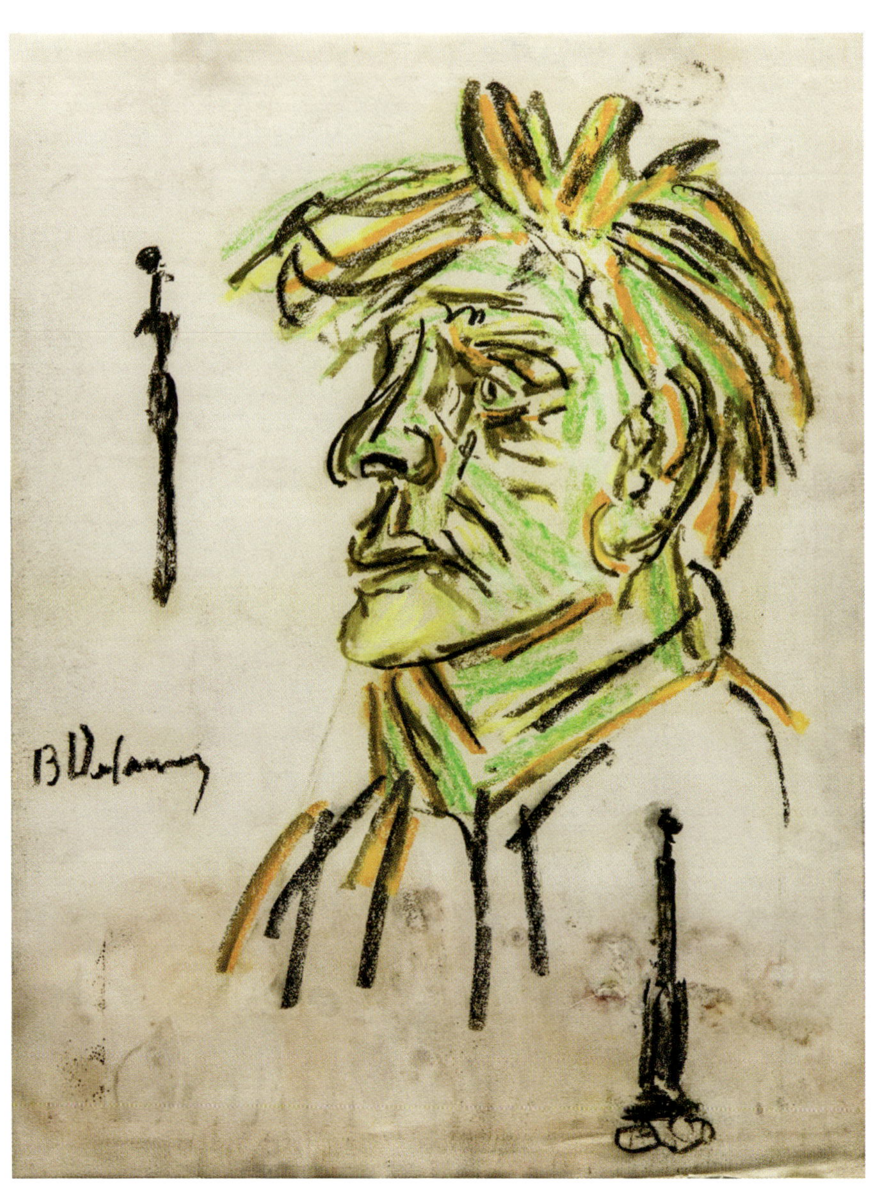

18

Beauford Delaney, *Untitled (Alberto Giacometti)*, ca. 1966. Pastel on paper, 20 × 16 in. (50.8 × 40.6 cm). The Estate of Beauford Delaney, Knoxville, Tennessee.

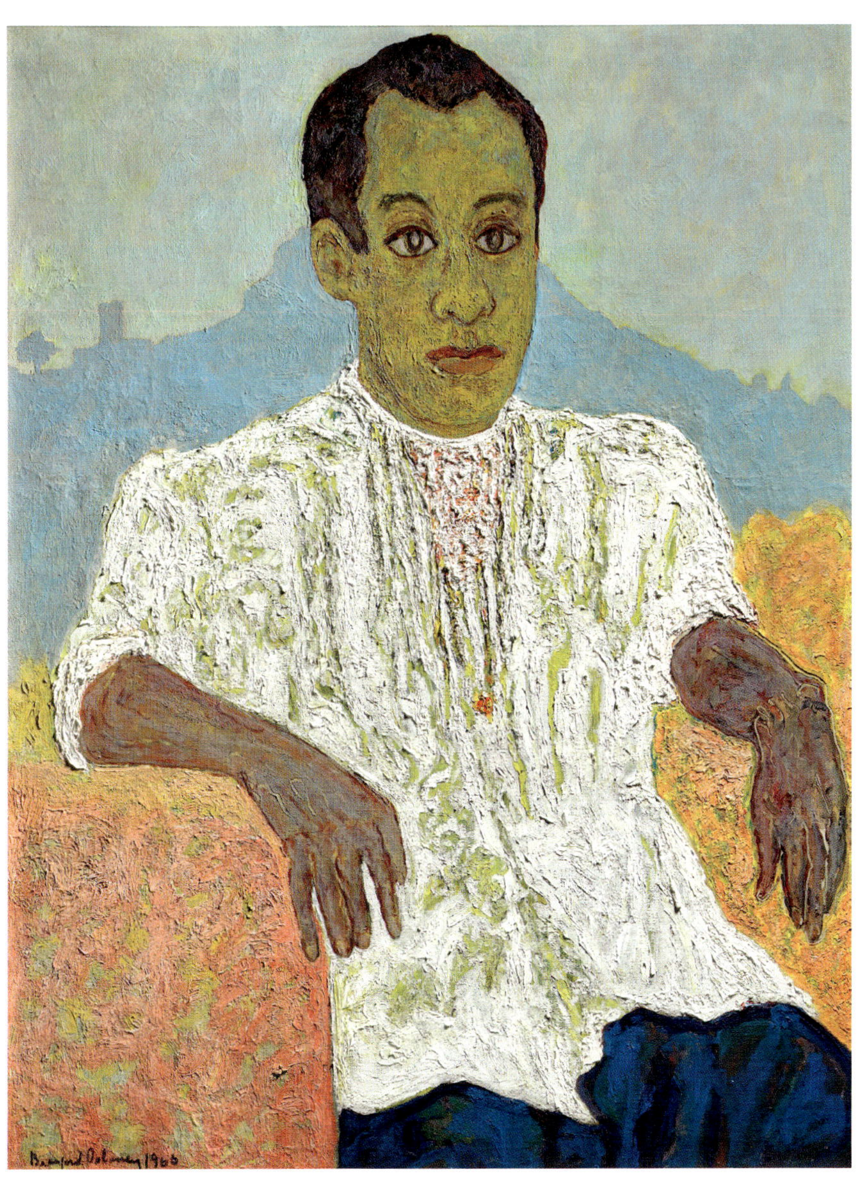

19

Beauford Delaney, *James Baldwin*, 1966. Oil on canvas, 39½ × 29⅞ in. (100.2 × 76 cm). Private collection.

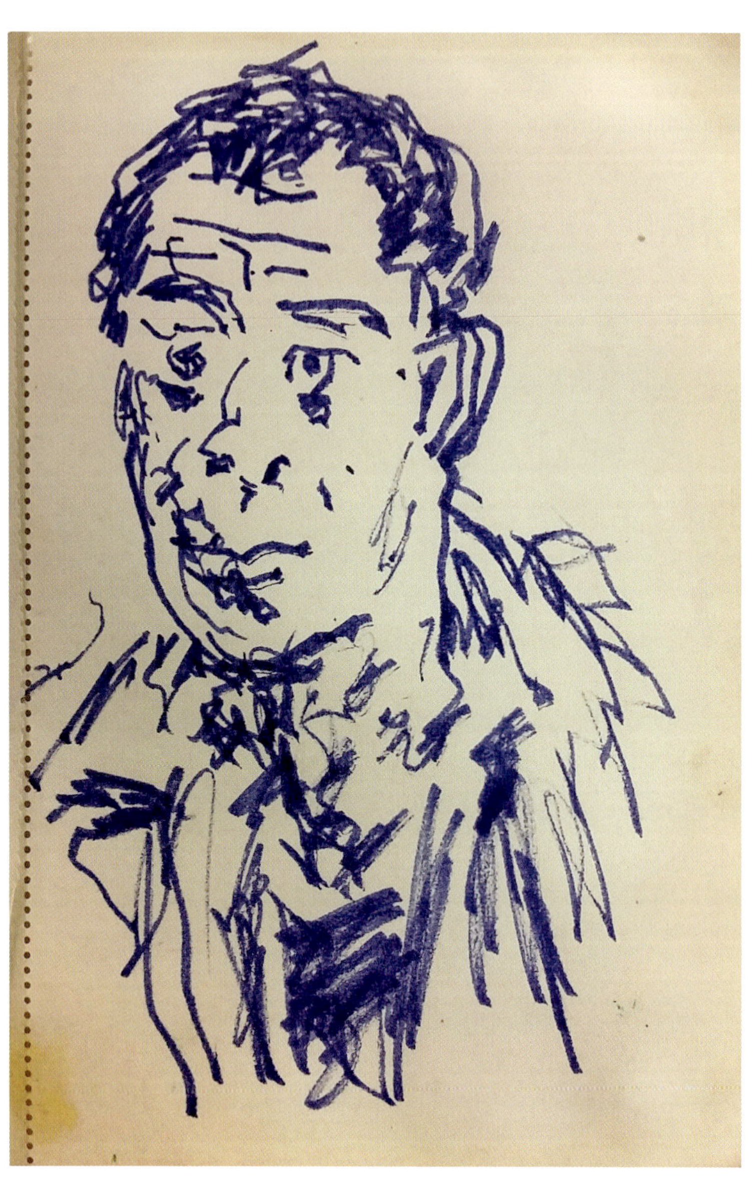

20

Beauford Delaney, *Sketch of James Baldwin*, ca. 1966. Ink on paper, 5½ × 3½ in. (14 × 8.9 cm). Knoxville Museum of Art. Photograph: Bruce Cole.

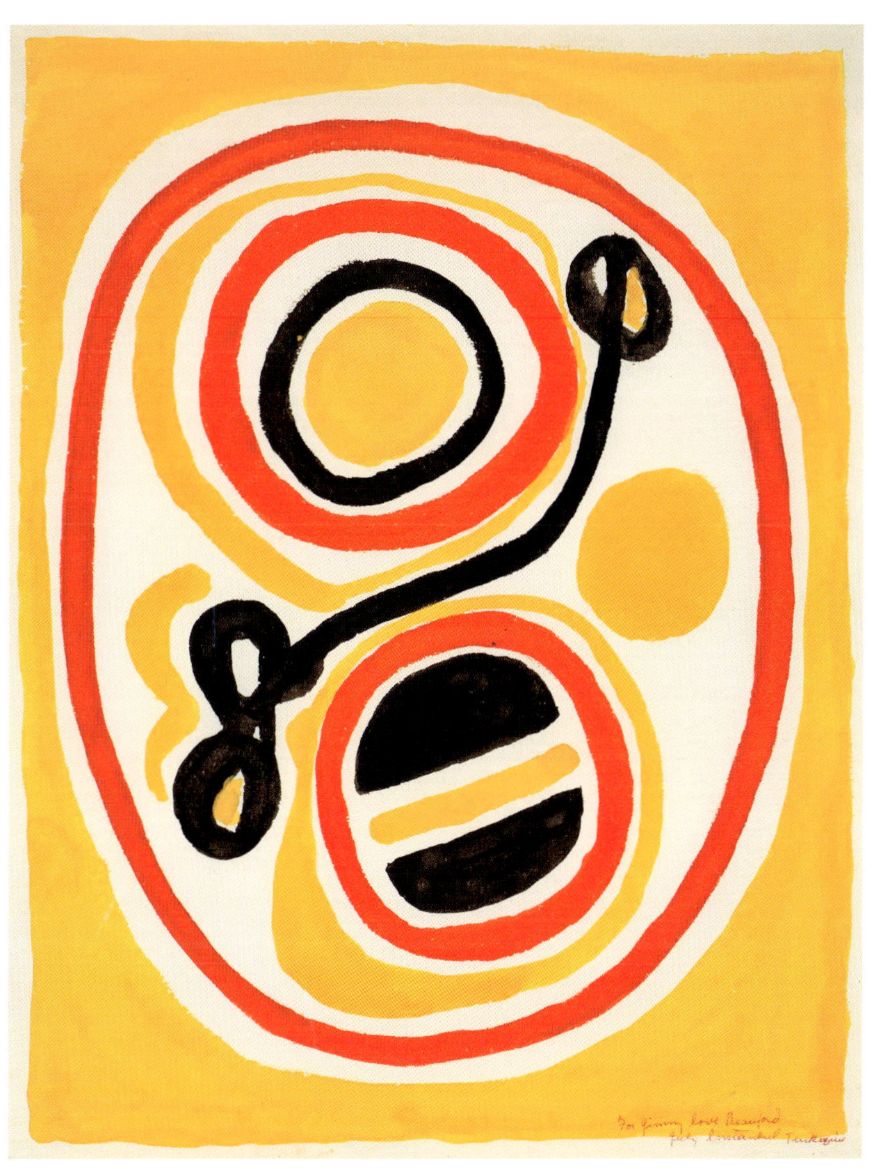

21

Beauford Delaney, *Untitled (Yellow, Red, and Black Circles for James Baldwin [Istanbul])*, 1966. Watercolor and gouache on paper, 25⅝ × 19 in. (65.1 × 48.3 cm). Knoxville Museum of Art. Photograph: Bruce Cole.

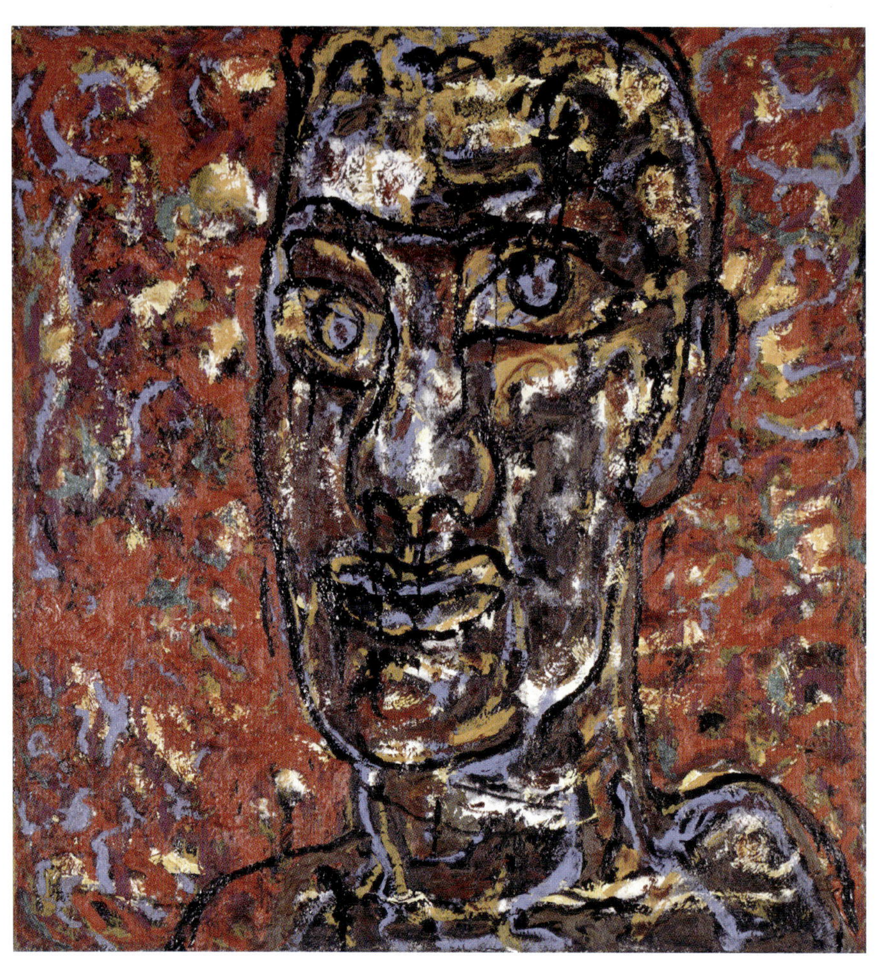

22

Beauford Delaney, *The Black Sage (James Baldwin)*, 1967. Oil on canvas, 35 × 33 1/16 in. Collection of Faye and Robert Davidson, Los Angeles.

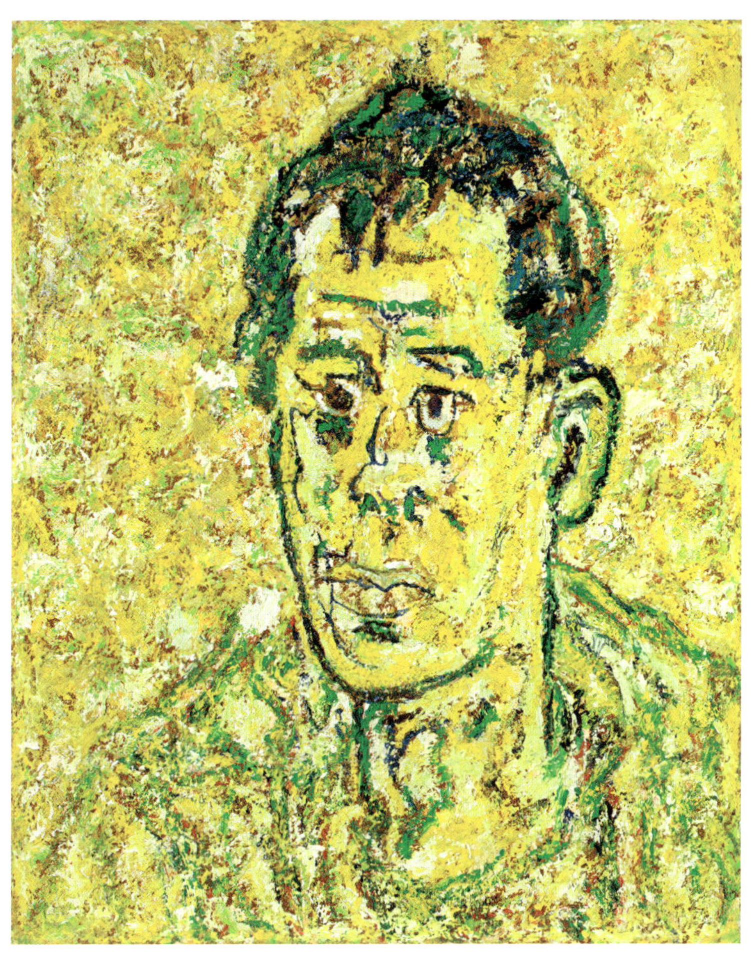

23

Beauford Delaney, *James Baldwin*, 1967. Oil on canvas, 39¼ × 31¾ in. (99.7 × 80.6 cm), signed. Private collection.

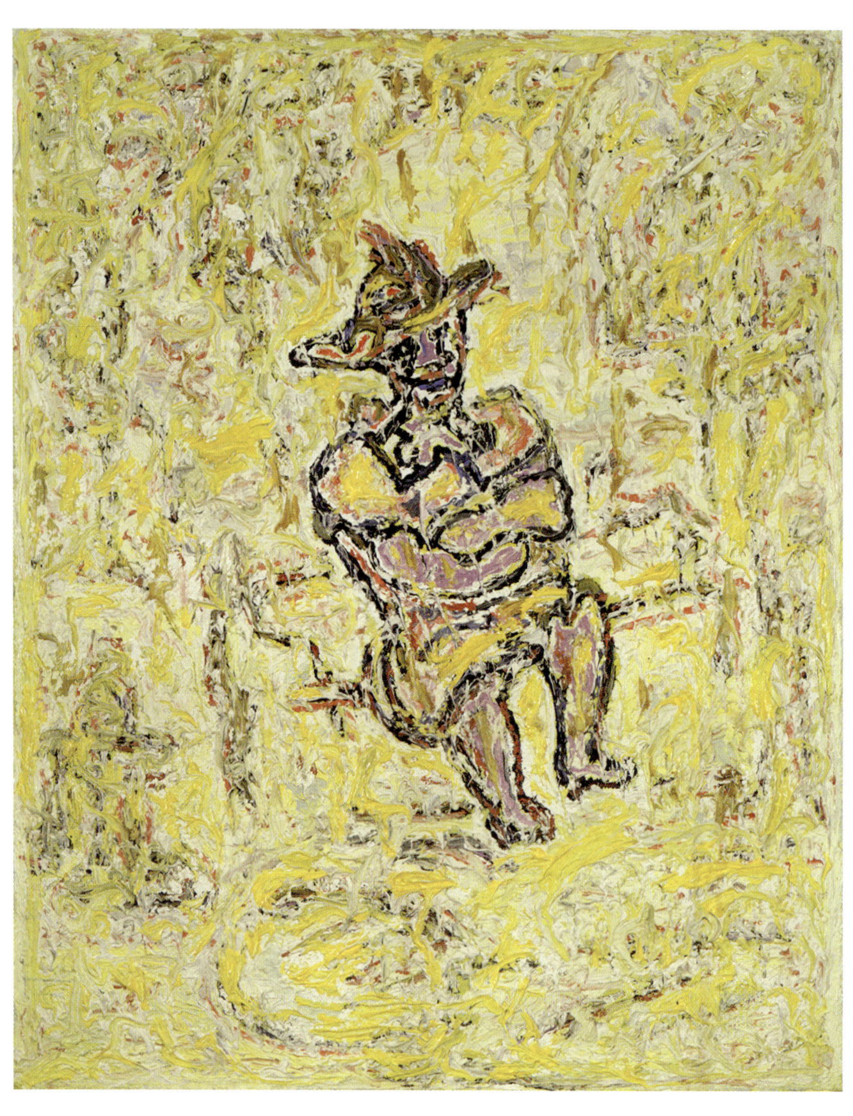

24

Beauford Delaney, *Rosa Parks*, 1967. Oil on canvas, 31¾ × 25½ in. (80.6 × 64.8 cm). Private collection.

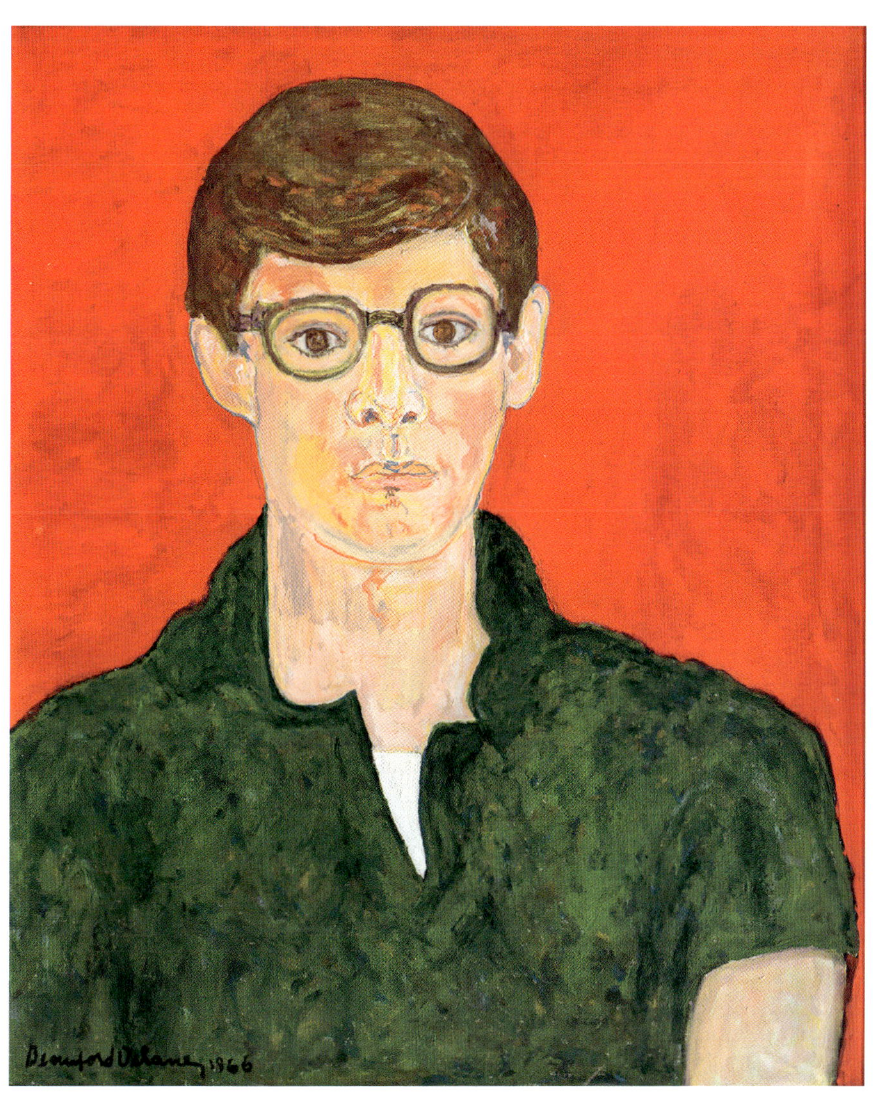

25

Beauford Delaney, *David Leeming*, ca. 1967. Oil on canvas, 24 × 28 in. (61 × 71.1 cm), signed. Collection of David Leeming.

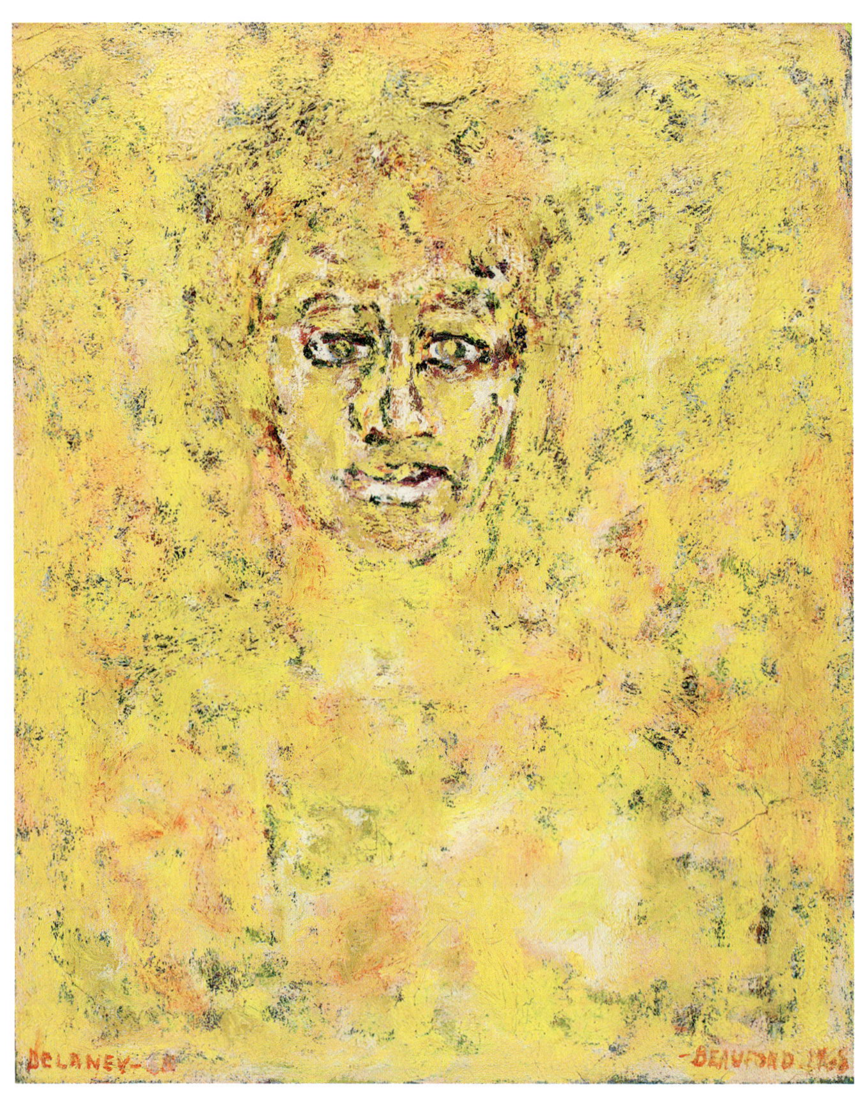

26

Beauford Delaney, *Portrait of Ella Fitzgerald*, 1968. Oil on canvas, 24 × 19½ in. (61 × 49.5 cm). SCAD Museum of Art, Savannah.

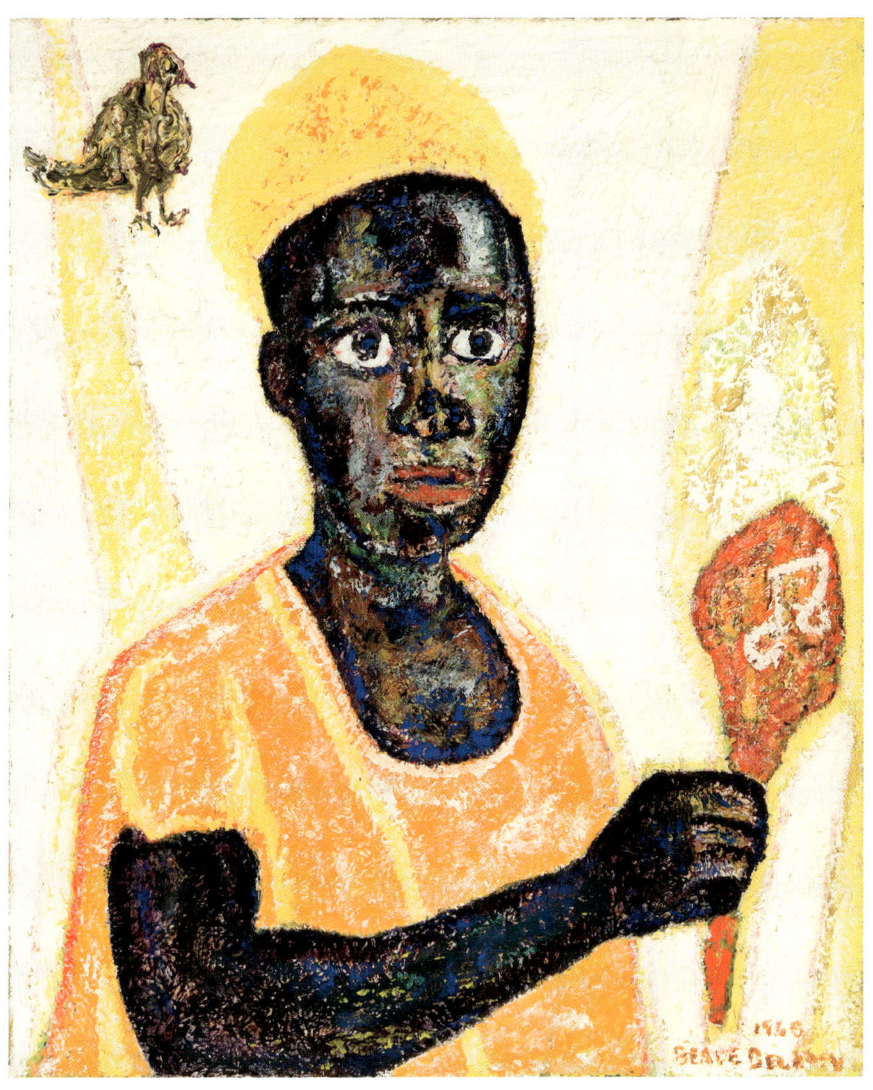

27

Beauford Delaney, *Charlie Parker*, 1968. Oil on canvas, 28¾ × 23½ in. (73 × 59.7 cm). Memorial Art Gallery of the University of Rochester. Photograph: Joshua Nefsky, courtesy of Michael Rosenfeld Gallery LLC, New York.

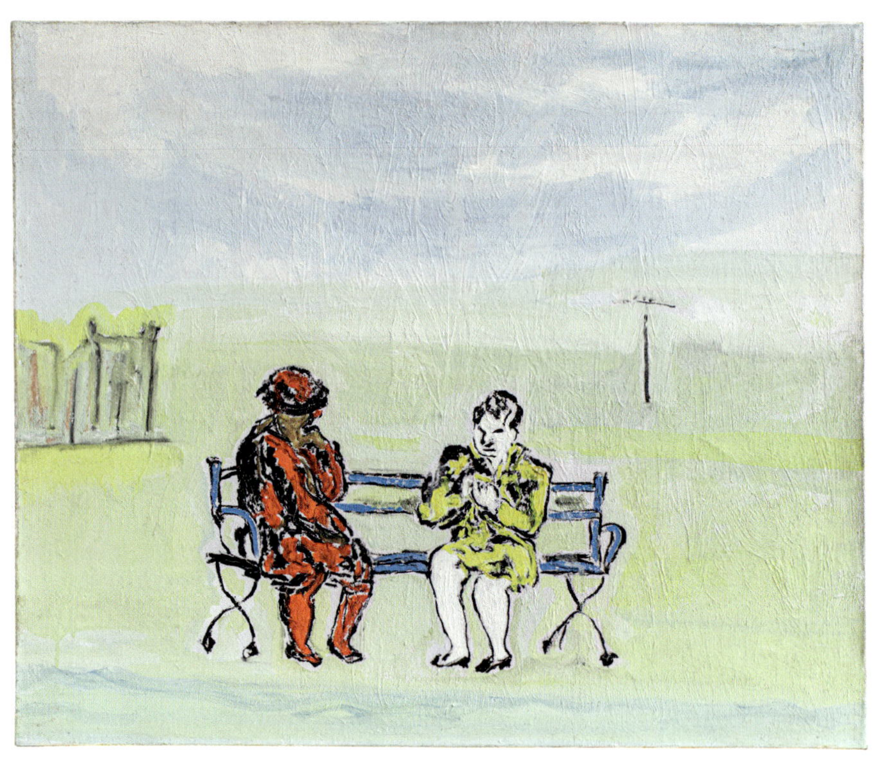

28

Beauford Delaney, *Untitled (Rosa Parks)*, ca. 1970. Oil on canvas, 21¼ × 25⅝ in. (54 × 65.1 cm), Beauford Delaney Estate stamp. Michael Rosenfeld Gallery LLC, New York, NY.

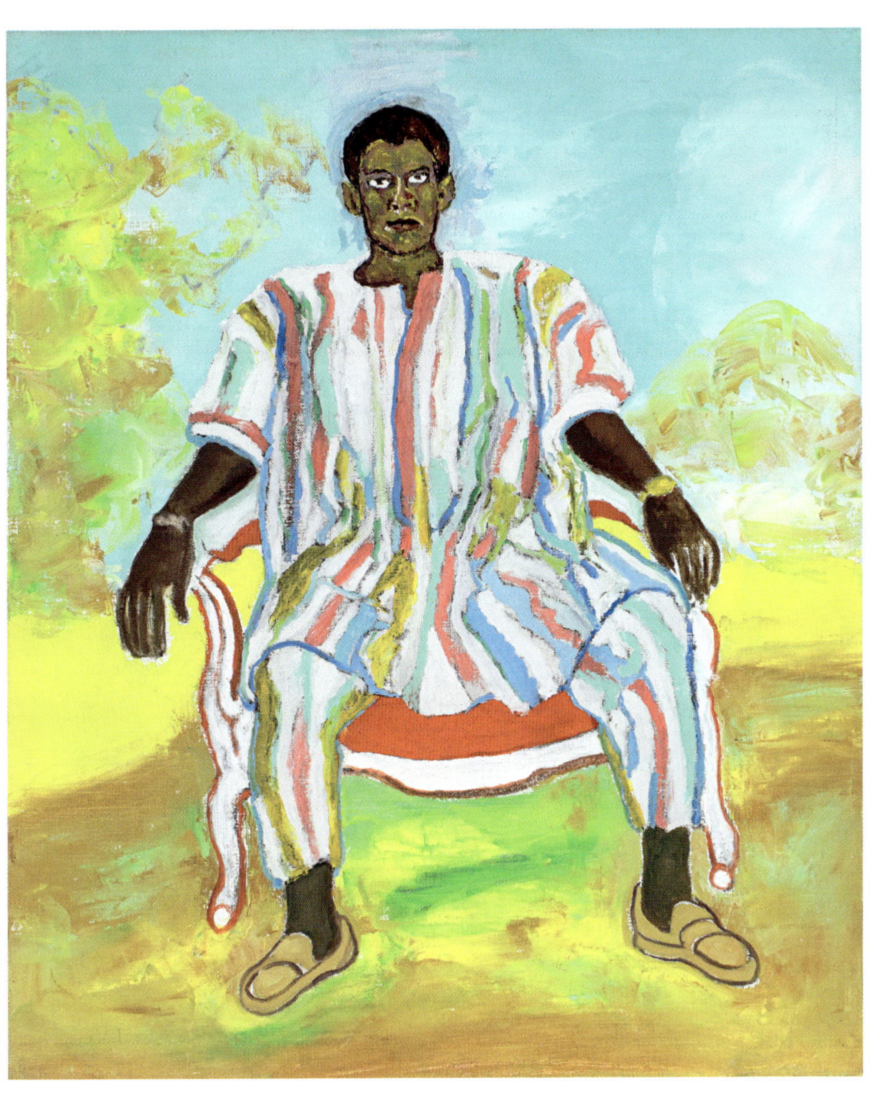

29

Beauford Delaney, *Untitled (Man in African Dress)*, ca. 1970.
Oil on canvas, 21⅝ × 18⅛ in. (54.9 × 46 cm), signed.
Michael Rosenfeld Gallery LLC, New York, NY.

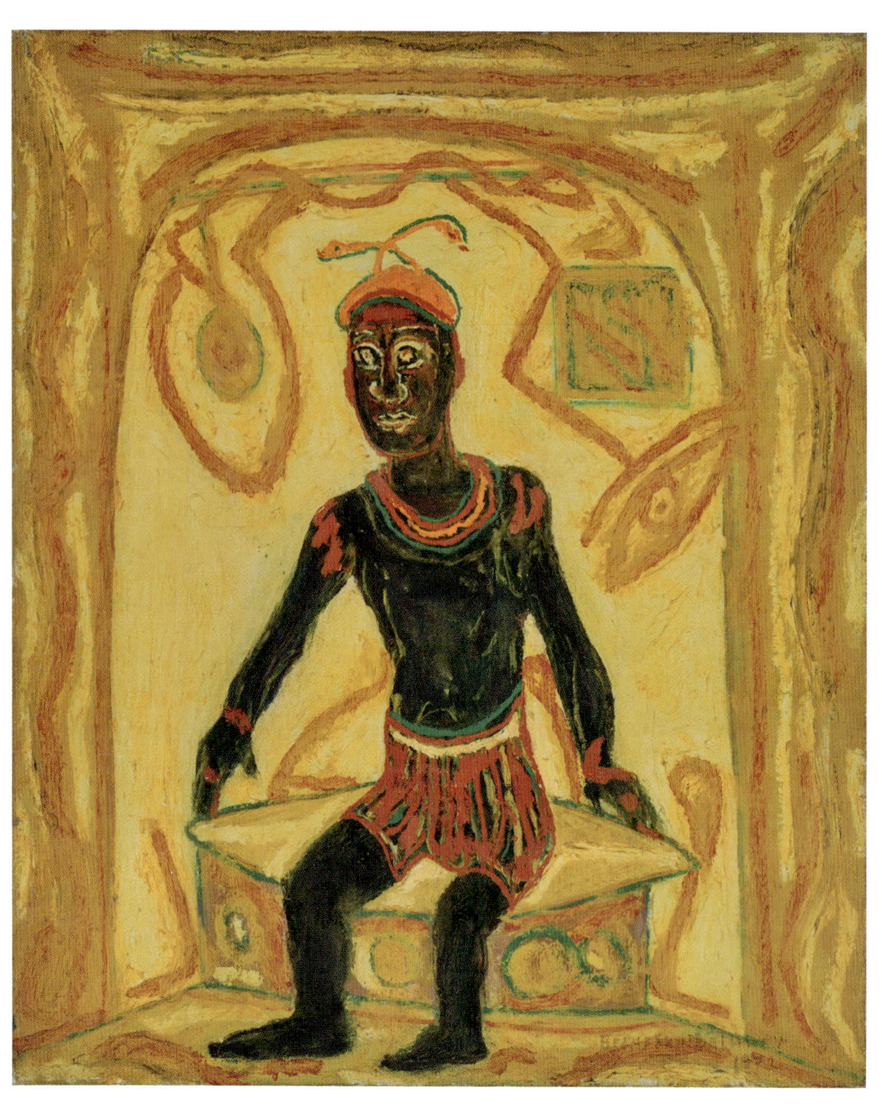

30

Beauford Delaney, *Self-Portrait in a Paris Bath House*, 1971. Oil on canvas, 21⅝ × 18⅛ in. (54.9 × 46 cm). Knoxville Museum of Art. Photograph: Bruce Cole.

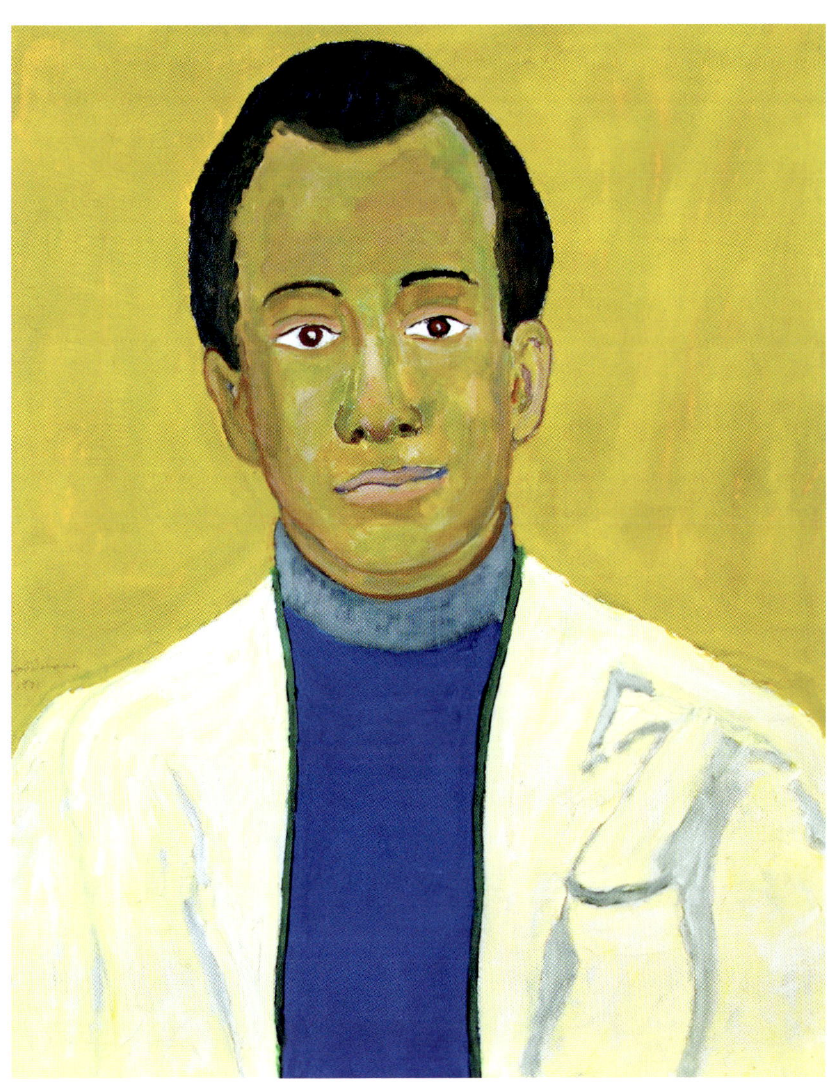

31

Beauford Delaney, *Portrait of James Baldwin*, 1971. Oil on canvas, 24 × 18 in. (61 × 45.7 cm), Clark Atlanta University Art Museum.

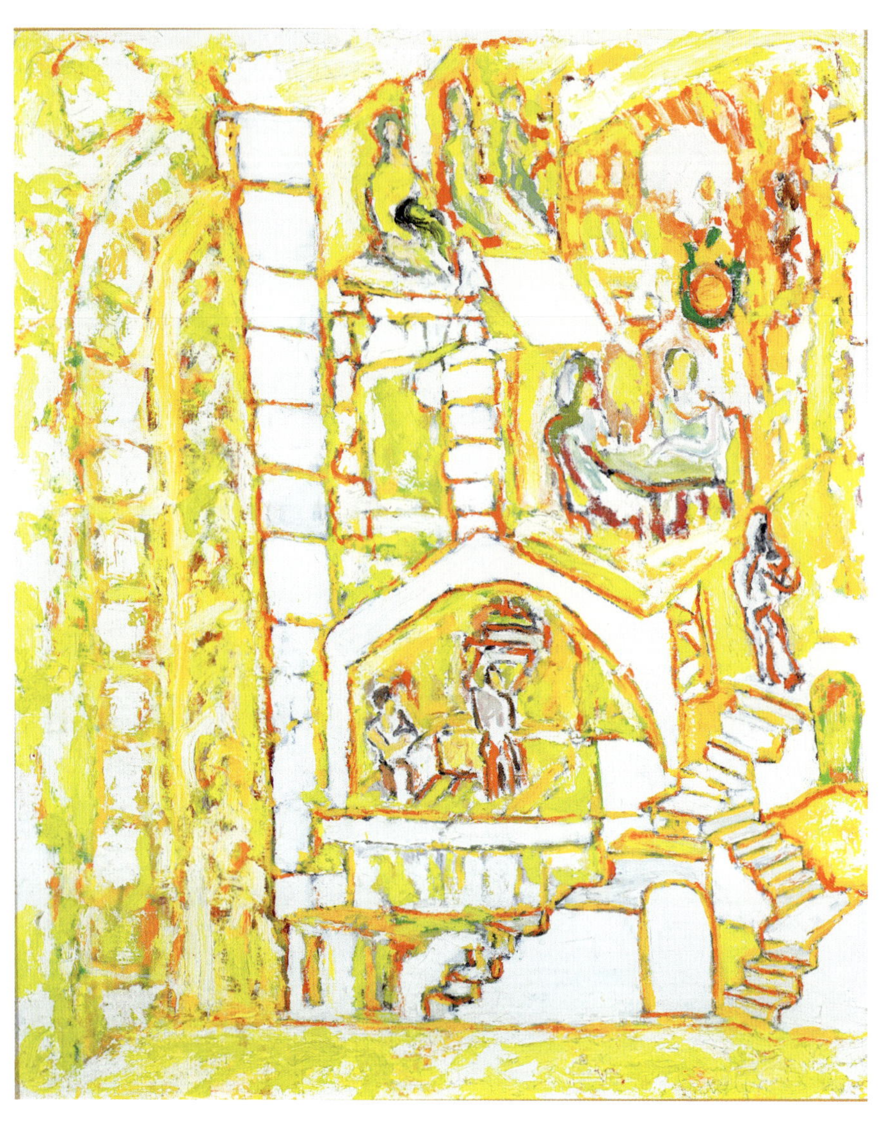

32

Beauford Delaney, *Village (Saint-Paul-de-Vence)*, 1972. Oil on canvas, 25¼ × 19½ in. (64.1 × 49.5 cm). Clark Atlanta University Art Museum.

PART II

Synesthesia and Arts in Dialogue

FIVE

Blue(s) as Cymbal

Beauford Delaney (Elvin Jones) James Baldwin

Fred Moten

I wanted the shirt Elvin Jones was wearing in the film *Different Drummer: Elvin Jones* (1979; figure 5.1) to have been painted by Beauford Delany. I wanted to talk about Beauford as the greatest painter of and with yellow in the history of this world and any other. That whole Apollonian symbolic chain that associates yellow with sun, light, enlightenment, intelligence, revelation, brilliance seems so clear, until you look long enough into the wreck of the collective head to see how and what yellow obscures and protects and enfolds and embellishes, not unto the disappearance of the object but rather unto the continually Dionysian reappearance of a way. And so, with Elvin's encouragement, and by way of the beautiful homophony that *cymbal* and *symbol* share and practice, I approach Beauford's yellow through his blue(s), which are, of course, not all blue.

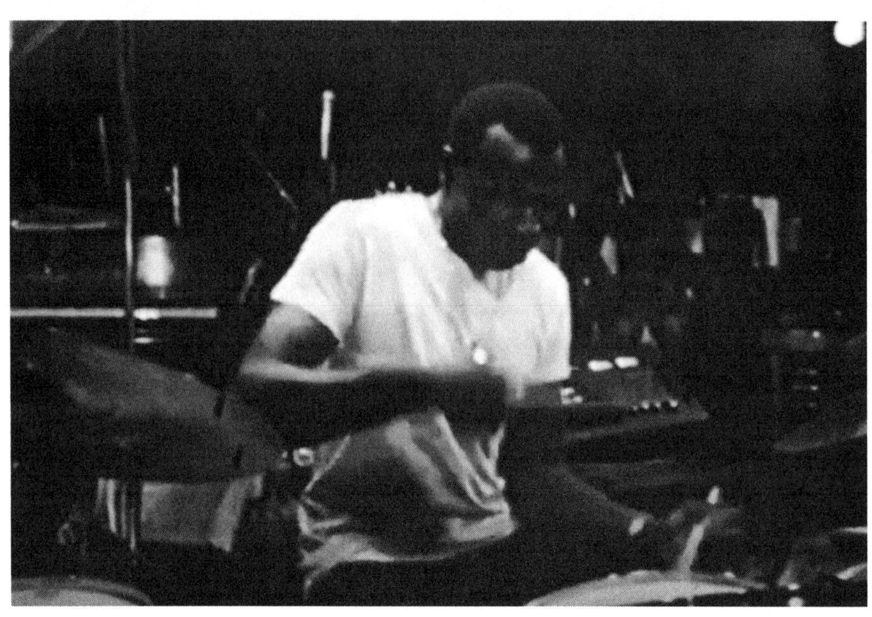

5.1

Elvin Jones in *Different Drummer: Elvin Jones*, 1979, directed and produced by Edward Gray. Courtesy of Edward Gray Films.

Imagine Delaney's painting *Blue-Light Abstraction* (ca. 1962; plate 13), then, as if it were a singer—let's call her Ethel, since in looking through the window of this painting, the sky is liquid with motion. Imagine that she sits in with Sonny, Creole, and the rest of the band that James Baldwin conjures, and then listens to so carefully, at the end of his story "Sonny's Blues" (1957).[1] As if she were Waters, Ethel asks, "Am I blue?" As if she were whispering to Miles Davis and Bill Evans, as if they were sitting at a table in the back of the Long Night Lounge taking notes and tones in analog swarm. "Yes," Ethel says, answering her own question, "more or less; yes, both more and less," she says. Her answer gives us leave to veer off a little bit and ask, about Delaney's painting, "Is blue in green, or is it green's background, or is green blue's structure—a skeletal frame that doesn't surround and contain but rather infuses and supports blue by being that through which blue can be seen, so that, then, blue can be seen through, too?" This seeing-through is not mirroring, but it's not a pure transparency, either: it's diffraction, and refraction, obliquity, and even opacity, and even obscurity. As Baldwin insists with regard to black, and thus to color in general, what matters is not held within the opposition between light's presence and absence; what matters to color is given in light's constant transformation. In this changing, what must be avoided, at all costs, are things becoming too clear. So, please join me in a mystery—which we can be, says Rita Dove, even if we can't be free.[2]

1.

I always wanted to be in a band, and over the last few years I have begun to realize that I have always been in a band. It's just that we often played remotely, not on the same stand or day, or in the same club or century. Was I just deluded, and, if so, what had been the agent of my delusion? Where did this desire to be in a band come from? What relation to possession could this thing that I wanted have? Did I, could I, have what I wanted even as I had it? Could what I wanted, and had, have me? What did it mean to desire what I had, or what had me? These are Hortense Spillers's questions. They have to do with slavery, slavery being, perhaps at its most fundamental, a radical interdiction of the capacity *to have*. The questions have to do, in turn, with how this incapacity to have—which is, in a culture based on possession, monstrous—might be the deepest and most fundamentally enabling thing imaginable. The incapacity to have may remind us to think deeply, in practice, this whole range of giving, sharing, passing, handing, holding, and releasing that *having* brutally obscures.

At the University of Tennessee, Knoxville, symposium about Delaney's and Baldwin's art in 2020, it was clear that critical inquiry had us sharing like a band, thriving on a riff, or some riffs—some texts and some problems—and the choruses I seemed to be taking on my own were really just me being taken, with love, and in love, by the chorus. An ensemble neither speaking for itself nor only to itself is beautiful. This beauty is hard, of course, because people always want to tell you how ugly—or, at least, how plain—it is to be leveled, to not stand out. And we say, yeah, it is, it's plain, like plainsong, which is rich and complex and open and constantly differentiated and differentiating in the depth of its textured, topographically uncountable surfacing. That musical surface is social, but there are no social relations; public and private haven't resolved into their opposites. In plainsong there are no bodies because no body is simply their own, and no one simply has one in the wake of this heritable inability to have, so that no one is not one, at all. All this feels oceanically beautiful but also terrible—when none can give any other description of how it might be truly *to live* than to associate living with leaving, and then leaving again, and with not quite living with what you leave, so that all your soul can do is look back and wonder how it got over the leaving, while always also wondering if getting over is all that it's cracked up to be in this loneliness none can have for sharing. The soul that looks back at the wreck of history is an angel in a way that lets you know that Walter Benjamin was always also sitting in with Beauford and Elvin and Jimmy'n'em. What Beauford continually had to leave of Knoxville, or Boston, or what he and Baldwin had to leave of Harlem, or Greenwich Village, or what Elvin had to leave of Detroit or of Trane, with Trane; whatever it is of what they're leaving wherever they are now; and what it is to see in leaving, and to see through leaving, and what it is to see through leaves: the word for that looking back and seeing through, for that refusal of foresight that is given in moving forward, in being dragged back into the future, arms flailing, flinging themselves away from the broken paradise of the very idea of a body or a home—that word is *improvisation*.

What if, in the interest of handing and handing on the gift of diffraction, we don't stand in front of paintings but off to the side of them, looking with them and through them, seeing the crowded texture of their surfaces? What if we stand not opposite but apposite to the painting, so that we can both better receive and better pass on its refractive practice, looking not at but with and through its disbursive eyes, so we can ask after this blue(s) we share? I hope this essay is about a militant refusal of a certain war of position, which is given in the full frontality that art, or its world, imposes upon us. I am made to stand against what I am looking at, which has become my object, *mein Gegenstand*, as the Germans more literally have it, hoping that my triumph over it in my acquisition of it will turn it into my mirror, so I can catch a glimpse of whatever self I'm trying be in affirmative opposition to, or faithful negation of, the forces that simultaneously impose selfhood and deny it. It's always a fight—a game of thrones, or honor—and victory is, in fact, conquest, appropriation, acquisition, and settlement of what is supposed to be unsettled and unsettling. The making and the buying of art are entangled in ways that ought to disturb us, even if we remain undisturbed by how so much of the making and buying of Black art simultaneously tends to and reopens the wounds that Black life suffers in being held in the entanglement of making and buying. It goes back to how we live this entanglement of self-making and self-buying across the divide that is supposed to separate slavery and freedom. Saidiya Hartman has written terribly beautifully about this, doing the indispensable work of telling us what we already know. We know because we know how Black families, by way of a range of structures in which care can be both opposed to and alloyed with abuse, send their children out into a range of variations of this fight because it seems to be the only way for them to survive the unrelenting war into which they are born. We send our children out into the world as if they were artworks whose mission is to change and thus survive it. We send our artworks out into the world as if they were children we want to protect from certain invasive and enveloping gazes while knowing that the world is nothing other than the aggregate of hostile looks and ruthless looking away.

This is an absolute and brutal irony. My family knew they had to send me, worked to send me, worked to instill in me the desire to go, but they didn't really want me to go. They had to send me so I could become myself, so that I could find or have a self, so I could have a life, because a life is what free people have. Sent out into the world of individuation and relation, all I could do, all I had—having been sent from the social aesthetic into which I was born and by which I was borne and by way of which I was always, happily, both more and less than I—was the religion of art that I found and refound daily standing in front of a Renoir at the Fogg Art Museum. Sent out from sociality into (anti)social relations (not sent as an individual but sent to find individuality, which is individuation's impossible aim and object), I found myself trying to find myself in a mirror called *Gabrielle en robe rouge*.[3] I was raised happy with and by the people who had no lives, or whose lives didn't matter, but who shared the irreducible materiality of a life in common. We were happy but we were brutalized, and sometimes we brutalized what chimerically appeared to us as one another, and we knew it, and we fought it. We spent vast amounts of time scheming and planning in and for this fight, and we did so joyously and we did so, as Baldwin would have had it, never wanting to be the equal or the semblance of the ones who brutalized us. Some of what we fought for took the form of certain aspects of citizenship, but, as Baldwin intimates, we wanted to be "other than citizens" (to use Charles Olson's phrase, which J. Peter Moore illuminates and amplifies) for specific reasons that have to do with the metaphysical foundations of politics and of citizenship.[4] We had no alternative metaphysics so much as we were constantly practicing an alternative to metaphysics, always fighting for that practice, and for how to retain it under the duress of a system that withholds and requires individuation in one fell and constant and vicious swoop.

What if the pragmatic decision regarding property that Baldwin speaks of at the end of "The Price of the Ticket" (1985)—when the founders of this country decided to extend the long, hostile tradition of the pseudointellectual subdivision of the earth in the direction of a distinction between property and persons, and to make distinctions among persons based on their access to and their being accessed as property, and to enshrine the murderous assertion of such access under the titles of freedom and democracy—is irreducibly and irrevocably linked to the constellation of fantasies and brutalities of individuation(-in-relation)?[5] Hilton Als brilliantly and beautifully refers to the connection Baldwin and Beauford have in their loneliness. He points to this connection as the hope we can draw from Beauford and Baldwin's relationship while also allowing and requiring us to understand that we do and must want more than that, that to want only that will have made us, finally, equal to the citizens and their state who place conditions upon us that tend to make this the horizon of our desire.

So, in Als's spirit, I hope, and in his wake, let's begin not only with the terrible beauty of connection in loneliness but also with its inadequacy. We might even consider that this particular and much-to-be-celebrated-and-lamented connection in loneliness that Baldwin and Beauford shared is their own incarceration in and escape from what Baldwin elsewhere calls "the male prison," where free and lonely personhood seeks a monogamy that, even in its seriality and sometimes even in its overlaps, is a wish to have, as Baldwin puts it, one's nakedness covered by some other one, even as, at the same time, what they share is enabled by and seeks a differentiating turn in, if not return to, a shared, ungendered, socialized maternity that is structured by substitution and dispossession always as if these could be a common practice rather than a sovereign demand. In this regard, the native's return is always to some elsewhere, as when Amiri Baraka, in his great poem "Return of the Native," writes of a Harlem that he, too, was only passing through, but beautifully, in beautiful recognition of its intensities: "Vicious the way it's made. / Can you stand such beauty? / So violent and transforming."[6] In being sent, only as if we were being sent from home, we were always headed to somewhere else from somewhere else, familiar, unfamiliar, like (fallen) angels.

2.

The image I get is one of a rickety bridge (sometimes a rickety boat) arching finer than a hair to touch down on the sands at, say, Abidjan. Listening to Burning Spear the other night, for example, I drifted off to where it seemed I was being towed into an abandoned harbor. I wasn't exactly a boat but I felt my anchorlessness as a lack, as an inured, eventually visible pit up from which I floated, looking down on what debris looking into it left. By that time, though, I turned out to be a snake hissing, "You did it, you did it," rattling and weeping waterless tears. Some such flight (an insistent previousness evading each and every natal occasion) comes close to what I meant by "cut."

Nathaniel Mackey, *Bedouin Hornbook*

To look is to have your head wrecked. Computer Style involutes the senses, puts them through a mental gymnasium, reassembles the sensorium ready for the hi-pressure future it depicts. It folds the mind into an origami state, a battle style. The senses are kinaesthetized into an orig army, armed for a contest of lines. To look is to be rocketed across the planes of the letter, shot along diagonals that charge space with acute dynamics, gradients that reverse gravity like skyscrapers that drill to the earth's core.

The letterform becomes a city of parallel lines of force. The word becomes a futurescape hostile to traditional sensoria. Surfaces converge to trap the optic nerve at a point of maximum impossibility. Stalked by angles, hunted by diagonals, the harassed eye wanders until it's impaled on the corner, pincered by a parallax plane. Vectors and horizontals join forces to push the retina to the razor's edge.

Kodwo Eshun, *More Brilliant than the Sun: Adventures in Sonic Fiction*

"Blue(s) as Cymbal" is concerned with two questions: Does the field of immersion in which the resonant localities of Baldwin's writing (whose particular refusal of the opposition or relation between fiction and nonfiction might be said to fail to achieve, and succeed in avoiding, narrative) and Delaney's painting (where the field of color is a zone of refusal of the opposition and relation of figuration and abstraction upon which realism can be said to be based) allow something else of Blackness to show up beyond the triangular nexus of personhood, narrative, and portrait? Is it possible that this largesse becomes sensible for us in and through the sub- as well as superphilosophical and synesthetic nonsense of the great drummer Elvin's theory of musical color?

In order to think about and around and with all this, we must consider the lonely percussive genius that miraculously emerges when a dialogue of drums in constant sexual differentiation is held in male virtuosity. This is part of the story Baldwin tells in "Sonny's Blues." He tells it by way of the story of the making of a musician, who emerges from loss and exile, addiction and incarceration, into a public, however cramped, that is capacious enough for him to speak. Now what if we augment Baldwin's telling of the terrible precedence of this birth into the particular loneliness of the artist with a little story about what precedes the particular loneliness of our birth into the particular loneliness of the broken and impossible Black self. In *The Half Has Never Been Told: Slavery and the Making of American Capitalism* (2014)—if we read it through Eshun's surfaces and Mackey's leaves—historian Edward Baptist describes the new forms of brutal(ly interdicted) individuation that mark the conditions of slavery in the era of cotton and of the institution's movement southward and westward from the tidewater to a somehow funkier, dirtier, deadlier South. He illuminates for us, in the wake of many other historians whose work enables his, the simultaneous financialization and mechanization of what R. A. Judy calls "sentient flesh," writing of how that flesh

> remembered that to pick quickly enough to turn cotton entrepreneurs' calculations into reality, one had to disembody oneself. Picking all day long until late at night, even by candlelight, they had to dissociate their minds from the pain that racked stooping backs; from blood running down pricked fingertips; from hands that gnarled into claws over a few short years; from thirst, hunger, blurred vision, and anxiety about the whip behind and before them. One had to separate mind from hand—to become, for a time, little more than a hand. Or two hands, like novice picker Solomon Northup's neighbor Patsey. While Northup lurched down his row, "the long cumbersome sack" making havoc with [cotton] branches," and groping single cotton bolls with both hands, Patsey worked both sides of her row in perpetual motion, right and left. She reached with one hand and dropped cotton in the bag hanging from her neck with the other, "lightning-quick motion was in her fingers as no other fingers possessed," Northup later wrote. She moved like a dancer in an unconscious rhythm, though of displacement rather than of pleasure.[7]

Baptist adds another quotation from Northup: "Patsey's hands—both of them, right and left—each did their own thinking, like those of a pianist."[8]

Moving sidewise, we might consider that the drummer, like the pianist, must also have what is called "independence of limbs." Playing polyrhythms depends on such independence. Consider, too, the disintegrated individuation of Elvin, which is activated so ensemble can reform! See how it is that from such brutal imposition a terrible beauty is born. What if the elsewhere Black music comes from and turns to in its constant evasion of origin and end is disindividuation? This will have been an anti- and ante-subjective condition of consent, rather than a subjective will to consent, not to be a single being, the line between imposition and voluntarity having blurred to fade in an undercommonness we share in/as practice, which is to say, deeper still, in a monstrosity we claim as our vessel, sociality thrown, together, overboard and broken.

Speaking of being thrown together, speaking of how shit go together, speaking of how we do:

> symbol (n.)
>
> early 15c., "creed, summary, religious belief," from Late Latin *symbolum* "creed, token, mark," from Greek *symbolon* "token, watchword, sign by which one infers; ticket, a permit, license" (the word was applied c. 250 by Cyprian of Carthage to the Apostles' Creed, on the notion of the "mark" that distinguishes Christians from pagans), literally "that which is thrown or cast together," from assimilated form of *syn-* "together" + *bole* "a throwing, a casting, the stroke of a missile, bolt, beam," from *bol-*, nominative stem of *ballein* "to throw" (from PIE root **gwele-* "to throw, reach").
>
> The sense evolution in Greek is from "throwing things together" to "contrasting" to "comparing" to "token used in comparisons to determine if something is genuine." Hence, "outward sign" of something. The meaning "something which stands for something else" first recorded 1590 (in "Faerie Queene"). As a written character, 1610s.[9]

Something that stands for something else, something thrown together, like two pieces of resonant metal, for the sound they make.

> cymbal (n.)
>
> "one of a pair of plates of brass or bronze which, when struck together, produce a sharp, ringing sound," mid-15c., from Old English *cimbal* and from Old French *cymbale* (13c.), both from Latin *cymbalum*, from Greek *kymbalon* "a cymbal," from *kymbē* "bowl, drinking cup." This previously has been connected with Sanskrit *kumbha-*, Avestan *xumba-* "pot"; Middle Irish *comm, cummal*. Beekes writes that, for structural reasons, "the word cannot be inherited. It is rather a 'Wanderwort', which fits a vessel term very well."[10]

The sense of "thrown together" remains in the short trip, the small wander, from symbol to cymbal. Is the blues something like a way of dealing with or living in Black variance to something Martin Heidegger calls thrownness? What it is to have been thrown, to have been cast out, into the world? What does this having been cast out (even as those voices cast us out to talk us in, in the way that Ed Roberson talks about in his poetry) have to do with what Baraka calls the loss of our *oom boom ba boom*, the interdiction of drumming as communion and communicability in slavery, which was thrown out not so much into an outer darkness but into the realm of impossible interiority, thrown together into thwarted individuation? I'm thinking of "Sonny's Blues" as cymbal. The pianist, who is, in Black music, always also a drummer, looks back and wonders. I am also thinking of this sense of cymbal as (broken, or at least, beaten) vessel, and not the emptiness so much as the outpouring, the spilling (as Alexis Pauline Gumbs would say, by way of Spillers) of the drum or jug. What's the relation between the Latin *cymbalum* and the Greek *symbolon*? What happens when these things are thrown together, compared, contrasted? Is the bowl thrown? When did people begin to speak of throwing pottery? How did shaping become known as throwing? What does this have to do with centering? And what does the breaking of the vessel, or the way the vessel breaks in thrownness, have to do with a necessary decentering? In speaking the intensity of the relation she sees between poetry and pottery, M. C. Richards says that "to center [the vessel in thrownness on the wheel] is to behave as a person," or to find an inner shape, to "fall into round."[11] But the throwing of hands or sticks that Elvin is engaged in is out of round, eccentric, centrifugal, as if in the interest, finally, of a profound selflessness that nothing seeming like something like a solo seems to give.

In this having been thrown together, what if we throw Richards's centering and Roberson's intervallic, integral, musical lucidity together into the resonant shimmer of the gathered means and meanings of their words? Wonder what blurry, blue-green repercussions might ensue? Perhaps "concrete experiences in thinking-with-the-organism, integrating perception and imagination and physical coordination—requiring study, observation, initiative, an ability to invent and to put things together. . . . A community where art is a central discipline is likely to develop an exceptional realism about the work to be done."[12] The resonance of words as a (per/reper)cussion:

throw (v.)

"to project, propel," c. 1300, from Old English *þrawan* "to twist, turn, writhe, curl," (past tense *þreow*, past participle *þrawen*), from Proto-Germanic **threw-* (source also of Old Saxon *thraian*, Middle Dutch *dræyen*, Dutch *draaien*, Old High German *draen*, German *driven* "to turn, twist"; not found in Scandinavian or Gothic), from PIE root **tere-* (1) "to rub, turn," with derivatives referring to twisting. Not the usual Old English word for "to throw" (*weorpan*, related to warp (v.) was common in this sense). The sense evolution may be via the notion of whirling a missile before throwing it. The sense of "put by force" (as in throw in jail) is first recorded 1550s; that of "confuse, flabbergast" is from 1844; that of "lose deliberately" is from 1868. To throw a party was in U.S. college slang by 1916.

To throw the book at (someone) is 1932, from notion of judge sentencing a criminal from a law book full of possible punishments. To throw (one's) hat in the ring "issue a challenge," especially to announce one's candidacy, first recorded 1917. To throw up "vomit" is first recorded 1732. To throw (someone) off "confuse by a false scent" is from 1891.[13]

warp (v.)

"to bend, twist, distort," Old English *weorpan* "to throw, throw away, hit with a missile," from Proto-Germanic **werpanan* "to fling by turning the arm" (source also of Old Saxon *werpan*, Old Norse *verpa* "to throw," Swedish *värpa* "to lay eggs," Old Frisian *werpa*, Middle Low German and Dutch *werpen*, German *werfen*, Gothic *wairpan* "to throw"), from PIE **werp-* "to turn, wind, bend" (source also of Latin *verber* "whip, rod"), from root **wer-* (2) "to turn, bend."

Connection between "turning" and "throwing" is perhaps in the notion of rotating the arm in the act of throwing; compare Old Church Slavonic *vrešti* "to throw," from the same PIE root. The meaning "twist out of shape" is first recorded c. 1400; intransitive sense is from mid-15c. Related: *Warped; warping.*[14]

warp (n.)

"threads running lengthwise in a fabric," Old English *wearp*, from Proto-Germanic **warpo-* (source also of Middle Low German warp, Old High German *warf* "*warp*," Old Norse *varp* "cast of a net"), from

PIE **werp-* "to turn, bend" (see *warp* (v.)). The warp of fabric is that across which the woof is "thrown." Applied by 1947 in astrophysics to the "bending" of space-time, and popularized in noun phrase warp speed (for faster-than-light travel) by the 1960s U.S. TV series "Star Trek."[15]

I.
because the final
confessions of a coarse air
bail the fire out
we are innocent of adduction.

taking the body down
we thought was a solo for fuel.
shoving it in for warmth
we cracked

our perpetual jar of things
to a more
naked jarring blast.
the crimes wch you wear my body for

I myself committed.[16]

Werfen (*geworfen*/*Geworfenheit*) is related to *weorpan* or *warp* and "our perpetual jar of things," thrown together like cymbals, like a symbol, like the drummer, cast out "to a more naked jarring blast," having been given some in having been abducted, and then in having thrown himself off or away after having been set on a throne so he can move without moving. This is ground flown over and under by Mackey and Eshun: having been taken, abducted, the drummer is guilty of adduction, this throwing together changed to more directly handed high-quickstep ride in forced and hard-row'd marching, or hand in weight on hambone, hard tap or shift, or shift on sand as if soufflé.

abduction (n.)

1620s, "a leading away," from Latin *abductionem* (nominative *abductio*) "a forcible carrying off, ravishing, robbing," noun of action from past-participle stem of *abducere* "to lead away, take away, arrest" (often by force), from *ab* "off, away from" (see *ab-*) + *ducere* "to lead," from PIE root **deuk* "to lead." As "criminal act of forcibly taking (someone)" by 1768; before that the word also was a term in surgery and logic. In the Mercian hymns, Latin *abductione* is glossed by Old English *wiðlaednisse*.[17]

Sonny started on the drums, then moved to piano, as if replicating in reverse the move from symbol to cymbal, so that we can see both instruments as elemental to the working through of the individuation of the sociopercussive. The piano intensifies that individuation by bearing melody's solitary, point-to-point seriality, which, in the story, by way of the blues, allows Sonny to enter the water, to immerse himself, to take the "immense suggestion that [he] speak for himself." At first, as Baldwin tells it, Sonny moved in halting utterance: "He and the piano stammered, started one way, got scared, stopped; started another way, panicked, marked time, started again; then seemed to have found a direction, panicked again, got stuck."[18] Later, this is what Baraka said—surely in a kind of echo, or better yet in constammerative duet with Baldwin, on the way to ensemblic articulation—that he heard in one of Trane's solos, as the solo's eternal preface to itself:

> After "Straight, No Chaser," Trane began to find out exactly what he was doing. But a great many times the chord jungle just caused him to run around and around hoping somehow to get into that thing he'd found and was trying to work out. I heard him several times during that period, just after he'd left Monk. One night he played the head of "Confirmation" over and over again, about twenty times, and that was his solo. It was as if he wanted to take that melody apart and play out each of its chords as a separate improvisational challenge. And while it was a marvelous thing to hear and see, it was also more than a little frightening; like watching a grown man learning to speak . . . and I think that's just what was happening.[19]

The tremulous throwing, the tremored, treme'd casting of a vessel, "the very cup of trembling,"[20] we bear as the feel of life, having been thrown on the wheel of life, as this entanglement of lushness and deprivation, sufferance and suffering, is how Baldwin hears in what he writes of the miracle of Sonny's centering, and how can I come up here, now, writing against that? How can I write against "the immense suggestion that Sonny speak for himself,"[21] having found freedom and made it his, or having made something his and, in that, having found freedom?

3.

To see with Baldwin is also to see with Delaney. A brown leaf on black asphalt; a blue sky through green leaves.

> And because I was seeing it with Beauford, because Beauford caused me to see it, the very colours underwent a most disturbing and salutary change. The brown leaf on the black asphalt, for example—what colours were those, really? To stare at the leaf long enough, to try to apprehend the leaf, was to discover many colours in it; and though black had been described to me as the absence of light, it became very clear to me that if this were true, we would never have been able to see the colour; black: the light is trapped in it and struggles upward, rather like that grass pushing upward through the cement. It was humbling to be forced to realise that the light fell down from heaven, on everything, on everybody, and that the light was always changing. Paradoxically, this meant for me that memory is a traitor and that life does not contain the past tense; the sunset one saw yesterday, the leaf that burned, or the rain that fell, have not really been seen unless one is prepared to see them every day. As Beauford is, to his eternal credit, and for our health and hope.
>
> Perhaps I am so struck by the light in Beauford's paintings because he comes from darkness—as I do, as, in fact, we all do. But the darkness of Beauford's beginnings, in Tennessee, many years ago, was a black-blue midnight indeed, opaque, and full of sorrow. And I do not know, nor will any of us ever really know, what kind of strength it was that enabled him to make so dogged and splendid a journey. In any case, from Tennessee, he eventually came to Paris (I have the impression that he walked and swam) and lived for a while in a suburb of Paris, Clamart. It was at this time that I began to see Beauford's painting in a new way, and it was also at this time that Beauford's paintings underwent a most startling metamorphosis into freedom. I know this sounds extremely subjective; but let it stand; it is not really as subjective as it sounds. There was a window in Beauford's house in Clamart before which we often sat—late at night, early in the morning, at noon. This window looked out on a

garden; or, rather, it would have looked out on the garden if it had not been for the leaves and branches of a large tree which pressed directly against the window. Everything one saw from this window, then, was filtered through these leaves. And this window was a kind of universe, moaning and wailing when it rained, light of the morning, and blue as the blues when the last light of the sun departed.[22]

Le clameur de Clamart. Clamor, black's latent and volatile chromaticism, which can be heard. That the relationship between cymbal and symbol is more than merely homophonic is borne out in Baldwin's analytic of the blues and in his entrance into Delaney's colors. What do the blues symbolize for Baldwin and how does all that fit into Delaney's symbolic economy? Clamart, clamor, but also various presences of light in blue indicate something not just as the basis for what yellow instantiates in the realm of value but also something alternative to that mode of measure. What if Baldwin is really trying to tell us something terrible about something terrible in this passage: "Beauford was the first walking, living, proof for me that a black man could be an artist. In a warmer time, a less blasphemous place, he would have been recognized as my Master and I as his Pupil. He became, for me, an example of courage and integrity, humility and passion. An absolute integrity: I saw him shaken many times and I lived to see him broken but I never saw him bow."[23] I want to say that whatever else it is, Baldwin's vision here is tragic when he describes this long apprenticeship in the impossible ways of individuation, which consciousness of oneself as an artist, or consciousness of oneself as having been claimed by that possibility, only intensifies. This interplay of seeing with and having been seen through, when reduced in and to the isolation of seeing what one stands against, is terrible. This concerns the reduction, abstraction, and dematerialization of the aesthetic as it is transformed, weaponized, and monetized into art, when sensibility and sensuality become financial instruments. How do we reconcile Baldwin's antipathy in "The Price of the Ticket" to the multitude or mob—which is only its own cowardice and submission to the state—with the clamor of the canvas, or the crowdedness of Harlem's surface, or the various intensities of congregation? Perhaps what is possible is not a reconciliation, but a revival such as occurs when Baldwin, as he often does, (re)turns to church for a lesson.

In the church I come from—which is not at all the same church to which white Americans belong—we were counselled, from time

> to time, to do our first works over. Though the church I come from and the church to which most white Americans belong are both Christian churches, their relationship—due to those pragmatic decisions concerning Property made by a Christian state sometime ago—cannot be said to involve, or suggest, the fellowship of Christians. We do not, therefore, share the same hope or speak the same language.
>
> To do your first works over means to reexamine everything. Go back where you started, or as far back as you can, examine all of it, travel your road again and tell the truth about it. Sing or shout or testify or keep it to yourself: but *know whence you came.*[24]

What are the differences between taking the suggestion to speak for yourself, learning to speak, and doing your first works over?

Can art be a method or an occasion to do our first works over? Or is it more often an obscuring of a certain work that is not, in fact, first, but whose belatedness requires something like the continual enshrinement of originarity? Is there a work that comes always and continually before the first work and, if so, how do we get to that, renew that, not just in its reiterative criticality but also in its anoriginal celebration in and of the church that criticism comes from? And how is that pursuit, that always and continually coming and going after, anything other than a condition of being spoken always and continually before yourself?

4.

The trap set—the ensemblic contraption of percussive instruments that we refer to, simply, as the drums—is a glorious invention, but I have been wondering about the horror that produced it ever since I began to come to grips with an intuition (again, anticipated by Mackey and Eshun, most especially) regarding its double origins in communal dispossession and imposed individuation. What the trap set bears, where it comes from, is borne, too, by the way we play the piano, a percussive encroachment on melody's linearity that always both records and prophesies catastrophe. That little toggle from drums to piano, which we take along with Sonny, hips us not so much to some first work to reexamine but, rather, to some prior work, some fucked-up precedence we have to deal with, an understanding of where the drummer be coming from, this continual exile in crowded surface, which is remembered, in futurial dismemberment, as wreck. The terrible banishment from texture to perspective, from contour to overview, is what's in store, and its refusal never requires or allows anything other than the most severe reckoning with roughness, which art approaches fretfully and dishonestly, which honest understandings of art readily admit, but only as if lying is the only, or at least the most reliable, method of truth.

If we continue to practice doing our first works over, we might also have to ask, at a level even more general than Baldwin offers us when he demands that we see how becoming white and becoming Black are unequal flipsides of one another: What if the price of the ticket is not precisely enough given in the phrase "becoming white"? What if becoming white is becoming one? What if it is individuation as such that is given in all this terrible and fateful christening and naming, which we imagine as having emerged from the natural condition of our separateness and our desired inaffectability? My name—either the one they gave me, or he gave me, or that I give myself—is understood to correspond to an individual capacity to have (oneself) that can only be questioned by way of its violation, rather than refused as a function of its necessary brutality. And how do we deal with the paradox that emerges when we are confronted with what appears to be such an absolute gift, the beauty of Baldwin, or Delaney, themselves in the wake of what is retrospectively fantasized as their decision, like Sonny, to speak for themselves?

What does it really mean to do our first works over? To see through them. Delaney's *Blue-Light Abstraction* is a lesson in seeing through. Now, what has blue-light abstraction to do with Elvin Jones? It's when he hits that cymbal, finally, and we hear and see with him through shimmer, extrasensually, not the world and the self as they are but, rather, that they are not. This follows from the way one can see that white people are not (white). To see through not only the terror of the obvious but also the depth that is supposedly hidden by the obvious, neither that standing out nor that depth having been grounded, so to speak, as surface. Perhaps when "apprehension began to beat the air," that is the moment of "a new confrontation with reality,"[25] such that the BangClash of vicious modernism, whether in Harlem or in Knoxville or in Paris, follows the exile/escapee everywhere he goes? Maybe the artist is just supposed to help us to identify and see and grasp our object, so we can protect ourselves from it with sufficiently murderous brutality? Maybe art is all and only that it "has this advantage, that you can see yourself in it, if you will bring yourself to it"?[26] But what if in looking at Beauford, the artist, Baldwin sees himself and is always trying to tell us the terror of that, and that derives from that? What if, above all, he is concerned with our discernment of the difference between seeing and being seen, on the one hand, and seeing through and seeing with, on that uncountable mass of other handing that we call Black social life?

NOTES

Epigraphs: Nathaniel Mackey, *Bedouin Hornbook*, Callaloo Fiction Series 2 (Lexington: University of Kentucky Press, 1986), 34–35; Kodwo Eshun, *More Brilliant than the Sun: Adventures in Sonic Fiction* (London: Quartet Books, 1998), 73–74.

1 James Baldwin, "Sonny's Blues," *Partisan Review*, Summer 1957, reprinted in *James Baldwin: Early Novels and Stories*, ed. Toni Morrison (New York: Library of America, 1998), 831–64.

2 Rita Dove, "Canary," in *Grace Notes: Poems* (New York: W. W. Norton, 1989), 64.

3 Pierre-Auguste Renoir, *Gabrielle in a Red Dress*, 1908, oil on canvas, 21¾ × 18¼ in. (55 × 46.5 cm), Harvard Art Museums/Fogg Museum, Cambridge, MA, https://hvrd.art/o/229048, accessed November 23, 2022.

4 Jonathan Peter Moore, "Other Than a Citizen: Vernacular Poetics in Postwar America," PhD diss., Duke University, 2016, https://hdl.handle.net/10161/12192.

5 James Baldwin, "The Price of the Ticket," in *The Price of the Ticket: Collected Nonfiction, 1948–1985* (New York: St. Martin's, 1985); reprinted in *James Baldwin: Collected Essays*, ed. Toni Morrison (New York: Library of America, 1998), 830–42.

6 LeRoi Jones, "Return of the Native," in *Black Magic: Poetry 1961–1967* (Indianapolis: Bobbs-Merrill, 1969), 147–48, reprinted in *The LeRoi Jones/Amiri Baraka Reader*, ed. William J. Harris, 2nd ed. (New York: Basic Books, 1999), 217, lines 3–5.

7 Edward E. Baptist, *The Half Has Never Been Told: Slavery and the Making of American Capitalism* (New York: Basic Books, 2014), 136–37. See also R. A. Judy, *Sentient Flesh: Thinking in Disorder, Poiesis in Black* (Durham, NC: Duke University Press, 2020).

8 Baptist, *Half Has Never Been Told*, 137.

9 Online Etymology Dictionary., "symbol (n.)," accessed December 30, 2019, https://www.etymonline.com/search?q=symbol.

10 Online Etymology Dictionary, "cymbal (n.)," accessed December 30, 2019, https://www.etymonline.com/search?q=cymbal.

11 Mary Caroline Richards, *Centering in Pottery, Poetry, and the Person* (Middletown, CT: Wesleyan University Press, 1964), 62, 108.

12 Richards, *Centering*, 108, 121.

13 Online Etymology Dictionary, "throw (v.)," accessed December 30, 2019, https://www.etymonline.com/search?q=throw.

14 Online Etymology Dictionary, "warp (v.)," accessed December 30, 2019, https://www.etymonline.com/search?q=warp.

15 Online Etymology Dictionary, "warp (n.)," accessed December 30, 2019, https://www.etymonline.com/search?q=warp.

16 Ed Roberson, *Voices Cast Out to Talk Us In: Poems by Ed Roberson* (Iowa City: University of Iowa Press, 1995), 11. © 1995 by Ed Roberson. Used with permission of the University of Iowa Press. All rights reserved.

17 Online Etymology Dictionary, "abduction (n.)," accessed April 22, 2019, https://www.etymonline.com/search?q=abduction.

18 Baldwin, "Sonny's Blues," 862.

19 LeRoi Jones, *Black Music* (New York: William Morrow, 1967), 59.

20 Baldwin, "Sonny's Blues," 864.

21 Baldwin, "Sonny's Blues," 863.

22 James Baldwin, "On the Painter Beauford Delaney," *Transition* 4, no. 18 (1965): 45; reprinted in Morrison, *James Baldwin: Collected Essays*, 720–21. (This quote is almost the entire short essay by Baldwin.)

23 Baldwin, "Price of the Ticket," 832.

24 Baldwin, "Price of the Ticket," 841.

25 Baldwin, "Sonny's Blues," 862; Baldwin, "On the Painter Beauford Delaney," 721.

26 Fred L. Standley and Louis H. Pratt, eds., *Conversations with James Baldwin* (Jackson: University Press of Mississippi, 1989), 31.

SIX

Baldwin and Delaney Tell the Story Using Yellows and the Blues

Robert G. O'Meally

"I warn you, Icarus, to fly in a middle course, lest, if you go too low, the water may weight your wings; if you go too high, the fire may burn them."

Ovid

En route to the floor of the ocean, the diver first passes through the "belt of the fishes." This is a wide band of light reflected from the surface of the sea. From this area he moves to a depth of water that cannot be penetrated by light above the surface. It is dark, foreboding, and eerie. The diver's immediate reaction is apt to be one of fear and sometimes a sudden spasm of panic that soon passes. As he drops deeper and deeper into the abyss, slowly his eyes begin to pick up the luminous quality of the darkness.

Howard Thurman

[T]hat light, that miracle, are what I began to see in Beauford's paintings, and this light . . . held the power to . . . redeem and reconcile and heal.

James Baldwin

In a talk at Columbia University in 2004, Toni Morrison offered a ringing manifesto for assessing African American art of the twentieth and twenty-first centuries. Her clear-sighted theory of reading directly informs my take on James Baldwin's "Sonny's Blues" (1957), in light both of what Baldwin calls his "uses of the blues" and of his kinship with the painter Beauford Delaney. Compartmentalizing fields of artistic practice "is convenient and useful for study, instruction in institutions," Morrison told her audience. The problem is that such divisions do not represent "how artists actually work. . . . The borders established for the convenience of study are, I believe, *not just porous, they are liquid*. Locating instances of this liquidity is vital if African American art is to be understood for the complex work that it is and the deep meaning it contains." To complete and sometimes just to start writing a narrative, she continued, "I need three kinds of information. . . . Once I've settled on an idea and the story through which to examine it, I need the *structure*, the *sound*, the *palette*—not necessarily in that order."[1] The same aesthetic "liquidity," as dynamic influence and interplay of elements in the works of James Baldwin (the bluesy picture-making writer) and Beauford Delaney (the polyphonic narrative painter), is the subject of my essay. As is the idea that their works' vibrating light and sound imply that we humans and more-than-humans must dedicate ourselves to loving each other more deeply.

Given that the word *blues* is nestled in the title of Baldwin's short story and that its main character is a jazz musician, we are evidently led to read (well, *try* to read) "Sonny's Blues" in terms of musicality—its jazz/blues sound, structure, and feeling. Musical references sound throughout the story. Along with "Old Ship of Zion" (which, the story's narrator confesses, has rescued no one lately), "Am I Blue?" may be the most significant of these soundings. Called for in "Sonny's Blues" as an instrumental in which the players are expected to "tell the story," as jazz players say (encouraging one another to play cliché-free narrative-like melodic lines, from the heart), "Am I Blue?" is closely associated with Billie Holiday, one of the blues-idiom musicians most frequently cited (and recited) by Baldwin. In the story's climactic scene, it's Creole who announces this song, thus conjuring the spare dramatic vibrato of Lady Day's interrogative and accusatory voice:

Am I Blue?
You'd be, too.
Ain't these tears in my eyes
Telling you?

Adding to the Billie-in-the-background musicality (and biographical storyline) of "Sonny's Blues" may be, among several models for Baldwin's character Sonny, the saxophone colossus Sonny Rollins, whom Baldwin knew and whose big-tone tenor eloquence the writer much admired.[2] Rollins's own experiences of separation from his father, drug addiction, and hard-bought cure, and the fatherly mentoring of Rollins by Thelonious Monk and Charlie "Bird" Parker—echoed in this story by Creole's guidance—all resonate throughout "Sonny's Blues."[3]

So does the short life of Parker, who, having struggled, quite publicly, with drug addiction, died soon after the publication of Baldwin's story. Who is this Bird? Sonny's brother wants to know. "He's just one of the greatest jazz musicians alive," Sonny answers, echoing Baldwin's own admiration, annoyed at the naïve question. "Maybe the greatest." The first sentences of "Sonny's Blues" compose a sparkling Parkeresque overture, unfolding an invitation to read the tale with jazz, and perhaps specifically with Parker, in mind. These introductory words create a halting but surging *poiesis*: a call-and-recall literary equivalent of the vibrating reed voice of Parker (or of his student Rollins). Watch/listen as Sonny's older brother, a Harlem secondary-school algebra teacher, seeks to parse the bad news of what's happened to Sonny, key phrases playing and replaying in the math man's mind:

> I read about it in the paper, in the subway, on my way to work. I read it, and I couldn't believe it, and I read it again. Then perhaps I just stared at it, at the newsprint spelling out his name, spelling out the story. I stared at it in the swinging lights of the subway car, and in the faces and bodies of the people, and in my own face, trapped in the darkness which roared outside.[4]

A few lines later, Bro Algebra (unnamed in this short story) evokes Bird again as he hears a schoolboy whistling a tune that was "at once very complicated and very simple, it seemed to be pouring out of him as though he were a bird, and it sounded very cool and moving through all that harsh bright air, only just holding its own through all those other sounds."[5]

Coming after the rhythmical dance step at the top of "Sonny's Blues," the brother's perception of the youngster's whistling "as though he were a bird" suggests that the math teacher too has developed an ear for Parker. He's absorbed elements of his aesthetic and begun to experiment with his own Bird-like improvised lines ("I read it . . . I read it . . . I read it again. . . . I just stared at it. . . . I stared at it"), "chasing the Bird," to paraphrase a Parker song title, in search of clarity through the urban chaos of "all those other sounds." As we shall see, Beauford Delaney, too, was mindful of Bird's example, as his shimmering painting called *Charlie Parker Yardbird* (1958; plate 10) made abundantly clear.

With these musical references in "Sonny's Blues" acknowledged, let us also see that like Morrison, who acknowledges having been "very generous to myself in getting ideas from painters,"[6] Baldwin visualizes on the printed page: picturing characters and scenes in words with deliberate uses of color, texture, and layers; enlisting strategies most closely associated with painting.[7] What is there to say about the liquid spaces in "Sonny's Blues," where visual and musical realms flow together, ever magnifying the fiction's meaning? What might Baldwin have drawn not only from Lady Day, Bird, and Rollins but also from his close friend, the painter Delaney?

The short form of my argument looks back to Morrison's term for the shared motives and methods of all the Black American arts: liquidity. This metaphor carries me to the story's end, to Bro Algebra's trembling Scotch-and-milk toast to Sonny: "He sipped from it and looked toward me, and nodded. Then he put it back on top of the piano. For me, then, as they began to play again, it glowed and shook above my brother's head like the very cup of trembling."[8] There's what Ralph Ellison calls "a heap o' signifying" in that cup of trembling, the masterful story's "*very* cup!"[9] Before turning to that image, note that the idea of trembling water, or rather, the idea of *trembling* itself, helps us appreciate the complex interflowing beauty of African American artworks and their lessons about how we earthly beings could love one another better. I have in mind the perpetual motion of our planet and all its members and elements, particles and waves; and I have in mind, further, as physicists have clarified for years, that we (the planet and all of us on it) tend toward "sympathetic resonance" or "sympathetic vibration."[10] Proximity makes vibrating strings pulse in tune; likewise, our heartbeats and other bodily cycles tend to sync up, to oscillate together. The philosopher Édouard Glissant (evidently vibing with "Sonny's Blues") declares that "we understand the world better when we tremble with it."[11] In other words, although trembling (primarily an involuntary response to fear or cold) is not the same as vibrating, an ethical dimension draws trembling and vibrating together. Both Glissant and Baldwin imply that one can *will* to empathize truly with others: one can *learn* to tremble. That's what this Baldwin story is about, most radically: one brother finally learning to tremble with the other.

Baldwin's recurring images of intermittent physical movement—reaching a crescendo in the story's last line, when the drink on Sonny's piano "glowed and shook like the very cup of trembling"—offers a key to the writer's connection with music, with visual art, and with the spirit world.[12] The motion of light that creates color and the vibrating waves that generate sound find counterparts in the rhythmical structures of "Sonny's Blues," both in the tectonic tremors that threaten to shake Harlem to pieces (echoing the biblical prophets' thundering proclamations of God's rage and judgment) and the positive sign of the waves trembling the drink on Sonny's piano.[13] Such images of vibration and trembling confirm the most profound meanings of "Sonny's Blues" as a liquid-space, a narrative of physics and metaphysics, of the love and trouble responsibilities of brother/sisterliness.

"You may not be able to stop nothing from happening," says Mama to numbers-inclined son concerning his brotherly responsibility toward Sonny. "But you got to let him know you's *there*."[14] "You don't have to be your brother's 'keeper,'" Rev. James A. Forbes told a Riverside Church congregation, "only your brother's *brother*."[15] Such an injunction to, at the very least, tremble together also confirms a kinship beyond biological bloodline. For kinship is one of the story's central concerns—the invisible interpersonal connections that form the basis of community-wide ties that bind: the stupefying, frightening tensions we share as well as the delivery of vibrations of love that Baldwin sometimes calls "witnessing."[16] In the biblical passage that Baldwin is quoting, the Hebrew word for "trembling" denotes monumental fear—the threat, in the book of Isaiah, of God's terrible wrath. We feel this when the daily news teaches us to fear for our planet—animal, vegetable, mineral, earth, sea, sky. But Glissant's insight that "we understand the world better when we tremble with it" suggests that we can learn to vibrate together as one world in relation; to model ourselves after a seasoned jazz combo, like the one at the end of "Sonny's Blues" that makes room for individual assertion and for 360-degree careful listening, each member offering the other a toast of love.

Where does the painter Beauford Delaney figure here? For starters, it is significant that Baldwin dedicated his collection of short stories *Going* to *Meet the Man* (1965), which introduced "Sonny's Blues" in book form, to the painter. And expansive ideas of "dedication" (from Latin *dedicare*, "to speak on behalf of, to affirm") as well as "influence" (Latin, "flowing in") underscore the subject of this chapter. To confirm profound levels of artistic dedication and fluidity, the first edition of Baldwin's book looks like it's gift-wrapped for Delaney. "For Beauford Delaney" graces the dedication page of *Going to Meet the Man*, whose dust-jacket title is printed in glistening yellow, the color most associated with Delaney's painterly aesthetic.[17] The hardback's binding, too, is done is sun-shimmering yellow cloth—ready to hand to Brother Delaney, who reportedly was very touched by the gesture.[18] Writes Baldwin:

> I learned about light from Beauford Delaney, the light contained in every thing, in every surface, in every face. . . . [T]hat life, that light, that miracle, are what I began to see in Beauford's paintings, and this light began to stretch back for me over all the time we had known each other, and over much more time than that, and this light held the power to illuminate, even to redeem and reconcile and heal. For Beauford's work leads the inner and the outer eye, directly and inexorably, to a new confrontation with reality. At this moment one begins to apprehend the nature of his triumph. And the beauty of his triumph, and the proof that it is a real one, is that he makes it ours.[19]

Delaney's *Portrait of Ella Fitzgerald* (1968; plate 26)—a portrait of the artist as an angel of light—is a case in point.[20] He depicts the First Lady of Song not in sweaty performance (as so often is the case in depictions of Black musical artists) but in a state of high-priestess contemplation—"the quiet place" from which, as Morrison has said, all art truly emerges.[21] Her mouth is closed, drawing the viewer to her wide-open eyes, welcoming inlets to her soul. These are the eyes of the supersubtle observer, the *curious* (in the Latin root sense of curative or healing, as well as hungry for knowledge) eyes of the artist as seer and singer of pulsating new worlds.[22] The self-composed, meditative Fitzgerald with this face and these eyes emerges from and radiates a full canvas of yellow light, filling its field of energy. These are *Delaney* yellows (not far from Van Gogh's brilliant "yellow, the color of divine clarity"): yellows of higher purposes, pure radiant energies that pulse and take you back to the spiritual glow of her eyes.[23] I return to the idea of this yellow as *curious*; this is an embers-like yellow that sparkles with intellectual capacity and holds "the power to illuminate, even to redeem and reconcile and heal." The portrait's many shades of yellow are intensified and broadcast from the canvas by a mix of other colors—daubs of white, green, orange, and brown. Again and again, Delaney's portraits—whether of Marian Anderson, Baldwin (his favorite subject), the artist himself, or unfamous persons whose names we do not know—all suggest the human's (and especially the artist's) extraordinary strengths, signaled by the prevalence of yellows from the bright world of the spirits.

Along with the gift of her perfect pitch, Ella Fitzgerald cultivated a surging power to swing that reminds one of her beginnings as a street dancer whose first performance stages were the pavements of New York City. Through never-ending practice (recalling Sonny's incessant woodshedding on the piano at the in-laws' house), she became one of the rare musicians who achieved a personal voice as a very young woman. At twenty-one years old, she was well on her way to becoming the swing era's competition-ready big-band balladeer and dancehall swinger who danced and sang on big-time stages—and who was soon to become Ella Fitzgerald, big-band leader. In this context, note Richard Powell's meditation on Fitzgerald's capacities for swing, which he sees in Delaney's *Ella Fitzgerald* as "a painterly game of peekaboo, playing on the viewer's expectation of an anticipated subject in the painting's standard portrait format and the resulting presence (Fitzgerald's face) and absence (Fitzgerald's upper body). In this respect, Delaney's portrait reminds one of his famous subject and her improvisatory genius in jazz and vocal 'swinging': an art form that Delaney described as possessing 'the authority to induce what we cannot perceive.'"[24] Fitzgerald's powerful sense of swing included a sea change in her style, reflecting her absorption of the lessons of Dizzy Gillespie and Charlie Parker, two coinventors of the quicksilver beats and changes of bebop. Step by step, she (along with young Sarah Vaughan and a few others) defined what it meant to be a bop improviser whose virtuoso instrument, her voice, could trade twelves with the best of the horns, rhythm, and dancers. In other words, like Bird, Fitzgerald was an artistic originator and agent of swing with the rare capacity for artistic self-reinvention. Her styles, early and late, had a radiance that I hear and see as a goldenness, shining—as Delaney's painting revealed—with fresh, new intellectual drive and the capacity for spiritual healing.

Enter, again, Mister Baldwin, master of musical storylines and colors. After the story's musical prelude, the broad arc of "Sonny's Blues" moves from the black-blue night of Sonny's drug addiction and incarceration to his achievement of a personal artistic voice as an improvising artist capable of telling his story in music. Another band across "Sonny's Blues" (for an aspect of what Morrison would term art's "layering"), another overlapping arc, takes the reader from the estrangement of Sonny and his brother to their reconciliation, signaled by the gift of "the very cup of trembling."[25] A third dark arc takes the reader from a Deep South nightmare road, where their guitar-player uncle, their father's brother, is run over in a crunch of bones, wood, and strings by a white man on a drunken car ride. There's also the storyline's move from those awful images, terrifying invisible sounds, and dark silences of the road of their uncle's death, to the story's conclusion, when Sonny is able, at last, to tell on the piano the night-road story and other grim tales, and when his brother is able, finally, to stand to hear it. "Sonny's Blues" narrates the dawning education of both these brothers, and, of course, of the reader who is invited to learn, as Farah Griffin has said, to "read until you understand."[26] We all need to be reminded of the eternal tale of human struggle that is "never new," as Baldwin says, for "there isn't any other tale to tell. . . . But always [it] must be heard."[27]

Before we revisit that resonant last scene, let us consider how Delaney's light plays early in the Baldwin story. Not only do the book's jacket, cover, and dedication announce it as a story flooded with Delaneyesque light, but also Sonny's name itself is an indicator. A young man coming of age, the family's youngest, at odds with his father, and then with his older brother and the in-laws who try to play for him parental roles, he is a son in search of a family—or rather, a new sense of kinship with the world. For this Sonny/"Sunny" also is the brother whose name cross-linguistically puns on "soul"/"sol."[28] He's the soul brother radiating hope, the Sun God/Son of God with the potential to be the One (the "sole") soul Savior.

While every scene in it is a carefully prepared light show, the story's first significant meditation on lighting figures in a scene set in the living room of the two brothers' Harlem apartment, where, after dinner, the adults regularly gather for intimate talk. Baldwin makes the darkness of that room the color both of night and of the encroaching menace of American racial violence, which, in one of his essays on Delaney, he terms the "black-blue midnight" of the painter's childhood in Tennessee.[29] In "Sonny's Blues," this is the darkness of "the world [that] waited outside, as hungry as a tiger. . . . That trouble [that] stretched above us, longer than the sky."[30] In the tenement front room's twilight—that late-evening time of mysteriously glowing clarity that photographers call the "magic hour" or the "golden hour"—the adults speak quietly of "where they've come from, and what they've seen, and what's happened to them and their kinfolk." The evening's uncannily revealing luminous darkness enables their talk of the encroaching black-blueness outside: "The darkness outside is what the old folks have been talking about," says the narrator. "It's what they've come from. It's what they endure." The dark-light time releases not only pained remembrances and "inside talk" but also sight and second-sight. In these nocturnal sessions, reports the narrator, the grown-ups "look at something a child can't see."[31]

The something that can't be seen is also something a child is too young to hear—the painful tale of human living. As the room goes darker and then, aside from street noises that include the dry rattle of tambourines, the room fades to black silence, the child drowsing on Mama's lap knows the adults won't talk any more that night. Baldwin's narrator explains that both adults and the boy-child overhearing them know that "if he knows too much about what's happened to *them*, he'll know too much about what's going to happen to *him*."[32] Morrison knew also that "this was not a story to pass on."[33] The fullness of the Black story in the United States, which, beyond personal truth-telling, is what I understand to be what jazz musicians mean when they urge one another to "tell the story"—something Fitzgerald could do with epic mastery—is too painful for the young to see or hear (much less to articulate) except in scat-like flits and flashes and in lights dimming to near-darkness and to the blackness of darkness.

Suddenly the room is bright again. Someone has snapped on the electric light, ending the adults' deep talk.

Baldwin's inclusion of the detail that what's turned on is an *electric* light is important here. For this electric light, silently staring, is a stark reminder of the official white American power system, with its addictive pulls and entrapping grid, against which the dark story of the Harlem adults must contend. That this hushed story, now hanging in the air, is one of trembling fugitivity does not make it one of paralyzing fear.[34] Just the opposite: it's a grown folks' tale of confrontation with the bluesy facts of life, and of readiness, anticipation, and resistance. A brainstorm session of Harlem maroons that's pronounced in defiance of the dull hum of the electric bulbs (of that era): a tale of willed trembling with the world. The Black Story; *The* Story.[35]

This Black Story/The Story that blues-idiom musicians urge one another to tell on their instruments defines jazz itself, Nathaniel Mackey implies, as a painful history flowing "from grief to grievance, from lover's lament, one might say, to slave narrative—to some extent erasing the line between the two."[36] It's a narrative of blues tragedy with split-second intimations of triumph, also in blue. Getting down to cases (and to the question of what are Sonny's blues), Sonny's sorrows are figured in images of confinement in Harlem's tenement buildings, then, by his in-laws, within the straitjackets of Black bourgeois respectability, and, all along, within the live-game trap-box that white America has set for him. "Smothering in these houses," the two brothers, as youngsters, and many others like them, "came down into the streets for light and air and found themselves encircled by disaster. Some escaped the trap, most didn't. Those who got out always left something of themselves behind, as some animals amputate a leg and leave it in the trap." Would-be escapees Sonny and his brother feel the loss: "It's always at the hour of trouble and confrontation," says the narrator, "that the missing member aches."[37]

Mackey refers to this painful missing member as a "phantom limb."[38] This recalls Glissant's definition of jazz as a music of those "who have escaped the abyss, and carry within them the abyss' dimension." It's a music of an injured people and of "echoes and traces," Glissant continues, that "is valid for everybody, not just Black people, because it's a music of a distraught memory."[39] Akin to phantom-limbed Sonny is the powerful one-armed Congo Square dancer-singer-instrumentalist Omar, who was his grandfather and the founder of jazz, according to New Orleans–born master clarinet and soprano saxophone player Sidney Bechet.[40] Sonny has inherited the scar of Omar, the aching invisible phantom limb that signals a fugitive spirit and his calling as a spiritual worker whose medium is the blues. Perhaps his brother, too, is on the road to higher equations, toward the spiritual/intellectual work of reconstructing both himself (figuring out his name) and a broken community. If so, it's the younger brother who's lighting Sonny's way, as he learns to confront and at last to tell The Story, in blues.

Before turning directly to the question of the color blue in "Sonny's Blues," let us note that like all colors, blue is produced by the motion of light. This matters, for this chapter emphasizes this story's insistence on motion and vibration and the Glissantian imperative for humans to learn to move together, to tremble together and with the world.

It's also crucial to draw a distinction between the blues as melancholy moods or worlds of trouble—both of which are frequently the subject of blues music—and the blues as a form of music springing from the single voice or one-string guitar straight toward the shout-chorus big bands of early Fitzgerald and Bird and the tight bebop combos where Sonny found his blues voice. Paradoxically, the primary purpose of blues music, be it vocal or instrumental, is to drive blue moods and worlds of trouble away—to stomp the blues, as Albert Murray puts it—and to accompany dances of courtship and fun, celebrating the fullness and joys of life in spite of its inevitable disappointments and woes. Blues music and its settings typically contradict the lyrics of the blues; the blues put the blues in perspective. Not, as Murray and this story remind us, that blues-troubles are ever really gone. One of the hardest moments in the short story comes when the young musician, now clean, says he can't be sure the demons that drove him into drug addiction won't be back; held in check for the moment by his music, where saving spirits live, blue devils, being blue devils, certainly will come knocking again! The struggle against them (reflecting Delaney's struggles against various demons, including drugs) is central to the meaning of "Sonny's Blues." So are the bright-light signs of hope that shine through "Am I Blue" and throughout the blues catalogue, where one finds the bold lyrics of Alberta Hunter: "I've got the world in a jug, stopper's in my hand."[41] Along with free-roaming troubles (blues running "around my house, in and out of my front door," says one Bessie Smith song), the blues often offers twists of levity.[42] In the essay "The Uses of the Blues" (1964), Baldwin quotes a blues song by Ray Charles that says: "You even cried so loud, you give the blues to your neighbor next door!"[43]

The blues figures in "Sonny's Blues" may be illuminated by what may seem an impossibly remote source: a file of letters from Henry James, the nineteenth- and early twentieth-century novelist whose sentence structures and structures of feeling provided significant models for Baldwin. In "The Uses of the Blues," Baldwin quotes part of an 1883 letter from James to a friend whose husband had recently died. James sends his friend the following tender words of consolation:

> Remember that every life is a special problem which is not yours but another's, and content yourself with *the terrible algebra* of your own. . . . We lighten the effort of others, we contribute to the sum of success, make it possible for others to live. *Sorrow comes in great waves*—no one can know that better than you—but it rolls over us, and though it may almost smother us it leaves us on the spot and we know that if it is strong we are stronger, inasmuch as it passes and we remain. *It wears us, uses us, but we wear it and use it in return; and it is blind, whereas we, after a manner, see.*[44]

Note James's phrase "the terrible algebra"—an important detail in our context, since Baldwin specifically identifies Sonny's brother as a teacher of algebra who's trying to figure things out. *Webster's* defines *algebra*, Arabic for "the reunion of broken parts," as the study of rules and symbols forming "a unifying thread of almost all of mathematics." In the context of "Sonny's Blues," we may regard algebra, writ large, as the radical study of searches for equation, strategies to reunite broken parts in the human soul and body politic. Algebra as spiritual strivings for new and better reconfigurations of our broken communities: new formulas for justice, equity, and the redistribution of wealth. In other words, like Sonny, whose vehicle for self-realization is his hard-won music ("Sonny was at that piano playing for his life"), the hardest subject for his math-teacher brother is the "terrible algebra" of life itself.[45]

Excruciating sorrows burden both Sonny and his brother: the blues they, their families, and Harlem neighbors have lived "wear" and "use" them both. Still, the two men learn to do as James has advised: to "use" the blues back, and in so doing, "after a manner," to *see*. They learn not just to battle with the blues but, paradoxically, to enlist them in the project of countering the blues. In "The Uses of the Blues," Baldwin seconds the words of James with a quotation from the Empress of the Blues (the jazz musician quoted by Baldwin even more than Holiday): "And Bessie [Smith] said: '*Good mornin', blues. / Blues, how do you do? / I'm doin' all right. Good mornin', / How are you*?"[46]

Through his music, Sonny uses the blues—the blues as sorrows, and music as the sorrow-blues' potent antidote—to confront, embrace, and transcend the blues story that is his life and the life of his family (and all of us).

To grasp the blueness of the light show in the final scene in "Sonny's Blues," let us return to that Icarus myth, shimmering in the story's background (conjuring, again, the presence of "Bird" Parker). As foil, Baldwin invokes the trials of Icarus and his father Daedalus, who, because Daedalus has assisted the Minotaur to escape the Labyrinth, are themselves condemned to incarceration there. Famously, the brilliant craftsman Daedalus improvises bird feathers so the two of them can fly to freedom.

> While fitting these ingenious wings to Icarus, he gave him careful instructions on how to fly safely: he must keep midway between earth and heaven, neither too low, where the sea-spray might weigh down his wings, nor too high, where the flaming sun might scorch them. . . . Fatally overtaken by the joy of flying freely through the air [Icarus] let his wings lift him higher and higher . . . toward the sun . . . so close that the wax of his wings melted in the heat, the feathers parted and he plummeted headlong into the sea below, still calling for his father as the waters engulfed him.[47]

It's with this olden tale in mind (and also evidently thinking of Delaney) that Baldwin sets his story's nightclub scene and prepares its complex lighting. The jazz room is darkly lit, "atmospheric." Bright beams spotlight the stage, and the musicians appear "most careful not to step into that circle of light too suddenly," as if should they move "into the light too suddenly, without thinking, they would perish in flame."[48] Once the players take their places on stage, the stage lights switch to "indigo," a dark blue (a "black blue") associated with Duke Ellington's moody masterpiece of 1930, "Mood Indigo." It's also the color of one of American slavery's most labor-intensive cash crops: that deadly blue dye.

The myth of Daedalus and Icarus teaches Baldwin's Sonny to negotiate a safe "midway" course between burning sun and drowning sea. ("Safe!" Sonny's father was known to say, "Safe, hell! Ain't no place safe for kids, nor nobody.")[49] Baldwin updates the Greek formula of the golden mean, such that Sonny must fly high enough to reach the sunlight associated with Delaney's yellows of hope and salvation without flying so high that he's destroyed by the flames of heroin addiction or other searing troubles. In Baldwin's bluesy version of Icarus, the flyer must dare to fly directly into the lights, risking his life. Rather than melting his wings and sending him to his death, the nightclub's bright (and then blue) lights cleanse him, temper and forge him "as a sword is forged."[50] In the brightness of the bandstand light, Sonny digs into the piano keys. Bro Algebra looks at Sonny's shining face, and his face was new: "The face I saw on Sonny I'd never seen before. Everything had been burned out of it, and, at the same time, things usually hidden were being burned in, by the fire and fury of the battle which was occurring in him up there."[51]

Baldwin further complicates the Icarus myth by specifying that while positioning himself in relation to saving/killing lights, Sonny also must learn to find his way through (not above) saving/killing waters. It's well remembered that Icarus flies too close to the sun, which melts his wings; less so that he plunges screaming to his death in the sea. An important example of the Icarus myth–inspired water imagery in "Sonny's Blues" comes when Baldwin describes Sonny's attempts to play the piano after a long spell in jail as standing in hesitancy at the music's "shoreline." The fatherly bandleader Creole, whose name suggests a New Orleans connection as well as a mix of cultural backgrounds, urges Sonny to use his music to risk moving beyond the water's edge, "to leave the shoreline and strike out for the deep water." Creole is "Sonny's witness that deep water and drowning were not the same thing—he had been there and he knew. And he wanted Sonny to know. He was waiting for Sonny to do the things on the keys which would let Creole know that Sonny was in the water."[52] Whether baptismal waters, amniotic fluid, or some other living water, Sonny wades his way in. Perhaps in this passage, and in the one featuring the "cup of trembling," Baldwin is reflecting on the pool of water that the Bible calls "stirred up" or "troubled" by an angel of God into a fluid that heals illnesses and wounds.[53] "Behold," Jesus tells one of those healed by the God-troubled water, "thou art made whole: sin no more, lest a worse thing come unto thee."[54] An artist who is also a spiritual seeker, Sonny cannot achieve what he wants by sailing the safe neutral zones between sky and sea, sun and water; to become a true artist—to tell The Story—he must risk going through the living gates of both these treacherous elements. Like Howard Thurman's swimmer, Sonny must swim the black waters until he reaches what the master-preacher called the "luminous darkness."

Like a Harlem preacher bringing the message home, Baldwin's narrator testifies that Creole is guiding Sonny onward, offering loving guidance that indicates a sense of kinship beyond the ties of family and bloodline. "Then Creole stepped forward to remind them that what they were playing was the blues. He hit something in all of them, he hit something in me, myself, and the music tightened and deepened." Creole reminds all present, particularly Sonny, "what the blues were all about. They were not about anything very new."[55] They were about Sonny's personal and family history, late and soon, but also The Story of Black People in America, which, again, when told with sufficient richness, is The Story of all of us. "There isn't any other tale to tell. It's the only light we've got in all this darkness." The musicians' job as retellers of The Story is to spell it out in fresh clear musical language:

> He [Creole] and his boys up there were keeping it new, at the risk of ruin, destruction, madness, and death, in order to find new ways to make us listen. For while the tale of how we suffer, and how we are delighted, and how we may triumph is never new, it always must be heard. . . . And he [Sonny] was giving it back, as everything must be given back, so that, passing through death, it can live forever. I saw my mother's face again, and felt, for the first time, how the stones of the road she had walked on must have bruised her feet. I saw the moonlit road where my father's brother died. And it brought something else back to me, and carried me past it, I saw my little girl again and felt Isabel's tears again, and I felt my own tears begin to rise. And I was yet aware that this was only a moment, that the world waited

> outside, as hungry as a tiger, and that trouble stretched above us, longer than the sky. Then it was over. Creole and Sonny let out their breath, both soaking wet, and grinning. There was a lot of applause and some of it was real.[56]

As he renders the moment of Sonny's epiphany, Baldwin's soaring sentences recall this writer's history as a preacher. Baldwin's account of Sonny's moment of truth also echoes the example of Charlie Parker, who, remember, Sonny names as his model for playing and whose virtuosic musical lines I believe Baldwin himself regarded as an artistic model. Parker said that in his searches for new ways to tell The Story on his saxophone, he "kept thinking there was something else": "I could hear it sometimes, but could not play it. . . . [And then, after endless experimentation,] "I found that by using the higher interval of a chord as a melody line and backing them with appropriately related changes, I could play the thing I'd been hearing."[57]

It's Parker the artist as seeker who brings us back to the questions of Delaney's influence on Baldwin and the uses of the blues by both painter and writer. Was "Sonny's Blues," begun at about the time of Parker's death, a eulogy prompting Delaney's portrait *Charlie Parker Yardbird* (see plate 10) as an amen expressed in lustrous oils on canvas? I want to focus on this early portrait of Bird because of its uniqueness in the Delaney collection of musical pieces; in the later one, from 1968, the artist returns to his signature yellows.[58] What's most striking about this painting, for all its luminosity, is its strict lack of yellows. In *Charlie Parker Yardbird* we find an abstract titled as a portrait, with no face looking back at us, no figures at all clearly delineated—and no yellows. Rather, what we witness here are intimations of a rose sunrise against a background of blues. Hinted lines of rose converge at the painting's center—or do they radiate from it, suggesting flowers about to bloom, a majestic dawning, or the sound emanating from the bell of Parker's sax? Most of all, I'm fascinated by this painting's uses of the blues. Step back for a moment. Whether bodies of water surrounding rosy islands or serene flashes of the infinite sky—or something abstract in search of visual equivalences of the blues—blue colors flow all through this large work, flickering infinite possibility as well as peril. In this "portrait," Delaney is not portraying Parker as much as he is painting Parker's music, sparkling with blues.

This Delaney portrait of Bird reminds us that, like Parker, Delaney found his voice as an artist through the blaring noise of blue devils. The bandleader Jay McShann, with whose band Parker first emerged as a powerful new player, described Bird as "a crying soul, a spirit as troubled by the nature of life. . . . The world had constantly disappointed Charlie Parker. For all the satisfactions of his music, for all the light jokes and deep laughs on the road, he was basically a melancholy and suspicious man, a genius in search of a solution to a blues that wore razors for spurs."[59] Against these sharp-edged blues, Bird could pronounce the twelve-bar blues, whether the slow blues or his double-time inventions flying top-speed over the train tracks of the blues—these latter improvisations, Bird's best biographer, Stanley Crouch, has said, executed "at the tempo of emergency."[60] Crouch calls Parker one of the greatest improvisers in the history of jazz, an artist who could "create a consistent stream of musical phrases that had life of their own—phrases that were marked by fluidity and emotional power, and that were made even stronger by the surrounding environment in which they were placed. [He] invented his own line, his own melody, and orchestrated it within the ensemble so that he was in effect playing every instrument. Only a few did that."[61] Bird was one, a master of extending and elaborating the blues, of executing them. But he was also a master of infusing songs not composed as blues with strong blues ingredients—something hinted at in the Delaney portrait's spray of blue lights. When the saxophonist performed "Summertime," for example, like Holiday he turned the operatic aria into an autobiographical chronicle of catastrophe somehow survived, a tale in blue now full of the jester's playfulness and I-can-do-anything spirit that characterizes so much of his music. On the wide walls of Delaney portraits, most of them in yellow (including, as noted, a fine yellow one of Parker), this painting for Bird casts its glow of hope as inklings of blue. Here, alongside Baldwin's complex blues for Parker and others, is Delaney's complex blues for Bird, persistently flashing blue hope through tragedy.

I compare this painting's take on Parker's blues with the last pages of "Sonny's Blues," where the young musician dares to leave the shorelines of "Am I Blue" for the depths of what the blues were all about. Here Baldwin's prose moves into the living waters shared, as we have seen, by all the arts (and I love the idea of blessed healing waters as waters that God has "troubled"). Powered by Greek mythology, Henry James, many twentieth-century American writers (William Faulkner, Richard Wright, Ernest Hemingway, and Ralph Ellison prominently among them), and by the promises and warnings of the Bible—all of these as much a part of Baldwin's artistic inheritance as the blues-idiom music of Bessie, Billie, Bird, Fitzgerald, and Rollins—Baldwin's Sonny begins to tell The Story in liquid terms, to own it and use it. But for me, above all, these final lines in Baldwin's greatest story most emphatically recall the shining lights of Beauford Delaney, whose life and work, whose masterful uses of color proved that there were trembling lights to guide us, yellows and blues we can use. Shimmering lights signaling that at the very least, we are there for one another. Perhaps, in all this darkness, these are the only lights we've got.

NOTES

Epigraphs: Ovid, *Metamorphoses* 8.203–6, trans. Frank Justus Miller (Cambridge, MA: Harvard University Press, 1916), 421; Howard Thurman, *The Luminous Darkness* (New York: Harper and Row, 1965), vii; James Baldwin, "On the Painter Beauford Delaney," in *James Baldwin: Collected Essays*, ed. Toni Morrison (New York: Library of America, 1998), 721.

1 Toni Morrison, "Abrupt Stops and Unexpected Liquidity: The Aesthetics of Romare Bearden," in *The Romare Bearden Reader*, ed. Robert G. O'Meally (Durham, NC: Duke University Press, 2019), 182–83.

2 Sonny Rollins is just one of the jazz tradition's numerous "Sonnys," among them Sonny Clark, Sonny Greer, Sonny Payne, and Sonny Stitt. Bluesmen Son House and Sonny Boy Williamson are among the many blues artists who also retained what's typically a childhood nickname, now a proud artistic title. As jazz and blues Sons and Sonnys turn gray, perhaps keeping the names to acknowledge their elders in the musical tradition, the names perhaps offer a nod to the aging players' formerly youthful selves and to the wish always to replenish an ever-youthful element in their playing: Sonny Boys Forever! Baldwinian Sonnys, too—always in search of new depths to sound, new heights to scale. It should be added that the self-naming of Sun Ra—known as "Sonny" to those close to him—was an important special case: Sonny as Black Man from Another Planet, futuristic life force close to the stars.

3 I am most thankful to Aidan Levy for this biographical information concerning Sonny Rollins, and to Mr. Rollins himself.

4 James Baldwin, "Sonny's Blues," *Partisan Review*, Summer 1957, reprinted in *Going to Meet the Man* (New York: Dial, 1965), 103.

5 Baldwin, "Sonny's Blues," 104.

6 Morrison, "Abrupt Stops and Unexpected Liquidity," 180.

7 That's what the art of painting is, says the writer's friend Romare Bearden: "putting something over something else." See Calvin Tomkins, "Profiles: 'Putting Something over Something Else,'" *New Yorker*, November 28, 1977, 72.

8 Baldwin, "Sonny's Blues," 141.

9 Ralph Ellison, *Invisible Man*, 2nd ed. (New York: Vintage International, 1995), 388.

10 See Herman Helmholtz, *On the Sensations of Tone as a Physiological Basis for the Theory of Music*, trans. Alexander J. Ellis (London: Longman, 1885); Benjamin Morgan, "Scale, Resonance, Presence," *Victorian Studies* 59, no. 1 (2017): 109–12; and Nicholas Rescher, *Metaphysical Perspectives* (Notre Dame, IN: Notre Dame University Press, 2017), 174–87.

11 Manthia Diawara, dir., *Édouard Glissant: One World in Relation*, produced by K'a Yéléma Productions (2009), film, 50 min.

12 Baldwin, "Sonny's Blues," 141.

13 For references in the King James Bible to the "cup of trembling," see Isaiah 51:17–22; and Zechariah 12:2.

14 Baldwin, "Sonny's Blues," 119.

15 Sunday service at Riverside Church, June 6, 1999. Noted by the author.

16 Baldwin discusses "bearing witness" in *The Fire Next Time* (New York: Random House, 1963), 45, 49. In his interview with Julius Lester, Baldwin elaborates on how he considered himself a witness: "Witness to whence I came, where I am. Witness to what I've seen and the possibilities that I think I see"; Julius Lester, "James Baldwin: Reflections of a Maverick," *New York Times Book Review*, May 27, 1984, 1, https://www.nytimes.com/1984/05/27/books/james-baldwinreflections-of-a-maverick.html?searchResultPosition=6.

17 For a discussion of this, see Richard J. Powell, *Beauford Delaney: The Color Yellow* (Atlanta, GA: High Museum, 2002).

18 David Leeming, *Amazing Grace: A Life of Beauford Delaney* (New York: Oxford University Press, 1998), 166.

19 James Baldwin, "On the Painter Beauford Delaney," *Transition* 4, no. 18 (1965): 45; reprinted in Morrison, *James Baldwin: Collected Essays*, 720–21.

20 Note that in 1957, Duke Ellington and Billy Strayhorn composed their own four-LP "Portrait of Ella Fitzgerald," a four-part suite in sections whose titles tell their own story of high respect: "Royal Ancestry," "All Heart," "Beyond Category," and "Total Jazz." *Ella Fitzgerald Sings the Duke Ellington Songbook*, Verve MGV 4008-2 and Verve MGV 4009-2, vols. 1 and 2, 1957. On "Portrait of Ella Fitzgerald," the Duke Ellington Orchestra "paints" a portrait of Fitzgerald, with Ellington's spoken commentary.

21 Morrison, "Abrupt Stops and Unexpected Liquidity," 183–84.

22 Ralph Ellison comments on Henry James's "super-subtle fry" in his introduction to the thirtieth anniversary edition of *Invisible Man*. Ralph

Ellison, *The Collected Essays of Ralph Ellison*, ed. John F. Callahan (New York: Modern Library, 2003), 486.

23 Powell, *Beauford Delaney*, 13. Powell quotes from René Huyghe, "Color and the Expression of Interior Time in Western Art," in *Color Symbolism: Six Excerpts from the Eranos Yearbook 1972* (Dallas, TX: Spring Publications, 1972), 129–65.

24 Powell, *Beauford Delaney*, 28.

25 Baldwin, "Sonny's Blues," 141.

26 Farah Jasmine Griffin, *Read until You Understand: The Profound Wisdom of Black Life and Literature* (New York: Norton, 2021).

27 Baldwin, "Sonny's Blues," 139.

28 See Nathaniel Mackey, "Cante Moro," in *Paracritical Hinge: Essays, Talks, Notes, Interviews* (Madison: University of Wisconsin Press, 2005), 188.

29 Baldwin, "On the Painter Beauford Delaney," 720.

30 Baldwin, "Sonny's Blues," 140.

31 Baldwin, "Sonny's Blues," 115.

32 Baldwin, "Sonny's Blues," 115.

33 Toni Morrison, *Beloved* (New York: Knopf, 1987), 275.

34 Baldwin defines a fugitivity in the spirit of Fred Moten and Nathaniel Mackey: as a restless, aggressive determination to go elsewhere, to find freer places to be and ways to live. Both explicitly associate this determination with Black music, Mackey with the jazz that Delaney means to represent. See Fred Moten, *In the Break: The Aesthetics of the Black Radical Tradition* (Minneapolis: University of Minnesota Press, 2003); and Mackey, "Cante Moro," 188.

35 On "a brainstorm session," see Moten, *In the Break*; and Mackey, "Cante Moro."

36 Nathaniel Mackey, *From a Broken Bottle Traces of Perfume Still Emanate*, vols. 1–3 (New York: New Directions, 2010), 120.

37 Baldwin, "Sonny's Blues," 112.

38 Mackey, "Cante Moro," 197.

39 Diawara, *Édouard Glissant*.

40 Sidney Bechet, *Treat It Gentle* (New York: Hill and Wang, 1960); Bryan Wagner, *The Life and Legend of Bras-Coupé* (Baton Rouge: Louisiana State University Press, 2019).

41 Cora "Lovie" Austin (music) and Alberta Hunter (lyrics), "Down Hearted Blues," first recorded by Hunter, Paramount 12005-A, 1922. This was made famous via Bessie Smith's recording the following year, Columbia A3844, 1923.

42 Bessie Smith, “In the House Blues,” Parlophone R2329, 1931.

43 Ray Charles, “Hey Now,” Swing Time 297A+, 1952.

44 Henry James to Grace Norton, July 28, 1883, in *The Letters of Henry James*, vol. 1, ed. Percy Lubbock (New York: Scribner, 1920), 101. Baldwin quotes the letter in “The Uses of the Blues,” *Playboy*, January 1964, reprinted in *The Cross of Redemption: Uncollected Writings*, ed. Randall Kenan (New York: Pantheon, 2010), 66 (italics added).

45 Baldwin, “Sonny’s Blues,” 125.

46 Baldwin, “Uses of the Blues,” 66 (italics added).

47 Jenny March, *Dictionary of Classical Mythology* (Philadelphia: Oxbow, 1998), 260.

48 Baldwin, “Sonny’s Blues,” 136. Consider again the artificiality of the electric lights, whatever their colored filters, and the temptation to choose a flight headlong into the killing suns of the American power system and, again, its addictions.

49 Baldwin, “Sonny’s Blues,” 114.

50 Baldwin mentions Ernest Hemingway as an important influence; quoted here is his *Green Hills of Africa* (New York: Scribner, 1953), 71.

51 Baldwin, “Sonny’s Blues,” 138.

52 Baldwin, “Sonny’s Blues,” 138.

53 The King James Bible, John 5:4, translates the Greek as “troubled”; the New Revised Standard Version translation is “stirred up.”

54 King James Bible, John 5:14.

55 Baldwin, “Sonny’s Blues,” 139.

56 Baldwin, “Sonny’s Blues,” 139.

57 Nat Hentoff and Nat Shapiro, eds., *Hear Me Talkin’ to Ya* (New York: Rinehart, 1955), 354.

58 I refer to Delaney’s work of 1968 (the same year as his *Ella Fitzgerald)* called *Portrait of Charlie Parker*. Here as in the tribute to Fitzgerald, Delaney goes back to his signature palette of yellows. This Parker could be a gold-winged angel or a priest in ritual robes and headpiece, the jazzman as apostle from God. Associated with a variety of African traditions, this Parker’s stance and diadem suggest royalty. This musical chieftain, musical notes on his staff, is attended not by a yardbird (a chicken, reportedly one of Parker’s favorite foods), nor, this time, by “Yardbird” in the work’s title—inside jokes with racial overtones that Delaney decides to do without. Instead, he’s attended by a bird standing on the yellow air, avatar of Parker/messenger set to fly to and from other worlds. Note again what I’ve called the subject’s visionary, seer’s eyes, defined, as in Fitzgerald’s

portrait, by their wide curiosity—the prophet observing the beyond. This wondrous work returns not only to the Bird himself and to yellows but also to other colors, associated with Delaney's James Baldwin. As Amy J. Elias has observed, the skin tones here match Delaney's most evocative portrait of James Baldwin, *Dark Rapture* (1941; plate 1), where the face is a black of many colors: "Though black had been described to me as the absence of light," writes Baldwin, concerning ongoing lessons from Delaney on the nature of color, "it became very clear to me that if this were true, we would never have been able to see the colour; black: the light is trapped in it and struggles upward, rather like that grass pushing upward through the cement." Blackness as a transcendent set of lights.

59 Quoted in Stanley Crouch, *Kansas City Lightning: The Rise and Times of Charlie Parker* (New York: HarperCollins, 2013), 17.

60 Crouch, *Kansas City Lightning*, 19.

61 Crouch, *Kansas City Lightning*, 18.

SEVEN

Chiaroscuro, Delaney's Aesthetic Vision, and Baldwin's "Sonny's Blues"

D. Quentin Miller

James Baldwin once wrote, disarmingly, "I don't know anything about music."[1] But Radiclani Clytus interprets this statement as rhetorically strategic: "By disavowing competency at the outset of his analysis, Baldwin shifts emphasis away from the technological terrain of music criticism and theory in order to enable his examination of the psychosocial origins of black expressive arts."[2] I concur with this interpretation, especially as it signals Baldwin's shift from musical analysis as an often technical exercise to musical analysis as a revelation of psychological complexity. I wish to consider the way Baldwin's short story "Sonny's Blues," often praised for its rendering of the jazz/blues aesthetic in fiction, explores psychology through the techniques of another expressive art: painting. Although "Sonny's Blues" invites the reader to carefully consider the importance of deep listening, it is actually a strikingly visual story. It consistently uses the interplay between light and darkness as a multivalent metaphor that reveals the unbridged distance between interior and exterior truths, knowledge and mystery, and self and other. Published in 1957, "Sonny's Blues" appeared at a point in Baldwin's career when his attention to visual aesthetics was catalyzed and refined by Beauford Delaney, the painter who had a profound effect on his vision, in multiple senses of that word. Reframing "Sonny's Blues" in terms of its visual elements both affords a deeper understanding of Delaney's influence on Baldwin and highlights the story's essential concerns with the revelation of a complex psychological self. The complete self emerges through the interplay of lightness and dark, metaphorical indicators of the interplay between surface and depth as well as the interplay between the facets of others we can perceive and the mysterious facets hidden in one's private interior.

The painting technique that corresponds to this verbal play is known as chiaroscuro, at its core an artistic emphasis on the contrast and interplay of light and darkness to reveal depth and dimension. The technique was identified in the Italian Renaissance and flourished in its aftermath, especially in paintings with somber, meditative subjects. The term mashes up the Italian words *chiaro* (clear) and *scuro* (dark). *Scuro* also suggests, etymologically, gloominess and figuratively connotes mystery, something being concealed. More than just a paradoxical term bringing together light and darkness, the word and the artistic technique it describes constitute an attempt to reveal the truth that hides beneath surfaces. When light and darkness are brought into close proximity, what seems like a struggle for dominance actually serves to highlight complexity. The two elements do not attempt to extinguish but rather to enhance each other and insist on their interdependence.

Delaney's fascination with light as perhaps the most important compositional component of his painting is well documented in David Leeming's biography, *Amazing Grace: A Life of Beauford Delaney* (1998). Leeming speaks of Delaney's fascination with light—singled out as the facet of experience he most "loved"—and of the fact that his first and most influential mentor, Lloyd Branson, gave him an explicit instruction which Leeming paraphrases as follows: "All painting . . . should be studies in light; the subject could be interesting in itself, but it was the interaction of the subject with light that made painting as opposed to mere representation."[3] This basic lesson helped Delaney develop and articulate his own aesthetic principles over time and encouraged him to privilege chiaroscuro. Describing an abstract sketch from the mid-1930s, Leeming writes, "The combination of light created by the glaze and the deep color could bring the 'mystery' and the dark memory of the inner life to the surface."[4] In this formulation, light exists in counterpoint to an underlying darkness, a psychological complexity that causes the viewer to attend to the darkness that light, paradoxically, illuminates. Deepening his appreciation through a study of the American modernists John Marin and Arthur Dove, Delaney "also found a concern for light and the possibility of using light and color abstractly to express the true 'reality' of a subject."[5] Examples of Leeming's analysis of the importance of light to Delaney's work recur throughout *Amazing Grace*, but what interests me is how this evolving principle in the painter's practice affected Baldwin's aesthetic and his philosophy quite specifically. Darkness and light, in short, are codependent in Delaney's work not just as aesthetic counterforces but as a means to suggest or reveal "dark memory" and "inner life" on the canvas, the psychological complexity I alluded to earlier. I will argue that the same effect is achieved through visual descriptions that strongly evoke chiaroscuro in "Sonny's Blues."

Delaney moved into his apartment in the Parisian suburb of Clamart in the mid-1950s, and the space struck Baldwin as a temple of the aesthetic imagination. Leeming tells us how Delaney "immediately covered the walls of the studio in white sheets to accentuate the light,"[6] and Baldwin wrote of this space as "a kind of universe . . . delicate with the first light of the morning and as blue as the blues when the last light of the sun departed."[7] Baldwin became keenly aware of the meaning of light in Delaney's paintings, a light that Baldwin believed "held the power to illuminate, even to redeem and reconcile and heal."[8] His essay "On the Painter Beauford Delaney" (1965) begins, "I learned about light from Beauford Delaney, the light contained in every thing," and continues, "Perhaps I am so struck by the light in Beauford's paintings because he comes from darkness—as do I, as, in fact, we all do."[9] The phrase "comes from darkness" is not entirely straightforward here, but knowing something of Baldwin's and Delaney's lives as well as the theme of Baldwin's fiction helps to contextualize the phrase. Darkness is suffering, felt and perceived especially deeply by those who live passionate, risky lives. The two brothers in "Sonny's Blues" support this interpretation. Sonny lives a life of spiritual, mental, and bodily risk and is attuned to the suffering of others; his brother lives an eminently safe life and assumes that suffering can be avoided if one attends to trappings of the material world and chases middle-class respectability. The story reveals how both brothers actually "come from darkness": the difference is that the narrator denies that fact.

Suffering in "Sonny's Blues" is both "repulsive" and necessary for a full understanding of what it means to be human.[10]

The mid-1950s marked the beginning of Baldwin's departure from Delaney's sphere, as the rising literary star became less attached to Paris and more confident in his ability to thrive as an artist. He was soon to write some of his most ambitious and accomplished works: *Giovanni's Room* (1956), *Another Country* (1962), *The Fire Next Time* (1963), and "Sonny's Blues," all of them arguably about risk-taking as a fundamental value of humanity. As he began his detachment, Baldwin implemented what Delaney had taught him, not only spiritually but also aesthetically. While Baldwin became one of the most celebrated African American artists of the early 1960s, Delaney began to succumb to his internal demons. Although Baldwin cherished the aesthetic wisdom of his mentor, he also became increasingly sensitive to Delaney's personal plight, and he blended psychological anguish with a concern with the interplay of shadow and light in his fiction. Baldwin repeatedly connected Delaney's struggle to the principles of light that the painter had articulated, both in his paintings and in explicit lessons to him, such as the oft-cited injunction to "look again" at something as mundane as water in a gutter until he recognized its beauty.[11]

In inventing a fictional figure to explore his ideas through a new aesthetic lens, Baldwin transferred some of Delaney's traits—artistic passion, mental instability, social anxiety, addictive tendencies—from a wise older mentor to a questing younger brother, a jazz musician rather than a painter. The figure of the jazz musician gave Baldwin considerable leeway to translate his mentor's story into one with broad cultural relevance, given the popularity and rich creative development of jazz in the mid-twentieth century. As the story suggests, jazz musicians were becoming larger-than-life culture heroes during this period: Sonny nearly worships Charlie Parker, one of many legends whose stories became popularized through audiovisual recordings and photography, expanding the scope of their genius beyond live performances. The aesthetic of jazz photography and portraiture that came to fruition in the mid-1950s (when "Sonny's Blues" was written) depends heavily on the contrast between light and darkness. In fact, jazz performers are frequently depicted as Black subjects emerging from dark backgrounds bathed in a light that essentially defines their form and being.[12] These photographic portraits are almost antisilhouettes. In photos of Ella Fitzgerald by Herman Leonard and Michael Ochs, for example, the chanteuse comes into focus in an arresting burst of light, with the remainder of the composition dominated by a deep black void (see figures 7.1 and 7.2).

In his 1968 portrait of Fitzgerald (plate 26), Delaney also emphasizes the subject's face emerging from a void, but he inverts the midcentury jazz portrait aesthetic by replacing darkness with a blinding yellow. Like the photos, his painting also provides high contrast between light and darkness, only using a different color palette to achieve a similar effect. The effect of chiaroscuro in both cases is to emphasize texture and dimension, drawing the viewer's eye to the face of a three-dimensional figure while suggesting many more facets that are not revealed as the subject's body dissolves into negative space. Delaney's Fitzgerald stares out of the void at the viewer, daring us to try to know her even more deeply than we are able to through hearing the voice that made her famous.

In 1962 Baldwin and others lobbied to get Delaney's work exhibited in New York. In a letter soliciting donations, Baldwin relies metaphorically on light to argue for Delaney's importance: his "spiritual father," as he called him, "brings great light out of the darkness of his journey."[13] In 1963, after Delaney was awarded a Fairfield Foundation grant, Baldwin wrote, "More than any other man I know, he has transcended both the inner and the outer darkness."[14] Baldwin's fullest expression of his appreciation of Delaney's use of light and its relationship to psychological darkness was published in a catalogue of Delaney's 1964 exhibition at the Galerie Lambert in Paris. Baldwin wrote there, "Though black had been described to me as the absence of light, it became very clear to me that if this were true, we would never have been able to see the colour; black: the light is trapped in it and struggles upward. . . . It was humbling to be forced to realize that the light fell down from heaven, on everything, on everybody, and that the light was always changing."[15]

To suggest that the above quotations could be read as margin notes to "Sonny's Blues," or that Delaney was the model for the character of Sonny, may sound like a stretch, but it's not that far from what I'm arguing.[16] It's worth noting that the 1965 story collection *Going to Meet the Man* (the centerpiece of which is "Sonny's Blues") is dedicated to Delaney. Versions of Delaney's story recur throughout Baldwin's fiction: he is the model of the victim-artist who takes on the cultural burden of his society and suffers in order to show us the value of the light that can "redeem and reconcile and heal." This description applies to Richard in *Go Tell It on the Mountain* (1953), Rufus in *Another Country* (1962), Fonny in *If Beale Street Could Talk* (1974), Arthur in *Just above My Head* (1979), and, of course, Sonny. If one is reluctant to see any immediate connections between Sonny and Delaney, it is at least fair to assert that there are parallels between the fictional

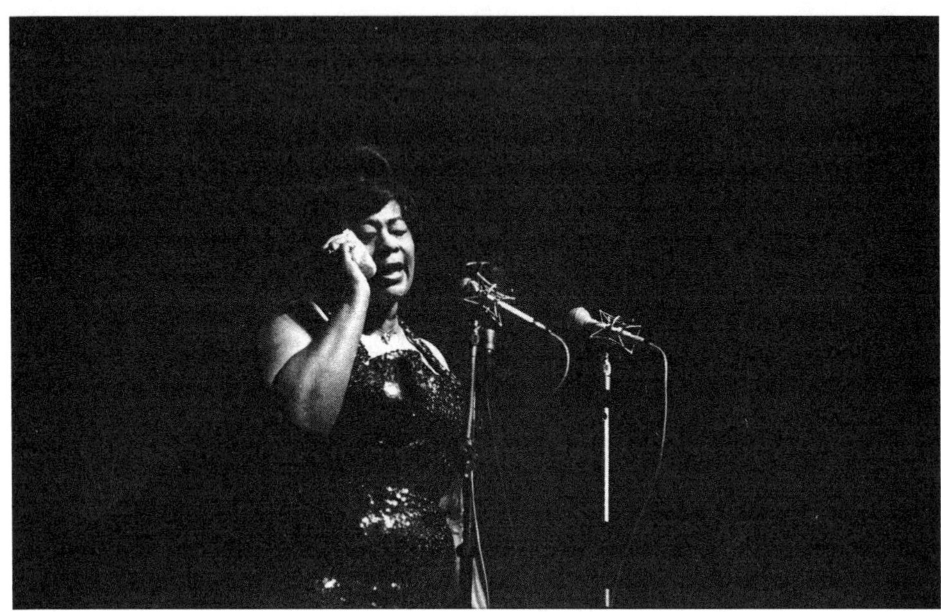

7.1

Michael Ochs, *Ella Fitzgerald*, 1960. Courtesy of Michael Ochs Archives via Getty Images.

relationship between Sonny and his brother and the "real life" relationship between Delaney and Baldwin. It is clear to any reader of the story that Sonny is the teacher (despite the fact that the narrator actually makes his living as a teacher) and that Sonny and Delaney both wrestled with internal demons (including substance addiction) that threatened their social relationships, that they both sought alternative paths to and definitions of wisdom, and that they were dedicated above all else to their art.

The correlation is solidified when we consider the motifs of light and darkness in Baldwin's tale. These are introduced in the magnificent opening paragraph of "Sonny's Blues," after the narrator has tried and failed repeatedly to comprehend the news of his brother's arrest. He says, "I stared at [the newspaper] in the swinging *lights* of the subway car, and in the faces and bodies of the people, and in my own face, trapped in the *darkness* which roared outside" (emphasis mine).[17] This scene reflects the narrator's confusion, reading paradoxically as if the narrator is simultaneously inside and outside the subway car. His face is both connected to and detached from the faces of others inside the car. It is a scene that causes the reader to do

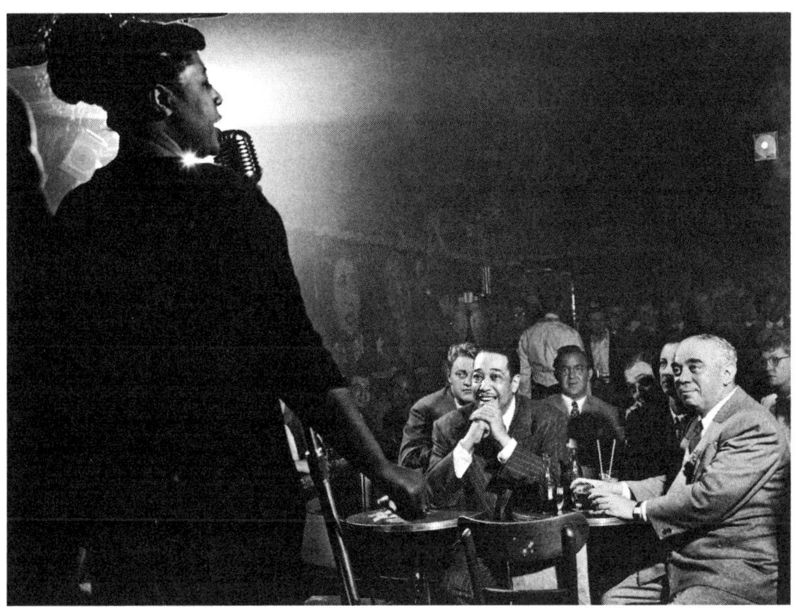

7.2

Herman Leonard, *Ella's Birthday, Downbeat Club, New York: Ella Fitzgerald, Duke Ellington, Stan Hasselgard, Benny Goodman, and Jack Robbins*, 1948.

what Delaney had encouraged the young Baldwin to do: look again. It is a strikingly visual scene, the effect of which is a kind of trompe l'oeil created by the darkness outside: a window becomes a mirror when backed by darkness. The narrator, searching in vain for reasons for Sonny's fate, discovers himself. In other words, looking outside causes him to look inside. And yet the outer darkness has trapped him. This visual trap is a precursor to the two most poignant metaphors in the story: the block of ice the narrator feels trapped inside his body that swells and increases throughout the story, until he is able to cry in the concluding paragraphs, and the hunting trap of Harlem that severs the limb of anyone who manages to escape, leaving behind phantom pains.

The way Baldwin plays with shadow and light in the story is as richly complex as the story as a whole. In the above passage the narrator is associated with the world of light: within the subway he is among other people, in the clear light of social interaction, and he thus believes he is safe from the darkness of Sonny's experience, the darkness of a life that has involved drug use, prison, a resistance to convention, and the dangerous but necessary psychological space of creativity. Throughout Baldwin's work, the belief in safety is an illusion, and that idea is expressed definitively in this story by the narrator's father, who cries out, "Safe! . . . Safe, hell! Ain't no place safe for kids, nor nobody."[18] In the story's opening paragraph, however, the safety (and light) of the subway car are dependent on the mystery (and dark) of what is outside. The narrator is led to see himself in both worlds and thus is encouraged to see the connection between his own path, which involves all the trappings of middle-class respectability (marriage, a home, a steady job), and Sonny's path, which does not. Neither path prevents anyone from suffering—or, put metaphorically, from inhabiting only the light without acknowledging the darkness that makes it possible. The narrator, who largely denies his own suffering, learns this lesson slowly throughout the story, but it is represented only as a visual metaphor in this opening scene.

The interplay between shadow and light continues throughout the story. For instance, when the narrator and Sonny reunite after Sonny is released from prison, Sonny "looked out from the depths of his private life, like an animal waiting to be coaxed into the light," and the narrator's doomed students are aware of "the darkness of their lives, which was now closing in on them."[19] Given space limitations for this volume, I will focus on two additional scenes. The first involves the narrator's recurrent memory of his mother on Sunday afternoons during his youth, when the old folks would gather in the living room and the children would become aware of "the night . . . creeping up outside."[20] The second is the famous closing scene in the nightclub where Sonny and his brother finally connect as Sonny struggles to play and the narrator struggles to listen.

The lengthy description of the first scene is abridged here to highlight the motifs of light and darkness:

> You can see the darkness growing against the windowpanes and you hear the street noises every now and again. . . . For a moment nobody's talking, but every face looks darkening, like the sky outside. . . . The silence, the darkness coming, and the darkness in the faces frighten the child obscurely. . . . In a moment someone will get up and turn on the light. Then the old folks will remember the children and they won't talk anymore that day. And when light fills the room, the child is filled with darkness. He knows that every time this happens he's moved just a little closer to that darkness outside. The darkness outside is what

> the old folks have been talking about. It's what they've come from. It's what they endure.[21]

What the children in this scene realize, even though it isn't spoken, is that they, like their elders, must also endure the darkness. As in the opening scene, it's a false distinction for the narrator to believe that he inhabits the world of light and Sonny the world of darkness: the window becomes a mirror as inside merges with outside, and the narrator feels his connection to Sonny even if he can't yet articulate it. Here, too, the distinction between the world outside this domestic scene and the world inside is false, just as the distinction between the young and old is false. The darkness creeps up outside and is reflected in the "darkening" faces of those inside. The light that is turned on is artificial and does not diminish the children's awareness of the dark: the torment of the past and the inevitable difficulty of the future. "*Everybody* tries not to [suffer]!" Sonny barks out at his brother at a key moment.[22] If the suffering is darkness, light is the will to rage against darkness, to attempt to respond to suffering even while realizing that there's no way to avoid it, as Sonny does through playing jazz.

Sonny, having passed repeatedly through the darkness, understands this principle; Sonny's brother, the narrator, is a master of denial who believes that the light is the only reality that matters, which is why he has such a hard time hearing or understanding his brother. He doesn't believe that Sonny can offer him anything, until the day his daughter Grace is buried, when he is taken by a realization: "I was sitting in the living room, *in the dark*, by myself, and I suddenly thought of Sonny. My trouble made his real."[23] Here the two brothers are united in the darkness, real and metaphorical, and it is Sonny's turn to lead his brother to a deeper understanding of shadow and light. Observing Sonny from a distance, the narrator notes, "The worry, the thoughtfulness, played on [his face] still, the way shadows play on a face which is staring into the fire."[24] Later, watching and listening to him try to express his deep thoughts, Sonny's brother observes, "The sun had vanished, soon darkness would fall. I watched his face."[25] In a story often praised for the way it describes sound, in this penultimate scene, versions of the verb "to watch" occur ten times and versions of "to look" occur four times. The important details are visual, even painterly: it is as though the narrator is scrutinizing a portrait of Sonny, as painted by Beauford Delaney.

Sonny is not capable of expressing most ideas in a way his ultrarational brother can understand. He is not great with words: his sentences are halting and incomplete through much of the story. But jazz is his true language, and the narrator must gradually learn to listen to this musical form that he once dismissed in order to hear Sonny's blues, which are also his blues. Although the entire story is about how the narrator needs to learn how to hear Sonny, the final scene depends heavily on vision: the nightclub is "very dim," and as they enter, they "couldn't see." As the narrator adjusts to the "atmospheric lighting," he notes, "heads in the darkness turned toward us."[26] The narrator is deliberately seated "in a dark corner" and observes how Sonny and the band "were being careful not to step into that circle of light [on the stage] too suddenly" for fear they might "perish in flame" if they moved into it too quickly.[27]

As the quartet begins to play, the light on the bandstand turns to "a kind of indigo"[28]—a visual confirmation that we are hearing the blues—and while the narrator *listens* to his brother's struggle in his music, he also *watches* that struggle in Sonny's face, and notes the movement of his fingers, and records the physical interactions between the band members. He concludes, "while the tale of how we suffer, and how we are delighted, and how we may triumph is never new, it always must be heard. There isn't any other tale to tell, it's the only light we've got in all this darkness."[29] The tale must be heard, but the story argues that it must also be seen, as confirmed by the return to a visual metaphor at the end of this key sentence, the recurrent metaphor of light and darkness. Sonny's blues are strongly evoked through the narrator's description, but the description, when one regards it in the context of Delaney's lessons and legacy, is profoundly visual. The narrator's revelation about suffering is described not as music, but as a series of visions of past suffering: "I saw my mother's face. . . . I saw the moonlit road where my father's brother died. . . . I saw my little girl again." The story in fact ends after Sonny and the band have stopped playing, and yet the narrator is still sitting "in the dark" and observing his brother talking to his bandmates "in the indigo light."[30] He is looking at Sonny in the light, and in the story's final gesture Sonny "look[s] toward" the narrator sitting in the dark and nods. This scene contains no music, and indeed no words. Instead, it depicts a deep reconciliation between two brothers in light and darkness under the glow of the drink the narrator has sent to the stage.

To recognize the strongly visual elements of Baldwin's celebrated story is not to diminish the aural ones, but rather to appreciate "Sonny's Blues" as a *Gesamtkunstwerk*, a complete work of art that employs multiple artistic modes to achieve its overall effect: language, music, and painting. When we "look again" at the visual content of the work, we are also closer to an understanding of Baldwin's indebtedness to Delaney, which was also multifaceted. In addition to showing Baldwin the meaning of light, he played the blues for him on a cheap phonograph in his Greenwich Village apartment. Nowhere is this influence more concentrated than in "Sonny's Blues," Baldwin's own version of the tale that is "the only light we've got in all this darkness."

NOTES

1 James Baldwin, "The Uses of the Blues," *Playboy*, 1964; reprinted in *The Cross of Redemption: Uncollected Writings*, ed. Randall Kenan (New York: Pantheon, 2010), 57.

2 Radiclani Clytus, "Paying Dues and Playing the Blues," in *The Cambridge Companion to James Baldwin*, ed. Michele Elam (Cambridge: Cambridge University Press, 2015), 70.

3 David Leeming, *Amazing Grace: A Life of Beauford Delaney* (New York: Oxford University Press, 1998), xii, 15.

4 Leeming, *Amazing Grace*, 49–50.

5 Leeming, *Amazing Grace*, 63.

6 Leeming, *Amazing Grace*, 129.

7 James Baldwin, "On the Painter Beauford Delaney," *Transition* 4, no. 18 (1965); reprinted in *James Baldwin: Collected Essays*, ed. Toni Morrison (New York: Library of America, 1998), 721.

8 Baldwin, "On the Painter Beauford Delaney," 721.

9 Baldwin, "On the Painter Beauford Delaney," 720.

10 James Baldwin, "Sonny's Blues," *Partisan Review*, Summer 1957; reprinted in *James Baldwin: Early Novels and Stories*, ed. Toni Morrison (New York: Library of America, 1998), 856.

11 Leeming, *Amazing Grace*, 69.

12 I am indebted to volume editor Amy Elias for this insight, and for directing me to these photographs of Ella Fitzgerald.

13 Leeming, *Amazing Grace*, 158.

14 Leeming, *Amazing Grace*, 161.

15 Leeming, *Amazing Grace*, 164.

16 Joan Dempsey provides a compelling argument that Delaney is the model for the character Creole in this same story; she describes Creole as "an artistic mentor, a father-figure, and a quasi-midwife." See Joan Dempsey, "Waiting for You: Beauford Delaney as James Baldwin's Inspiration for the Character Creole in 'Sonny's Blues,'" *Obsidian*, 12, no. 1 (Spring/

Summer 2011): 62. It should be noted that the two men were physically dissimilar: Creole is “enormous,” with “a big voice” (Baldwin, “Sonny’s Blues,” 859), in stark contrast to the diminutive and soft-spoken Delaney.

17 Baldwin, “Sonny’s Blues,” 831.

18 Baldwin, “Sonny’s Blues,” 840.

19 Baldwin, “Sonny’s Blues,” 837, 832.

20 Baldwin, “Sonny’s Blues,” 841.

21 Baldwin, “Sonny’s Blues,” 841–42.

22 Baldwin, “Sonny’s Blues,” 857.

23 Baldwin, “Sonny’s Blues,” 852, emphasis mine.

24 Baldwin, “Sonny’s Blues,” 849.

25 Baldwin, “Sonny’s Blues,” 859.

26 Baldwin, “Sonny’s Blues,” 859.

27 Baldwin, “Sonny’s Blues,” 860.

28 Baldwin, “Sonny’s Blues,” 861.

29 Baldwin, “Sonny’s Blues,” 862.

30 Baldwin, “Sonny’s Blues,” 863.

EIGHT

Yellow Light, Black Abstraction

Jazz, Writing, and Ethical Shattering in Baldwin's and Delaney's Works

Walton Muyumba

At the end of James Baldwin's "Sonny's Blues" (1957), the unnamed narrator attends a musical performance that includes his pianist brother, Sonny. During the final number of the set, Creole, the band's bassist, leads Sonny into the depths of the blues. Through Creole's guidance, Sonny slowly gains insight about musical improvisation and also about his own recovery from heroin addiction. Noting the poignancy of Creole's blues-idiom mentorship, Sonny's brother takes up a central tenet of critical noticing. Normally someone who tightly controls his actions and beliefs, he immerses himself in the music, and as a result, the sonic and symbolic scene tugs both him and the story's readers out from the story's dark, layered, historical depths toward a kind of enlightenment:

> Creole began to tell us what the blues were all about. They were not about anything very new. He and his boys up there were keeping it new, at the risk of ruin, destruction, madness, and death, in order to find new ways to make us listen. For, while the tale of how we suffer, and how we are delighted, and how we may triumph is never new, it always must be heard. There isn't any other tale to tell, it's the only light we've got in all this darkness.[1]

Though the narrator suggests that listening closely will not reveal something new about the only "tale to tell," he does believe that attending critically to the risks that artists take in telling the tale anew will illuminate otherwise obscure human truths. Moreover, just as Creole's disquisition on "the uses of the blues" moves his bandmates to improvise innovative musical statements, the narrator's description of this blues-idiom moment stands as a guide for the story's readers (listeners?) to envision new social arrangements.

Importantly, Joan Dempsey has suggested that we read Creole in this short story as a "rendering of—and a tribute to—the critical, mentoring role that Beauford Delaney played in Baldwin's life."[2] Just as Creole's example instructs the brothers, Delaney's blues mentorship informs Baldwin's literary art and arts criticism. Yet while the claim is provocative that "Sonny's Blues" may be Baldwin's homage to Delaney, the story's richness thickens when we notice that the author has rendered versions of himself within it: Sonny, the improvising artist, and his brother, the narrator-as-critic, are both stand-ins for Baldwin. This doubling leads me to a line of inquiry: during the 1950s and 1960s, Delaney began using the language of abstraction more frequently and assertively in his paintings. At the same time, in his fiction and cultural criticism, Baldwin's writing veered away from epiphanic endings or final, certain judgments and toward a kind of critical abstraction. What Baldwin arrives at, under the influence of Delaney's abstract paintings, is a credo of ethical shattering: for Baldwin, telling us "what the blues were all about" means leading the reader/viewer/listener into an abstractionist self-interrogation, one that shatters our preconceptions and drives us to that place where we must disassociate ourselves from ourselves in order to do the close interrogation needed for social renewal.

Delaney first met Baldwin, then sixteen years old, in 1940. With his "extraordinary eyes," imbued with what seemed to be X-ray vision, Delaney recognized the young writer's visceral need for artistic instruction.[3] The painter taught his protégé how to envision and represent those unseen (or ignored) elements of human experience. Baldwin, in his tribute essay "On the Painter Beauford Delaney" (1965), describes how his own recognition of color, under the painter's influence, "underwent a most disturbing and salutary change." To look with intention and a desire for apprehension at, say, a leaf, "was to discover many colours in it; and though black had been described to me as the absence of light, it became very clear to me that if this were true, we would never have been able to see the colour; black: the light is trapped in it and struggles upward."[4]

Delaney was "living proof . . . that a black man could be an artist."[5] He "opened the door," and just as Creole leads Sonny into the blues as a place of truth-telling self-expression, Delaney ushered his "pupil" into the blues as his true home. Creole can guide Sonny into and through the blues because he's had to learn how to navigate those waters himself. Likewise, Baldwin recognized that Delaney's ability to represent and re-create the play of light and darkness on canvas sprang from his courage and "absolute integrity": "The darkness of [Delaney's] beginnings, in Tennessee . . . a black-blue midnight indeed, opaque, and full of sorrow," gave life to his aesthetic.[6] Baldwin presses this blue-black detail into biographical and existential truth: we all come from darkness, but only a few have learned how to turn this fact into art. As the narrator realizes in "Sonny's Blues," the process of learning the blues, surviving them, delighting in them, and narrating them triumphantly is "the only light we have to hold up against the darkness."

Delaney's abstract paintings from the 1950s through the 1970s offered visions of psychological and spiritual liberation beyond the clamor of the battles that Baldwin described in his essays. His canvases—often dominated by yellow light, sometimes with varicolored, jagged striations—visualize communal spaces yet to be achieved. Though Delaney painted figures and scenes from the Black musical world, portraits and stills that blend abstraction and representation, I'm interested in canvases that encourage viewers to imagine alternative spaces but do so without figurative prompting.[7]

Take, for example, Delaney's *Charlie Parker Yardbird* (1958; plate 10), a work that seems to pulsate syllabically: bebop, rebop, bebop. The painting's rhythms also exhibit a respiratory action: atop a stormy gray-blue background, Delaney's quivering streams in red, rose, and brown run from the canvas's center out to its edges like the rapidly stated melodic ideas of Parker's improvised solos. Even as our eyes follow the flow of these tributaries, we are pulled back to the image's middle space as though we were riding the saxophonist's inhalation as he prepares to blow another statement through his horn.

Untitled (Abstraction I) (ca. 1960) exemplifies an even more emphatically counterrepresentational mode: Delaney's impasto (his brushwork jots and swerving across the yellow foundation) and color choices (cerulean blue, mustard, chartreuse, pale rose) evoke the sensation breaking through or crossing over from limitation into illuminated possibility.[8] Reviewing the 2016 exhibition *Beauford Delaney: Resonance of Form and Vibration of Color*, Joseph Nechvatal describes abstracts similar to *Untitled (Abstraction I)* as projecting "a strong and vivid performance of social innocence where no actual innocence exists."[9] Nechvatal argues that Delaney's abstractionist paintings offer exits from the contemporary world's bleakness (school shootings, beheadings, terrorist attacks, police shootings of unarmed Black people, the dehumanization of LGBTQI people). Crossing through those exits, viewers encounter a "universal inner spirituality, offering us the chance to widen our focus and consider the warm swirling incontestable fundamentals of a person."[10] This interpretation suggests that Delaney's abstracts do more than project meaning through realist representation: these paintings encircle viewers, reflecting back to them pictures of their own "swirling incontestable" selves. Richard Powell in fact has argued that Delaney's paintings contain spiritual properties that are "inherently radical."[11] Like Nechvatal, Powell sees Delaney's abstract paintings as presenting points of transition: visual platforms for imagining forms of being alternative to the cultural and political status quo. Abstraction provided Delaney with "an entrée into a figure or form which, by its very nature, is already enigmatic and abstract."[12]

For example, in *Moving Sunlight* (1965; plate 15), Delaney generates texture, structure, and movement by shifting across yellows from sunny to goldenrod and manipulating the paint thickness with a palette knife, raising swirls and ridges on the canvas and creating a spiral effect in the painting's midsection. Onlookers may feel as though they are entering a chamber of cycling light. *Moving Sunlight* offers entry to a space wherein the self, one's vision, and visions of one's self can be adjusted, enhanced, and revitalized. Delaney's painting offers what Baldwin accepted at the threshold of the painter's Greenwich Village studio in 1941: passage toward renewed practices of seeing and imagining. "I walked through that door into Beauford's colors," Baldwin explains, "on the easel, on the palette, against the wall."[13] Baldwin's description emphasizes "those portals through which interior and exterior space are managed."[14] Entering Delaney's studio, Baldwin stepped into "a liminal space of shifting referential coordinates" and gained access to the older artist's "transformative and transportive power."[15]

Baldwin's writings mirror what *Moving Sunlight* and *Untitled (Abstraction I)* accomplish.[16] Baldwin's own abstractions arrived in books that offer readers access to liminal, imaginary spaces of "shifting referential coordinates": his recollection of the 1960s Black Liberation movement, *No Name in the Street* (1972), and his study of Hollywood cinema and racial mythologies, *The Devil Finds Work* (1976).[17] Like Creole in "Sonny's Blues," Baldwin leads readers into "deep waters" in two ways. First, using his own experience and person as a locus for interrogating the sociopolitical landscape, he blends memoir and criticism to critique the various forces occluding Black liberation and the radical reconstruction of American community. In this way, Baldwin merges the roles that Creole and the narrator serve in the short story: he simultaneously performs as teacher/leader and as critic. Second, his interpretive narratives draw readers toward intellectual thresholds beyond which lie abstract vistas. Looking across the brink, readers can imagine the yet-to-be-created alternatives to the cultural and political status quo and see reflections of their fathomless, intricate selves. Directing readers beyond the thresholds of his books, Baldwin argues that we will see our fundamental human complexity reflected in abstraction.

In *No Name in the Street* and *The Devil Finds Work*, in particular, Baldwin's experimental and digressive technique is a "kind of mimetic evocation" of his mind at work. In her review of Eddie Glaude Jr.'s *Begin Again: James Baldwin's America and Its Urgent Lessons for Our Own* (2020), Sara Collins suggests (by way of the French philosopher Blaise Pascal) that we read Baldwin's approach as "la peinture de la pensée," thought painting.[18] We might also liken Baldwin's essayistic efforts to those of Michel de Montaigne, who described his own compositional practice as akin to painting. Montaigne characterized his essays as having been "patched and huddled up together of diverse members without any certain or well-ordered figure, having neither order, dependency, or proportion, but casual and framed by chance."[19] This description suggests that the essay form arises from a mode of collage that veers away from "any certain or well-ordered figure," that is, away from any concrete, singular directive and toward a presentation of experience as an engagement with abstraction. I think that Baldwin shaped his book-length essays similarly.

Baldwin directs his readers' "inner and the outer" eyes toward inexorable "confrontation[s] with reality."[20] His theorization "develops as an integrated part of his larger project of exposing the delusions that perpetuate inequality and injustice"—namely, the mythologies of white innocence and the scourge of historical amnesia.[21] From Baldwin's angle of critique,

Koritha Mitchell writes, only by "facing reality," relinquishing mythology, and addressing American history honestly can "Americans grapple with the injustice of social hierarchies and thereby recognize their connection to one another."[22] This can occur, Mitchell continues, through Baldwin's examination of the "meaning-making power of performance whether in the form of blues and gospel singing or the theatricality of everyday life." Reading "the theatricality of everyday life" as a kind of ideological performance helped Baldwin demonstrate that mythologies of Black inhumanity, white supremacy, and white innocence are the controlling narratives of American consciousness. In *No Name in the Street*, Baldwin counters "everyday theatricality," and the US televisual-film culture that supports it, by detailing his participation in the civil rights movement, his friendships with movement leaders, and the ways that violent resistance to the movement and American ahistoricism defer African American freedom while blocking the possibility of radical community building.

Baldwin argues that a radical community cannot form until white Americans confront the nation's racial history, understand that their own freedom is enmeshed with Black liberation, and embrace African Americans as equal citizens. His notion of refashioned, radical community is related to John Dewey's conception of "great community": while "society" is born of the nation-state's political arrangements, "great community" is an unrestricted, diverse array of associated groups bound in solidarity through mutually recognized humanity and dignity.[23] Radical solidarity will come to fruition only after Black Americans lovingly "force [their white] brothers to see themselves as they are, to cease fleeing from reality, and begin to change it. . . . We can make America what America must become."[24]

No Name in the Street not only recollects a tumultuous decade, it also argues that even after the direct-action protests, the murders and assassinations, and the political victories, African Americans were still bound to a nation they could not "honorably defend—which they were compelled, indeed, endlessly to attack and condemn—and who yet spoke out of the most passionate love, hoping to make the kingdom new, to make it honorable and worthy of life."[25] Baldwin engages this irony narratively. On the one hand, he presents the book as a canvas for reconceptualizing Black liberation and Black participation in democracy, even in the face of violent resistance to both. On the other hand, Baldwin's narrative design expresses the book's meaning: he understood that his readers would not see the moral and existential problems born out of Black unfreedom unless his story delivered readers to the threshold of an imaginative-intellectual space wherein community could be renewed.[26]

In fact, Baldwin's mixed forms work to counter the structures of everyday theatricality and Western televisual-film culture. Those structures support a matrix of mythologies about gender, sexuality, race, and capital, a "mythos [that] acts as a social imaginary, enabling the putatively white individual to construct a 'provisional,' fantasy self, which, in turn enables him or her socially and politically to oppress African Americans (without any sense of moral culpability)."[27] However, as Baldwin's critique of *Lawrence of Arabia* (1962) argues, because supposedly "white" people govern and gain cover from this self-perpetuating visual narrative system, they need never confront themselves existentially. Yet naked self-interrogation is fundamental to identity formation: "This nakedness reveals the various abject conditions of mortality, sexual hunger, dispossession, and historical guilt or shame that universally constitute [for Baldwin] 'real' selfhood," Ryan Jay Friedman explains.[28]

Friedman's reading helps explain why, in *No Name in the Street* and *The Devil Finds Work*, Baldwin tries to cut exit routes out from the cul-de-sac of American society's white supremacist organization. "Escaping the trap that legalized white supremacy created requires being willing to let go of both what appears to be using people as objects and cherished avenues of resisting objectification," writes Christopher Freeburg.[29] Among the cherished avenues of resistance are those standardized literary forms that would keep Baldwin's life-writing categorically distant and separate from his criticism. Freeburg suggests that Baldwin's new writing, in response to his attentive listening to Bessie Smith's music, offered readers points of perception where the blues can be heard communicating "its racial and existential significance to getting over things, not once and for all, but to begin again."[30] The blues, of course, is an autobiographical form; it swings poetically, expressing the pendulum of lived experience in all its exuberance and all its low-down dirty shamefulness. As Houston Baker writes, the blues "constitutes an amalgam that seems always to have been in motion in America—always becoming, shaping, transforming, displacing the peculiar experiences of Africans in the New World."[31]

The Devil Finds Work enacts that amalgam—the blues in motion—melding memoir and film criticism improvisationally; Baldwin's formal arrangement allows him to simultaneously interrogate the social imaginary *and* narrate his ongoing self-questioning and self-becoming. Baldwin seems to have first practiced this "patched up and huddled" form of life-writing-as-criticism in *No Name in the Street*. Recounting the process of adapting *The Autobiography of Malcolm X* (1965) for screen; the author's memories of his activism in the civil rights movement; his relationships with Martin Luther King Jr., Medgar Evers, and Malcolm X; the rise of the Black Power movement; and his frustrations with the Hollywood film industry all model the kind of naked self-interrogation he believes is crucial to recognizing one's own complex selfhood.

Baldwin's critique—of the ideological conflicts among African Americans, of the film industry, of the burgeoning mass incarceration of young Black men,[32] of historical amnesia and political violence in the United States, of himself—springs from blues-idiom practices.[33] Blues-idiom critics must first attune themselves anew. These new equalizing adjustments are meant to both sharpen listeners' auditory experiences and expand readers' visualizing capacities. Writing through Black vernacular culture, Baldwin's mixed-genre works also describe a "manner" of seeing differently. These new visual possibilities occur, Freeburg contends, at a "threshold . . . which indicates obscurity and a new self or group relation at the same time."[34] Baldwin brings his readers, newly attuned blues-idiom critics, to these thresholds in the elliptical, open-ended, closing pages of both *The Devil* and *No Name*. Detailing the fiery, murderous end to the 1960s in *No Name*, Baldwin argues that the struggle for African American liberation will ultimately remain stunted because white people fail to comprehend the ironies central to Black experience. Even worse, he adds, is that that failure manifests as whites' mockery and hatred of Black life. Baldwin finds all this "moving because it is so blind: it is terrible to watch people cling to their captivity and insist on their own destruction. I think Black people have always felt this about America, and Americans, and have always seen, spinning above the thoughtless American head, the shape of the wrath to come."[35]

Because Baldwin's vision of spinning wrath in *No Name in the Street* mimics his warning at the end of *The Fire Next Time*— "*God gave Noah the rainbow sign, No more water, the fire next time*"—it's possible that he decided to supplement *No Name* with an epilogue.[36] After all, political conflagrations did engulf many cities across the United States during the second half of the 1960s. But those signs weren't heeded, and no long-standing sociopolitical improvements followed those acts of resistance. The most significant moment in *No Name* may be when Baldwin notes that Tony Maynard and Angela Davis remain incarcerated and in danger and that the Jackson brothers, George and Jonathan, have entered "the royal fellowship of death," and then explains that "this book is not finished [and] can never be finished."[37] The work's incomplete condition places readers in a breach. And on the gap's other side, I argue, is a space for creative reversals and innovations.

Effectively expressing a conception of social justice attuned to Black liberation theology, Baldwin ennobles the Jackson family, leaving *No Name in the Street* with a final image of a pietà in Black: "And one may say that Mrs. Georgia Jackson [mother of George and Jon] and the alleged mother of God have, at last, found something in common. Now, it is the Virgin, the alabaster Mary, who must embrace the despised black mother whose children are also the issue of the Holy Ghost."[38] This image in fact reverses the narrative's closing warning by asserting that there are some Black people—Davis, Evers, King, the Jacksons, Malcolm, Maynard—willing to risk or sacrifice their lives in order to save the nation from itself. Their example may, in fact, keep heavenly wrath at bay. Baldwin's "sculptural" allegory posits African American radical resistance as a rejection of the nation's main mythological symbol: the White Savior. Those blindly clinging to white supremacy cannot understand Baldwin's image. To see and apprehend that image, readers must cross the author's threshold, entering into the abstract imaginary beyond its edge.

The inability or unwillingness to relinquish white supremacist mythos is a central theme of the film criticism in *The Devil Finds Work*. Baldwin's cultural criticism asks readers "to brave escaping or being released in new political histories (and traps) far beyond our comfort zones, levels of trust, and firmly held beliefs about racial difference and the seemingly never-ending need for collective racial politics."[39] Baldwin illustrates over and again that Hollywood films trap their viewers in a kind of mirrored fun house. Rather than reflecting the complexities of American life, the film industry's predominant narratives protect white dreams of innocence, general historical ignorance, and white supremacy. On screen, Black experience is represented through tropes that inevitably flatten Black humanity and obscure African American history. At the movies, Black heroines and heroes "must always be left at society's mercy: in order to justify white history and in order to indicate the essential validity of the black condition."[40] Because we consume output from this system so frequently, Baldwin might say, we have learned to misperceive ourselves within those distorted images. And that kind of visual training weakens our interpretive abilities: we fail to identify possible exits from that repeated narrative loop.

However, *The Devil Finds Work* is also Baldwin's attempt to point out exits and to prompt his readers to imagine abstract alternatives to the

Hollywood status quo. Focusing on certain screen actors, especially Black ones, Baldwin argues that they can sometimes defy white mythologies with their powerful performances. And when a performance breaks through, it can crack the screen's smooth, dreamy continuity and express truths about the lived experience of racialized American life that are otherwise obscured. For example, writing about Sidney Poitier's now-canonical performances in *Guess Who's Coming to Dinner* (1967), *In the Heat of the Night* (1967), and *The Defiant Ones* (1958), Baldwin argues that all three film narratives are founded upon conceptions of white supremacy/innocence and narrow characterizations of Black life that mute or diminish the actor's special talent for veracious representation.

But Baldwin also illustrates how the force of Poitier's physical and facial expressiveness in *The Defiant Ones* can sometimes "shatter" the film's mythos-verse. Poitier's visage in close-up can create indelible, miraculous moments that deliver information from "beyond the confines of the script: hints of reality, smuggled like contraband into a maudlin tale, and with enough force, if unleashed, to shatter the tale to fragments."[41] From their own experiences, Baldwin explains, Black viewers are steeped in the "unspoken," subtextual source material that Poitier draws from to arrange his mien dramatically. Baldwin seizes upon these shattering moments to establish "an oblique analytical perspective." From that interpretive angle, he can point out a film's "internal contradictions" while also pointing toward alternative narrative possibilities.

Baldwin's critique of Poitier's shattering look illuminates a passage to abstract spaces where practices of looking and imagining are revitalized. However, rather than a portrait of Poitier made from an extracted still image, I imagine that Baldwin has drawn our attention to a frozen frame, blown up in order to detail the actor's eyes and furrowed brow. The detail's distorted, fractured quality emphasizes the unspoken and inscrutable information about Black experience in the set of Poitier's gaze. Perhaps Poitier splinters the screen at those moments when his characterization interpolates blues-idiom knowledge from the subtextual reality onto the film's surface. When viewers engage the actor's stare in these moments, they gain entry to a culturally rich visual space wherein visions of one's self in relation to Poitier's gaze must be adjusted, enhanced, and revitalized, just as viewers of Delaney's *Moving Sunlight* are prompted to enter a liminal space where one's self-conception as well as one's conception of "reality" can be reformed.

At the end of *The Devil Finds Work*, interrogating the inanities of William Friedkin's *The Exorcist* (1973), Baldwin raises the stakes of his criticism by demonstrating how our willingness to imagine and perceive abstraction may, in fact, liberate us and, thus freed, help us to begin again sorting ourselves into a great democratic community. To educate readers about this final threshold of possibility, Baldwin analyzes the easy and deceptive version of evil presented in Friedkin's film.

At the close of *The Exorcist*, Regan MacNeil (Linda Blair), the child character who becomes the corporeal host for Satan, has been possessed, exorcised, liberated, unburdened of any memory of her demonic trial, and thus returned to innocence. Writing on the brink of America's bicentennial, Baldwin argues that "Americans should certainly know more about evil" than the "mindless and hysterical banality" displayed in the film. In fact, he continues, those Americans pretending ignorance of evil "are lying." And those best prepared to call out this lie are the ones who've "been treated as the devil," those marginalized and oppressed within the national culture—people of color, and even white children—are the ones who recognize "the devil when they meet."[42]

This isn't a theological argument. Baldwin's claim is political and philosophical: because we maintain the tenets of US racial mythology and refuse to accept one another, we also fail to recognize our own "possession." "For, I have seen the devil," Baldwin writes, "by day and by night, and have seen him in you and in me. . . . This devil has no need of any dogma. . . . He does not levitate beds, or fool around with little girls: we do."[43] And so, at the end of *The Devil Finds Work*, Baldwin shatters the narrative of American innocence that relies on false scapegoats to carry the nation's burdens or sins, in the manner of Hollywood's allegorization of evil into symbolic family horror tales. And those who recognize the devil among and within us constitute the very "shape of the wrath to come": "In the eyes and hearts and perceptions of the wretched everywhere, and in the ruined earth of Vietnam, and in the orphans and the widows, and in the old men, seeing visions, and in the young men, dreaming dreams: these have already kissed the bloody cross and will not bow down before it again: and have forgotten nothing."[44] Here, Baldwin follows Delaney's lead, framing this final image as a reflection of his readers' own "swirling, incontestable, fundamental" selves.

Delaney's mode of abstract painting allowed him to make the blues-in-motion visible. Following his mentor's lead into the deep waters of abstract expression, Baldwin attempts something similar in both *The Devil* and *No Name*: within the thick litanies closing both works are an array of contingent images invoked to make the blues-in-motion visible and imaginable. But instead of finality, Baldwin's visions, if you will, give both books a feeling of open-endedness, as though leaving us readers on the threshold of an uncomfortable, unframed space of blues abstraction. That zone exists beyond both the accepted and hegemonic models of political resistance, the reified mythologies of everyday theatricality, and the televisual-cinematic matrix. To engage abstraction is to understand the permeability of boundaries: "To encounter oneself is to encounter the other: and this is love. . . . Neither of us, truly, can live without the other: a statement which would not sound so banal if one were not endlessly compelled to repeat it, and further, believe it, and act on that belief."[45] Across those thresholds, entering the breach, Baldwin argues, we can confront ourselves nakedly, reimagine ourselves critically, and begin again to achieve a renewed radical community.

NOTES

1 James Baldwin, "Sonny's Blues," *Partisan Review*, Summer 1957; reprinted in *James Baldwin: Early Novels and Stories*, ed. Toni Morrison (New York: Library of America, 1998), 862.

2 Joan Dempsey, "Waiting for You: Beauford Delaney as James Baldwin's Inspiration for the Character Creole in 'Sonny's Blues,'" *Obsidian: Literature in the African Diaspora* 12, no. 1 (Spring/Summer 2011): 62.

3 James Baldwin, "The Price of the Ticket," in *The Price of the Ticket: Collected Nonfiction, 1948–1985* (New York: St. Martin's, 1985); reprinted in *James Baldwin: Collected Essays*, ed. Toni Morrison (New York: Library of America, 1998), 830.

4 James Baldwin, "On the Painter Beauford Delaney," *Transition* 4, no. 18 (1965); reprinted in Morrison, *James Baldwin: Collected Essays*, 720.

5 Baldwin, "Price of the Ticket," 832.

6 Baldwin, "On the Painter Beauford Delaney," 720.

7 For figurative works by Delaney that blend abstraction and representation, see his *Portrait of Ella Fitzgerald*, 1968 (plate 26); *Untitled (Jazz Band)*, 1965, illustrated in "All That Jazz," *Les Amis de Beauford Delaney* (blog), http://lesamisdebeauforddelaney.blogspot.com/2019/11/all-that-jazz.html; and *Marian Anderson*, 1965, Virginia Museum of Fine Arts.

8 For *Untitled (Abstraction I)*, ca. 1960, see "Beauford at the Indianapolis Museum of Art (Newfields)," *Les Amis de Beauford Delaney* (blog), December 9, 2017, http://lesamisdebeauforddelaney.blogspot.com/2017/12/beauford-at-indianapolis-museum-of-art.html.

9 Joseph Nechvatal, "Beauford Delaney: Resonance of Form and Vibration of Color," *Brooklyn Rail*, May 1, 2016, https://brooklynrail

.org/2016/05/artseen/beauford-delaney-resonance-of-form-and-vibrationnbspofnbspcolor.

10 Nechvatal, "Beauford Delaney."

11 Richard J. Powell, *Beauford Delaney: The Color Yellow* (Atlanta: High Museum of Art, 2002), 16.

12 Powell, *Beauford Delaney*, 20.

13 Baldwin, "Price of the Ticket," 830.

14 Emma Cleary, "'Here Be Dragons': The Tyranny of the Cityscape in James Baldwin's Intimate Cartographies," *James Baldwin Review* 1, no. 1 (2015): 96.

15 Cleary, "'Here Be Dragons,'" 96.

16 See Baldwin's manipulation of narrative time in *Another Country* (1961) and *Tell Me How Long the Train's Been Gone* (1968) and his use of "echo-effect" in *If Beale Street Could Talk* (1974).

17 In both books, Baldwin locates or links himself to a litany of places, including Harlem, Hollywood, Algeria, Angola, Istanbul, and Saint-Paul-de-Vence, France.

18 Sara Collins, "The US through James Baldwin's Eyes," *The Guardian*. February 18, 2021, https://www.theguardian.com/books/2021/feb/18/begin-again-by-eddie-s-glaude-jr-review-the-us-through-james-baldwins-eyes.

19 In Michel de Montaigne's essay "Of Friendship," essay writing is related to the painter's process of creation and composition. See *Shakespeare's Montaigne: The Florio Translation of the Essays: A Selection*, ed. Stephen Greenblatt and Peter Platt, trans. John Florio (New York: New York Review Books, 2014), 40.

20 David Leeming, "Beauford, Abstraction, and Light," in *Beauford Delaney: Liquid Light: Paris Abstractions, 1954–1970* (New York: Michael Rosenfeld Gallery, 1999), unpaginated.

21 Koritha Mitchell, "James Baldwin, Performance Theorist, Sings the *Blues for Mister Charlie*," *American Quarterly* 64, no. 1 (2012): 34.

22 Mitchell, "James Baldwin, Performance Theorist," 33.

23 See "All Safety Is an Illusion," in *Trained Capacities: John Dewey, Rhetoric, and Democratic Practice*, ed. Gregory Clark and Brian Jackson (Columbia: University of South Carolina Press, 2014), 159–73.

24 James Baldwin, "My Dungeon Shook," in *The Fire Next Time* (New York: Random House, 1963), reprinted in Morrison, *James Baldwin: Collected Essays*, 294.

25 James Baldwin, *No Name in the Street* (New York: Dial, 1972), reprinted in Morrison, *James Baldwin: Collected Essays*, 474.

26 See Walton M. Muyumba, "Movement III: Cutting Session: Baldwin as Prizefighting Intellectual, Baldwin as Improvising Intellectual," in *The Shadow and the Act: Black Intellectual Practice, Jazz Improvisation, and Philosophical Pragmatism* (Chicago: University of Chicago Press, 2009).

27 Ryan Jay Friedman, "'Enough Force to Shatter the Tale to Fragments': Ethics and Textual Analysis in James Baldwin's Film Theory," *ELH* 77, no. 2 (2010): 386.

28 Friedman, "'Enough Force to Shatter the Tale to Fragments,'" 386.

29 Christopher Freeburg, "James Baldwin and the Unhistoric Life of Race," *South Atlantic Quarterly* 112, no. 2 (January 2013): 237.

30 Freeburg, "James Baldwin and the Unhistoric Life of Race," 237. Baldwin considers Smith's music several times throughout his oeuvre. For examples see *Another Country* (1961) and his essays "Stranger in the Village" and "The Use of the Blues."

31 Houston Baker, *Blues, Ideology, and Afro-American Literature* (Chicago: University of Chicago Press, 1987), 5.

32 The imprisonment story of Tony Maynard, Baldwin's sometime personal assistant and chauffeur, is a central narrative thread in *The Devil Finds Work.*

33 For some definitions of blues-idiom practices, see Albert Murray's many critical works, especially *The Blue Devils of Nada* (1996) and *Murray Talks Music* (2016). Also see Ralph Ellison's essays on literary artists and musicians, especially "Richard Wright's Blues." Alongside their individual book-length studies of blues-idiom musical and literary aesthetics, Robert O'Meally, Brent Edwards, and Farah Jasmine Griffin have coedited two anthologies central to ethnomusicological critical theorizing: *The Jazz Cadences of American Culture* (1998) and *Uptown Conversation* (2004).

34 Freeburg, "James Baldwin and the Unhistoric Life of Race," 237.

35 Baldwin, *No Name in the Street*, 474.

36 James Baldwin, *The Fire Next Time* (New York: Random House, 1963), reprinted in Morrison, *James Baldwin: Collected Essays*, 347. Italics in original.

37 Baldwin, *No Name in the Street*, 475.

38 James Baldwin, "Epilogue: Who Has Believed Our Report?," in *No Name in the Street*, 475.

39 Freeburg, "James Baldwin and the Unhistoric Life of Race," 237.

40 James Baldwin, *The Devil Finds Work* (New York: Dial, 1976), reprinted in Morrison, *James Baldwin: Collected Essays*, 564.

41 Baldwin, *Devil Finds Work*, 554.

42 Baldwin, *Devil Finds Work*, 571.

43 Baldwin, *Devil Finds Work*, 571.

44 Baldwin, *Devil Finds Work*, 572.

45 Baldwin, *Devil Finds Work*, 571.

NINE

Baldwin/Delaney/Cazac

Nicholas Boggs

When James Baldwin's boldly experimental "child's story for adults," *Little Man, Little Man: A Story of Childhood*, was originally published in 1976, it didn't resonate with critics. They were confounded by its loose and episodic story of three Black children navigating the pleasures and dangers of their Harlem neighborhood, as well as by its childlike narrative voice rooted in the vernacular Black English of Baldwin's youth. In fact, apart from a dismissive review in the *New York Times Book Review*, in which Julius Lester called it "not especially exciting or disappointing," it was hardly remarked upon at all and went quickly and quietly out of print.[1] Even with the resurgence of interest in Baldwin that gathered momentum at the turn of the twenty-first century and accelerated in the era of Black Lives Matter, *Little Man, Little*

Man remained conspicuously absent from the larger cultural conversations about the author's life and work.

That all began to shift in 2018, when Duke University Press published a new edition of *Little Man, Little Man* for which Jennifer DeVere Brody and I had the honor of serving as coeditors. An early review from *Kirkus* raved: "Pulled from the past, this is a brilliant exploration of black childhood with profound emotional depth."[2] *Entertainment Weekly* included *Little Man, Little Man* in its list of the "50 Most Anticipated Books of 2018," calling it "brilliant, essential."[3] And during the week of its publication, an extensive feature article appeared on the front page of the *New York Times* books section with the headline "A James Baldwin Book, Forgotten and Overlooked for Four Decades, Gets Another Life." A number of positive reviews followed in the popular press, with the consensus that the book (as Alexandra Alter put it in the *Times*) "couldn't be more timely."[4] Yet scholarly engagement with *Little Man, Little Man* remains limited, especially in comparison with literary and cultural criticism addressing Baldwin's other works.[5]

This chapter responds to this gap by digging deeper into the influence of two essential figures in the book's overlooked history: Baldwin's mentor, the painter Beauford Delaney, to whom it was dedicated, and the French artist Yoran Cazac, who provided its illustrations. In the process, I suggest that *Little Man, Little Man* is best understood not as the product of a sole author (James Baldwin), or even as a collaboration between Baldwin and Cazac. Instead, drawing on new biographical information, I show how the aesthetic originality of *Little Man, Little Man* should be read as a particularly productive confluence of the artistic sensibilities of all three men. Their collaboration began to take shape when they collectively gazed out of the window of Delaney's studio on the outskirts of Paris more than a decade and a half before the book's publication. In its final form, I argue, *Little Man, Little Man* weds Baldwin's political vision and linguistic virtuosity with the imprint of Delaney's influence on him as an artist, and it refracts this union through Cazac's dreamy watercolor illustrations. Through this process, these men created an unprecedented literary work that produces a mode of seeing—the gift of what Baldwin called Delaney's "double vision"—that we are only now beginning to apprehend in all of its subversive glory.

Baldwin, Delaney, and Cazac at the Window

I discovered an original copy of *Little Man, Little Man* over two decades ago at Yale University's Beinecke Rare Book and Manuscript Library when I was an undergraduate in search of a subject for a senior thesis. A few years later, in 2003, I tracked down Baldwin's collaborator, Yoran Cazac, and conducted a series of interviews with him in his Montmartre studio in Paris (see figure 9.1). He also gave me a copy of an untitled essay I had never seen before, which Baldwin wrote about him and his work for a 1977 exhibition at the Orangerie of the Chateau de Maintenon (now available online).[6] It begins as follows:

> I met Cazac in Paris, in 1959. I was introduced to him by our friend Beauford Delaney. Cazac was very young then, but so possessed, and so utterly individual, that he was sometimes as exasperating as a boy of ten, and sometimes as inaccessible as a man of ninety. Delaney appeared to understand him completely, but I didn't. Cazac said that he was French, and he is, but the French appeared to find this claim somewhat dubious, and so did I. It helped, but not by very much, to be informed that the Cazac family had roots in Finland and Brazil. For Cazac's real antecedents are to be found in the history—the mystery—which, ruthlessly, produces and shapes the artist.

It was a few months before this introduction that Delaney had met Cazac for the first time himself at Galerie Facchetti, where he had already participated in a group show and would later have a solo exhibition. By this time the fifty-eight-year-old Delaney was already an established artist, having made his way to Paris from his hometown of Knoxville, Tennessee, by way of Boston and then New York City (Baldwin joked to his former personal assistant and biographer David Leeming that his mentor had walked all the way across the Atlantic Ocean).[7] Cazac, meanwhile, was a fiery and charismatic twenty-one-year-old Frenchman who had recently come to Paris from the nearby provinces to pursue his passion for painting.

Despite their obvious differences in age and background, Delaney and Cazac were kindred artistic spirits—outsiders, visionaries, and highly enigmatic figures. In the essay, Baldwin alludes to Cazac's mysterious origins. (Yoran was not even his real name; he was born "Bernard.") Elsewhere Baldwin famously refers to Delaney as "a cross between Brer Rabbit and Saint Francis of Assisi," obliquely echoing Henry Miller's description of him,

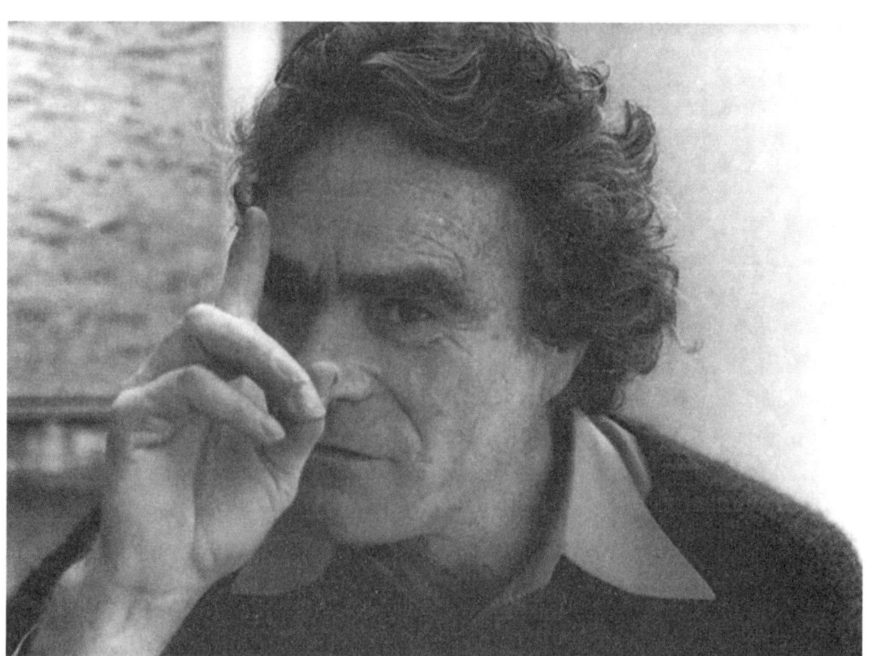

9.1
Yoran Cazac. Courtesy of Beatrice Cazac.

in the essay *The Amazing and Invariable Beauford DeLaney*, as a Buddha-like figure.[8] Similarly, the biographer Judith Thurman, a longtime friend of the Cazac family, described Yoran to me as "wild, mystical, untutored" and "a life force."[9] Indeed, even when I interviewed Cazac at the age of sixty-five, he retained the childlike yet ancient aura that matched Baldwin's description from decades earlier.

After Cazac showed me the essay Baldwin wrote about him, he told me more about that warm summer evening in 1959 when Delaney introduced them on a terrace at a café on boulevard Saint-Germain near Café de Flore. They hit it off immediately, and the three men stayed up together laughing and drinking until dawn, as they were later wont to do. Importantly, in the ensuing weeks, Baldwin and Cazac visited Delaney in his apartment in the Parisian suburb of Clamart several times, and they all spent hours talking as they looked out of his window together. This experience had a profound impact on both Cazac and Baldwin, as the latter recalled in his 1965 essay "On the Painter Beauford Delaney":

> There was a window in Beauford's house in Clamart before which we often sat—late at night, early in the morning, at noon. This window looked out on a garden; or rather it would have looked out on a garden if it had not been for the leaves and branches of a large tree which pressed directly against the window. Everything one saw from this window, then, was filtered through these leaves. And this window was a kind of universe, moaning and wailing when it rained, light of the morning, and blue as the blues when the last light of the sun departed.[10]

This description is the centerpiece of Baldwin's homage to how he "learned about light from [Delaney], the light contained in every surface, in every face." He harkens back to earlier days when they walked down the streets of Greenwich Village and he marveled at how Beauford was "*seeing* all the time," using the example of learning to stare at a leaf long enough to "discover many colours in it" to illustrate how "the reality of [Delaney's] seeing caused me to begin to see."[11] He confesses that what he was struck by then, even more so than the paintings, was Delaney's idiosyncratic way of noticing everything around him, as an artist does. That appreciation would come later, after that window in Clamart offered him a portal to understanding Delaney's midcareer transition from portraiture and figurative painting to what Stephen Wicks calls his "intensified experiments in abstraction."[12] "It was at this time that I began to see Beauford's painting in a new way," Baldwin writes, "and it was also at this time that Beauford's paintings underwent a most striking metamorphosis into freedom."[13]

It was a metamorphosis that also thrilled Cazac, who had recently undergone his own transformation, the first of many, and who would later tell me these viewings in front of Delaney's window alongside Baldwin helped to further awaken his own interest in abstraction. At eighteen years old he had produced a realist painting he hated. A friend joked that he should burn it. So Cazac did. "The matter became something extraordinary," he told me. "I had invented a process of burnt matter. It was a way of creating an aesthetic, an antipainting."[14] With their reddish underworlds bubbling up on the surface of the canvas, he called them *brûlages*. "These struck me with their violence," Baldwin wrote, "and, also, their depth. There was a violence on the surface which immediately assaulted the eye—and the surface, because the texture, or *la matière*, seemed volcanic. One sensed the danger which accompanies the unknown, or revelation. But, as one studied, or lived with, these beginner's voyages, one began to be pulled beneath the surface, into another depth, the depth, perhaps, from which a volcano erupted. Or a Cazac."[15]

These paintings, along with Cazac's further experiments with *les aquarelles*, or watercolor-absorbent paper, drew the interest of Delaney, as well as of Baldwin and notable figures in the Parisian art world, including the art historian Gaetan Picon and the gallerists Karl Flinker and Edouard Loeb. Yet despite the successes Baldwin, Delaney, and Cazac were experiencing amid the intense aesthetic and interpersonal affinities that took flight between them during this period, the triumvirate was short-lived, at least in its Paris iteration.[16] Baldwin was pulled back to the United States by the fight against racial injustice in the early 1960s, and soon enough it was Istanbul that became his place of respite and escape. Delaney, who told Cazac many times that it was "impossible to be a Black man and an abstract painter in the States," remained in Paris, where his interest in abstraction gathered velocity.[17] And by 1965 Cazac's own voyages took him from experiments with mescaline alongside Henri Michaux in Paris to the Villa Medici in Rome. There he was mentored by Balthus, who encouraged his return to figurative painting, but with an important difference that was heightened by recent visits he had made to the countryside outside of Florence. "In Tuscany, I would open a window and there *was* an abstraction," he told me, explicitly relating his epiphany there to the experience of staring out the window at Delaney's apartment in Clamart. "In nature, the depths of the hills *are* abstractions." He recognized that from the *brûlages* period onward, he had in fact always been an abstract painter. "All painting," he said, "even if it's figurative, it is abstract. Even a photograph of your face is an abstraction."

Baldwin admired Cazac's growth as an artist as he moved from his "frustrating and innumerable experiments" to "evolving a new palette, in oils and in a new landscape," in what would become his home for years to come: Tuscany. "The tension between the surface and depth in Cazac has become greater, more beautiful, and more demanding since those early, fiery, volcanic years," he writes in his essay on Cazac as it builds toward its sublime conclusion, an implicit recognition of how Cazac's paintings from this period exist at the productive intersection of figuration and abstraction: "The Tuscan landscape solicits us with stones, trees, waterfalls, figures decipherable and undecipherable, here, a house, here, a clump of trees, again a waterfall, a pilgrim, hunters, the horizon rising relentlessly, repeating itself at each new height, the landscape pulling us into it, hill upon hill, rising, rising, until the very idea of a horizon grows dim, and we are left, within ourselves, with the beauty and the inexorability of the earth, the hope and the tyranny of the sky."

By the end of the 1960s, Baldwin himself was about to enter a new era of experimentation, much of it inspired by Cazac. This included his novel *If Beale Street Could Talk* (1974), which he dedicated to Cazac and in which he dared to write from the first-person perspective of a pregnant Black woman, Tish. It also included the book-length essays *No Name in the Street* (1972), dedicated to Delaney, and *The Devil Finds Work* (1976). These two genre-bending works pushed against the conventional boundaries of nonfiction writing, weaving the personal essay with a political critique, respectively, of the failures of the civil rights movement and the racism of Hollywood films. But the backdrop for these transformations was not Paris or Istanbul: it was the sprawling farmhouse in Saint-Paul-de-Vence, France, that became Baldwin's final home in 1970 and where his perhaps most experimental work of all, *Little Man, Little Man*, was also conjured into being.

The book was written at the behest of Tejan, Baldwin's young nephew back in the States, who implored his famous uncle to write a story about him. Delaney visited frequently, and he loved to paint in the garden, a calming environment he sorely needed as his physical and mental decline gathered momentum. His 1970 *Self-Portrait* captures his emotional distress at that time even as its saturated yellows signal his effort to find solace in vibrant color.[18] Yellow, after all, was his favorite color because, as Baldwin wrote in his essay on Delaney, the light it contained "held the power to illuminate, even to redeem and reconcile and heal."[19] The use of this color continued in Delaney's final two known paintings, *Village (Saint-Paul-de-Vence)* (plate 32) and *Yellow Cyprus*, each likely composed in 1972.[20] Both aptly illustrate his effort to find peace in Baldwin's new home even as the voices and hallucinations closed in on him and his "memory banks" became, as his friend Charley Boggs told Leeming, "depleted."[21]

Delaney was slated to contribute the illustrations to *Little Man, Little Man* and had even completed a handful of preliminary sketches. But by late 1973 the damage to his physical and mental health had proved to be irreversible. He could scarcely remember who anyone was, except Baldwin and perhaps one or two others. In 1974 he had to be institutionalized at Saint Anne's Hospital just outside of Paris. After a ten-year hiatus, Baldwin and Cazac had reconnected in the early 1970s, and now they both lamented Delaney's poor state. It was decided that Cazac would pick up where Delaney had left off and illustrate the book himself, and they would dedicate the book to their mutual friend. No doubt Delaney's and Cazac's shared interest in light and the relationship between abstract and figurative painting, as well as the memory of their intense conversations in front of Delaney's window in Clamart, helped convince Baldwin that the book would still bear the imprint of his mentor's lessons.

Baldwin felt that because Cazac had never been to the United States, let alone Harlem, this lack of knowledge would actually allow him to "see" the Harlem neighborhood with the fresh eyes that Delaney had taught them to value. Nonetheless, Baldwin still showed Cazac a number of sources, including *The Black Book* (1974), a compendium of images from African American history that featured everything from patents by Black inventors to posters from Black Hollywood films.[22] He also gave him photographs of the neighborhood and his family as models for the characters. These sources, along with Baldwin's conversational descriptions, allowed Cazac to begin work on capturing a Harlem he had never seen or experienced in person. He finished a full draft of the book in wax crayon (see figure 9.2) before realizing he needed to work with pencil and watercolor instead, as they would better allow him to channel Delaney's vision and, as he put it, "imagine the unimaginable" (see figure 9.3).

The final published version was a series of illustrations characterized by sketchy lines and bleeding colors, from the faces of neighbors sitting on stoops to the streetscapes of Lenox Avenue. It was Harlem and it was not Harlem, figurative *and* abstract—for somehow it was also Saint-Paul-de-Vence, and Tuscany, too, and also none of them at all. Or rather, it was a Harlem reimagined and made strangely, unexpectedly beautiful. Baldwin and Cazac enacted Delaney's abiding lesson in the art of seeing differently by asking readers to look through the metaphorical "window" of *Little Man, Little Man* in order to revalue and find beauty in what had been routinely cast aside as marginal, irrelevant, even ugly by dominant culture—namely the varied lives, landscapes, and languages of Black children in Harlem. And no wonder Baldwin chose Cazac to join him for this task. Baldwin's descriptions of the two artists—Delaney and Cazac—in fact echo one another, showing their shared artistic perspectives. Baldwin wrote about Delaney, "For Beauford's work leads the inner and the outer eye, directly and inexorably, to a new confrontation with reality."[23] And about Cazac, he wrote, "The artist is probably the only real visionary because what he sees is real. He helps us to see what we have always known. He leads us back to reality again. So we can endure it, rejoice in it, and, even, begin to change it."[24] Both artists predicated their work on a vision of "looking again" and blending engagement with real life with an abstraction that causes us to see that reality anew.

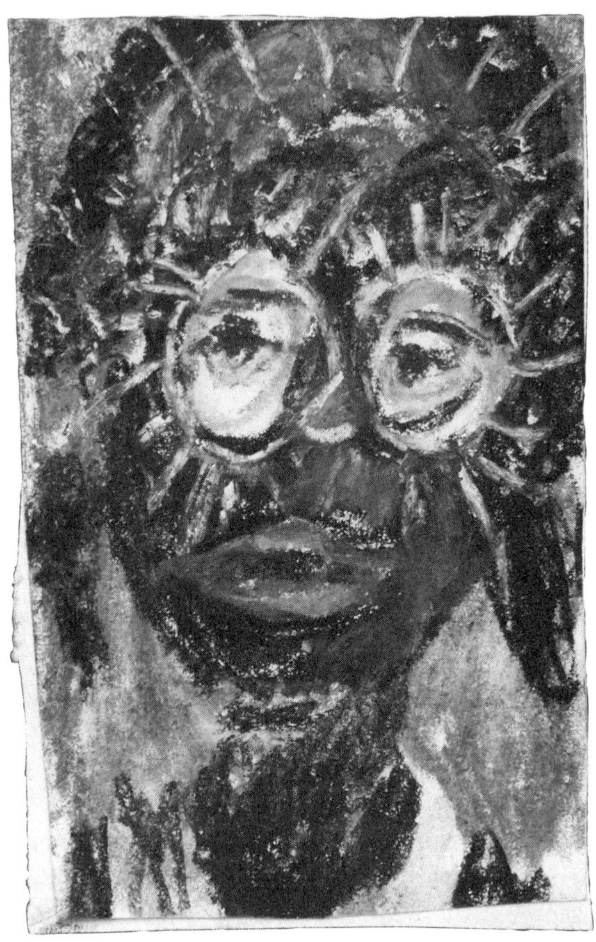

9.2

Yoran Cazac, crayon drawing of Blinky. Courtesy of Beatrice Cazac and Nicholas Boggs.

Blinky and the Double Vision of Looking Again

James Baldwin very much seems to have understood that the book he wrote with Cazac would illustrate what has by now become a famous anecdote of Delaney's tutelage: the story of how, when he was a teenager standing on Broadway, Baldwin was told by Delaney to look down at a gutter. When he did and saw nothing, Delaney told him to "look again." Then Baldwin saw

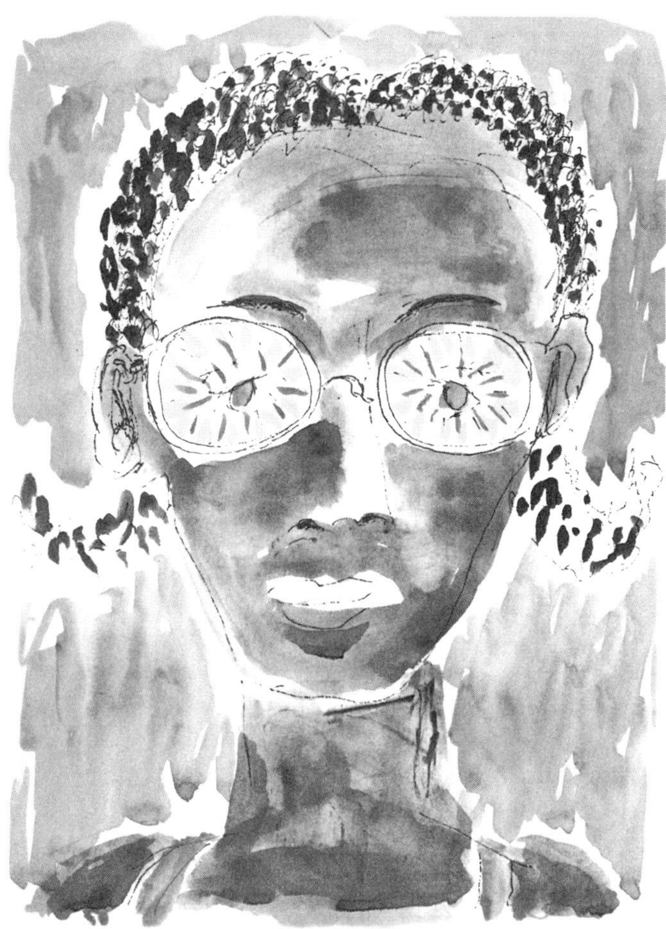

9.3

Yoran Cazac, watercolor drawing of Blinky, published in James Baldwin, *Little Man, Little Man: A Story of Childhood* (New York: Dial, 1976). Courtesy of Beatrice Cazac and Nicholas Boggs. Source: Duke University Press.

something spectacular: the reflection of buildings "in the oil moving like mercury in the black water of the gutter," distorted and radiant.[25] "Looking again" would become a central theme and reading strategy in *Little Man, Little Man*.

The transformative possibilities inherent in "looking again" surface most saliently in *Little Man, Little Man* in the character of Blinky, an eight-year-old Black girl whose window-like eyeglasses "blink" in yellow hues reminiscent of Delaney's paintings (see figure 9.3). In addition to exemplifying, as

I have argued elsewhere, a surprising model for the possibilities of gender performance and Black female masculinity, she clearly embodies the gift of what Baldwin, in the course of retelling Leeming the story of the puddle on Broadway, called Delaney's "double vision."[26] Indeed, to blink is precisely to "look again," and in so doing to see differently and usually more truly. As the children move through Harlem together, playing ball, skipping rope, and running errands for neighbors, Blinky increasingly acts as a surrogate older sister for the younger boys, four-year-old TJ and seven-year-old WT. At first her eyeglasses are a source of skepticism for TJ, since he can't see out of them and some "white folks at school" bought them for her. (This is quite possibly a reference to Black "double-consciousness" as articulated by W. E. B. Du Bois.) But several pages later, TJ is already coming to understand that Blinky's "own skin color changing all the time. She always make TJ think of the color of sunlight when your eyes closed and the sun inside your eyes. When your eyes is open, she the color of real black coffee, early in the morning."[27]

Elsewhere it is noted that other characters are "the color of tea after you put in the milk," "the color of chocolate cake with no icing on it," and "the color of peaches and brown sugar." This attention to difference within the category of blackness, to the range and spectrum of shades and hues that fall outside of and complicate the binary of black and white upon which racism depends, is central to the radical content of *Little Man, Little Man*. Indeed, TJ's dawning realization of the problem of defining the color "black" echoes lessons Baldwin learned from Delaney in Greenwich Village and later in Clamart: that "to stare at a leaf long enough, to try to apprehend the leaf, was to discover many colours in it; and though black had been described to me as the absence of light, it became very clear to me that if this were true, we would never have been able to see the colour; black."[28] Or, as Cazac told me when describing his use of color and light in the book, and why it features characters whose faces often appear only partly painted: "In the full light, no one is fully black or fully white."

These earlier scenes of instruction between Delaney, Baldwin, and Cazac help us better understand the particularities of the book's radical literary form. For not only does *Little Man, Little Man* give readers a way of seeing the world from a rearranged angle of vision attuned to variations of color and depths of experience usually overlooked and even suppressed. It also insists that there are messages that we learn early and that intervention must be aimed at a child's understanding, even if written for an "adult audience." This is why they called it a "child's story *for* adults" (emphasis added). The book encourages readers to see *through* the double vision of the child's perspective. As Margo Natalie Crawford has suggested, the watercolor wash makes it seem to readers that they are wearing Blinky's eyeglasses that make everything look as though it were rained on, creating what she calls "a new way of seeing that occurs when people try to move past the realism of race in order to find the language and pictures that race does not name."[29] Often saturated in Cazac's evocation of Delaney's beloved yellows, the book teaches readers to "look again" and see the beauty of Harlem as well the social ills depicted in the book—including police brutality, drug addiction, alcoholism, and the racist distortions of the mass media—from a Black child's perspective, which, crucially, as Jennifer DeVere Brody and I have argued elsewhere, is not innocent.[30]

Finally, and perhaps most poignantly, the book also invites us to see the world from the perspective of arguably the most important member of its intended audience: the man it was dedicated to, Delaney himself. Leeming told me that in his final years, as his body shriveled and his mannerisms became increasingly childlike, Delaney became "the little man of Saint-Paul-de-Vence."[31] Baldwin would scoop him up and carry *him*, a reversal of their lifelong relationship in which Baldwin called him his "spiritual father." And in 1985, six years after Delaney's death and two years before his own, Baldwin told Leeming in Saint-Paul-de-Vence, "Watching Beauford all those years, looking and seeing, even on the edge of madness, down here going mad, he still *saw*. And when he could no longer do that, he stopped painting."[32] But fortunately for us, Cazac, in Delaney's stead, did not. On the contrary, drawing on the elder painter's enduring lessons, he and Baldwin created a work of art they hoped would lift the dying man's spirits as he languished in his hospital room. They yearned to return to him, if only momentarily, the gift of the double vision he had bequeathed to them in front of that window in Clamart, where everything was "filtered" through those rain-soaked leaves—"light of the morning" and evening sky "blue as the blues"—and which *Little Man, Little Man*, by challenging readers to see the world differently and anew, now makes available to us all. For "the beauty of [Delaney's] triumph," as Baldwin wrote, "and the proof that it is a real one, is that he makes it ours."[33]

NOTES

1 Julius Lester, "Little Man, Little Man," review of *Little Man, Little Man: A Story of Childhood* by James Baldwin and Yoran Cazac, *New York Times Book Review*, September 4, 1977, 22.

2 "Little Man, Little Man: A Story of Childhood," *Kirkus Reviews*, June 15, 2016, https://www.kirkusreviews.com/book-reviews/james-baldwin/little-man-little-man-baldwin/.

3 David Canfield, "The 50 Most Anticipated Books of 2018," *Entertainment Weekly*, December 26, 2017, https://ew.com/books/most-anticipated-books-2018/.

4 Alexandra Alter, "A James Baldwin Book, Forgotten and Overlooked for Four Decades, Gets Another Life," *New York Times*, August 20, 2018, https://www.nytimes.com/2018/08/20/books/review/james-baldwin-little-man-picture-book.html.

5 See Nicholas Boggs, "Of Mimicry and (*Little Man Little*) Man: Towards a Queersighted Theory of Black Childhood," in *James Baldwin Now*, ed. Dwight McBride (New York: New York University Press, 1999), 122–60; Hortense Spillers, introduction to "James Baldwin," special issue, *African American Review* 46, no. 4 (Winter 2013): 563–72; Nicholas Boggs, "Baldwin and Yoran Cazac's 'Child's Story for Adults,'" in *The Cambridge Companion to James Baldwin*, ed. Michele Elam (New York: Cambridge University Press, 2015), 118–33; Michele Elam, "Baldwin's Boys," *CR: The New Centennial Review* 16, no. 2 (2016): 17–30; Magdalena Zaborowska, *Me and My House: James Baldwin's Last Decade in France* (Durham, NC: Duke University Press, 2018), 258–60; Nicholas Boggs and Jennifer DeVere Brody, introduction to *Little Man, Little Man: A Story of Childhood*, by James Baldwin and Yoran Cazac, ed. Nicholas Boggs and Jennifer DeVere Brody (Durham, NC: Duke University Press, 2018), xv–xxii; and Kyle DeCoste, "Music All up and down the Street: Listening to Childhood in James Baldwin's *Little Man, Little Man*," *Journal of Popular Music Studies* 31, no. 3 (2019): 57–72.

6 James Baldwin, untitled essay, 1977, "Collaboration with James Baldwin," Yoran Cazac, https://yorancazac.com/#baldwin (accessed July 6, 2022).

7 James Baldwin, interview with David Leeming, Saint-Paul-de-Vence, France, June 24, 1985, in the David Leeming Collection of James Baldwin Research, James Weldon Johnson Collection in the Yale Collection of American Literature, JWJ MSS 172, b.1 39900210488627l, Beinecke Rare Book and Manuscript Library, New Haven, CT.

8 David Leeming, *Amazing Grace: A Life of Beauford Delaney* (New York: Oxford University Press, 1998), x.

9 Judith Thurman, interview with the author, fall 2002, New York City.

10 James Baldwin, "On the Painter Beauford Delaney," *Transition* 4, no. 18 (1965); reprinted in *James Baldwin: Collected Essays*, ed. Toni Morrison (New York: Library of America, 1998), 721.

11 Baldwin, "On the Painter Beauford Delaney," 720.

12 Stephen C. Wicks, "Beauford Delaney's 'Metamorphosis into Freedom,'" in *Beauford Delaney and James Baldwin: Through the Unusual*

Door, ed. Stephen C. Wicks (Knoxville: University of Tennessee Press, 2020), 25. My essay is influenced by Wicks's keen insights into the importance of the Clamart scene in particular, as well as his attention to puddles, windows, and other transparent, reflective surfaces in general for understanding Delaney's development as an artist.

13 Baldwin, "On the Painter Beauford Delaney," 721.

14 Yoran Cazac, interview with author, May 17, 2003, Paris.

15 Baldwin, untitled essay.

16 See David Leeming, *James Baldwin: A Biography* (New York: Henry Holt, 1994), 319.

17 Cazac, interview with author.

18 Beauford Delaney, *Self-Portrait*, 1970, Collection of David Leeming.

19 Baldwin, "On the Painter Beauford Delaney," 721.

20 Beauford Delaney, *Yellow Cyprus*, ca. 1972, Clark Atlanta University Museum. Both *Village (Saint-Paul-de-Vence)* and *Yellow Cyprus* were given to the Clark Atlanta University Museum in the bequest of James Baldwin.

21 Leeming, *Amazing Grace*, 192.

22 *The Black Book* was largely assembled by Toni Morrison when she was an editor at Random House, though only her coeditors were named in the publication. See Harris et al., *The Black Book*.

23 Baldwin, "On the Painter Beauford Delaney," 721.

24 Baldwin, untitled essay.

25 See Baldwin, "On the Painter Beauford Delaney"; and Jordan Elbrably, "James Baldwin: The Art of Fiction No. 78," *Paris Review* 91 (Spring 1984), https://www.theparisreview.org/interviews/2994/the-art-of-fiction-no-78-james-baldwin.

26 Baldwin, interview with David Leeming.

27 James Baldwin and Yoran Cazac, *Little Man, Little Man: A Story of Childhood* (London: Michael Joseph, 1976), 13.

28 Baldwin, "On the Painter Beauford Delaney," 720.

29 Margo Natalie Crawford's unpublished essay, "Adding Watercolors to *The Black Book*: The 'Eye-Glasses' Blinking between James Baldwin and Yoran Cazac," and our conversations about it have influenced my understanding of the use of watercolor in the book.

30 See Boggs and Brody, introduction to *Little Man, Little Man.*

31 David Leeming, interview with author, November 10, 2005, New York City.

32 Baldwin, interview with David Leeming.

33 Baldwin, "On the Painter Beauford Delaney," 721.

TEN

Singed Innocence

Baldwin, Delaney, and the Problematic Black Child

Robert F. Reid-Pharr

Blame it on the times; blame it on indecision, urgency, resilience, and hope; blame it on wars and rumors of war; blame it on the never-ending, never-satiated pessimism of the American people; blame it on the bright cold washing through the room in which I write; blame it on whatever you will. But somehow I cannot stop thinking of fire. Fire is the rapid oxidation of a base material in the exothermic chemical process of combustion that releases heat and light while radically altering the original reactive material, such that in the most extreme examples, only smoke and ash reference the essence of the thing burned. Fire is elemental but not substantial. We perceive it through its effects, not its essence. It lacks material, body, and constituency. It cannot be stopped or even exactly slowed, but only extinguished or blotted out. We can never directly approach it. Our understanding of its status, its "thingness," instead comes largely from observations of infinitely slower oxidative processes, such as digestion or rusting. Still, even with all the vagueness and inelegance with which we attempt to draw near this fundamental process, African Americans—intellectuals and laypersons alike—have obsessively returned to images of flame and burning in our efforts to name not so much "the self" as the inexplicability of our awkward identity, the vulgarity of a people stretched across time, space, ideology, and culture.

One imagines that it was damp on that day in 1959 when James Baldwin was first introduced to the young painter Yoran Cazac on the Left Bank of Paris. Baldwin (age thirty-five) and Cazac (age twenty-one) were both refugees of sorts. Baldwin was escaping the smugly comfortable white supremacy of postwar America; Cazac, the tight conservatism of staunchly Catholic central France. Both had come under the tutelage of the woefully undervalued modernist painter Beauford Delaney, the person who first recognized in an adolescent Baldwin the sparks of the adult genius that would soon come to captivate the globe. Delaney and Baldwin met each other in New York's Greenwich Village in 1940, when Baldwin was sixteen years old and beginning his last year as a boy preacher. "Beauford was the first walking, living proof, for me, that a black man could be an artist," he later remembered.[1] It is telling (remarkable, really) that the individual who most decidedly encouraged Baldwin as an artist, the only person the maestro ever saddled with the label "mentor," was not a writer but a painter, a man obsessed with processes of seeing and visual representation, processes that he helped Baldwin to understand and to capture in his own work.

More important still, it was Delaney who began training Baldwin to see, to force himself to look beyond the expected in order to perceive the dynamism, the life, of the scenes and objects that met his gaze. In a now famous remembrance of a day spent with the artist in the winter of 1940, Baldwin relates the tale of standing on a corner, carefully avoiding the puddled water shimmering next to the curb. Delaney told Baldwin to look down and tell him what he saw. Baldwin complied but grasped nothing. Delaney told him to look again. This time Baldwin recognized the complexity of what the older artist was trying to teach. He saw "oil moving like black mercury in the water," creating a reflection that could not adequately reveal the literal concreteness of the buildings standing above them but that could, in fact, help demonstrate both the instability of those structures and the shocking amputations and excisions of perception that we enact in order to ignore and cover over that instability.[2]

Given Baldwin's apprenticeship with Delaney, it surely came as a surprise to no one that he immediately recognized an intellectual kinship with Yoran Cazac. The younger artist represented a sort of carnivalesque image of Baldwin's teenaged self. Cazac also had become another of Delaney's protégés, and he was equally concerned with attempting to represent movement, process, surprise, and difficulty in his art. However, unlike a young Baldwin standing on a garbage-choked Manhattan corner contemplating the complexity of dirty water, Cazac was concerned with the possibilities opened up through the use and consideration of fire, especially the *brûlage* technique favored by the surrealists. Taking its name from the French nominative of *brûler* (to burn), the process involves various forms of singeing, flaring, scorching—or, in the case of photography, the heating of glass-plate negatives to the point at which the image begins to decompose. *Brûlage* was part of the arsenal of techniques that allowed for the production of what the surrealists named "automatism," the destruction of a clear connection between an object and the representation of that object. At the same time, coming to international prominence in the periods between the First and Second World Wars, the ruined nature of *brûlage* art—its ugliness—reminded shocked and disturbed viewers of the oily violence and the churning of human bodies that underwrote and suffused the whole of so-called European high culture and that continues to do so today.

I suggest that what Baldwin began to understand as he consumed Cazac's early experiments with *brûlage*—as he fingered the rough, puckered edges of canvases intentionally "ruined" by exposure to heat, smoke, and fire—was that he might attempt similar deformations in his own writing. Baldwin's introduction to Cazac took place during an interstitial period in his career in which the economy and precision of his first two brief and diamond-hard novels, *Go Tell It on the Mountain* (1953) and *Giovanni's Room* (1956), gave way not only to the aptly named collection of essays *The Fire Next Time* (1963) but also to his creased and rambling 1962 work *Another Country*, a text that came under sustained criticism for being unfocused, antidiegetic, preachy, and yet somehow morally vague. The perfection of Baldwin's early career had been spoiled. He had become, we are told, too concerned with the demonstration of his considerable style, the cascade of words describing mood and mise-en-scène, the unrelenting sermonizing that never seemed to reveal a properly established center.

In the process of mounting something like a defense of Baldwin I would argue that what we see in the mature writer is his reiteration of the lessons first learned by the side of Beauford Delaney on a damp Manhattan sidewalk and relearned as he made his acquaintance with Yoran Cazac. In the many portraits that Delaney did of Baldwin, we see an absolute refusal of any flatness of surface. In Delaney's capable hands, Baldwin's face is a landing for all color. The paint is thickly visible on the canvas, the drawing childish and carnivalesque. The personality and ego of the artist are ever visible; the viewer is never invited to forget that what they are witnessing is *artificial* creation. Each image that Delaney mounts is one in which the unnamed logics of our barely examined techniques of seeing are made visible.

This is evident in Delaney's work *Dark Rapture*, his first portrait of Baldwin, painted in 1941 (plate 1). While the piece is not a *brûlage*, it certainly is meant to evoke painterly stress. The surfeit of color is wrong. The intensely drawn angularity of the model's body is wrong. The lack of precise distinction between surfaces (bed, boy, couch, tree, floor, sky) is wrong. More telling still, the mottling of the model's skin, the imprecision (or is it *over*precision?) of the artist's palette suggests a thing that is falling apart. Baldwin appears as so much cooked meat, meat made more delectable in the process. And lest his viewers ignore or forget the seriousness of the experiments that Delaney is attempting, he resolves the painting with one bit of certainty, that spot of dark black-blue-green color between the boy's thighs, representing the possibility, the story, of genitalia.

The Black child is an impossibility. Though it is infrequently noted, the development in Europe and the Americas during the seventeenth and eighteenth centuries of the concept of a distinct period of life known as childhood coincided directly not only with the production of racialist thought, but also with European colonization and the Atlantic slave trade. The fantasy of an unmarked white childhood rested—and rests—directly on the buying, selling, killing, maiming, raping, and slaving of Africans, Asians, and the many Indigenous populations of both the Atlantic and the Pacific. We know that slave traders preferred the importation of young persons, such that at least a quarter of the individuals transported on ships plying the Atlantic trade were adolescents and young children. We know that particularly in South America and the Caribbean, harsh working conditions, lack of proper nutrition and housing, and the prevalence of disease produced an exceedingly high mortality rate among the enslaved population, such that the continual importation of newly enslaved persons was a necessity that skewed the age ratio on the American plantations even further. Part of the reason, in fact, that Americans and Europeans continue to be so enamored of images of old slaves, Mammy and Uncle Tom, is that these types of individuals were so rare. I must rush to say, however, that I am in no hurry either to salvage Black childhood or to mourn our loss of innocence. Instead, I want to make plain how we *see* so-called childhood, or more to the point, how we can burn and deform the media that allow for that process of "seeing" so that we might begin to wean ourselves from some of the clumsier lies about how our various cultures are structured and maintained.

The remarkable 1976 collaboration between James Baldwin and Yoran Cazac, the children's book *Little Man, Little Man*, forces us into this process. Called by Baldwin a "child's story written for adults," the book concerns the lives of three children: four-year-old TJ, the narrator of the text, and his friends seven-year-old WT and eight-year-old Blinky. It also continues the aesthetic politics that Baldwin and Cazac helped each other to develop and that had been so forcefully and skillfully nurtured by Delaney, to whom the book is dedicated. *Little Man, Little Man* is precious largely because it demonstrates so clearly Baldwin's deeply sophisticated understanding of the complicated relationship between visuality and language. It is a work that troubles not only the boundaries surrounding "children's literature" but also those that demarcate the preciously clumsy concept of "the child," for which so many tears have been shed and so much violence enacted. At the same time, the experimental—and indeed political—nature of the text proved to be its undoing. The book went largely unnoticed after it was published, eliciting only one tepid review, and it quickly went out of print, coming back into the public purview in 2018 only through the efforts of the texts' editors, Nicholas Boggs and Jennifer Devere Brody.[3]

For his part, Yoran Cazac realized with remarkable clarity the unbelievably complicated visual codes that he and Baldwin wanted to represent in their art. In particular, he suggests that part of what we euphemistically label "maturation" is, in fact, a process by which children are forced to give up on more involved modes of viewing the world and articulating what they see in favor of methods that are less elastic but more serviceable in communities obsessed with the strict policing of distinctions of race, class, and gender. This fact is made particularly evident in the character of Blinky. Though Blinky is described as a girl, that label is always rendered suspect and held in abeyance: "One thing TJ understand about Blinky. She don't like nothing that wears dresses. She don't hardly never wear a dress herself. She always in blue jeans. Look like she do everything she can to be a boy. But she ain't no boy. Blinky is a girl. But she don't like girls."[4]

The gender trouble that Blinky represents has nothing to do with identity. It is instead entirely a matter of the visual, and most especially the sartorial.

The jeans, and what those jeans represent, are the problems. Blinky wants to play, be rambunctious, run errands for neighbors, eat candy, dance, act the fool, and occasionally fight, all of which are pleasurable activities for both males and females, children and adults. The exigencies of what Cedric Robinson has called racial capitalism, but which I will call raced and gendered capitalism, are such that the enforcement of class/race/gender distinctions is key to the production of what we name "childhood."[5] Cazac and Baldwin's collaborative insights, however, suggest that they recognize that these distinctions have no particular depth. They are entirely matters of surface and style. TJ is wrong in his assessment. Blinky evinces no actual hostility toward girls. She does, however, forthrightly resist the imposed trappings of girlhood. She especially hates the tight skirts and the insubstantial high-heeled shoes reserved for females, commenting on Miss Lee, wife of the superintendent of TJ's building and the undisputed beauty of the block, "Here come Miss Lee. Look like she can't hardly walk."[6]

There are, however, consequences associated with this resistance— sometimes serious and even violent consequences for nonconforming children like Blinky. Her name comes from the fact that she has poor vision and wears thick glasses. She sees differently, and that fact initiates a cascade of anxiety in both adults and children. Cazac's drawing of the child is remarkable. He expends almost no effort representing the glasses as prosthetics separate from the fleshy reality of Blinky's body. Instead, the devices seem to be embedded in her face, not so much covering or shielding her eyes as overtaking them. "She say she can't see without them," Baldwin writes. "Maybe that true, if she say so. But TJ put them on one time and he couldn't see nothing with them on. He couldn't see across the street. Everything looked like it was rained on. So TJ ain't too sure about Blinky. It was some white folks at school bought them glasses. If *he* can't see out them, how *she* going to see out them? And she older than he is. She eight years old. She ought to know better: But she a girl."[7] Baldwin and Cazac stretch the contradictions of this character to their extremes. It is impossible to decide whether TJ's words are simple evidence of childish phobias regarding disability or if he is, in fact, right to be suspicious of the corrections given to his friend by unnamed "white folks at school." And of course all of this is made that much more complicated by the spectacle of Blinky's ill-fitting girlhood. "But she a girl," TJ complains, suggesting that her gender is a defect, one that troubles both her cognition and her good common sense.

It may seem that I have moved quite a distance from consideration of the images of fire and singeing with which I began this essay. Yet this question of the utility of heat and flame is, in fact, omnipresent in *Little Man, Little Man*. In the portrait of Blinky, Cazac's palette is full of oranges, yellows, reds, and pinks. Blinky's eyes are rendered as large iridescent globes, looking almost exactly like a child's drawings of the sun. Moreover, the beautiful Miss Lee is married to Mr. Man, the janitor of TJ's building, who lives with his wife in a basement apartment *next to the furnace*. "Sometime he take them down the basement where the furnace is and he tell them stories and he give them ginger snaps and the furnace keep huffing and puffing . . . and it get real red hot and Mr. Man grin with all them teeth and it real nice then," Baldwin writes.[8] This image of the red-hot furnace obviously evokes Richard Wright's 1940 classic novel *Native Son*, in which the work's antihero, Bigger Thomas, disposes of the dismembered body of his employer's daughter, Mary Dalton, in the flames of the family's boiler.

Again, however, what most shocks—if not exactly surprises—is Baldwin's own deft iteration of this motif. In his novel *Another Country*, published in 1962, Baldwin reaches his stride as a novelist, introducing his reader to the character Eric, an actor born into a well-to-do white southern family, who escaped his isolation by seeking solace with his parents' servants, Grace and her husband, Henry. Henry was a man who drank too much and who made the furnace room his particular zone of escape and renewal. When young Eric encounters Henry crying alone in the heat and gloom, he throws himself into the man's arms, unleashing a confused set of emotions slipping between, fear, rage, and a not yet named—or nameable—desire. "It was the first time he had felt a man's arms around him," Baldwin writes. "The first time he had felt the chest and belly of a man. . . . He had been terribly frightened, but he had not, as the years were to prove, been frightened enough."[9]

In the final scene of *Little Man, Little Man*, TJ, WT, and Blinky are playing outside when a bottle falls from the roof and shatters on the pavement in front of them. WT steps on a piece of glass and severely cuts his foot, his shoes so worn that there are holes in the soles. The children then retreat to the basement of TJ's building, seeking the assistance of Mr. Man. In the action that follows we find that it is Mr. Man's wife, Miss Lee, who has dropped the bottle from the roof, a place to which she retreats to drink. The scene undercuts readers' probable assumptions that the couple's relationship is lovely and a model for others. The scene in fact reveals that Miss Lee, the grand beauty, is also an alcoholic. Her husband, meanwhile, is at once kind and severe, warning her in front of the children that "I been telling you about that roof. One of these days I'm going to have to put you away again."[10] Once more, a man is shown to police the behavior and comportment of a woman—a policing that Blinky, dressed in her jeans and thick glasses, attempts to resist. Still, it is Miss Lee who brings the scene back into order, arriving with peroxide, iodine, and bandages to tend WT's wounds. She ends by offering all the children glasses of Pepsi-Cola and laughs as Blinky and TJ dance for WT to cheer him up. Finally, it is Ms. Lee who first uses the phrase "Little Man, Little Man," her hands caressing WTs face and wiping away, if not extinguishing, his fear.

Little Man, Little Man is an unruly piece of fiction. It is scorched and flaming. The form of the children's books to which it refers has been warped, demonstrating the ways in which such texts are more often than not wholly inadequate to the needs not only of Black children but of all children. I suspect, in fact, that the work was so poorly received when it was first published because it does not shy away from representations of children in danger. WT lives with his junkie older brother and a single mother who is always working. Blinky lives with an aunt who took her in after the girl was abandoned and orphaned. And while TJ lives securely with loving parents, he still witnesses drug use, drunkenness, and the killing of a man by police, all of which provoke bouts of sleeplessness as he stares into the darkness afraid that his parents will be taken from him.

This is not to say, however, that the book is in any way macabre. Instead, Baldwin and Cazac refuse the idea that there is a necessary opposition between danger and hope, childhood fun and inebriation. On the contrary, they opt for what I call a "singed aesthetic," in which the beauty of the story that they tell is altogether caught up with threat and vulnerability. Those of us interested in modern culture often fail to promote—and provoke—the same flat-footed, dry-eyed bravery and decisiveness in our work that we see in *Little Man, Little Man*. The critic who reads this brief and wondrous work is reminded immediately of just how safe and stale so much of our literature, and especially our literary criticism, actually is. The burn of the text is that it at once shames and challenges us. It insists that artists and intellectuals of all types would be well served by confronting and deforming their most cherished conceits and methods, breaking away from a need to reproduce pretty narratives. We are invited to a different path, to seek ways to tear, scorch, scratch, overcook, and otherwise warp our materials and techniques. Clean bits of paper and pristinely acceptable forms of thought might allow one's works to be seen and perhaps published, but they cannot assure the validity, the power, or the ethics of what one has to say.

1 James Baldwin, "The Price of the Ticket," in *The Price of the Ticket: Collected Non-Fiction, 1948–1945* (New York: St. Martin's, 1985), xi.

2 James Baldwin, "On the Painter Beauford Delaney," *Transition* 4, no. 18 (1965); reprinted in *James Baldwin: Collected Essays*, ed. Toni Morrison (New York: Library of America, 1998), 720.

3 In addition to the introduction by Brody and Boggs to the 2018 edition of *Little Man, Little Man*, see Nicholas Boggs, "Of Mimicry and (*Little Man Little*) Man: James Baldwin and the Politics of Race and Sexuality," in *James Baldwin Now*, ed. Dwight A. McBride (New York: New York University Press, 1999), 122–60; Nicholas Boggs, "Baldwin and Yoran Cazac's Child Story for Adults," in *The Cambridge Companion to James Baldwin*, ed. Michele Elam (New York: Cambridge University Press, 2015), 118–32.

4 James Baldwin and Yoran Cazac, *Little Man, Little Man: A Story of Childhood*, ed. Nicholas Boggs and Jennifer DeVere Brody (1976; repr., Durham, NC: Duke University Press, 2018), 31.

5 See Cedric J. Robinson, *Black Marxism: The Making of a Black Radical Tradition* (1983; repr., Chapel Hill: University of North Carolina Press, 2000).

6 Baldwin and Cazac, *Little Man, Little Man*, 31.

7 Baldwin and Cazac, *Little Man, Little Man*, 8.

8 Baldwin and Cazac, *Little Man, Little Man*, 6.

9 James Baldwin, *Another Country* (New York: Vintage Books, 1962), 198.

10 Baldwin and Cazac, *Little Man, Little Man*, 89.

PART III

Visibility, Performance, Abstraction

ELEVEN

Baldwin and Delaney

The Politics and Performance of Black Sight

Indie A. Choudhury

A single eye in monochrome grayscale looks out from a black face occupying the April 1964 cover of *Playbill*.[1] This image illustrates the original stage production of James Baldwin's play *Blues for Mister Charlie* (1964), which opened the same month at the ANTA Theatre on Broadway (see figure 11.1).[2] The white typography of Baldwin's title floats dramatically against the black face, but the eye remains the arresting feature of the artwork, challenging the viewer to return its gaze. It may seem a curious image for a play about the fatal consequences of racialized seeing in the civil rights era, but *Blues for Mister Charlie* is also about the paradoxical desire for, and disavowal of, Black sight. In his second play, Baldwin utilizes the dramatic genre to enact the conjunction between sight, visibility, and performance in representing Black subjectivity.

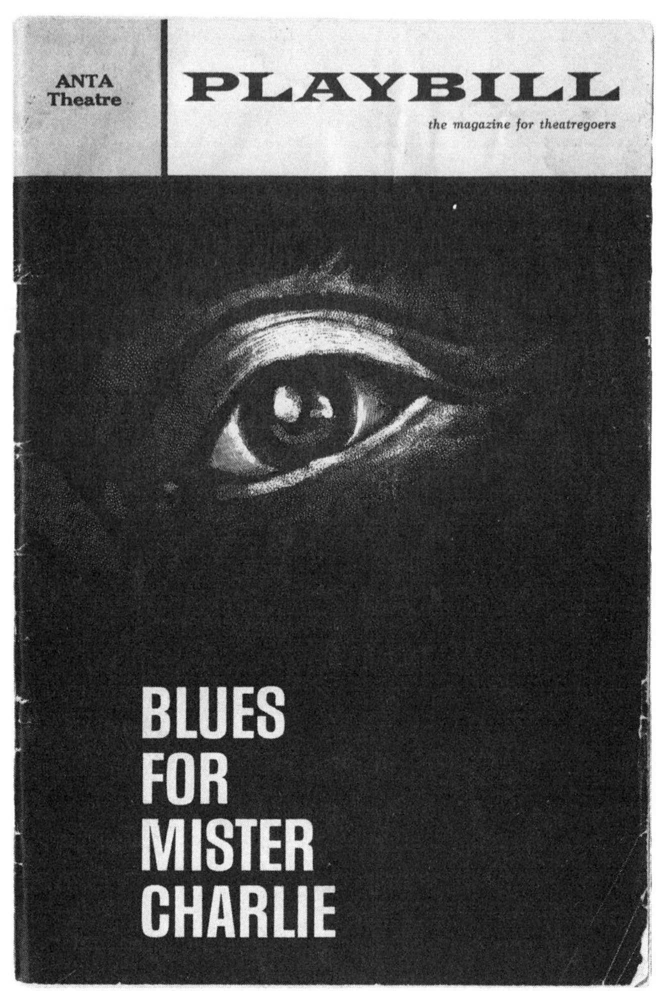

11.1

Playbill cover for James Baldwin's *Blues for Mister Charlie*, produced at the ANTA Theatre, New York, April 23–August 29, 1964. Used by permission. All rights reserved, Playbill Inc.

Baldwin not only shared this convergence of ideas with Beauford Delaney, but in many ways, it may have been inspired by his friend and mentor. Delaney's self-portrait eye studies made in 1962 (plates 14a and 14b) parallel the *Playbill* cover, in that Delaney's single eye is the only feature of the sketches, exemplifying the importance of sight within his own oeuvre. Eyes are a central feature in many of Delaney's portraits, often accentuated by thick outlining and the additional contrast of bright white pigment.[3] In the 1962 sketches, it is Delaney's subjective eye that draws one's attention. As is common in self-portraiture, rather than viewing an object of the artist's gaze, Delaney is both the subject and the object of the work. Both the *Playbill* artwork for Baldwin's *Blues for Mister Charlie* and Delaney's 1962 eye sketches serve as visual synecdoches for the politics of "seeing" configured by the performance of Black sight.

My interest in this essay lies in the ways that Delaney and Baldwin conflated sight and visibility and how performance became the functional apparatus that mediated the relationship between these modes. Performance offered the opportunity not just to perceive Blackness but also to render it visible—to consider, in Baldwin's terms, the evidence of things not seen that constituted Black existence. It signified a mode of self-determination conjoined with an act of mediation. In this sense, performativity became a way to both navigate and displace already given codes and stereotypes about the expectations associated with race and gender—notably, with Black male sexuality.[4]

Baldwin recalled of Delaney on their first meeting in 1940, "He had the most extraordinary eyes I'd ever seen," eyes that had the capacity to at once perceive and apprehend completely the fifteen-year-old Baldwin through "an instant X-ray."[5] It was this capacity, as also conveyed in Delaney's artistic practice that, for Baldwin, "leads the inner and outer eye, inexorably and directly to a new confrontation with reality" and that enabled his own "inner eye" to be activated.[6] More specifically, Baldwin linked Delaney's almost extrasensory sight to the growth of his own visual acuity in the same year that *Blues for Mister Charlie* was published and first performed, stating, "He is *seeing* all the time; and the reality of his seeing caused me to begin to see."[7]

The reality of Delaney's seeing offered Baldwin a new apprehension of Blackness. This is demonstrated in an evocative passage Baldwin wrote as part of an introduction to Delaney's 1964 exhibition at the Galerie Lambert in Paris: "Though black had been described to me as the absence of light, it became very clear to me that if this were true, we would never have been able to see the colour; black: the light is trapped in it and struggles upward, rather like the grass pushing upward through cement."[8] Baldwin's full introduction is an extraordinarily beautiful movement of seeing blackness through a journey—not of darkness seeking light, but of an inner black light striving to be fully visible and free. In Baldwin's statement, the grass pushing upward functions as both a metaphor for Delaney's and Baldwin's own evolution toward visibility as artists and as a larger allegory for how

Black life might see and be seen. Baldwin's introduction culminates in an image of Delaney's "metamorphosis to freedom" that evokes continual transformation and, significantly, resists the notion of fixed identities.[9] In citing Delaney's freedom, Baldwin alludes to all freedoms: the possibility and self-actualization of racial and sexual as well as artistic freedom that Delaney embodied.[10] For Baldwin, the lesson of Delaney's *seeing* was that visual acuity was connected to a perceptual, cognitive, and synesthetic acuity that for the artist and the writer were linked intrinsically to Black sight and the capaciousness of Black existence beyond the binaries of light or dark, black or white.

The dichotomy between visibility and invisibility was just one of the binaries that defined Delaney's career, yet it has remained the most potent one.[11] Acknowledging that "nobody knows my face" in an undated journal entry from between 1923 and 1928, Delaney signaled that his sense of invisibility was aligned with a lack of agency arising from racial inequality.[12] Delaney's sense of obscurity, derived from discrimination, anticipated Ralph Ellison's *Invisible Man* (1952) and Baldwin's second essay collection, *Nobody Knows My Name* (1961). While W. E. B. Du Bois had encapsulated the double bind of Black sight through his concept of double consciousness as "precisely this sense of always looking at one's self through the eyes of others, of measuring one's soul by the tape of a world that looks on in contempt and pity,"[13] Baldwin would use Delaney's lesson to invert this double bind: "I, speaking now as a black witness to the white condition, see you in a way that you cannot afford to see me."[14] By positing the nominative first person *I* at the beginning of his statement, Baldwin asserted his reclamation of the Black subject position from that of the passive Black object being viewed only through the eyes of others. Moreover, Baldwin imbued the act of Black seeing with a capacity that was rendered operative by the very inequity of Black invisibility: "I . . . see you in a way that you cannot afford to see me." For Delaney and Baldwin, "seeing" was a fundamentally political act, and it was conjoined to the way that Black as well as queer visibilities could be either conferred or deferred within their work, by activating perceptual subjectivities that engendered slippages between seemingly immutable categories.

James Baldwin's Blues *for Mister Charlie* is predicated on the politics of racialized seeing. The play's underlying theme is how Black people and white people reinforce a racial dialectic through their mutual gaze.[15] By employing the blues for "Mister Charlie," a contemporary Black colloquialism for a white man (usually one deploying racist behavior), Baldwin signals how the tragedy of what he called the "plague" of race affected both whites and Blacks.[16] Baldwin's title is also a profound statement about the blues as a Black expressive form and its capacity for a consciousness born out of Black sight.[17] The blues could both lament and triumph over a tragic situation but required the ability to *see* the truth of that situation.[18] Baldwin's proffer of the blues for white people activates the Black subject position, echoing his own positionality as "a black witness to the white condition."[19] In invoking the blues to mourn his own condition and also that of the very group that denied Black subjectivity, Baldwin validates the power of a Black performative mode as a form of universal witness and empathy.[20] In "Notes for Blues," Baldwin's preface written for the ANTA production, Baldwin explains that just as Black people were defined by race, the "white man" was, similarly, "locked in the prison of his color."[21] And in another essay from the same year, "Words of a Native Son," in which Baldwin examined the impetus behind the play and his choice of genre, he further clarified, "there's a dead boy in my play; it really pivots on the dead boy. No one is innocent of it. Neither black nor white."[22] Initially inspired by Emmett Till's lynching in 1955, Baldwin completed the play in October 1963, after the murder of his friend and associate civil rights activist and NAACP field operative Medgar Evers five months earlier in June 1963.[23] The play is dedicated to Evers, his widow, and his family, and to the four girls killed in September 1963 in the 16th Street Baptist Church bombing in Birmingham, Alabama. Outside of nonfiction writing, notably *The Fire Next Time* (1963), *Blues for Mister Charlie* most directly reflects the turn, from 1963, at which Baldwin's work takes on a deeper political fervor and a more pointedly activist role. As with the essay collection, the play also reflects Baldwin's return to the South that year, which serves as the backdrop of the play.[24]

The reality of African American life in 1964 is demarcated physically in the staging of *Blues for Mister Charlie* by the set, via an aisle between Whitetown and Blacktown in Plaguetown in an imaginary American South. Richard Henry's racially motivated murder begins the play. We see him shot by Lyle Britten, a white store owner, and his body falls into a gulf between the two towns. The dramatic form of the play cuts across this physical divide through a nonlinear narrative and temporal disruptions in the form of flashbacks, acoustic echoes through songs or monologues, and the perpetual psychic presence of Richard as corpse, ghost, or interlocutor on stage. The juxtaposition of the physical space with these narrative dislocations and the shifts between past and present mean that the audience cannot remain within the color line and their dialectically opposed Black or white viewpoint. The dislocated nature of Richard's presence as one who is ostensibly dead yet also alive on stage means that he occupies both a subject and object position simultaneously. While the audience first sees him as Baldwin's "dead boy," the play ensures that we also see Richard as an active character, in a way that humanizes such lives and deaths beyond the fiction of the play.

There are two pivotal moments of racialized seeing in the play, both between Richard and Lyle. The first is an initial moment of antagonism, when the two first meet in act 1, and the second precedes Richard's murder.[25] Their first encounter in act 1 occurs as Richard dances with Juanita in Papa D.'s bar and she is knocked, not accidentally, by Lyle. Consequently, the two men hold each other's gaze in a charged moment of mutual acknowledgment and challenge. Baldwin provides few stage directions in this play, but here he directs the characters: "*On Lyle's way out, he jostles Juanita. Richard stops, holding Juanita at the waist. Richard and Lyle stare at each other.*"[26] These three spare directives instigate the entire power dynamic between them that will end in Richard's death. Lyle's provocative act of touching Juanita, a Black woman, even seemingly inadvertently, is an action that Richard can never make toward a white woman, inadvertent or otherwise, despite being accused of attempting far worse with Lyle's wife, Jo, later in the play. Baldwin packs the drama with these dualities to reinforce the ever-present color line and, at the same time, to acknowledge its redundancy. The held gaze between these two men is encoded as a performance of what cannot be said or enacted between them. In contrast, the Black bar owner Papa D.'s deferential spoken intervention to "Mister Lyle" on Richard's behalf in this scene demonstrates that if language is the master's tool here, sight can operate powerfully outside of speech or a direct act, albeit not without repercussions. This reflected moment of *seeing* both asserts the two characters' racial difference and erodes it. Similarly, it engenders a fraught yet complex power relation between them in which any mutuality is simultaneously affirmed and refuted.

Baldwin establishes the weight of this exchange by mirroring it again in the final act at Papa D.'s bar. Papa D. recounts the incident between the two characters at the trial in act 3: "He [Richard] played his record. Lyle Britten never moved from the door. And they just stood there, the two of them, looking at each other."[27] To ensure that we understand that Richard is aware of his impending death, a flashback precedes this exchange, of Lyle's murder of Old Bill, another Black man. Immediately after the flashback, Papa D. tells Richard he can settle his account the next day, and Richard replies, "What do I owe you Papa D.? I'm not sure I can pay you tomorrow."[28] The past and future murders echo each other, while Richard's past, present, and future are suspended in a single statement of teleological comprehension. Richard's perception of the inevitability of his murder rebounds back to Old Bill and forward to his own murder, functioning outside of the narrative form of the play world as a larger social commentary about the inevitability of racially motivated murders toward the Black community which often culminate without legal parity or recourse. Yet Richard's perceptual second sight of his own tragic fate can be shared by the audience, as we have already witnessed his murder at the start of the play. These temporal splices throughout the play allow us, the audience, to experience Black insight through these shifting perspectives.

Baldwin offers the most potent summation of the desire to possess and revoke Black sight, ironically, through the failed intermediary of the play, the white journalist and part-time businessman Parnell James. For Parnell, seeing Blackness manifests the self-revolt felt in the desire to both possess and destroy the Other when one's subjectivity is always weighted against seeing oneself through another:

> Blackness in front of your eyes. Boys and girls, men and women—you've bowed down in front of them all. And then hated yourself. . . . Black boys and girls. I've wanted my hands full of them, wanted to drown them, laughing and dancing and making love—making love—wow—and be transformed, formed, liberated out of this grey-white envelope. Jesus! I've always been afraid. Afraid of what I saw in their eyes? Blackness. What is it like to be black? To look out on the world from *that* place.[29]

Parnell's final question and rejoinder are the essential crux of the play. By asking the audience to look out from *that* place, Baldwin asks us to dissolve the color line and perceive the world with Black sight.[30]

Parnell's monologue also articulates the entanglement of perceiving Blackness with the fear of Black sexuality that is at once a threat to whiteness and a marker of its distinction. Parnell states what Lyle cannot acknowledge: to see "blackness in front of your eyes" may be a form of liberation and transformation. It is significant that Richard's final words to Lyle are not just a sexual taunt about his interaction with his wife, Jo; they also introduce the possibility of Lyle's desire for Richard: "Don't let her [Jo] near no nigger. She may get to like it. *You may get to like it, too*."[31] Richard's words demonstrate how racial constructions are pivoted against sexuality, especially with respect to Blackness, and how upholding racial difference is used to mask desire. By voicing the possibility of interracial homosexual desire, Richard negates both the racial and sexual constructions built on these purported differences.

Neither Beauford Delaney nor James Baldwin was primarily a dramatist. Yet Delaney was also fascinated by the stage. His painting *The Time of Your Life* (1945; plate 4), focuses on interracial exchange, as did Baldwin's *Blues for Mister Charlie*, but with a different perspective on Black sight and spectatorship. The work references Armenian American novelist and playwright William Saroyan's play *The Time of Your Life* (1939), set in San Francisco in October 1939 and dramatizing the interactions of a diverse and marginalized group of characters in a downtown bar, Nick's Pacific Street Saloon, Restaurant and Entertainment Palace. Saroyan's play opened on Broadway in 1939, and Delaney may have seen it then or in its second run in 1940, after it won the Pulitzer Prize for best American drama.[32] As much as Saroyan's play is about marginalized lives, it is also about the power of social community that the keenly strung tension of Baldwin's *Blues for Mister Charlie* precludes. For Delaney, as a marginalized figure himself in various ways, this may have been the play's appeal.[33] Despite Delaney's quotation of Saroyan, the painting is more than a representation of the play. Discordant colors and reiterated outlining are used to designate geometric zones, gesturing toward the abstract. However, Delaney also uses these techniques narratively, diminishing the unity of the group by creating individual units imposed by this zoning. As a result, the figures or groups of figures are presented in one social space but are, nonetheless, isolated. Similarly to Baldwin's staging of racial division, Delaney uses color and space to infer social divisions. Delaney does not, however, present the collective segregation of *Blues for Mister Charlie*; his characters occupy more singularly divided spaces.[34]

Looking closely at *The Time of Your Life*, one can see that the two central male actors in the painting are disproportionately larger than the surrounding cast. The two men are diagonally parallel and face each other, dividing the stage space. Aside from their skin tone, they are visually rhymed in their clothes, shoes, and stance. Their racialized identities, nonetheless, are emphasized further by their doubling. The Black male is the only clearly Black figure in the work and the only figure turned away from the viewer. However, not all the characters are discernibly racialized.[35] The central white male smokes a cigarette in a holder while the Black male carries a tray and holds a carafe with one hand. If the Black man is a bar employee, possibly Wesley in Saroyan's play, the white man appears to be a patron. Yet the racial and socioeconomic distinctions between them are disrupted by their open, rhymed posture and clothing.

The two men are engaged in a circuit of looking, holding each other's gaze in an interchange, like Baldwin's Richard and Lyle. But this is a different type of interaction. They are transgressing the boundaries produced by their differences, even if just for a moment. Their locked gazes, in tandem with their size and rhymed figures, focus the viewer's attention upon them. There is a stillness in this captured moment, however fleeting, despite the jarring colors and angular lines and the other social groups and individuals around them. Their fixed gaze is conspicuous when seen against that of the other bodies in the center of the canvas, particularly the unreturned gaze between the seated heterosexual couple in the foreground. And indeed, the presence of the couple casts a different inflection on the dynamic between the two men. If this is some encoded moment of interracial cruising, it is indeterminate and made more so by the Black actor's back turned to the viewer. His denial of visual access is emphasized further by the fact that he is on a stage and singularly contrasted to the other figures on view. His turned body paradoxically asserts his agency to deny visual access despite his status or race. Nevertheless, he presents himself to his white counterpart, keeping the exchange between them somewhat furtive and ambivalent.

One might argue that Delaney's painting addresses the relationship between performance, visibility, and privacy that he experienced in his own life. Performativity marked Delaney's life as a queer Black artist. From early on, he sensed that his sexuality—and more visibly, his race—required him to play a part in public. As a young adult, Delaney felt he had to make "good nigger compromises" in his self-presentation to avoid persecution in life, "telling his mother's stories of the old South, avoiding any indication of anger at white people, occasionally singing a spiritual, and making people laugh."[36] Yet Delaney used performativity in his own practice to mediate how one apprehended experiences that he did not wish to make visible. For Delaney, this meant that his art should possess "an authority to induce what we cannot perceive."[37] Although performativity did not mark his own personal life in the same way, like Delaney, Baldwin understood the performance of visibility, especially Black visibility, but his calling was to make it manifest in real-life terms.[38] *Blues for Mister Charlie* represents Baldwin's objective that "everything in a play . . . be terribly concrete, terribly visible."[39] Delaney's painting presents Black visibility while denying its spectatorship, whereas Baldwin's play hinges upon the dialectic between them. In *Blues for Mister Charlie*, Richard's murder affords spectatorship but also makes visible the life prior to it. On Delaney's stage, the Black actor's visible presence is registered, but he refuses his gaze.[40] Each invokes a different type of Black seeing, one that by necessity demands viewership while another is presented as provisional, circumspect, or even largely hidden from view. Both imbricate the viewer within a performance of Black sight that mediates the politics of spectatorship and how Blackness may be visible but not always seen.

In *The Time of Your Life*, only the world of the play occupies the canvas; the perspective of the painting is essentially that of an audience member seated in the theater watching the play. Yet Delaney's rendering of a disjointed and abstracted stage set also reinforces the construction of different ways of seeing that support the refusal of Black spectatorship by the central Black actor. Like Baldwin's *Blues for Mister Charlie*, this is a work about the politics of Black sight and spectatorship and, simultaneously, the performance of different forms of viewership through various configurations of color, texture, perspective, and depth. Despite being bounded within the play world, we are also offered possibilities to move through and beyond it. The doorways within the set, for example, are outlined repeatedly, drawing the eye in and offering a means of entry and escape. Linear shading adds to an effect—that the eye can see both in and out of Delaney's composite world. In an imagined letter to Delaney in 2015, Glenn Ligon described this quality in Delaney's practice: "In your paintings, the line between figuration and abstraction is always porous. This has inspired a similar fluidity in my paintings which often turn text (a kind of figuration, I suppose) towards abstraction."[41] Extending Ligon's line beyond genre and reading with Baldwin's 1964 introduction, we are able to apprehend that, for Delaney, seeing is "always porous." This permeability is visible in all of Delaney's works, whether abstract or figurative, and as Baldwin noted, his work moves beyond any form of hermeneutic closure. Citing both Delaney and Baldwin as his "queer predecessors," Ligon manifests a similar correlation between seeing and visibility in regard to Blackness and queerness in his work.[42] As Hilton Als observes of Ligon's 1996 *Stranger* series, inspired by Baldwin's essay "Stranger in the Village" (1953), "Like Baldwin's essay, Ligon's work—certainly in this series—is about being seen and not seen at the same time. The surfaces of the painting, their layers upon layers of coal dust and handiwork, both draw you close and push you away (but where to? To the artist's imagination? And what would you find there, in that queer universe influenced by queers who belonged to a generation in which you could say who you were only through metaphor, if even then?)."[43]

Delaney's ultimate lesson was that seeing itself could be a performative act, one in which the play between seeing and not seeing was constantly shifting, and through this perpetual play, offer the possibility for one's subjectivity to shift also. His paintings assert a position in which one could be visible without always being seen, and vice versa. Within the metaphorical and material interstices of this visual performativity, the fluidity of Blackness and queerness could be enacted and perceived. Ligon's use of coal dust as a medium in the *Stranger* series juxtaposes the darkness and immutability of its mark-making capacity against the ephemerality of its material fragments. As such, the latter quality breaks down the figurative into the abstract, as the letters visibly disintegrate into abstract forms. Delaney described an equally protean quality within his own practice as "a penetration of something that is more profound in many ways than the rigidity of form. A form if it breathes some, if it has some enigma to it, it is also the enigma that is abstract."[44] For Delaney, "seeing" involved not the resolution of form wholly into mimesis but the metaphorical possibility of remaining an enigma.

One example may suffice. In his *Portrait of Ella Fitzgerald* (1968; plate 26), Delaney blurs the tension between figure and ground similarly to Ligon's coal-dust works. Fitzgerald's face floats out of an intangible abstract space, while the outline of her body is less discernible. Delaney's choice of Fitzgerald, a Black female singer steeped in jazz and the blues tradition, reflects the inheritance that he would bestow on Baldwin.[45] Here, as in Baldwin's *Blues for Mister Charlie*, the blues pare down the essence of a situation and give clarity of vision—yet, at the same time, the blues often convey actions and emotions beyond what sight may bear.[46] Given Delaney's preoccupation with eyes in his paintings, it is not unexpected that Fitzgerald's eyes are the most prominent feature in this work, and, in a queered transposition, seem to echo Delaney's own eyes and haunting expression in his 1962 sketches. The background envelops Fitzgerald through Delaney's signature yellow tonal values in tandem with a reiterated swirling pattern that moves rhythmically and cursively. As with Ligon's coal-dust letters that seemingly dissolve into abstraction, Delaney's abstract forms appear to have an almost graphic legibility. Within the yellow clouds, like luminescent smoke fumes, Fitzgerald is both concealed and revealed, dissipating the contours of her female form so she is only voice, only eyes, only performance. Here is something of Delaney's enigmatic penetration, in which Fitzgerald's presence, not merely her physical form, conflates both the subject and object relations of the work and, in turn, collapses the subject and object position of the viewer.

Is Fitzgerald acting upon us to see her, or are we making her visible by activating her presence? Perhaps this is Baldwin's "metamorphosis of freedom" enacted through a performance of seeing that Delaney allows us to choose.

NOTES

1 *Playbill* 1, no. 4 (April 1964). The dust jacket of the first edition of the published script uses the same image; see James Baldwin, *Blues for Mister Charlie* (New York: Dial Press, 1964).

2 *Blues for Mister Charlie* premiered on April 23, 1964.

3 Referencing Derrida's "monocular stare," Catherine St. John identifies the emphasis on outlining and asymmetrical eyes in Delaney's self-portraits as indicative of vacancy rather than sight; see Catherine St. John, "A Narrative of Belonging: The Art of Beauford Delaney and Glenn Ligon," in *Proceedings for the School of Visual Arts Eighteenth Annual National Conference on Liberal Arts and the Education of Artists: Art and Story*, 45–46, https://www.academia.edu/1411170/INTERPRETATION_NARRATIVE_AND_THE_STUDENTS_SEARCH_FOR_AN_ARTISTS_INTENTIONS.

4 On the Black male as an ideological construction, especially with reference to the body, sexuality, and performance in American visual culture, see *Black Male: Representations of Masculinity in Contemporary American Art*, ed. Thelma Golden (New York: Whitney Museum of American Art, 1994). See also bell hooks, "Reconstructing Black Masculinity," in *Black Looks: Race and Representation* (Boston: South End Press, 1992), 97–113.

5 James Baldwin, "The Price of the Ticket," in *The Price of the Ticket: Collected Nonfiction, 1948–1985* (New York: St. Martin's, 1985); reprinted in *James Baldwin: Collected Essays*, ed. Toni Morrison (New York: Library of America, 1998), 831.

6 James Baldwin, "Introduction to Exhibition of Beauford Delaney Opening, December 4, 1964, at the Galerie Lambert," in *Beauford Delaney: A Retrospective*, ed. Richard A. Long (New York: Studio Museum in Harlem, 1978), n.p.

7 Baldwin, "Introduction to Exhibition of Beauford Delaney," n.p. In a much-quoted passage, Baldwin described Delaney teaching him to "see" again in a 1984 interview, recalling the moment of Delaney pointing to reflections cast in rain puddles as a "great revelation": "I looked and all I saw was water. And he said, 'Look again,' which I did, and I saw oil

on the water and the city reflected in the puddle. He taught me how to see, and how to trust what I saw. Painters have often taught writers how to see. And once you've had that experience, you see differently." Jordan Elgrably, "James Baldwin: The Art of Fiction No. 78," *Paris Review* 91 (Spring 1984), https://www.theparisreview.org/interviews/2994/the-art-of-fiction-no-78-james-baldwin.

8 Baldwin, "Introduction to Exhibition of Beauford Delaney," n.p.

9 Baldwin, "Introduction to Exhibition of Beauford Delaney," n.p.

10 Baldwin stated, "Beauford was the first walking, living proof, for me, that a black man could be an artist" and he modeled the freedom that being an artist entailed as a Black man. Baldwin, "Price of the Ticket," 832.

11 Delaney's history is characterized by obscurity, even though he exhibited his work steadily until the end of his life; see Eleanor Heartney, "Whatever Happened to Beauford Delaney?," *Art in America*, November 1994, 116–19; and Theresa Leininger, "Beauford Delaney: An Abstract Expressionist Who Wasn't Part of the New York School" (1989, unpublished). Ann E. Gibson situates critical inattention to Delaney's contribution within the wider neglect of African American abstract artists during the postwar period in her *Abstract Expressionism: Other Politics* (New Haven, CT: Yale University Press, 1997); and "Two Worlds: African American Abstraction in New York at Mid-century," in *The Search for Freedom: African American Abstract Painting, 1945–1975* (New York: Kenkeleba Gallery, 1991), 12–14.

12 Beauford Delaney, cited in David Leeming, *Amazing Grace: A Life of Beauford Delaney* (New York: Oxford University Press, 1998), 26.

13 W. E. B. Du Bois, "Of Our Spiritual Strivings," in *The Souls of Black Folk* (Greenwich, CT: Fawcett, 1961), 16–17.

14 James Baldwin, "Of the Sorrow Songs: The Cross of Redemption (1979)," in *The Cross of Redemption: Uncollected Writings*, ed. Randall Kenan (New York: Pantheon, 2010), 151. For Baldwin, Delaney was his "principal witness"; see Leeming, *Amazing Grace*, 69.

15 On the relationship between the Black gaze and subjectivity, see Frantz Fanon, "The Fact of Blackness," in *Black Skin, White Masks*, trans. Charles Lam Markmann (New York: Grove, 1967), 109–12; bell hooks, *Black Looks: Race and Representation* (Boston: South End, 1992); Toni Morrison, "The Source of Self-Regard," in *The Source of Self-Regard: Selected Speeches, Essays, and Meditations* (New York: Vintage, 2020), 304–21.

16 James Baldwin, "Notes for Blues," in *Blues for Mister Charlie*, 7.

17 For Baldwin, the blues refers to "a state of being." James Baldwin, "The Uses of the Blues," *Playboy*, January 1964; reprinted in Kenan, *Cross of Redemption*, 80. On the importance of the blues as a Black expressive form,

see that essay and also James Baldwin, *The Fire Next Time*, in Morrison, *James Baldwin: Collected Essays*, 311. In Baldwin's 1957 short story "Sonny's Blues," Creole, a character thought to be based on Delaney, explicates the power of the blues. James Baldwin, "Sonny's Blues," *Partisan Review*, Summer 1957; reprinted in *Going to Meet the Man* (New York: Dial, 1965), 139–40.

18 For Baldwin's commentary on the relationship between the blues and sight, see "Uses of the Blues," 82, 86, 90.

19 Baldwin described the play as his own attempt to "bear witness"; see "Notes for Blues," 8. Baldwin's statement here mirrors Creole's description of the blues bringing light out of darkness in "Sonny's Blues," 139.

20 Baldwin explained this capacity for universality arising from Black experience in "The Uses of the Blues": "The blues are rooted in the slave songs; the slaves discovered something genuinely terrible, terrible because it sums up the universal challenge, the universal hope, the universal fear" (89). On the use of the blues for the white condition in *Blues for Mister Charlie*, see David Leeming, "*Blues for Mister Charlie*," in *James Baldwin: A Biography* (New York: Knopf, 1994), 232; and Koritha Mitchell, "James Baldwin, Performance Theorist, Sings the Blues for Mister Charlie," *American Quarterly* 64, no. 1 (2012): 55.

21 Baldwin, "Notes for Blues," 7.

22 James Baldwin, "Words of a Native Son," *Playboy*, December 1964; reprinted in Morrison, *James Baldwin: Collected Essays*, 712.

23 Elia Kazan had suggested that Baldwin write a play inspired by Till's murder in 1958, presuming that Kazan would direct and the Actor's Studio in New York would produce it; see James Baldwin, "Notes for Blues," 5; and Leeming, "*Blues for Mister Charlie*," 230.

24 Critical scholarship on *Blues for Mister Charlie* is scant, focusing predominantly on form or performance history; see, for example, Mitchell, "James Baldwin, Performance Theorist," 33–60; Nicholas K. Davis, "Go Tell It on the Stage: *Blues for Mister Charlie* as Dialectical Drama," *Journal of American Drama and Theatre* 17 (Spring 2005): 30–42; and Soyica Diggs, "Historicizing the Sound of a Ghastly Sight: James Baldwin's *Blues for Mister Charlie*," in *Sonic Interventions*, ed. Marijke de Valck, Sylvia Mieszkowski, and Joy Smith (Amsterdam: Rodopi, 2007), 193–210. Leeming's biography provides background and context, including Baldwin's relationship with the Actor's Studio, his political and artistic aims for the play, and its reception; see Leeming, "*Blues for Mister Charlie*," in *James Baldwin: A Biography*, 230–42.

25 Ironically, the actual confrontation between Lyle and Richard that begins after the exchange between Richard and Lyle's wife Jo is less important

here; that confrontation is one we will see and hear rehearsed and then reiterated in act 3's trial by different characters, as apparent witnesses.

26 Baldwin, *Blues for Mister Charlie*, 48.

27 Baldwin, *Blues for Mister Charlie*, 119.

28 Baldwin, *Blues for Mister Charlie*, 120.

29 Baldwin, *Blues for Mister Charlie*, 140.

30 Tina M. Campt reinforces Baldwin's point: "Rather than looking at Black people, rather than simply multiplying the representation of Black folks, what would it mean to *see oneself through* the complex positionality that is Blackness—and work through its implications on and for oneself?"; Tina M. Campt, "How Black Artists Are Shaping a Distinctly Black Gaze," *Hyperallergic*, August 22, 2021, https://hyperallergic.com/671547/how-black-artists-are-shaping-a-distinctly-black-gaze-tina-m-campt/.

31 Baldwin, *Blues for Mister Charlie*, 120 (italics added).

32 According to Patricia Sue Canterbury, Delaney's work may have originated from witnessing a rehearsal of the play through his association with the actor Canada Lee, who was cast as Wesley. Delaney had painted Lee's portrait in 1942. See Canterbury, "Transatlantic Transformations: Beauford Delaney in Paris," in *Beauford Delaney: From New York to Paris*, ed. Jodie L. Ahern and Chad Dayton (Minneapolis: Minneapolis Institute of Art, 2004), 48.

33 On Delaney's preoccupation with marginal lives, particularly social exclusion and Black privation, compare, for example, Delaney's *The Time of Your Life* with his *Can Fire in the Park* (1946), which depicts a group of African American homeless men. See Virginia M. Mecklenburg, "Commentaries on the Artworks: Beauford Delaney," in *African American Art: Harlem Renaissance, Civil Rights Era, and Beyond*, ed. Richard J. Powell and Virginia M. Mecklenburg (New York: Smithsonian American Art Museum, 2012), 77–79.

34 Delaney's motif of using color and line to "zone" areas can also be seen in works such as *Jazz Quartet* (1946) and, for both individuals and groups, *Untitled (Jazz Club)* (1950). In contrast to the latter, however, the spatial lines of zoning in *The Time of Your Life* emphasize disparity rather than unity.

35 Another Delaney motif in his group portraits was mixing racially identified subjects with figures who were not discernably identified by race, thus making the lone Black male figure in *The Time of Your Life* especially prominent as the single Black-identified figure in the work.

36 Delaney, cited in Leeming, *Amazing Grace*, 21.

37 Delaney, cited in Leeming, *Amazing Grace*, 61.

38 Both Delaney's father and Baldwin's stepfather were preachers, which lent a shared understanding of the importance of performance to their practices. Baldwin referred to the performativity of the Black church in *The Fire Next Time*, 306. Baldwin also noted the necessity of performance within Black life, echoing Delaney's sense of performing for others; see James Baldwin, *No Name in the Street* (1972), in Morrison, *James Baldwin: Collected Essays*, 261.

39 Baldwin, "Words of a Native Son," 710.

40 Delaney further complicates this performance between Black sight and spectatorship in that we are seeing Saroyan's play depicted through his gaze.

41 Glenn Ligon, "Letter to Beauford Delaney," in *Glenn Ligon: Encounters and Collisions*, ed. Glenn Ligon, Alex Farquharson, and Francesco Manaconda (London: Nottingham Contemporary, 2015), 49.

42 Glenn Ligon, "Artist's Artists: Ligon on Delaney," *Frieze*, October 10, 2015, https://frieze.com/article/artists-artists-glenn-ligon.

43 Hilton Als, "Strangers in the Village," in *Glenn Ligon: America*, ed. Scott Rothkopf (New York: Whitney Museum of Art, 2011), 211.

44 Delaney, cited in interview with Richard A. Long, in Long, *Beauford Delaney*, n.p.

45 Baldwin discovered through Delaney a new way of perceiving Black music, and noted, "I really began to *hear* Ella Fitzgerald"; see Baldwin, "Price of the Ticket," 831.

46 On the blues as a form for bearing suffering, see Baldwin, "Uses of the Blues," 82. See also note 17 above.

TWELVE

Shared Subjects

Rachel Cohen

Am today still trying to bring together color compositions from the strange and many-faceted thing that is my life.

Beauford Delaney to Larry Wallrich, June 2, 1958

Which Is the Eye?

Two paintings by Beauford Delaney: a self-portrait, and a landscape. You see them in a storage facility, almost back-to-back, hung on metal dividers.[1] Both paintings are radical concatenations of colors, built out of thickly applied oil paints. In one, *Untitled (Village Street Scene)* (1948; plate 6), you are on a street in Greenwich Village, and on the sidewalk, in the bottom right of the painting . . . is that an eye? It is a puddle, reflecting light, and it is also so like an eye, a turquoise color within, a black oval rim, angle of brows above.

In the second painting, *Self-Portrait* (1944; plate 3), you look at the man, his clothes, his red hat, each of his two eyes in turn—one especially, his left, the eye of a man self-considering and meeting your gaze.

But how similar they are—the puddle on the sidewalk, the left eye—in shape and orientation, in the angle of maroon above, in the variable thickness of pigment, sometimes heavy, sometimes so thin the weave of the canvas shows through. The eye is the window of the soul, we say, and the puddle is the window of the city street, a showing through, a place of coalescence, meeting, outwardness and inwardness.

> I remember standing on a street corner with the black painter Beauford Delaney down in the Village, waiting for the light to change, and he pointed down and said, "Look." I looked and all I saw was water. And he said, "Look again," which I did, and I saw oil on the water and the city reflected in the puddle. It was a great revelation to me. I can't explain it. He taught me how to see, and how to trust what I saw. Painters have often taught writers how to see. And once you've had that experience, you see differently.[2]

This passage by James Baldwin is often quoted, but it looks different with Delaney's eye and puddle in mind. Stop. Look. Wait for the light to change. Oil on water. When you see a puddle, you are seeing a kind of involuntary painting. A painting happens when a subject—a city or a person, a feeling or an understanding—is reflected, and changed, in a puddle of oil and water.

Delaney worked very personally, and also, in some interesting way, *im*personally, just as a city might harbor the reflections of the people moving through it. Writing to his friend Don Freeman in the spring of 1938 about the beautiful sights he saw walking near his Greene Street apartment at Washington Square Park, Delaney noted how one sight may come through another: "The old houses around Washington Square seem like large out of shape flowers blooming softly thru the trees." This brought him directly to ambitions for his own work: "I so wish it were possible for me to put into the words the deep felt things which are so obvious and tangible . . . and real like great alive forces working thru the deep unconscious tracts of our inner consciousness."[3]

The surface of a puddle, that thin membrane, may seem like the closest we can come to the touching of the inward and the outward. The curator and scholar Stephen C. Wicks, turning over the ways that Delaney might have understood city surfaces, thinks of the "protean iridescence" when oil interacts with water and wonders if this is a kind of "visual pathway into a shifting arena of light and movement."[4] Wicks notices a similar voyage into sight and back out again in these words from a note Delaney wrote to his family, probably in the 1940s: "It seems possible to have an articulate contact with majesty and omniscience by . . . perhaps observing the prismatic color of a drop of water held so as to reflect the sunlight, or perchance glance into the eye of anyone we might happen upon any expression whatsoever reflected back in evidence of . . . vastness and scope."[5] As in the paintings, there is again the "drop of water" and the "glance into the eye" that brings us to a majesty and omniscience Delaney hoped to share with those dearest to him.

Shared experiences of looking were often how Delaney made contact with other people, contact that might turn into relationships lasting over long periods of time. Baldwin often told the story, for instance, about looking at the city puddle with Delaney. In his *Paris Review* interview, Baldwin in fact tells a version of the story some forty years after it happened, and some years after Delaney's death. It was still vivid to Baldwin—a deep, ongoing practice of attention shared by the writer and the painter.

When, at age sixteen, in 1940, Baldwin first entered Delaney's Village apartment, he was astounded: "I walked through that door into Beauford's colors—on the easel, on the palette, against the wall—sometimes turned to the wall—and sometimes (in limbo?) covered by white sheets."[6] Those walls and their paintings were a part of his inheritance and his future: "Beauford was the first walking, living proof, for me, that a black man could be an artist." And this example was not only an inspiration, but, Baldwin wrote, "an enormous protection."[7] The first half of the 1940s was an eventful period in Delaney and Baldwin's shared history of looking closely. Delaney painted the very young Baldwin in *Dark Rapture* in 1941 (plate 1). Right at the time of the 1943 Harlem insurrection, there came the summer days when Baldwin buried his father with the help of money found by Delaney, and then moved down from Harlem to Greene Street, first to live with Delaney and later to live in an apartment nearby. When Baldwin was living at 181 Greene Street, Delaney's studio was filled with sketches and portraits of him, and of Delaney himself, and of the Village streets they walked together. Baldwin would have seen the great Delaney *Self-Portrait* of 1944 that now hangs at the Art Institute of Chicago. A few years later, in 1948, Baldwin wrote the essay "The Harlem Ghetto" and made the difficult separation, leaving in November for Paris. Before his departure, he would have seen Delaney at work on another of the great streetscapes of Greenwich Village, *Untitled (Village Street Scene)*. Perhaps the puddle that is like an eye in the painting is watching out for Baldwin in the city streets.

In a painter's studio or apartment, work retains its contingency; there is the sense that it was just made and could be made again. Seeing a work on a museum wall, it is hard to return to this sense of possibility. I had first read descriptions of Delaney's studio around 2003, when I was at work on my book *A Chance Meeting: Intertwined Lives of American Writers and Artists* and was writing about the friendship between Delaney and Baldwin. At that time, I was interested to learn from David Leeming's biography of Delaney that the artist covered his walls in white sheets, to make the colors of the paintings vivid and central, and I was interested that he had even painted his Victrola—music and painting being closely related for him. But even having these details, it was hard to imagine the effect on Baldwin of entering the space of the paintings, to see the paintings while the artist looked, too, and to see *through* Delaney's way of seeing.

Seventeen years later, in Chicago in January 2020, I was preparing to speak at the Knoxville, Tennessee, symposium "In a Speculative Light: The Arts of James Baldwin and Beauford Delaney" and had a rare chance to immerse myself in two works by Delaney. I now live in Chicago, and I contacted the Arts of the Americas department at the Art Institute about doing research on their *Self-Portrait* of 1944, which was then in the storage facility, on its return from a major exhibition. The department's collection manager, Julie Warchol, let me know that in fact they were temporarily holding another Delaney painting, *Untitled (Village Street Scene)*. I could look at both.

On the appointed day, I went with Warchol into storage, down a long institutional corridor, and through a door she held open for me. In the room we entered, she pulled out one of the sliding metal racks onto which the stored paintings are hung. Then she rigged up a bright, soft conservation light to one side, offered me a chair, and sat down at some distance. The paintings—no longer received judgments on museum walls or in flattened reproduction, but palpable, vibrating color compositions—stepped out. First, *Self-Portrait*. Then, two racks beyond and facing the other way, *Untitled (Village Street Scene)*. I asked, and Warchol obligingly pulled both out at once for me, so I could go back and forth around them for a good half an hour, sitting on the floor, varying the distance, leaning in as close as I dared. I not only noticed, but really *felt*, the puddles in the street, the eyes in the self-portrait; I began to understand differently the recollection of Baldwin's famous story of looking at the puddles with his friend and mentor. I took picture after picture, peered into the pools of paint, which were so thick and defined in the rare raking light of the conservation lamp.

The question of how to think about Delaney's ongoing double pursuit of portraits and abstract compositions is one that fascinates artists and scholars who love his work. Thinking about the eyes and the painted puddles in Delaney's works has been a way into this question for me. Turning back to David Leeming, I find a set of thoughts that are newly suggestive. Leeming quotes Delaney from an interview with the artist in the *New York Telegraph* in 1930: "I paint people. People—and in their faces I hope to discover that odd, mysterious rhythm."[8] To Delaney, a face is a surface like the surfaces of a city, or of a Victrola, to be painted and rendered in paint. Moreover, later in his book, Leeming quotes Henry Miller's sometimes problematic and sometimes insightful essay *The Amazing and Invariable Beauford DeLaney*, written in the first half of the 1940s, in which Miller reflected on why Delaney was painting his friend Dante Pavone again and again and again (see plate 7). "Why not?" wrote Miller, "Some men paint the same landscape over and over again. Dante was a wonderful landscape for Beauford: he had cosmic proportions."[9] Leeming follows this quotation with an observation of his own that now holds my attention: "Miller's remarks are perceptive. He realized that Dante was indeed Beauford's primary 'landscape' for exploration, that Beauford's need was to fathom Dante's mystery because Dante was at the center of Beauford's attempt to understand himself."[10]

For Delaney, perhaps there is always a relationship between portraiture and landscape work, but this becomes especially pronounced as he studies the faces most important and familiar to him: those of the men he loved and whose portraits he frequently painted, such as Dante Pavone—and later, and over the course of a longer period and more profoundly, James Baldwin. Of course, the face whose terrain he knew best of all was his own. The three genres become like a triptych in which each pair overlaps: the landscape and the portrait; the portrait and the self-portrait; the self-portrait and the landscape.

Which Is the I?

For the exhibition, the curator has carefully arranged a wall of Delaney's abstractions—the famous abstractions from the Clamart period, with their all-over movement, their beautiful verticality, their endless patterning that is so spatial, or like the experience of space, a space you can move in. . . . Though is it movement like taking a walk, or movement like a movement of the soul?

A Delaney self-portrait catches your eye (plate 12); it was painted in 1962, and the figure and ground are held together by an all-over pattern of yellow curving lines. You are reminded of another Delaney painting, *The Black Sage* (1967; plate 22), in which Baldwin's head is patterned in paint that seems wound together with the patterns of the red background.

> Well, that life, that light, that miracle, are what I began to see in Beauford's paintings, and this light began to stretch back for me over all the time we had known each other, and over much more time than that, and this light held the power to illuminate, even to redeem and reconcile and heal. For Beauford's work leads the inner and the outer eye, directly and inexorably, to a new confrontation with reality. . . . And the beauty of his triumph, and the proof that it is a real one, is that he makes it ours.[11]

Written for the exhibition catalogue of the solo show at the Galerie Lambert in 1964 that was one of the most important in Delaney's lifetime, "On the Painter Beauford Delaney" is Baldwin's fullest attempt to say in print what he thought mattered most in Delaney's paintings. Baldwin's essay reflected a very close period of shared subjects.

In history, and in friendship, it is sometimes possible to point out two periods of time that reflect one another, the same again, but differently. If the first half of the 1940s is one crucial period between Baldwin and Delaney, that between 1958 and 1964 is another. In both of these blocks of time, the two men sometimes lived together, Baldwin living in a small space with Delaney—the two cooking meals together, looking together. In both time spans, Delaney painted abstract landscapes, self-portraits, and portraits of Baldwin, and, as he wrote to Larry Wallrich in 1958, made significant leaps in his efforts to "bring together color compositions from the strange and many-faceted thing that is my life."[12]

That summer of 1958 was the one in which Baldwin lived with Delaney in the studio at Clamart. This was the period of the opening out of the very beautiful abstractions, so often vertical, with their greens, yellows, roses, and reds. Were they, the colors, inside, or outside? That same June, Delaney also wrote to Henry Miller that he thought his work was becoming "more personal or impersonal; they are both about the same it seems to me."[13]

Baldwin would describe the summer with Delaney using interestingly impersonal constructions. He wrote that when he had first gone *looking*, walking the Village streets with Beauford during their first period of time together, the effect on his own vision had been that "the very colors underwent a . . . salutary change."[14] Now, in this second period of radical experimentation, he wrote as if the paintings were themselves alive, that the "paintings underwent a most striking metamorphosis into freedom."[15]

That summer, they were both paying attention in a fervent, maybe even a devout, way. Leeming writes that "Baldwin was in France primarily for Beauford that summer." Baldwin, Leeming continues, wrote to their close friend Mary Painter "that he had never listened to anyone so closely, never tried so hard to," as Baldwin phrased it, "'put myself in someone else's skin.'"[16] How close could you get to seeing what someone else did? Very close. "He makes it ours," Baldwin concluded, in his essay six years later—a change in pronouns and plurality, subjects shared.

I brought my photographs of painted eyes and of streets with their puddles to show to my colleagues and fellow writers at the "In a Speculative Light" symposium at the University of Tennessee in Knoxville, where Delaney grew up. The conference had been carefully timed to coincide with the exhibition *Beauford Delaney and James Baldwin: Through the Unusual Door* (2020), curated by the Knoxville Museum of Art's Barbara W. and Bernard E. Bernstein Curator, Stephen C. Wicks.[17] On my last day in Knoxville, I spent several hours immersed in the exhibition. I saw it alone, and I saw it with Wicks. There was a special area of the exhibition where, he later told me, he had really tried to evoke the window in Clamart that Baldwin described. For the show, Wicks sequenced the colors of the abstractions to suggest the changing light in the course of a day. Many have been taken by Baldwin's description of the important window in Delaney's Clamart studio and have worked to understand Delaney's painting through that passage:

> There was a window in Beauford's house in Clamart before which we often sat—late at night, early in the morning, at noon. This window looked out on a garden; or, rather, it would have looked out on a garden if it had not been for the leaves and branches of a large tree which pressed directly against the window. Everything one saw from this window, then, was filtered through these leaves. And this window was a kind of universe, moaning and wailing when it rained, light of the morning, and as blue as the blues when the last light of the sun departed.

Well, that life, that light, that miracle, are what I began to see in Beauford's paintings.[18]

That space of Clamart in the exhibition asked viewers not only to stand still and be absorbed, but to range around, as you might in the studio of a friend. I sat on a bench and watched not only the changing light but also the other people going up and down to look closely at the paintings. Among the painting-windowed walls was created a space through which people moved like dancers. It was unforgettably beautiful and in motion.

A window is a place that reflects landscape, where landscape and painting meet in quadrangle. Delaney's Clamart abstractions are like his earlier abstract streetscapes—a territory, marked by geometric and color understanding, that can be set back-to-back or side-to-side with the portraits and with the self-portraits. In my earlier research, I had been able to join Delaney's 1944 *Self-Portrait* to his *Untitled (Village Street Scene)*. And it was at this point, in the light of that space at the Knoxville Museum of Art, thinking of those tall abstractions as a kind of landscape painting, that an understanding of two Delaney portraits began to come through to me differently.

In the years after that summer of 1958—when he and Baldwin moved together among the paintings, through the light of the studio together—Delaney went on painting portraits of himself, his friends, and Baldwin. One, *Self-Portrait,* from 1962, in the collection of Michael Rosenfeld, shows Delaney in a beret, smoking a cigarette; there is a vivid red-orange background and squiggles of yellow-ochre lines over the whole of the figure, his clothing and face, and the ground. The other is a portrait I have often looked at in reproduction but never seen: *The Black Sage*, Delaney's portrait of Baldwin from 1967. In this painting, the head of the sitter stretches up to the very top of the canvas and seemingly beyond, suggesting that the viewer might be within that person—or the whole world might be. Lines of a striking periwinkle blue course around the face and shoulders and through the background, as does an ochre yellow that seems as though it might be similar to that in the 1962 self-portrait. A pattern of colors is running through the atmosphere and the person.

In the portrait and the self-portrait, patterns of all-over abstraction make of the figure and ground some strange many-faceted color composition in which the inner life is background and foreground, or the face is a landscape, or the landscape is alive, or the colors, in all their plurality, are themselves, and ours.

We have nothing but profound friendship. Our century is exploding in infinite ways. Perhaps, this has always been so, however we must continue in the midst of the seemingly impossible moments when words spoken are not heard by unfortunately the immediate unhappiness. At such times one must, if speech is impossible, simply be silent. All of us must be ourselves and contain our belief in the healing of wounds which time, we hope, can bring about.[19]

These reflections of Beauford Delaney's, written in 1967, the year he painted *The Black Sage*, leave an open space. Six words in this passage form a Delaney koan, like the puddles in the street that ask us to look again: "All of us must be ourselves." The words imply at first only that a person has an authentic self, one we come to with difficulty, trying to heal our wounds. But after spending time with Delaney's work, one sees another meaning below the surface: that each of us must be our several selves, our many selves, our overlapping and sometimes conflicting identities. And finally, as we look with Delaney and Baldwin, we realize that the phrase could also mean the most difficult thing to imagine: that all of us must be one another's selves, and that conceivably one is oneself or oneselves alongside another themself or themselves, and that these may run together inwardly, issuing forth as enmeshed selves, both oneself and themselves, as light—Delaney's beloved light—is both particle and wave.

NOTES

Epigraph source: Quoted in David Leeming, *Amazing Grace: A Life of Beauford Delaney* (New York: Oxford University Press, 1998), 139.

1 For closeups of these details, see Rachel Cohen, "Beauford Delaney Eyes," *Rachel Cohen* (blog), June 5, 2020, https://rachelecohen.com/blog/The_Frederick_Project/c/1075.

2 Jordan Elgrably, "James Baldwin: The Art of Fiction No. 78," *Paris Review* 91 (Spring 1984), https://www.theparisreview.org/interviews/2994/the-art-of-fiction-no-78-james-baldwin.

3 Quoted in David Leeming, *Amazing Grace: A Life of Beauford Delaney* (New York: Oxford University Press, 1998), 58.

4 Stephen C. Wicks, "Beauford Delaney's Metamorphosis into Freedom," in *Beauford Delaney and James Baldwin: Through the Unusual Door* (Knoxville: University of Tennessee Press, 2020), 9.

5 Beauford Delaney, handwritten note, ca. 1940s, Beauford Delaney Letters, ScMG 217, Schomburg Center for Research; cited in Stephen C. Wicks, "Beauford Delaney's Metamorphosis into Freedom," 10.

6 James Baldwin, "The Price of the Ticket," in *The Price of the Ticket: Collected Nonfiction, 1948–1985* (New York: St. Martin's, 1985); reprinted in *James Baldwin: Collected Essays*, ed. Toni Morrison (New York: Library of America, 1998), 830.

7 Baldwin, "Price of the Ticket," 832.

8 Beauford Delaney, interview in *New York Telegraph*, March 27, 1930, quoted in Leeming, *Amazing Grace*, 37.

9 Henry Miller, *The Amazing and Invariable Beauford DeLaney* (New York: Alicat Bookshop, 1945), quoted in Leeming, *Amazing Grace*, 57.

10 Leeming, *Amazing Grace*, 57.

11 James Baldwin, "On the Painter Beauford Delaney," *Transition* 4, no. 18 (1965); reprinted in Morrison, *James Baldwin: Collected Essays*, 721.

12 Beauford Delaney, letter to Larry Wallrich, June 2, 1958, quoted in Leeming, *Amazing Grace*, 139.

13 Beauford Delaney, letter to Henry and Eve Miller, June 24, 1958, quoted in Leeming, *Amazing Grace*, 139.

14 Baldwin, "On the Painter Beauford Delaney," 720.

15 Baldwin, "On the Painter Beauford Delaney," 721.

16 James Baldwin, undated letter, 1958, quoted in Leeming, *Amazing Grace*, 140.

17 *Beauford Delaney and James Baldwin: Through the Unusual Door*, Knoxville Museum of Art, February 7, 2020–October 25 2020, https://knoxart.org/exhibitions/beauford-delaney-and-james-baldwin-through-the-unusual-door/; catalogue available at https://www.bibliovault.org/free_ebook_request.epl?ISBN=9780998825250&format=acsmpdf. I interviewed Wicks for the Les Amis de Beauford Delaney blog, and he spoke carefully of the guidance he found in having Baldwin as "my co-curator": see Rachel Cohen and Stephen C. Wicks, "Stephen Wicks and Rachel Cohen Discuss Baldwin Portrait—Part 2," *Les Amis de Beauford Delaney* (blog), December 11, 2021, http://lesamisdebeauforddelaney.blogspot.com/2021/12/stephen-wicks-and-rachel-cohen-discuss_01943507523.html.

18 Baldwin, "On the Painter Beauford Delaney," 721.

19 Beauford Delaney, letter to Richard A. Long, October 9, 1967, quoted by Richard Long at the end of his introduction to *Beauford Delaney: A Retrospective* (New York: Studio Museum in Harlem, 1978), n.p.

THIRTEEN

Choosing Both

Abstraction and Singularity in Beauford Delaney and James Baldwin

Monika Gehlawat

The happy, if belated, recognition of Beauford Delaney's exquisite work would be incomplete without acknowledgment of his peculiar, career-long talent for incorporating both abstraction and figuration in his paintings. While there have certainly been abstract painters, like Willem de Kooning, who worked with the figure, few have so gleefully incorporated both the radical freedom of abstraction *and* the particular pleasures of figuration in so many canvases and across such a broad body of work. Delaney is less a painter of definitive "phases" than one who generated an expansive freedom in artistic experimentation that was not afforded him in life. While in his personal experience, according to David Leeming, Delaney compartmentalized the different aspects of his identity (his sexuality, artistic practice, and religious background),[1] in his paintings, he shifts nimbly between and overlaps genres, endowing his figurative work with an expressive range that recalls the fauvist influence of Henri Matisse, while often invoking surrealist landscapes or natural imagery in his abstract paintings. There is a kind of insatiability that characterizes Delaney's paintings—their vivid colors, myriad portraits, whimsical landscapes, and most of all, insistent play with any and all formal methods at hand.

What has any of this to do with James Baldwin? In this essay, I hope to show that Baldwin and Delaney share certain experimental methods that can be discerned more readily through juxtaposition. Specifically, Delaney's proclivity for *choosing both* abstraction and figuration in fact links his painting to Baldwin's nonfiction, for though they worked in different media, both artists coordinate the freedom of abstraction with the singular authority of figuration to achieve formal and political ends. Specifically, in several essays and speeches, Baldwin uses pronoun play as a rhetorical strategy to enact a vision of democracy he finds lacking in America. If we consider his linguistic methods alongside Delaney's experiments with abstraction and figuration, we can see more clearly how Baldwin refuses to surrender the authenticity of his own personhood even as he demands that the value of human life in American be equally and interchangeably valid. Thus, in language, he lays claim to both the resources of personhood (as figuration) and the symbolic status of citizenship (as abstraction). As Black American artists, Delaney and Baldwin balanced the historical pressure and emotional urgency to represent the particularities of Black life with the artistic freedom to transcend the limitations of their so-called minority status.

In his essay "On the Painter Beauford Delaney" (1965), Baldwin writes that "Beauford's work leads the inner and the outer eye, directly and inexorably, to a new confrontation with reality."[2] Baldwin implies that Delaney's paintings invite our engagement with not only the particularities of reality but also the vicissitudes of memory—both personal and collective—and thus engage trauma, imagination, and emotion. He achieves this intervention by audaciously working in both figurative and abstract modes, resourced according to the pressures of the moment. halley k harrisburg of the Michael Rosenfeld Gallery, who organized a solo show of Delaney's work in 2016, has stated, "It was really courageous for African-American artists of Delaney's generation to be abstract painters. They faced pressure from both the black and white communities to paint the black narrative as Jacob Lawrence and Romare Bearden did. To abandon representation—and specifically representation of the African-American experience—took extraordinary bravery, but for artists like Delaney it was in their soul. They were abstract painters and it is very gratifying to see that they are now being accepted as abstract painters."[3]

Yet rather than reading Delaney's midcareer shift toward abstraction as inherently better, because freer or somehow truer to his "soul," I want to highlight his persistent commitment to both the creative experimentation of the abstract mode and the distinctive gratifications of personhood afforded by figuration. Although his turn to abstraction predated painters like Jackson Pollock, Barnett Newman, Franz Kline, and others who became known as leading abstract expressionists, Delaney irreverently skirted their dogmatic rigor and continued to allow thematic content, and thus forms of subjective singularity, to define his painting, alongside radical abstraction.

Notably, among the figurative paintings Delaney produced after his turn toward abstraction are his celebrated portraits of James Baldwin. Consider *Dark Rapture*, painted in 1941 (plate 1), which situates its subject as a nude in a surrealist forest, recalling the elongated forms pictured in Matisse's *Bathers by a River* (1909–16) while invoking the bright color palette of his *Bonheur de vivre* (1905). Undoubtedly an homage to his fauvist predecessor, Delaney's portrait of Baldwin charges its subject's body with a vitality enlivened by myriad brushstrokes that juxtapose contrasting chromatic angles, making it "colored," and thus subverting the historically pejorative meaning of that term. Instead, the subject projects toward us as intensely as the landscape that surrounds him, as the fantasy of freedom that issues from this painting departs from the concrete context or stable backdrop we expect from portraiture. The figure is seated on what might be brightly colored carpets, in a swirling and animated landscape. As a nude, he is pictured as archetypal, a supernatural man, neither primitive nor worldly. At the same time, however, the sitter's facial features are clearly delineated; this is a man, not simply a figure, who manifests a somber, almost spiritual, self-composure that balances the painting's spirited tonal palette. The subject's alert watchfulness countermands the one-directionality of the gaze upon the Black body in America. Not quite regarding the viewer, the seated figure's eyes seem meditative and observant, an embodiment of the inner and outer eye that Baldwin felt Delaney cultivated in him. At once a painting of a man and of *this* man, *Dark Rapture* enacts the composite plurality Baldwin would later elaborate in his writing as "I," "you," "one," "he," and "we."

Just as Delaney was inspired by Matisse for his vivid emphasis on color and his own play with figuration and abstraction, so would Baldwin often invoke Henry James as a literary forefather. For Baldwin, working in creative nonfiction and the essay form, the play with pronouns became both an homage to the influence of Henry James and a political gesture geared toward a solution to problems posed in Baldwin's essays. James's late novels are known for their enveloping abstraction, an obscuring of the particularities of personhood, or character, in favor of a finely textured narrative voice that becomes the very atmosphere of consciousness itself. James's movement from the specific embodiment of characterization to the abstraction of self-reflective thought finds a radical counterpart in Baldwin's essays. Specifically, Baldwin uses "I," "you," "one," "he," and "we" interchangeably as subjects in any given sentence or passage, in order to enact a kind of utopian abstraction that seeks to overcome the limitations of, and therefore the biases against, racial and sexual identity in American democracy.

To consider language, and nonfiction in particular, in terms of abstraction may seem to deviate from the concrete power that is typically assigned to the genre, but Baldwin capitalized on the discursive freedom afforded by the essay form precisely in order to challenge the false transparency of political categories and historical narratives, even as he remained anchored in thematic arguments. While the distinctions between figurative and abstract painting in Delaney's work are at first more readily apparent, Baldwin too finds purchase in pivoting between a stark representation of reality and the transcendence of it. Thus both Baldwin's and Delaney's works exhibit a complex understanding of what it means to be a gay, Black, American artist, at once demanding the forms of subjective and creative singularity their white counterparts enjoy *and* speaking to their shared racial history and the unique, and ongoing, suffering of Black Americans.

When asked in February 1960 to speak on the subject of minority rights, Baldwin responded with characteristic defiance, delivering a speech titled "In Search of a Majority: An Address." In it, Baldwin repeatedly distinguishes himself from the term "Negro" in order to subvert its objectifying power and expose it as an abstraction connoting failure. He does so by speaking as a "we," a category he uses to condemn the blind fear that drives Americans' collective unconsciousness: "We could never, never allow Negroes to starve, to grow bitter, and to die in ghettos all over the country if we were not driven by some nameless fear that has nothing to do with Negroes."[4] This "we" is strategic, as Baldwin's audience at Kalamazoo College was likely white, upper-middle class, and educated—a liberal population to whom he considered himself equal and sought to awaken from a political complacency he loathed. He demands that his audience consider this question: If "we" are not fearful, why do we accept this extreme dehumanization? He is "in search of a majority" that is still inchoate, so his deliberate appropriation of the pronoun *we*, and his self-assertion within its sphere of influence, can be read as at once critical and visionary.

Toward the end of the speech, Baldwin juxtaposes a dizzying array of pronouns to create distinctive positions in an intersubjective arena in which he situates himself, his audience, and the figure of the "American Negro":

> No one in the world—in the entire world—knows more—knows Americans better or, odd as this may sound, loves them more than the American Negro. This is because he has had to watch you, outwit you, deal with you, and bear you, and sometimes even bleed and die with you, ever since we got here, that is, since both of us, black and white, got here—and this is a wedding. Whether I like it or not, or whether you like it or not, we are bound together forever. We are part of each other. What is happening to every Negro in the country at any time is also happening to you.[5]

This insight continues to prove timely to our contemporary moment in a number of ways. The pervasive use of "we" toward the end of the passage signals his grim acceptance of the inextricable ties between white and Black Americans: "We are bound together forever." But the complexity and pathos that comes with that realization depends upon naming "I" and "you" as historically distinct. For as Baldwin demonstrates, this is not an equal marriage—a state he condemns by identifying with the American Negro. Now humanizing this canny subject by referring to him in the third person, Baldwin reminds his audience of the discerning personhood behind the abstraction "Negro," for "he has had to watch you, outwit you, deal with you, and bear you." Thus "he," "I," "you," and "we" take on specific symbolic functions in Baldwin's rhetorical argument. Each represents a distinctive form of subjectivity: Baldwin is an embodied and singular "I" speaking to an audience that serves as a white abstraction, a collective "you" seated in the auditorium, rendered like brushstrokes on a canvas. "He" and "we," meanwhile, require imaginative work from this audience to generate sympathetic understanding of a life they have not lived (who is "he"?) and desire for a new and more inclusive collectivity (who can "we" be?).

The play of signification that characterizes Baldwin's nonfiction, abstract *because* political, was misunderstood by certain intellectuals on both the left and the right. Douglas Field reports on how some found his rhetorical, and indeed cultural, plurality irresponsible (the citation of Morris Dickstein is his):

> Baldwin's use of racially interchanging pronouns infuriated and bemused a number of black and white critics alike. [Note: See also Morris Dickstein . . . where he notes that "Baldwin's 'we' sometimes wobbles in the early essays, acting out his predicament by assuming now a white, now a black face."] Langston Hughes, for example, bemoaned that "Baldwin's viewpoints are half-American, half-Afro-American, incompletely fused." Hughes's suggestion that Baldwin's writing is somehow bastardized—neither authentically white nor black—is most acutely illustrated in the writing of the white critic, Robert Bone, in his survey of African American literature, *The Negro Novel in America*, first published in 1958. In his chapter on Baldwin, Bone's writing demonstrates profound anxieties about the ways in which *Giovanni's Room* and other "raceless" novels merge dangerously with the body of "white" American literature.[6]

Given Baldwin's intention to undermine multiple social and symbolic binaries, he was bound to dismay those critics whose political perspective depended on maintaining fixed racial affects and identities. As a Black gay artist, Baldwin was marginalized by the Nation of Islam, the Black Panther movement, and even Martin Luther King Jr. He himself never disavowed these groups, advocating for Black civil rights throughout his career, even as he cultivated friendships with Jewish, white American, and Pan-African artists, as well as with lovers in both Europe and America.

While this broad range of cultural, political, and personal behavior caused some in the politically polarized 1960s to view him as compromised or apolitical, Baldwin's complex extroversion clearly relates him to his mentor and friend Beauford Delaney. Indeed, just as Baldwin's formally inventive pronoun play received mixed reviews from his contemporaries, so too have some art historians attributed Delaney's long-neglected career to his failure to fit neatly into expectations for the Black American artist. Eloise Johnson, for instance, explains:

> [Delaney] was not given to overt political representations, as were so many African-American artists of his generation (although he was acutely aware of the climate of racial discrimination that permeated his world). On the contrary, Delaney's style—a Fauvist-infused abstraction that ranged from figuration to nonfiguration—defies assumptions about artists of color at mid-twentieth century. As a result, his achievements and talent went largely unacknowledged until the

end of the twentieth century, when new postmodern readings and exhibitions focused long-overdue attention on Delaney's art.[7]

Notably, Johnson credits the more recent appreciation of Delaney's work to "postmodern readings" that presumably destabilize formal oppositions such as between abstraction and figuration as well as identity markers such as Black and white, gay and straight, or American and Other. Throughout their careers, Baldwin and Delaney depended on, and had to live with the consequences of, disrupting these categories. In particular, the two men shared a common sense of alienation, or un-homeliness, in face of their families and of America in general. This estrangement derived from the widespread rejection of what was most important to them: their race, sexuality, and artistic identity. Feeling as if none of these fundamental aspects of their personhood were honored or even accepted in the country of their citizenship, Baldwin and Delaney forged a kind of kinship in exile, a family of their own.

In an essay he wrote for the *New York Times Magazine* titled "The American Dream and the American Negro" (1965), Baldwin explains this painful experience: "It comes as a great shock to discover that the country which is your birthplace and to which you owe your life and identity has not, in its whole system of reality, evolved any place for you. The disaffection and gap between people, only on the basis of their skins, begins there and accelerates throughout your whole lifetime. You realize that you are 30 and you are having a terrible time."[8] Here Baldwin deliberately writes in the second person in order to compel his white liberal readers to envision his fraught personal history—an experience that is at once acutely his own and suffered by all Black Americans—and to underscore how foreign it is from that of his white audience. Rather than "you" being an opposing abstraction, as it was in the Kalamazoo speech, here it becomes a way of obliging curiosity and care through a kind of thought experiment. "Imagine if" is the haunting, unspoken preface to this passage. The raw simplicity of its last line, "You realize you are 30 and you are having a terrible time," makes his innocent message accessible to all readers, while reminding them of the spiritual darkness with which artists like Baldwin and Delaney had to struggle throughout their lives.

Delaney's portraits of Baldwin and other Black figures, I want to suggest, use abstraction and figuration in order to attempt to picture this dislocation as well as the artist's power to overcome the void of alienation. Paintings such as *Moving Sunlight* (1965; plate 15), *Portrait of Ella Fitzgerald* (1968; plate 26), and *Marian Anderson* (1965) share not only the luminous yellow that pervades Delaney's work from this time but also his play with abstraction and figuration.[9] This trio showcases his incredible flexibility with genre even as it establishes an authoritative aesthetic disposition that prioritizes color as a formal device for abstract painting. In his *Portrait of James Baldwin* (1965; plate 16), painted twenty years after *Dark Rapture* (see plate 1), Delaney uses his then-preferred tone of yellow to establish an intense all-over color field that blurs the distinction between figure and ground, so that the sitter's head looms profoundly and disproportionately large against varying shades of yellow.

In *Portrait of James Baldwin* (1965), we reencounter the pronounced particularity of facial features that contrasts with the otherwise abstract image, as in *Dark Rapture*. In the later painting, both figure and ground are energized by the yellow color field, just as they often are in other paintings by dynamic brushstrokes and impasto layering. Delaney chooses both figuration and abstraction, and this pair of portraits of the same subject reveals the expressive range of his inclusive choice. In *Portrait of James Baldwin* (1965), Delaney is keen to validate the distinctive personhood of his subject, not only in his well-wrought face but also, more subtly, in the slight tonal distinction that separates figure from ground. Baldwin's shirt is a darker, umber tone of yellow that allows his slender shoulders to be defined against the chartreuse background. This distinction, as well as the grave expression in his eyes and the subtle outline of his tie, lends the sitter a kind of dignified poise reminiscent of the subject in *Dark Rapture*. Thematically, then, Delaney insists that the openness of the abstract field contends with the delineated composure of his subject.

Abstraction and figuration can be done differently and jointly, Delaney demonstrates, so that the very argument of these paintings stems from their reluctance to stay in one lane. These are thus at once pictures of refusal and of radical incorporation; in that regard, they are pictures of freedom. Just as Baldwin ventures boldly into any and all subject positions in his writing, so too does Delaney take liberties with what *ought to be* abstraction or figuration, effectively transgressing the limitations of each genre. Baldwin in these portraits is at once legitimized for his, and *only his*, unmistakable subjectivity while still allowed to float freely in a strange and as yet unrealized world: a vivid nude on his forest throne, a naked face in brilliant light. In that respect, Delaney gives us pictures of Baldwin's aspiration "to prevent myself from becoming *merely* a Negro; or even merely a Negro writer. I wanted to find out in what way the *specialness* of my experience could be made to connect me with other people instead of dividing me from them."[10]

And indeed, whether seated naked and serene or looming large on the yellow canvas, Baldwin's figure in these paintings awaits and invites a connection between viewer and subject. He is pictured as at once powerful and vulnerable, a sensitive persona that reflects the voice we hear in his essays.

In his essays, Baldwin rigorously challenges the imaginations of his readers—or what we might for our purposes call their powers for abstract thinking—in order to expose them to a reality they do not share. He reimagines who "we" might be, ventriloquizing how "he" sees "you" and conflating both speaker and reader into a "you" who suffers. In essence, he abstracts personhood through pronoun play, blurring the lines between subject and object, context and interiority. One sees this most dramatically in his experiments using the first person: "I am speaking very seriously, and this is not an overstatement: I picked cotton, I carried it to the market, I built the railroads under someone else's whip for nothing. For nothing."[11] Here, with dreadful detail, Baldwin recalls the long historical oppression of Black Americans and its inevitable generational impact. The "I" who speaks is at once singular and multiple, denoting a singular narratorial consciousness named "James Baldwin" and an abstract, collective consciousness encompassing all Black Americans. He insists that "this is not an overstatement" because he has personally inherited the agony of those men and women who came before him and whose labor he now dramatizes. All that misery was, by definition, "for nothing," given that systemic racism persists in America. "For nothing" catapults the reader back into the present moment, when Baldwin emerges as still-suffering. His implication is that his own fate, speaking now as an embodied "I," relates not only to the vast historical crime of slavery, but also to the present-day "case of the American Negro." It is this existential pain that connects Baldwin to Delaney, as does their turn to art as a means of self-expression and personal salvation.

While Baldwin's linguistic experiment with pronoun play is more explicitly political, I would argue that Delaney's paintings reflect his own desire also to supersede the racial, sexual, political, and geographic categories that inhibited his organic evolution as a person and artist. In art, he created the world as he would have it. His paintings produce the vision of what could have been, and what *could be*—a futurity that explains why they appear, as does Baldwin's writing, so incredibly fresh, contemporary, and prescient now. Take the late painting *Village (Saint-Paul-de-Vence)* (1972; plate 32), which was part of Baldwin's private collection and painted while Delaney visited his friend at his home in the South of France. At once figurative and abstract, *Village* portrays a discernible workaday world, with figures walking, eating, and going about daily life. Yet it is constituted by an illuminating tonal palette that makes it seem an otherworldly landscape. Notably, Delaney uses white paint as a structural device to constitute the steps and architecture of the ancient town, a formal choice that allows the painting to express the solidity of proportional planning but without weight, so that, combined with its yellows, celery greens, and brief, disciplined crimson outlines, *Village* evokes a sunlit, ethereal mood. Its atmosphere speaks at once of holiday and the everyday, of the transcendent and the earthly, a kind of secular spirituality felt in so many of Delaney's paintings. Villagers are both recognizable as figures and rendered in abstract brushstrokes, and they interact and live in a kind of harmonious, enlightened realm, as if a lustrous, verdant filter had been placed on the world as we know it, effectively re-creating it as paradise, a dream to dream.

Why not? Delaney's paintings seem to ask. Why not redefine the meanings of our labels of majority and minority, of abstraction and figuration, of figure and ground, indeed even of color? By retaining the particularities of personhood that arise in portraiture or personal memory, Delaney and Baldwin honor the authentic and traceable subjectivity of each individual they represent. Any collectivity worth its salt must maintain and honor the eccentricities of its individual constituents, their right to be different within and among themselves. Such pictures and narratives are needed. Yet abstraction within and beyond these representational practices advances toward the unknown, the as-yet-unrealized, the work of the imagination that makes both the past and future understandable and thus has the potential to activate personal and collective transformation. In juxtaposing their work, we find that Baldwin and Delaney are united not only in friendship and a shared identity, but also in their unrelenting entitlement to *choose both*, indeed to choose *all*.

NOTES

1 See David Leeming, *Amazing Grace: A Life of Beauford Delaney* (New York: Oxford University Press, 1998).

2 James Baldwin, "On the Painter Beauford Delaney," *Transition* 4, no. 18 (1965); reprinted in *James Baldwin: Collected Essays*, ed. Toni Morrison (New York: Library of America, 1998), 721.

3 halley k harrisburg, quoted in Sara Roffino, "Abstraction in Focus," *Blouin Art and Auction* 39, no. 7 (March 2016): 29.

4 James Baldwin, "In Search of a Majority: An Address," in *Nobody Knows My Name: More Notes of a Native Son* (New York: Dial, 1961); reprinted in Morrison, *James Baldwin: Collected Essays*, 219.

5 Baldwin, "In Search of a Majority," 220–21.

6 Douglas Field, *All Those Strangers: The Art and Lives of James Baldwin* (Oxford: Oxford University Press, 2016), 38. Field quotes Morris Dickstein, *Gates of Eden: American Culture in the Sixties* (New York: Basic Books, 1977), 173; and, for Langston Hughes, cites David Leeming, *James Baldwin: A Biography* (New York: Arcade, 1994), 101.

7 Eloise Johnson, "Out of the Ashes: Cultural Identity and Marginalization in the Art of Beauford Delaney," *Notes in the History of Art* 24, no. 4 (Summer 2005): 46–55.

8 James Baldwin, "The American Dream and the American Negro," *New York Times*, March 7, 1965; reprinted in Morrison, *James Baldwin: Collected Essays*, 715.

9 Beauford Delaney, *Marian Anderson*, oil and egg tempera emulsion on canvas, unframed: 63 15/16 × 51 5/16 × 1½ in. (162.4 × 130.33 × 3.81 cm), Virginia Museum of Fine Arts.

10 James Baldwin, "The Discovery of What It Means to Be an American," in *Nobody Knows My Name: More Notes of a Native Son* (New York: Dell, 1961); reprinted in Morrison, *James Baldwin: Collected Essays*, 137.

11 Baldwin, "Discovery of What It Means to Be an American," 715.

FOURTEEN

"Architects of the Spirit"

Color and Intimacy in Beauford Delaney's Post-1950 Abstractions

Abbe Schriber

In Beauford Delaney's abstract paintings, color demands attention. There is, of course, the glowing intensity of the hues, but also the nuance and specificity of the term *color* itself at midcentury. Delaney's dear friend James Baldwin wrote in 1962, "In Negro speech, the word 'colored' has very special reverberations. . . . The same phrase can also be applied to someone who is direct, warm, unaffected, and unconquerable."[1] Seen within the privacy of shared Black reference to which Baldwin alludes, "color" is deeply felt and reinhabited in the face of its being externally projected. For Baldwin, color is tenderness between people racialized, and spatialized as such, in the United States. One of Delaney's earliest full abstractions, the oil painting *Composition 16* (1954–56; plate 8), begins to suggest ways of thinking of his paintings in these terms. *Composition 16* challenges many critics' desires to read Delaney's paintings through his psychological states, for it exemplifies a sensual tactility that is born of paint rendered as a malleable material. A thicket of tubular, yellow squiggles dance across the canvas, converging toward a diffuse atmospheric center; at the bottom, dense strokes of blue, teal, green, and hot, bright orange interlace with the yellow. Pushing out to each edge, Delaney's expansive swirls set a precedent for later works, moving color right to the surface's very limit and advancing an unframed, unbounded field.

Composition 16 shows that Delaney's canvases elicit new expressive modes through redefining vision as visual, tactile, and interrelational. This essay argues that for Delaney, intimacy can be understood as an extension of seeing, and that his relationships with Baldwin and other close artist friends such as Herbert Gentry are essential to reading his paintings as such.[2] Delaney's paintings do not immediately index any form of social intimacy: their process of making does not record collective creation or partnership, nor does it register intimate, bodily production beyond that of brush to hand. According to Ann Eden Gibson, Delaney's brushstrokes bear more textural similarities to how his mentor Stuart Davis applied paint than to the grand gestures of abstract expressionists: "a material application of pigment decoratively applied as if it were textured plaster on a wall."[3] Yet in the worked, dense chromatic surfaces of Delaney's canvases, there is an intimacy born not only of multisensory stimuli, but also of affiliations and social exchanges embodied in the complexity of color.[4]

Baldwin offers the richest and most consistent example of an intimate contact, from his first meeting with Delaney as a young man in 1945 in Greenwich Village to his role as primary trustee of Delaney's estate at the end of the artist's life. As I use the term here, "intimacy" comprises not only sexual or romantic relations, but also interactions that are "publicly mediated" and therefore sited liminally between the familial and the familiar.[5] Beyond the traditional spaces of the domestic and the interior, queer intimacy extends by necessity into spheres beyond the heterosexually coded nuclear family that has been co-opted into a privatized conception of the intimate. As it did for Baldwin and Delaney, this intimacy can span day-to-day companionship, the extension of parental or stand-in parental care, pragmatic financial and emotional support, close physical but not sexual proximity, long dinners, and nights of drinking, talking, and listening to records until dawn.

However, according to his biographer David Leeming, Delaney also "kept his life in compartments."[6] He was often shy to acknowledge or act upon sexual desires that could increase his vulnerability to danger, even in 1940s bohemian New York.[7] Attacks on Black residents of Greenwich Village, where Delaney lived, were commonplace and documented in detail by newspapers such as *PM* and Adam Clayton Powell Jr.'s *The People's Voice*. In August 1946, jazz singer Sarah Vaughn and musicians George Treadway, Naomi Wright, and J. C. Heard were assaulted after leaving the popular jazz venue Café Society.[8] Delaney himself had been the victim of an assault in the Village in 1942.[9]

In 1950s Paris, Delaney fostered relationships with Black American men in addition to Baldwin: painters, poets, composers, and sculptors such as Gentry, Romare Bearden, Howard Swanson, Ed Clark, Larry Potter, Ted Joans, and Haywood "Bill" Rivers. Most had arrived in Paris funded by the GI Bill or on art-school fellowships. Delaney met Gentry on his first overseas trip to Paris. Gentry remarked repeatedly on the bond they formed: "I never really tell people all my problems. All of a sudden . . . I'm talking to him and opening up and feeling better, I mean really. I realized . . . how important it is to have someone to talk to, have a dialogue, or have someone you can talk to and they would listen, maybe advise."[10] To the *New York Times*, he described Delaney as "a lyrical expressionist who wasn't about selling, but was about painting and people. . . . His strong point was as the philosopher, the giver."[11]

It was Gentry who, along with Romare Bearden, actively lobbied the Whitney Museum of American Art about the possibility of a solo exhibition for Delaney in 1973, just after Bearden's major retrospective had opened at MoMA—a major coup in the fight for increased museum representation.[12] The care that Bearden and Gentry extended to their friend is evident in a note Gentry scribbled at the end of a letter to Delaney's Paris gallerist, Darthea Speyer: "P.S.: I talked to Romare again last nite regarding this matter and we both decided to go to the Whitney right after Romare's opening. March 28."[13] Bearden and Gentry ultimately paused their efforts because of interest from another potential exhibitor, Ornette Coleman's Artist House, the experimental loft-space venue at 131 Prince Street. However, a Delaney retrospective would not materialize until 1978, at the Studio Museum in Harlem.[14]

Despite the interpersonal generosity between Delaney, Gentry, and Bearden, expectations for Black masculinity were not uniformly agreed upon among the broader groups back in Paris. For instance, Delaney and Baldwin only occasionally fraternized with Richard Wright's circle at Café Tournon, where the two encountered a palpable discomfort with homosexuality.[15]

What Lauren Berlant and Michael Warner call a "national heterosexuality" could not detach itself from certain notions of a permissible Black American masculinity, even across the Atlantic in self-imposed, diasporic exile.[16] Indeed, the threat queer sexuality posed to nationhood and conceptions of home has been powerfully linked to Baldwin's own artistic choices and his desire for a more complexly nuanced, intersectional Black nationalism.[17] Theorist E. Patrick Johnson notes that "some marginalized groups like black gay men are willing to take risks that might endanger their lives just so that they can experience intimacy—through touch, sweat, heat—in ways that they never experience living in white supremacist society that constantly rejects them."[18] However, wary of the vulnerability posed by this form of relation, Delaney found in abstraction new pathways to intimacy in the face of violent cultural reaction to Black being and queer attachment. His paintings retranslate, into forms of freedom, the circumscription of queerness that resulted from heteronormative conventions of care shaped by US homophobia and racial segregation in the 1950s and 1960s.

In "Color," first published in *Esquire* in 1962 and reprinted in his *The Price of the Ticket* (1985), Baldwin recognized the power of shared recognition within all-Black spaces. His words are worth quoting at length:

> Color, for anyone who uses it, or is used by it, is a most complex, calculated, and dangerous phenomenon. One will probably find more color in Small's Paradise, for example, even on an off night, than I, anyway, have usually managed to encounter in any nightclub downtown. It is not that the music is intrinsically so much better—always—but the people playing it and the people hearing it have more fun with it, and with each other. They know, on one level, everything concerning each other that there is to know: they are all black. And this produces an atmosphere of freedom which is exactly as real as the limits which have made it necessary. . . . And while they are dancing and listening to the music and drinking and joking and laughing, with all their finery on, and looking so bold and free, they know who enters, who leaves, and on what errands: they are aware of the terrible and unreachable forces which yet rule their lives.[19]

For Baldwin, "color"—and its correlate in the affect of "coloredness" in an environment for and by Black people—offers one of the few sites of intimacy in which the constraints of "respectable" behavior and self-presentation to the white world fall away. Within these bounds, color becomes a kind of care, allowing for creative expression among kin united by the baseline persistence of implicit or explicit racism. Color, to rehearse Baldwin's words, "produces an atmosphere of freedom which is exactly as real as the limits which have made it necessary." Baldwin suggests that the intimacy of color offers ways to work, think, and imagine past abstraction as original trauma irrevocably entwined with, as Leigh Raiford phrases it, "the concept of abstract personhood."[20] "Blackness in abstraction" has been prominently theorized as a conceptual paradigm, particularly in the deployment of black monochrome pigment intended to "negotiate and exhaust the paradigm of black representation in visual art."[21] Already in 1968, a sole tube of "lamp black" paint anchored the cover of Edmund Barry Gaither's exhibition catalogue *Afro American Artists: New York and Boston*. Edited by the director and curator of the Museum of the National Center of Afro-American Artists (NCAAA), the catalogue was a powerful reminder of the condition of "coloredness" that anchored the 158 works by 70 Black artists (see figure 14.1).

Following Baldwin, Delaney's work prompts viewers to imagine for artists of African descent the formal and conceptual possibilities of color beyond the immediacy of black pigment. His abstractions formally incorporate the full range of the color spectrum, suggesting color as a lens for viewing and inhabiting the world, especially at midcentury or just after. We might see Delaney's vibrant, gestural strokes foregrounding color and "coloredness" beyond that concept's externally imposed, structurally imposed connotations, and instead as what Baldwin conveyed as "vivid, many-hued, e.g. the rainbow, and warm and quick and vital, e.g. life."[22]

Historically, abstraction has been forced to rationalize its "motivation" or stated purpose apart from representation.[23] Yet for many European and American theorists of modernist painting, albeit from vastly different standpoints, if line and color are decoupled from representation, they become superfluous, and therefore risk straying too close to artificial, redundant, or exaggerated form.[24] Modernist ideas (what Caroline A. Jones calls "the spectre of the decorative" and what Douglas Crimp calls "the decorative unconscious") saddled abstraction with (then) pejorative associations with queerness and/or femininity.[25] Delaney's watercolors, gouaches, and impasto-laden oils all appear to dismiss of any such threatening critical evaluation. In an untitled watercolor from 1960 (plate 11), for example, an ebullient palette of popsicle-hued arabesques is contained by a square yellow outline. The squiggled curlicues of seemingly random, vibrant colors create a tension with the heavily outlined square that binds them, though this

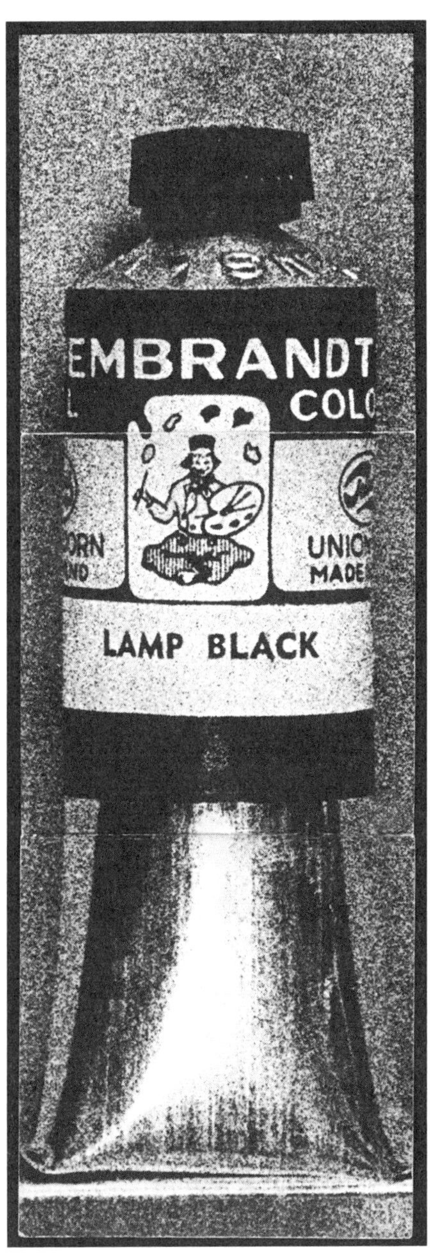

14.1

Cover of the exhibition catalogue *Afro-American Artists: New York and Boston*, edited by Edmund Barry Gaither (Boston: Museum of Fine Arts Boston, 1970). Photograph © 2025 Museum of Fine Arts, Boston.

outline too is in yellow, and broken through by other colors. The painting allows us to ask how the inclination to flourish, to aestheticize, can give new association to color and line when detached from mimesis.

For Black artists, nonrepresentational abstraction has historically provided a multifaceted relation to care: flight from the perceived legibility of race, gender, and sexuality; resistance to identitarian expectations through new or inscrutable forms; recoding of formal gesture into private, shared communication; or sustained examination of color and line in translation across transnational, diasporic pathways.[26] Raiford has powerfully argued that abstraction can work against the limits imposed by the abstracting of personhood that is baked into white supremacy. From a related standpoint, but in response to the concept of an easily extractable, perceptible social identity, David Getsy has argued for late twentieth- and twenty-first-century abstraction as a counter to essentialism and even homophobia that pigeonholes and narrows personhood: "Abstraction is one tactic for refusing the power of this marking and for resisting the visual taxonomies through which people are recognized and regulated. . . . Abstraction makes sense as a vehicle for queer stances and politics because it is unforeclosed in its visualizations and open in the ways in which it posits relations."[27]

For Delaney, strategies of opacity or subversion operate not as deflection, but as intimate invitation.[28] He remained an astute student of European and American painting throughout his artistic development and sought to earn a living through making work invested in its traditions. As Nikki A. Greene points out, in Boston, Delaney visited the studio of John Singer Sargent after the older artist's death. It is possible that he made his portrait of a nude Baldwin, *Dark Rapture* (1941; plate 1), in dialogue with Sargent's *Thomas McKeller,* the portrait of his nude Black model. Already in 1941, Greene notes, it is through color and brushstroke that Delaney effects his intimate affection without sensationalizing Baldwin's nudity: "Although Delaney created a nude portrait of Baldwin, the writer appears 'dressed' here in multicolor pigments. . . . As a black man, Delaney respectfully and upliftingly renders Baldwin's black, male body not in code or in hiding. Baldwin is not under erasure. In fact, Baldwin is boldly proclaimed and celebrated with every brushstroke!"[29]

Delaney rejected the naturalism and dark palette of Sargent as well as the discourses of abstraction emerging alongside abstract expressionism at midcentury, which increasingly congealed into a dogma of autonomy, medium specificity, and optical hegemony under the influence of Clement

Greenberg. If abstract expressionism proffered artistic individuality as a crucial component of these discourses, it did so paradoxically through collectivity—socializing in gatherings and discussions in downtown New York locales such as the infamous Cedar Tavern. Yet the physical architectures of a storied site like the Cedar Tavern are inextricable from collective and bodily safety, which in turn lead to different expectations, and artistic translations, of interpersonal intimacy. After all, it was Baldwin who pointed to the dangers of the Village, and the risks of Delaney's living Black and queer in that space, despite its history of welcoming gay and lesbian congregation: "His example operated as an enormous protection: for the Village, then, and not only for a boy like me, was an alabaster maze perched above a boiling sea. To lose oneself into the maze was to fall into the sea. . . . Racially, the Village was vicious, partly because of the natives, largely because of the tourists, and absolutely because of the cops."[30]

Paris offered an environment that was, if not free from racism, at least unbound from its pernicious effects in the United States. The artists congregated in spaces like Chez Honey, a restaurant, jazz club, nightspot, and gallery on rue Jules-Chaplain in Montparnasse run by Gentry and his wife.[31] Here, Delaney's community of African American painters and sculptors expanded the limits of abstraction through the combined material and optical properties of color. Darby English has mapped the extension of these discourses into Greenbergian formalism in the 1960s and early 1970s—a time when Black artists making late-modernist paintings were often dismissed by white critics as derivative of white modernists, and by Black critics as insufficiently communicative or legible to Black audiences.[32] For English, "artifactual color" suggests a tension between color's metaphorical and lived valences.[33] By this account, formalist doctrine should have been open to the contingency and diversity of social life, yet it remained averse to formal *and* social "deviance." Indeed, modernism policed the subjective experience of looking.[34] Thus in the slight crack of a perceptual window that opened late modernism to new phenomenological possibilities through color, still unresolved was the social specificity of late modernism's corporeal address (its addressing of Blackness, queerness, able-bodiedness, or whiteness itself) for both viewers and makers.

If a conversation is to be had about the convergences of color's literal, metaphorical, and physical meaning, it cannot occur without accounting for what, in 1928, Zora Neale Hurston so famously called being "thrown against a sharp white background," or the visual imposition of race as it occurs in societies shaped by white supremacy.[35] The visual and affective are interlinked in Hurston's account, as she frames the experience of *feeling* colored as inextricable from being seen as such, with the social demarcations of space impacting that feeling. In other words, when Hurston relates that "my color comes" at the jazz club, she is both liberated to color and made all the more aware of it relative to whiteness, particularly that of the white patron. In "Color," Baldwin's point is to attend to the self-determined, if temporary, intimacy to be found within Black spaces: "The atmosphere of a Harlem nightclub *must* be different from that of the Copacabana because of the way of life which has produced it, and the peculiar needs it serves."[36] These spatial dimensions of color shape how we view Delaney's abstraction.

Delaney's peers, such as Romare Bearden and Herbert Gentry, held longstanding, dedicated investments in his work and saw in his paintings modes of relation that extended abstraction to mutual care. Of his own painting practice, Gentry noted, "My base is African American, also it's in my paintings, the people I've met throughout the world, American, African American, but I've met people throughout the world who are my friends who actually I love and we've done things together, so this appears in my work."[37] Here, Gentry directly equates his formal choices with his social configurations, particularly as a Black man among Black artist peers. Gentry's words, and especially his expressionist, quasi-abstract oils, watercolors, and prints, reveal dialogue not only with Delaney's lived ethos but also with his abstractionist works. Gentry's 1962 *Autumn Path*, for example, reveals an open weave of overlapping circles, sticks, and whorls, which wrap and radiate outward from a central vertical band (see figure 14.2). The muted palette of burnt reds, yellows, taupes, and olive greens painted in dry, blunt strokes become indistinguishable from line, dissolving a separation between color and line. One might compare the open composition of this work to that of Delaney's watercolor *Untitled* (1960), discussed above, whose yellow border, Stephen C. Wicks claims, evokes the sill of the Clamart window that looked out at tree foliage, a view that Delaney often shared with Baldwin.[38] Delaney's pastel and mixed-media *Untitled (Abstract Circles)* (ca. 1956; plate 9) relies on similarly active gestures, showing a scumbled composition of circles and whorls in yellow, burnt orange, and indigo. The effect produces an intense optical haze, yet gives the illusion of depth through pastel layered in varying thickness and texture. We can trace such apparently superficial

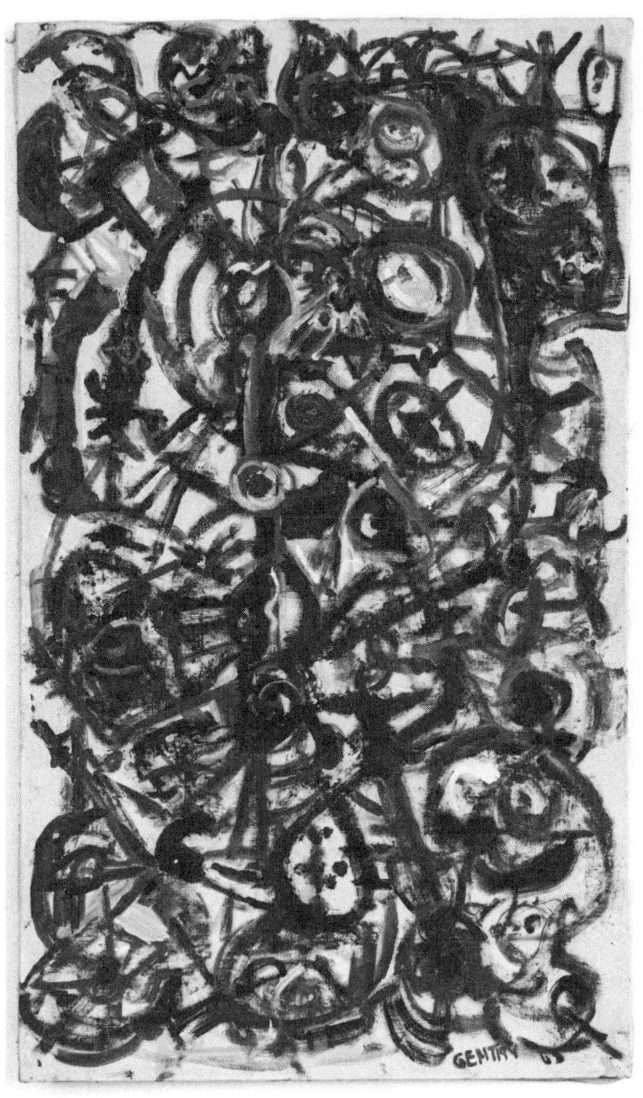

14.2

Herbert Gentry, *Autumn Path*, 1962. Oil on canvas, 53 × 31½ in. (134.6 × 80 cm). © Herbert Gentry. Courtesy of the estate of the artist and RYAN LEE Gallery, New York.

formal affinities between Gentry and Delaney to the intimacy of kin that does not get visualized in abstraction, but only felt.

Art historians have long affirmed that US postwar abstract artists probed the unconscious, spontaneous gesture, yet did so within discursive fields that created the "unconscious" as something historically and socially conditioned. As Michael Leja put it in 1990, "The individual experiences the unconscious, and all of psychological reality, in a form defined and shaped by a culture and its models of self, subject and identity."[39] For Delaney, what bubbled to the surface to animate form was not the same as what emerged for, say, Pollock. Here, again, is where we find the contingencies of "color" and all its associations as part of what each artist brings to the canvas. At stake are the intimacies that abstract painting refuses to render visible to the eye by means of conventional representation, yet which correspond to the physical spaces that offered shared understanding and mutuality. If, as Adrienne Edwards has suggested, "Blackness is the original abstraction" in

the myths invented to justify racist ideology,[40] then we can return to the idea of abstraction deployed by Black modernist painters as inferring the possibility of Black sociality, an insistence on color as alive, mutable, mutually and tenderly regarded.

Delaney noted in a 1970 interview that "abstraction, ostensibly, is simply for me a penetration of something that is more profound in many ways than the rigidity of a form. A form if it breathes some, if it has some enigma to it, it is also the enigma that is the abstract, I would think."[41] Returning to the painting with which we started, *Composition 16*, one can see how its near-calligraphic squiggles surge with breath, a breath imbued in form. It is telling that breath, which gives life, is the metaphor Delaney uses to animate his view of abstraction, the "enigma" of which he understands as deeper and more compelling than form by itself. Instead of indexing an inner, unconscious emotion or sealing himself off into a self-contained world, Delaney's gestures mark subjectivity in and through surrounding relationships, on the premise of building something with a viewer, a peer, or a friend. The warmth with which Delaney held his close friendships and acquaintances—his intimates—is palpable in his post-1950 abstractions, an observation that was not lost on him. In a 1965 letter, he articulated it: "Something has happened to my color and the paintings seem to have sunlight and the feeling sometimes of all you wonderful people it has been my privilege to have as friends and architects of the spirit."[42]

Thank you, Amy Elias, Lauren Mackler, Daonne Huff, Chloe Johnston, Autumn Ahn, and Ashley James for your comments and care in reading this essay.

1 James Baldwin, "Color," *Esquire* , December 1, 1962, 225; reprinted in *The Price of the Ticket: Collected Nonfiction 1948–1985* (New York: St. Martin's, 1985), 319.

2 For prior examples that constellate Delaney's abstraction through care and friendship, see Jamillah James's 2013 exhibition *Brothers and Sisters* at the Studio Museum in Harlem, March 28–June 30, 2013, https://studiomuseum.org/exhibition/brothers-and-sisters; Amy J. Elias, "Yellows and Blues: Delaney, Baldwin, and Synesthetic Expressionism" (paper presented at the College Art Association Annual Conference, February 15, 2019); and James Smalls, "Picturing Jimmy, Picturing Self: James Baldwin, Beauford Delaney, and the Color of Light," and Tyler T. Schmidt, "Lessons in Light: Beauford Delaney's and James Baldwin's 'Unnameable Objects,'" both in *Of Latitudes Unknown: James Baldwin's Radical Imagination*, ed. Alice Mikal Craven and William E. Dow (New York: Bloomsbury, 2019), 35–49, 49–71.

3 Ann Eden Gibson, "Gay and Black in Greenwich Village: Beauford Delaney's Idylls of Integration," in *Beauford Delaney: From New York to Paris*, ed. Patricia Sue Canterbury (Minneapolis: Minneapolis Institute of Art, 2004), 15.

4 The role of New York City, and of Greenwich Village specifically, in the development of Delaney's work is analyzed in Gibson, "Gay and Black in Greenwich Village," 12–31.

5 Lauren Berlant and Michael Warner, "Sex in Public," *Critical Inquiry* 24, no. 2 (Winter 1998): 553.

6 David Leeming, *Amazing Grace: A Life of Beauford Delaney* (New York: Oxford University Press, 1998), 52.

7 See Leeming, *Amazing Grace*, especially 51–55.

8 The papers of Charles White at the Archives of American Art document these occurrences in newspaper clippings and articles saved by the artist. See, for instance, clippings in Charles White Papers, Archives of American Art, Smithsonian Institution, Washington, DC: "'Village' Hoodlums Beat Charlie White, Friend," *The People's Voice*, n.d.; and "The 'Melting Pot' Boils Over in Greenwich Village," *PM*, May 5, 1947, 12.

9 Leeming, *Amazing Grace*, 71.

10 Herbert Gentry, oral history interview with Liza Kirwin, May 23, 1991, Archives of American Art, Smithsonian Institution, Washington, DC,

https://www.aaa.si.edu/collections/interviews/oral-history-interview-herbert-gentry-11493#transcript.

11 Quoted in C. Gerald Fraser, "Beauford Delaney, Painter, Dies; Portraitist of the Famous Was 77," *New York Times*, April 1, 1979, 34, https://www.nytimes.com/1979/04/01/archives/beauford-delaney-painter-dies-portraitist-of-the-famous-was-77.html.

12 See Herbert Gentry, letter to Darthea Speyer, March 23, 1973, box 2, folder 9: correspondence, 1969–73, Galerie Darthea Speyer records, Archives of American Art, Smithsonian Institution.

13 Gentry, letter to Darthea Speyer.

14 In Paris, Ornette Coleman attended Delaney's 1973 exhibition at Speyer's gallery, and there discussed with Delaney the prospect of a show. By August of that year, however, Artist House had contacted Edmund Barry Gaither at the National Center of Afro-American Artists and ceded the exhibition planning to him. See Anne Weber, undated letter to Darthea Speyer, box 2, folder 9: correspondence, 1969–73, Galerie Darthea Speyer records, Archives of American Art, Smithsonian Institution.

15 Leeming, *Amazing Grace*, 115.

16 Berlant and Warner, "Sex in Public," 549.

17 Dwight A. McBride, "Straight Black Studies: On African American Studies, James Baldwin, and Black Queer Studies," in *Black Queer Studies: A Critical Anthology*, ed. E. Patrick Johnson and Mae G. Henderson (Durham, NC: Duke University Press, 2005), 68–89. James Smalls also notes that "exile" was very carefully noted by Baldwin—and also Delaney—in contrast to "expatriate"; see Smalls, "Picturing Jimmy, Picturing Self," 43.

18 E. Patrick Johnson, introduction to *No Tea, No Shade: New Writings in Black Queer Studies* (Durham, NC: Duke University Press, 2016), 9.

19 Baldwin, "Color," 322.

20 Leigh Raiford, "'Burning All Illusion': Abstraction, Black Life, and Unmaking White Supremacy," *Art Journal* 79, no. 4 (Winter 2020): 80.

21 Adrienne Edwards, "Blackness in Abstraction," *Art in America*, January 2015, 68.

22 Baldwin, "Color," 321.

23 For the canonical arguments about "motivation" in abstraction, see Yve Alain Bois, "Strzemiriski and Kobro: In Search of Motivation," in *Painting as Model* (Cambridge, MA: MIT Press, 1990), 123–57; and Rosalind Krauss, "The Motivation of the Sign," in *Picasso and Braque: A Symposium*, ed. Lynn Zelevansky (New York: Museum of Modern Art, 1992), 261–86.

24 One could think of Piet Mondrian, Kasimir Malevich, or Aleksandr Rodchenko within this rubric. Mondrian and Malevich are discussed by

Briony Fer in *On Abstract Art* (New Haven, CT: Yale University Press, 1997), in terms of how canonical modernism became "entrenched in a language of absolutes, predicated on the belief that certain forms had the capacity to express a higher, ideal reality" (57). Recent revelations about an inscription embedded in the underpainting of Malevich's *Black Square* have removed any doubt about the racist unconscious that is additionally tied to certain canonical modernist repressions.

25 Caroline A. Jones, *Eyesight Alone: Clement Greenberg's Modernism and the Bureaucratization of the Senses* (Chicago: University of Chicago Press, 2005), 231; and Douglas Crimp, *Before Pictures* (Chicago: University of Chicago Press, 2016), 29. For other arguments about modernism's negation of superfluous or superficial form, mass cultural pleasure, and especially the association of these with queerness and/or femininity through Greenbergian modernism, see Andreas Huyssen, "Mass Culture as Woman: Modernism's Other," in *After the Great Divide: Modernism, Mass Culture, Postmodernism* (Bloomington: Indiana University Press, 1986), 44–62; Amelia Jones, "The Pollockian Performative," in *Body Art/Performing the Subject* (Minneapolis: University of Minnesota Press, 1998); Amelia Jones, "Art History/Art Criticism: Performing Meaning," in *Performing the Body/Performing the Text*, ed. Amelia Jones and Andrew Stephenson (London: Routledge, 1999), 39–55; Marcia Brennan, *Modernism's Masculine Subjects: Matisse, the New York School, and Post-Painterly Abstraction* (Cambridge, MA: MIT Press, 2004); Tom Folland, "Robert Rauschenberg's Queer Modernism: The Early Combines and Decoration," *Art Bulletin* 92, no. 4 (December 2010): 348–65; and Christa Noel Robbins, "The Sensibility of Michael Fried," *Criticism* 60, no. 4 (Fall 2018): 429–54.

26 For a noncomprehensive set of examples discussing these varying "uses" of abstraction for African American and Afro-Caribbean artists, see Frank Bowling, "Discussion on Black Art," *Arts Magazine* 43, no. 18 (April 1969): 16–20; Frank Bowling, "Discussion on Black Art, II," *Arts Magazine* 43, no. 7 (May 1969): 20–23; Frank Bowling, "Formalist Art and the Black Experience," *Third Text* 2, no. 5 (1988): 78–82; Frank Bowling, "Some Notes toward African American Abstraction," in *The Search for Freedom: African American Abstract Painting 1945–1975*, ed. Ann Gibson (New York: Kenkeleba Gallery, 1991), 125–28; Adrian Piper, "Flying," in *Adrian Piper: Reflections, 1967–1987*, ed. Jane Carver (New York: Alternative Museum, 1987), 24–33; Ann Eden Gibson, *Abstract Expressionism: Other Politics* (New Haven, CT: Yale University Press, 1997); Kobena Mercer, introduction and "Black Atlantic Abstraction: Aubrey Williams and Frank Bowling," in *Discrepant Abstraction*, ed. Kobena Mercer (Cambridge, MA: MIT Press, 2006), 6–29; Jacqueline Goldsby, "The Art of Being Difficult: The Turn to Abstraction in African American

Poetry and Painting during the 1940s and 1950s" (lecture, Humanities Lecture Series, Brigham Young University, March 7, 2014), https://www.youtube.com/watch?v=pqKe8k4skzs; Philip Brian Harper, *Abstractionist Aesthetics: Artistic Form and Social Critique in African American Culture* (New York: New York University Press, 2015); Amber Jamilla Musser, "Architectures of Blue: Race, Representation, and Black and Brown Abstraction," *Brooklyn Rail*, October 5, 2017, https://brooklynrail.org/2017/10/art/Architectures-of-Blue-Race-Representation-and-Black-and-Brown-Abstraction; Kyla Wazana Tompkins, "Crude Matter, Queer Form," ASAP/*Journal* 2, no. 2 (May 2017): 264–68; Daonne Huff, "On Abstraction: Things You Can't Tell Just by Looking at Us," *Studio Magazine*, https://studiomuseum.org/article/abstraction-things-you-cant-tell-just-looking-us; Sarah Lewis, "African American Abstraction," in *Routledge Companion to African American Art*, ed. Eddie Chambers (London: Routledge, 2019), 159–72; and Ayanna Dozier, *Rebellious Inventions: Abstraction in the Black Diaspora*, exh. cat. (New York: FALSE FLAG Publication, 2020).

27 David J. Getsy in conversation with William J. Simmons, "Appearing Differently: Abstraction's Transgender and Queer Capacities," in *Pink Labour on Golden Streets: Queer Art Practices*, ed. Christiane Erharter et al. (Berlin: Sternberg Press, 2015), 43–44. See also Jennifer Doyle and David Getsy, "Queer Formalisms," *Art Journal* 72, no. 4 (Winter 2014): 58–71; and David Getsy, *Abstract Bodies: Sixties Sculpture in the Expanded Field of Gender* (New Haven, CT: Yale University Press, 2015). For recent work that advances the discourses about queer abstraction, see "Queer Form," ed. Kadji Amin, Amber Jamilla Musser, and Roy Pérez, special issue, ASAP/*Journal* 2, no. 2 (May 2017).

28 Richard A. Long notes that Delaney rarely directly engaged the aesthetic debates of the moment. See "Interview with Richard A. Long," in *Beauford Delaney: A Retrospective* (New York: Studio Museum in Harlem, 1978), n.p.

29 Nikki A. Greene, "Thomas McKeller *sous rature*: John Singer Sargent's Erasure of a Black Model," in *Boston's Apollo: Thomas McKeller and John Singer Sargent*, ed. Nathaniel Silver (Boston: Isabella Stewart Gardner Museum, 2020), 77–78.

30 James Baldwin, "The Price of the Ticket," in *Price of the Ticket*, xi.

31 See "Herbert Gentry," in *Explorations in the City of Light: African-American Artists in Paris, 1945–1965*, ed. Audreen Buffalo (New York: Studio Museum in Harlem, 1996), 54.

32 This is not to say that this split did not definitively exist or that it was not deeply felt by a cohort of artists in New York, but rather that continuing to rely on it precludes us from more deeply attending to works that

tried distinctly to blend these categories—as well as continues to cast Black Arts movement artworks in vastly overgeneralized terms without assessing *their* formal power.

33 Darby English, *1971: A Year in the Life of Color* (Chicago: University of Chicago Press, 2016), 9. In *1971*, the many types of abstraction available in this moment get distilled to, and then become interchangeable with, the definition supported by Clement Greenberg and Michael Fried, even when the work of the artists under discussion, such as Ed Clark or Al Loving, cannot be categorized so easily under this rubric.

34 For an excellent argument on this point, see Robbins, "The Sensibility of Michael Fried."

35 Zora Neale Hurston, "How It Feels to Be Colored Me" (1928), in *I Love Myself When I Am Laughing . . . And Then Again When I Am Looking Mean and Impressive*, electronic revised ed., ed. Alice Walker (New York: Feminist Press at the City University of New York, 2020).

36 Baldwin, "Color," 323.

37 Gentry, oral history interview with Liza Kirwin.

38 Stephen C. Wicks, in *Beauford Delaney and James Baldwin: Through the Unusual Door*, ed. Stephen C. Wicks (Knoxville: University of Tennessee Press, 2020), 120.

39 See Michael Leja, "Jackson Pollock: Representing the Unconscious," *Art History* 13, no. 4 (December 1990), 544.

40 Seph Rodney, quoting Adrienne Edwards, in "How to Embed a Shout: A New Generation of Black Artists Contends with Abstraction," *Hyperallergic*, August 23, 2017, https://hyperallergic.com/389105/how-to-embed-a-shout-a-new-generation-of-black-artists-contends-with-abstraction/.

41 Beauford Delaney, interview with Richard Long, September 5, 1970, quoted in *Beauford Delaney: A Retrospective*, ed. Richard Long (New York: Studio Museum in Harlem, 1978), n.p.

42 Beauford Delaney, letter to Henry Miller, November 3, 1965, quoted in Leeming, *Amazing Grace*, 166.

FIFTEEN

Feeling Modernist

Beauford Delaney's *Self-Portrait* (1944)

Levi Prombaum

As with the work of many Black modern artists who have been the subject of renewed scholarly and critical attention, the interpretation of Beauford Delaney's work is bound up in modernist art history's pervasive racialism and economies of study that pronounce Black modernisms derivative. This modernist gaze places Black artists' work in proximity to the formal or critical strategies of the Western (European and North American) modernist canon as a pretext for recognition.[1] Emerging from unchallenged assumptions about centers and margins and unilateral flows from past to present, such a view reinscribes a racial hierarchy of meanings even when positive revaluation of an artwork is the critic's intent.[2] This gaze further delimits the artwork's originality by circumscribing its perspective—what the work looks *like*, what it looks *at* or *back to*, what it looks *after*—to a rigidly understood set of values derived from a narrowly formalist tradition.[3] These entrenched practices become a performative engine of art history's whiteness when they displace the racializing tendencies of reception and interpretation onto the work itself.[4] When an artwork comes to bear the responsibility of critiquing this problem—and furthermore, when such critique is framed in terms that misconstrue this ongoing interpretive violence as past, measurable, and reparable—processes of objectification and marginalization continue unabated.[5]

Beauford Delaney's *Self-Portrait* (1944; plate 3), currently in the collection of the Art Institute of Chicago, is one of the artist's most assertive announcements of his identity as a modernist, and it is an invaluable entry point for a discussion of the influence of European modernism on his work, because it instantiates alternative interpretive patterns germane to Delaney's *uses* of these traditions. The self-portrait's monumental visage, invested with reverberating motion and emotion, combines Delaney's study both of more recent histories of painting and of classical histories, and it shows how Delaney was at the vanguard of modern painting's presents and futures. Delaney places himself neither outside nor in opposition to European painting traditions: on the contrary, his work positively emanates from, and reterritorializes, the modernist frequencies into which he taps. *Self-Portrait* can be appreciated as part of the artist's pursuit of the porous promises of an early twentieth-century modernist subjectivity. It exemplifies Delaney's affecting and transformative means of deploying the self, an approach that would deeply impact the work of his protégé, James Baldwin.

Delaney's orchestration of modernist feeling demands that we reconsider art historical questions of formal and iconographical analysis in tandem with performance theories of substitution and genealogies of modern subjectivity emerging from affect studies. Iconographical analysis and considerations of Delaney's critical inhabitation of art historical forms lay the groundwork for exploring how Delaney attends to, and tarries with, the critical assumptions and normative operations of the dominant European modernist lineage of his time. From these perspectives, *Self-Portrait* marks a journey through, with, and against an emerging narrative of European modernism rife with teleologies, colonial sensibilities, and patriarchal pretensions. Returning to the painting with affect studies in mind shows how Delaney's critique of art historical traditions is an outcome of his abiding interest and creative investment in the kind of modernist subjectivity that emphasized the fluidity of interior and exterior, self and other, present and past. *Self-Portrait* is irreducible to a painted representation of the artist. Instead, the visions of selfhood that emerge here are strategies for orienting the work in multiple worlds, searching declarations of historical attachment, and distillations of modes of feeling within and beyond the confines of the self.

Questions of Form

From the 1940s onward, Delaney developed an expressionist portraiture practice that emphasized his identity as a modernist. In *Self-Portrait* (1944), Delaney turns away from the realist imperatives and bourgeois expectations of traditionally representational portraiture. He appropriates the specific forms of iconic modernist self-portraits from the turn of the twentieth century while tapping into the cult of authorship that has marked the interpretation of self-portraiture for centuries.[6] Delaney's *Self-Portrait* is a meditation on previous expressions of artistic identity that attempted assertively to reimagine painting's limits and possibilities. Creating scenarios of likeness and substitution using his own image, Delaney grounds his artistic identity in the mobilization of received histories of Western European modernism. With this strategy, Delaney situates himself as an uncontestable heir to the work of artists he studies and admires, but he also uses their portrait forms as devices that can do other historical work entirely.[7]

Self-Portrait (1944) presents itself to students of Western European modernism as a series of formal encounters between Delaney's painterly persona and three central figures of modern painting: Vincent van Gogh, Henri Matisse, and Pablo Picasso. In *Self-Portrait*, the rich golden-green background, the trembling, all-over impasto, and the immediate graphic impact of the work suggest (as do so many of Delaney's paintings) an important reference point in the formal strategies of Van Gogh. Yet Richard Powell, in his 2001 exhibition catalogue *The Color Yellow*, suggests instead that Delaney's visage bears a remarkable likeness to a well-known portrait of Matisse: "Although there is no hard evidence of Delaney's closely studying Matisse and his writings, Delaney's *Self-Portrait* of 1944 . . . bears a strong resemblance to and affinities with Matisse's *Self Portrait in Striped Outfit* of 1906, of which reproductions would have been widely available in New York."[8] Distinguished by its bust length and oversized reproduction, Matisse's *Self Portrait in Striped Outfit* is, John Klein suggests, "the most intense and confrontational self portrait of [the artist's] career."[9]

Powell's observation is based on the shared formal and psychological affinities between Delaney's and Matisse's portraits. Delaney's oversized portrait shares the Matisse portrait's assertive presence because it also uses color expressively and architectonically to structure the viewer's experience. The artists' visages are similarly monumental, entering imposingly into the viewer's space through their angled and receding bodies as well as through piercing looks marked by expressively raised eyebrows and a downturned mouth. Some viewers encounter these portraits as expressions of cool distance, as if the artists are hyperaware of themselves and the viewer both; in contrast, for other viewers, the vivid greens and blues appear so heavily worked across figure and ground that they produce an atmosphere of melancholy and exertion.

According to Kirk Varnedoe, Matisse's portrait conveys a "gruff, rusticated masculinity" that offered a major departure from the image of propriety, distance, and studiousness that he usually embodied in his self-portraits. It is a result of the painter's different experiments at this moment, some driven by angular, agitated line and others by fauvist color.[10] The work is also a signature example of his attempts to synthesize classical and modern art. Alfred Barr, for example, described *Self Portrait in Striped Outfit* as drawing from both Cézanne's experiments with color modeling and the "apostolic dignity" of fifth-century Roman mosaics.[11] As Delaney stakes himself both as a modernist practitioner in the vein of Matisse, with his vibrant color and sketchy brushwork, and as a potent synthesizer of different artistic vernaculars, it is significant that he reflexively draws on a bold moment of self-presentation that redefines Matisse's public image. Delaney, too, announces himself with an uncharacteristically unapologetic quality that also reinforces how well studied he is in a particularly Matissean manner.

While Delaney enters into a dialogue with Matisse and the modernism that he inhabits, *Self-Portrait* (1944), I'd argue, is just as visually engaged with Pablo Picasso's *Self Portrait* of 1907.[12] Delaney re-creates Picasso's dramatic structuring outline, and he appropriates his petrifying stare—a gaze that arrests, but that refuses to be arrested. He uses graphic lines to unify different elements of the composition, in the vein of Picasso's own "weighted angular slashes and rhythmical arcs, potently locked together by insisted parallelisms, repetitions and alignments."[13] Picasso's dramatically architectonic treatment of his face, which troubles relations of depth and flatness, is modeled on his recent study of African masks and reflects his colonialist worldview, in which the root of African masks' formal power and sophistication is inextricable from their psychological alterity. Varnedoe describes Picasso's Africanizing *Self Portrait* as at once a split and amalgamated figure: a composite image of the different personas that Picasso captures in previous self-portraits, which "compete for ascendance with the figuration of a death's head."[14] As Delaney courts Picasso's forms, channeling a persona marked by his encounter with otherness, he also wields the striking signatures of Picasso's unabashed primitivism.

In light of these resemblances, theories of substitutive performance, such as Joseph Roach's notion of "surrogation," can help track the different registers of relation and critique that Delaney stages in tandem here.[15] Roach emphasizes surrogation as a mode of cultural continuity founded on repetition, a way of creating "myths of legitimacy and origin" that depend on the forgetting and reinvestment of meaning into historical forms. "In its improvisatorial behavioral space," Roach explains of surrogation, "memory reveals itself as imagination."[16] Thus in Delaney's ur-modernist visage, one might see continuity and timelessness achieved via forgetting: Delaney appears in the mid-twentieth century as *the* vanguard of painting's pasts, as heir rather than Other to these traditions.

At the same time, with regard to Black diasporic form, Roach emphasizes

how surrogation is a "monumental study in the pleasures and torments of *incomplete* forgetting" under the conditions of whiteness.[17] As Delaney adapts Picasso's line, courting its psychological gravity, he also avoids Picasso's physiognomic exaggerations. *Self-Portrait* (1944), from this perspective, reflects Delaney's refusal merely to reproduce the racist underpinnings of the tradition that he inherits.[18] In his proclamation as successor, Delaney intentionally surfaces and activates what would otherwise remain repressed in the histories and forms that he champions.[19] This inhabitation of Picasso's primitivist vernacular, his ability to wear *it* as a mask, interrupts the metaphorical economy through which Picasso reinforces a connection between African ritual objects and negativity. In the remade contours of Picasso's abstracted forms, Delaney presents himself in and against this projection of otherness. He registers neither mimicry nor emulation, but rather a peculiar attention to, and kinship with, the various imaginaries that have irrevocably marked his body.

As a painter who closely studied Picasso's work, Delaney would have known that he was entering into a moment of historical dialogue *between* Picasso and Matisse, whose portraits and personas developed in close conversation with each other at this moment. It was Matisse who provided Picasso, in their early meetings, with one of his first introductions to the formal study of African masks, and both artists, steeped in the primitivism of their time, used "the mask as a solution to a crisis in representation."[20] In the version of modernism that Alfred Barr introduced at the Museum of Modern Art in the late 1930s, Matisse's fauvism and Picasso's cubism would represent competing aesthetic programs. As Delaney enmeshes these figures in a single visage, he underscores their shared values, including their primitivism, in place of their perceived aesthetic differences.[21] In collapsing this rivalry into a single image, *Self-Portrait* (1944) acknowledges and troubles the narratives of Barr's modernism that rest on a portraiture connoisseurship that easily elides political and social issues, as well as nationalities and geographies, to establish a broader teleology of style.[22] Delaney's substitutive gestures offer, in place of a notion of succession, a past that is present in intimate encounters between artists, evoking relation and dialogue over unidirectional progression, influence, and authority.

While *Self-Portrait* (1944) thus shows evidence of Delaney's thorough study of European modernism, it also remains a testament to Delaney's own synthetic study of modern and classical traditions. In one of Rachel Cohen's rich meditations on *Self-Portrait*, for example, she suggests that we take seriously the undulant quality of Delaney's spatial construction, which she surmises could be related to his interest in the work of Florentine painters.[23] Cohen references the red cap that Delaney dons in this portrait, a staple of the artist's mid-1940s Greenwich Village persona, as an iconographical lead in this direction.[24] Delaney's archives support a view of his abiding interest in Italian Renaissance painting: in addition to reproductions of Florentine sitters that would hang on his Parisian studio walls, journals from the 1940s suggest Delaney's engagement with a treatise by philosopher Pico della Mirandola, *Oration on the Dignity of Man*. "With free choice and dignity, you may fashion yourself into whatever form you choose," Delaney transcribed, echoing a tradition of humanism that, in this context, underscores his choice to work capaciously within the different formal traditions he desired.[25] Across the painting's many references and substitutive operations, the bold proclamations and critiques of *Self-Portrait* are also multiplicative and recuperative. *Self-Portrait* resurfaces rich histories of encounter and affinity, and it functions as an expansive repository of contradictory styles, politics, and personalities. In place of one tradition, or break from tradition, is a concept of formal innovation and identity attuned to multiple traditions' cumulative and accumulative forces. The personas that abound with close looking also congeal into an unrivaled personality.

Modes of Feeling

Matisse's and Picasso's expressive portraitures from the early twentieth century are often appreciated in terms of their dramatic ruptures with mimetic representation.[26] But in Delaney's experimental *Self-Portrait* (1944), I would argue, these artist's self-portraits are taken up less for their surgeries on representation than as affective vessels. That is, their portraits are utilized for the kind of self that they picture: they are templates for the modern artist as a radically self-differing subject; and they affirm the possibilities that come with bold assertions of the artist's alterability in pursuit of innovation. In this section, I'm interested in further considering the "historically and socially-coded" nature of the expressive self that Delaney deploys in *Self-Portrait*.[27] I want to think about Delaney's portrait as a way of *feeling modern* (and not only "looking modern") by digging closely into one moment in which Delaney invites affective encounters within his work's surfaces that index his own process of close viewing and listening.

To set the terms of modernist selfhood that captured Delaney's imagination as he engaged the creative personas of the aforementioned painters, it is useful to consider Lisa Blackman's genealogical inquiry into conceptions of the affectable self in Western Europe in the nineteenth and early twentieth centuries. Blackman argues that notions of the self as corporeally and temporally porous were not merely prevalent in the late nineteenth and early twentieth centuries, but fully "authorized" as they became problems of scientific study.[28] Modern artists, in process and posture, tapped into notions of their bodies as conduits for affects that "circulate between the self and other, the human and the non-human, the physical and the ethereal." This was especially the case for artists with symbolist affinities, such as Matisse and Picasso: symbolism's notion of expressive selfhood was based on the idea of the self's radical indeterminacy, emphasizing the unrivaled power of the imaginary space built in dynamic reciprocity with others.[29]

In its sustained formal and historical dialogues, *Self-Portrait* (1944) is a testament to Delaney's belief in a kind of self-realization that can only take place in the imaginary space of the work of art. It is also a statement of Delaney's interest in his predecessors' ability to transmit feeling through such declarations of identity. Throughout the 1940s, Delaney was similarly preoccupied with achieving a form of artistic expression and originality that would emotionally involve the viewer. In his journals, he wrote how he closely studied the work of other artists, distinguishing between the act of merely *looking* at a work and the act of *observing* it in order to grasp its underlying logics.[30] Delaney courted the latter for his own art, seeing the production of sustained observation as a hallmark of his authenticity. Artistic personas could also provoke interpretation: Delaney kept lists of musicians and visual artists he admired who had an "aura" about their personality and work that directed its reception. So too did he return in his writing during this period to the word *enigma*, with its evocations of psychological feeling, as he tracked his painting's development.[31]

In another of her close studies of *Self-Portrait* (1944), Rachel Cohen remarks how the painting's emotional force is conveyed through potent details embedded in the work's layers, which, in her words, appear "a bit as if you are looking at a sculpture made of paint."[32] Cohen's writing is a beautiful example of the way that Delaney's painting invites and rewards deep and slow attention. It also attests to the fact that no transparent insight is granted to the study of a Delaney surface, which is more likely to raise questions than offer revelations. As with other Delaney works from this period, with this portrait it is not possible to neatly retrace the order of the application of layers of paint, nor is there a sense of procedure marked by a clear beginning or end. Each area of the canvas, with its sculptural accumulation of paint, has accumulated layers in a different order and with different emphases. Attention to any given detail relays the sense of a process that involved multiple steps of careful reworking to produce the final image. The black, graphic outlines across the figure, for example, are a peculiar kind of structural element: they are sometimes painted first, other times laid down last, and more frequently overpainted and remarked throughout. The swirling background, as another example, is marked by visible strokes of green vigorously mixed into a golden ground, which itself encases and draws attention to the layers of brushwork concealed beneath the unified plane of color.

With Delaney's distinctive approaches in mind, it is worth turning to one of the most enigmatic details of this painting: a prominent slash at the artist's neck. Cohen notes of the slash that "the sculptured paint seems to have special significance around what looks like a scar at the figure's neck. Some art historians think this was a place where Delaney changed the proportions of the figure. Others imagine this as a more direct comment on history and its violence."[33] In what appears to be a swift move of the palette knife, Delaney scrapes the flesh tones off this figure to reveal dark washes of blue and purple beneath, which are worked back into the surface with tints of blue and green. Faint black lines, almost inscription-like, linger atop the exposed layer of paint, signaling a further depth of accumulation as well as a further emphasis on indecipherability. In contrast to Cohen's interpretation of this detail, I am stuck on one possible origin story for it: an X-ray analysis done by the Art Institute of Chicago shows that the canvas for this portrait was originally torn, and then repaired, along the horizontal line where Delaney both slashes the neck of his figure and prominently paints his signature.[34] Such an origin frames *Self-Portrait*'s sensibility as reparative: with attention to, and care for, things that gather at the seams. One could metaphorize the slash as a reparative art historical critique, in which Delaney is gesturing to the fibers of a European modernist tradition that itself needs repair. Reworking a teleology of painting predicated on ethnic as much as aesthetic values and founded in the colonial abstraction of otherness, the slash in *Self-Portrait* could be cast as a Derridean tear, disrupting the self-same logic that founds the modernist lineage Delaney engages.[35] In this reading, the wound is materialized with a Picassian slash and sutured with an effluence of Matissean color, so that as Delaney brings together these brilliantly spirited and intensely pained resemblances, he revisits and supplements the received histories of his time.

Delaney puts his signature on the same horizontal plane as the slash, emphasizing this moment of violence or rupture as the place at which his artistic subjectivity is founded. (I would underscore that Delaney's paintings open up such possible readings through his sustained interest in the kind of artistic selfhood developed in mental conversations with his modernist forebears.) Delaney's use of the signature with-and-as slash reproduces a trope of the modern artist's authorship as paramount to the experimental nature of the work.[36] It's also a further sign of his investment in a paradigm of modernist self-portraits that functioned not only as statements of aesthetic purpose and painterly verve but also as potent denials of bourgeois subjectivity and values.[37] In such portraits, selves are pushed to their limits: malleable and in formation, lodged between self and other, offering autobiographical statements that have little interest in the bounded, autobiographical self. As a painter who additionally had to navigate racializing closures and expectations around his work, Delaney had ample reasons to deploy the form of the bourgeois self against and beyond itself. With the slash as extended signature, and vice versa, Delaney marks an identity that is formed out of an underneath, an inside, and a beyond within the world of the painting, that attends to what lies both beyond the visual and beyond the self.

In addition to its surplus of rich formal and symbolic meaning, Delaney's declaration of selfhood is heavy with an affective weight that tends to the haptic and aural dimensions of feeling, using the visual as a means rather than an end. In her consideration of innovative deployments of affect studies that rhyme with spiritualist formations of the affectable self, Blackman also surveys studies of diasporic subjectivity and "intergenerational exchange, where the other or the past is embodied as a voice or trace registered corporeally." She focuses on approaches that identify "gaps and cleavages," as well as silences and indecipherability, as telling forms of relational and historical constellation in which perception can be distributed "across space and time, carried by mediums other than the speaking subject."[38] In Delaney's *Self-Portrait*, such attunement is present in the distribution of sensation differently across every area of Delaney's canvas. The mysterious slash does not merely invite the viewer's attention; it exemplifies his signature mode of invoking a lingering, looking, and listening in the space of rupture.

Self-Portrait, that is, locates itself thoroughly "in the break."[39] The "voices and forces" that Fred Moten understands as being animated by and deployed by Delaney's work can be found everywhere in *Self-Portrait*'s idiosyncratic visual tensions and energies, its haptic excesses and modes of expressive selfhood. This is underscored most dramatically at the slash, by the giving and taking of voice at the site of the throat.[40] The surfaces of *Self-Portrait* (1944), I've argued, provide additional textures for understanding Delaney's particular affective-discursive mode: his concerted break with a tradition of breaking from tradition, his recuperative consideration of the histories that break upon the present, and his extension of a tradition of artistic subjectivity that uses the form of the self to get elsewhere. These are all part of what makes Delaney's work an important node in constellations of avant-garde art and performance and what distinguishes his painting's "feeling modern": his sensory encounters and arresting images both symbolize and enact the profound possibilities of "living singularity in the face of multiplicity."[41]

Feeling Modernist with James Baldwin

In the early 1940s, during years in which he frequently visited the Museum of Modern Art and watched Delaney's *Self-Portrait* (1944) take shape, James Baldwin inherited some enduring lessons in feeling modernist from his principal witness. I'm tempted to see some of Delaney's articulations in *Self-Portrait* reflected in the strategies of *Go Tell It on the Mountain* (1953), a novel initially praised for its "unusual substantive powers" yet mischaracterized as exhibiting "conventional ingenuity in form."[42] There are resonances with Delaney's work in Baldwin's construction of an autobiographical protagonist; in his careful layering of the narrative, symbolic, and emotive registers of the diegesis; in the critical navigation of the authoritative literary figures and discourses of his time; and in his unconventional formal attention to history's intergenerational transmissions and affective substances.[43] This is part of what is at stake when Baldwin tells his biographer, David Leeming, that in some ways, his first novel was "all about Beauford."[44]

But a more modest and direct point of intersection may first be warranted: with regard to articulating a relationship to Western European culture, one might consider Baldwin's essay "A Stranger in the Village" (1953), and the repeated references that Baldwin makes to Chartres Cathedral. This icon of European civilization, as a rhetorical device, is first invoked as a symbol of Baldwin's alienation from European narratives of cultural achievement, narratives which are readily available to the villagers: "Chartres says something to them which it cannot say to me, as indeed would New York's Empire State Building, should anyone here ever see it. Out of their hymns and dances come Beethoven and Bach. Go back a few centuries and they are in their full glory—but I am in Africa, watching the conquerors arrive."[45]

In its second appearance, however, Chartres is instead the bearer of the racist myths that underpin the church's complicity in European imperialism and that interpellate him in Europe:

> The cathedral at Chartres, I have said, says something to the people of this village which it cannot say to me; but it is important to understand that this cathedral says something to me which it cannot say to them. Perhaps they are struck by the power of the spires, the glory of the windows. . . . I doubt that the villagers think of the devil when they face a cathedral because they have never been identified with the devil. But I must accept the status which myth, if nothing else, gives me in the West before I can hope to change the myth.[46]

This latter passage is frequently interpreted as Baldwin's "declaration of the outsider's voice entering into the conversation," the "foregrounding of his distance" from a European cultural tradition which he is now able to claim.[47] What this repetition makes explicit, however, is that it is *not* Baldwin who has claimed something, but *Chartres itself*. Eleanor Traylor explains that Chartres becomes "not a paragon, but a speaking subject—a voice from the past."[48] Baldwin is compelled to tend to what lies beyond the marvelous sight of Chartres's spires or stained glass, and to listen to its utterances—both as its addressee and also as a historian of those myths that it refuses to speak to him directly.

"People are trapped in history and history is trapped in them," Baldwin informs the reader in "Stranger." Yet Baldwin also offers in this essay a mode of feeling, and a kind of listening, that affirms an artistic subject position that takes as its object the dynamic reciprocity between past and present, art and subjects, history and people. Such unparalleled attunement to myth's hold and sensitivity to its cleavages and gaps is how history is freed to do new work—by Beauford Delaney, and also by those, like James Baldwin, who claim his work as their inheritance.

NOTES

1 The Art Institute of Chicago's description of this essay's subject, Delaney's *Self-Portrait* (1944), is a striking example of this tendency. See "Beauford Delaney, Self-Portrait," https://www.artic.edu/artworks/111629/self-portrait.

2 For an example of the debates that such issues of comparison continue to inspire between pathbreaking scholars in the field, see Huey Copeland, "One-Dimensional Abstraction," *Art Journal* 78 (2019): 111–16.

3 On the interpretive binds of formalist imagination, see Denise Ferreira da Silva, "In the Raw," *e-flux* 93 (2018), https://www.e-flux.com/journal/93/215795/in-the-raw/.

4 On the humanities' extensions of the sociological problematization of blackness, see Fred Moten, "The Case of Blackness," *Criticism* 50 (2008): 177–218.

5 This essay marks my response to a comment made by Robert O'Meally at the February 2020 symposium "In a Speculative Light: The Arts of James Baldwin and Beauford Delaney" held at the University of Tennessee, Knoxville. In response to my presentation considering Delaney's relationship to the painterly vocabularies of Vincent van Gogh, O'Meally invoked the advice of Delaney scholar and curator Richard Powell: "Beware the default position of dismissing Beauford Delaney as merely derivative. . . . People will say, 'It's Cézanne,' 'It's Van Gogh,' 'It's Rousseau,' 'It's others.'" O'Meally then asked: "What's the best answer to the people who say that? That's what we have with Jacob Lawrence and many others. When and where does [Delaney] enter that would show that they're wrong?"

6 Vivien Gaston, *The Naked Face: Self-Portraits* (Melbourne: National Gallery of Victoria, 2010), 18.

7 On traditions of anti- and nondepictive portraiture in American art, see Anne Collins Goodyear, Jonathan Frederick Walz, and Kathleen Merrill Campagnolo, *This Is a Portrait if I Say So* (New Haven, CT: Yale University Press, 2016).

8 Richard J. Powell, *Beauford Delaney: The Color Yellow* (Atlanta: High Museum of Art, 2001), 16.

9 John Klein, *Matisse Portraits* (New Haven, CT: Yale University Press, 2001), 129. Henri Matisse, *Self Portrait with Striped Shirt*, 1906, oil on canvas, 22 × 18 in. (55.9 × 45.7 cm), Statens Museum for Kunst, Copenhagen. © 2022 Succession H. Matisse / Artists Rights Society (ARS), New York, online catalogue https://open.smk.dk/en/artwork/image/KMSr78?q=matisse%20self&page=0.

10 Kirk Varnedoe, "1," in Elizabeth Cowling, Anne Baldassari, John Elderfield, et al., *Matisse, Picasso* (London: Tate Publishing, 2002), 27.

11 Alfred Barr, *Matisse: His Art and His Public* (New York: Museum of Modern Art, 1951), 94.

12 Pablo Picasso, *Self Portrait*, 1907, oil on canvas, 22 ½ × 18 in. (56 × 46 cm), Narodni Galerie, Prague. © 2022 Estate of Pablo Picasso / Artists Rights Society (ARS), New York, https://sbirky.ngprague.cz/en/dielo/CZE:NG.O_8021

13 Kirk Varnedoe, "Picasso's Self Portraits," in *Picasso and Portraiture: Representation and Transformation* (New York: Museum of Modern Art, 1996), 136.

14 Varnedoe, "Picasso's Self Portraits," 136.

15 Joseph Roach, *Cities of the Dead: Circum-Atlantic Performance* (New York: Columbia University Press, 1996), 3.

16 Roach, *Cities of the Dead*, 28–29.

17 Roach, *Cities of the Dead*, 7 (italics added).

18 In this way, Delaney's use of surrogation in self-portraits rhymes with adaptations of the concept of surrogation in which substitutive performance becomes a method of retooling overdetermining fantasies of race, gender, and sexuality, expanding the political stakes and possibilities of well-worn cultural figures and narratives. See Daphne Brooks, *Bodies in Dissent: Spectacular Performances of Race and Freedom, 1850–1910* (Durham, NC: Duke University Press, 2006); and Jack Halberstam, *The Queer Art of Failure* (Durham, NC: Duke University Press, 2011).

19 David Lomas, *The Haunted Self* (New Haven, CT: Yale University Press, 2000), 95.

20 John Klein, "The Mask as Image and Strategy," in Paloma Alarcó, Malcolm Warner, Francisco Calvo Serraller, et al., *The Mirror and the Mask: Portraiture in the Age of Picasso* (New Haven, CT: Yale University Pres, 2007), 26.

21 On productively complicating the Picasso-Matisse mythologies of rivalry and difference, see Yve-Alain Bois, *Matisse and Picasso* (Paris: Flammarion, 1998).

22 Susan Noyles Platt, "Modernism, Formalism, and Politics: The 'Cubism and Abstract Art' Exhibition at the Museum of Modern Art," *Art Journal* 47 (1988): 286.

23 Rachel Cohen, "Delaney, Self-Portrait with a Red Hat," *Rachel Cohen* (blog), June 4, 2020, https://rachelecohen.com/blog/The_Frederick_Project/c/1055.

24 A picture of Delaney in a similar cap appears in the excerpt from Henry Miller's *The Amazing and Invariable Beauford DeLaney* (1945) in *Beauford Delaney: A Retrospective*, ed. Richard A. Long (New York: Studio Museum in Harlem, 1978), n.p.

25 The full quote in Delaney's journal reads: "We have made you neither of heavenly nor of earthly stuff, neither mortal nor immortal, so that with free choice and dignity, you may fashion yourself into whatever form you choose. To you is granted the power of degrading yourself into the lower forms of life, the beasts, and to you is granted the power, contained in your intellect and judgment, to be reborn into the higher forms, the divine." Beauford Delaney sketchbook, ca. 1943, box 9, Beauford Delaney Estate, Knoxville Museum of Art.

26 For an example of an investigation into experimental portraiture rooted in this well-established semiotic approach to modernist portraiture's form, see E. J. van Alphen, "The Portrait's Dispersal: Concepts of Representation and Subjectivity in Contemporary Portraiture," in *Portraiture: Facing the Subject*, ed. Joanna Woodall (Manchester: Manchester University Press, 1997), 239–56.

27 In the same way that art history has built on social and historical critiques of the neutrality of vision, I want to further explore critiques of the post-Enlightenment self with affect studies. Delaney's *Self-Portrait* additionally marks an opportunity to consider how affect studies' attention to materiality and encounter with a work can supplement poststructuralist approaches to portraiture that study the reflexive and deconstructive gestures of the artist. See Veerle Thielemans, "Beyond Visuality: Review on Materiality and Affect," *Perspective* 2 (2015), https://journals.openedition.org/perspective/5993.

28 Lisa Blackman, *Immaterial Bodies: Affect, Embodiment, Mediation* (London: Sage, 2012), 119.

29 Marja Lahelma, "The Open-Ended Artwork and the Symbolist Self," in *The Symbolist Roots of Modern Art*, ed. Michelle Facos (London: Routledge, 2017), 67–68.

30 See Beauford Delaney sketchbooks, ca. 1943, box 9, Beauford Delaney Estate, Knoxville Museum of Art.

31 See Beauford Delaney sketchbooks, ca. 1940, box 9, Beauford Delaney Estate, Knoxville Museum of Art.

32 Rachel Cohen, "Beauford Delaney Eyes," *Rachel Cohen* (blog), June 5, 2020, https://rachelecohen.com/blog/The_Frederick_Project/c/1075.

33 Cohen, "Beauford Delaney Eyes."

34 "Examination Report/ Treatment Proposal," internal file for Beauford Delaney's *Self-Portrait* (1944), Art Institute of Chicago, 1991.

35 Anais N. Spitzer, *Derrida, Myth and the Impossibility of Philosophy* (London: Bloomsbury, 2011), 45.

36 On signatures and strategic forms of authorship, see John Wilmerding, *Signs of the Artist: Signatures and Self-Expression in American Paintings* (New Haven, CT: Yale University Press, 2003).

37 Malcolm Warner, "Portraits about Portraiture," in *The Mirror and the Mask: Portraiture in the Age of Picasso* (New Haven, CT: Yale University Pres, 2007), 12.

38 Blackman, *Immaterial Bodies*, 94, 127.

39 Fred Moten, *In the Break: The Aesthetics of the Black Radical Tradition* (Minneapolis: University of Minnesota Press, 2003), 33–38.

40 This also resonates with Rizvana Bradley's extension and refraction of Moten's aesthetic project through her observation that "the quest(ion) of blackness" is one that "can only be enunciated through losing one's voice, or rather through yielding to the polyvocality that is always already the condition of possibility of speech." Rizvana Bradley and Denise Fereirra Da Silva, "Four Theses on Aesthetics," *e-flux* 120 (2021), https://www.e-flux.com/journal/120/416146/four-theses-on-aesthetics/.

41 Blackman, *Immaterial Bodies*, 24.

42 Donald Barr, "Go Tell It on the Mountain," *New York Times*, May 17, 1953, https://archive.nytimes.com/www.nytimes.com/books/98/03/29/specials/baldwin-mountain.html.

43 On Baldwin's automythographical presentation, see Wallace Graves, "The Question of Moral Energy in James Baldwin's *Go Tell It on the Mountain*," CLA *Journal* 7, no. 3 (1964): 215–23. On Baldwin's navigation of authoritative literary discourses, see Keith Clark, "Baldwin, *Communitas*, and the Black Masculinist Tradition," in *New Essays on "Go Tell It on the Mountain*," ed. Trudier Harris (Cambridge: Cambridge University Press, 1996), 133.

44 Many thanks to Mary Campbell, who shared with me her transcription of Baldwin's conversation with David Leeming from June 24, 1985, from series 1 of the David Leeming Collection of James Baldwin Research, Beinecke Rare Book and Manuscript Library, New Haven, CT.

45 James Baldwin, "Stranger in the Village," *Harper's Magazine*, September 1953; reprinted in *James Baldwin: Collected Essays*, ed. Toni Morrison (New York: Library of America, 1998), 121.

46 Baldwin, "Stranger in the Village," 128.

47 Michaela Bronstein, *Out of Context: The Uses of Modernist Fiction* (Oxford: Oxford University Press, 2018), 21.

48 Eleanor W. Traylor, *The Humanities and Afro-American Literary Tradition* (Washington, DC: D.C. Community Humanities Council, 1988).

SIXTEEN

"The Giacometti Effect"

Reconsidering Beauford Delaney's 1966 Portrait Bust of James Baldwin

Stephen C. Wicks

The Knoxville Museum of Art's 2020 exhibition *Beauford Delaney and James Baldwin: Through the Unusual Door* examined the relationship between painter Beauford Delaney and writer James Baldwin and the ways their ongoing intellectual exchange shaped one another's creative output and worldview. The selection of paintings and archival objects called attention to Baldwin's central role in Delaney's life as protégé and muse and to Delaney's seemingly inexhaustible desire to explore Baldwin as a portrait subject. Over the course of his career, Delaney portrayed with equal intensity those he knew well and those he admired but never met. His special attention to Baldwin as a subject reflects the writer's central position in the artist's life over a thirty-eight-year period. Several images of Baldwin reflect the technical and expressive breadth of Delaney's attempts to depict the writer's evolving persona. Canvases ranging from the idyllic figure study of 1941, *Dark Rapture* (plate 1), to the restrained 1971 bust in *Portrait of James Baldwin* (plate 31) provide compelling evidence of the writer's ability to inspire some of the artist's most adventurous and varied artistic responses. This variability also stems from Baldwin's inconsistent presence in Delaney's life, which at times forced the artist to rely on memory or photographs of the writer as portrait references.

One particular painting, *James Baldwin* (1966; plate 17), stands apart from all of Delaney's portraits of the writer in its atypically narrow color scheme of yellow and black, tangled angular contours, openwork structure, and absence of physical likeness. Evidence suggests this unusual handling may have been triggered by circumstances related to a prominent artist in Delaney's orbit: Swiss sculptor Alberto Giacometti (1901–66). In this short piece, I aim to explore possible influences on Delaney's work by Giacometti, as they circled one another in only occasionally intersecting social and artistic orbits.

According to writer David Leeming, Delaney began painting *James Baldwin* while he, Baldwin, and friends were nestled in a scenic Istanbul retreat on the Bosporus from July 7 through late August 1966.[1] Delaney convinced Baldwin to sit for him several times before the artist returned to Paris at summer's end; he took the unfinished canvas with him and continued to develop it in Paris before sending the completed work to Baldwin in Istanbul later that year.[2] Yet, despite the fact that Baldwin sat for Delaney over an extended period in their Istanbul quarters, recognizable references to Baldwin and his surroundings are glaringly absent in the final composition. While there is no written account of the sitting, Leeming recalls that "the portrait changed quite a lot between Istanbul and Paris" and "became more abstract in the process."[3] Without Baldwin there as an anchor to the visible world, Delaney likely felt free to venture into more subjective abstractionist territory.

Such a venture was by no means unprecedented for him. Once questioned about the abstracted nature of many of his portraits, Delaney explained that abstraction was simply his attempt to depict "something I saw in my mind," rather than a visual transcription of an actual sitting.[4] Indeed, Delaney's portrait subjects may appear unrecognizable to those who knew them, inserted as they often are into connotational settings formed of arbitrary hues and emotive brushwork. In some cases, color environments surrounding portrait subjects take the form of auras or veils composed of loose swirling strokes. Transformed on the canvas by the artist's active imagination and powers of association, sitters can assume new identities and appear in an endless variety of seemingly ambiguous contexts. One need only consider two of the artist's portraits of jazz great Charlie Parker to witness the spectrum of this approach. The first is a 1958 canvas that transforms the musician into an abstract field of undulating color bands emanating from a central point, as if Parker were metamorphosed into waves of sound radiating from the bell of his saxophone (plate 10). The second is a 1968 painting that depicts him allegorically, as a bold figure in African attire holding a scepter in place of his signature instrument (plate 27). In both cases, Delaney reimagines his portrait subject, the real human being Charlie Parker, as a mythic or affective presence based on the painter's own aesthetic values and pictorial concepts. Regardless of what form Delaney's subjects assumed, the artist's priority, as Baldwin once observed, was to penetrate external appearances in order to reveal "the light contained in every thing; in every surface, in every face."[5] For Delaney, portraits were as much a form of self-portraiture—manifestations of his own explorations of form and his own internal landscape—as they were physical representations of those he sought to depict.

Given Delaney's unconstrained and allegorizing approach to portraiture, Leeming's account as well as visual evidence make more plausible the notion that when painting *James Baldwin* (1966) while separated from his subject, the artist shifted from a mode of direct observation to one dictated by his mind's eye, a mode of seemingly infinite possibilities. An examination of the final composition hints at the reductive transformation that must have occurred after the artist left Istanbul. It presents a hollowed-out bust whose outer surface has been entirely peeled away, revealing distorted angular contours that appear as if branded into a nebulous gleaming backdrop. Although a skeletal framework of the sitter's image remains visible, the overwhelming presence of the surrounding color environment approaches the totality of that seen in the 1958 nonobjective painting of Parker.

Based on its degree of figural reduction, linear angularity, and chromatic contrast, the 1966 Baldwin portrait represents a significant departure from Delaney's other paintings of his protégé, even those produced around the same time. For example, *James Baldwin* (1967; plate 23) presents a luminous visage whose transparent anatomy permits the penetration of background hues, as in the 1966 Baldwin bust. Despite the loose overall construction of the figure using dabs of thick paint, its distinctive heavy-lidded eyes and double-arched upper lip represent an unmistakable likeness of Baldwin. In addition, a rare sketch related to the 1967 canvas (ca. 1966; plate 20) indicates the artist did not stray far from the contours of his original composition.

Even more recognizable as a Baldwin portrait is *Portrait of James Baldwin* (1965; plate 16), which like the 1966 abstract portrait also depicts the sitter amid a radiant field of color. However, the 1965 painting features a clearly described Baldwin, whose attentive face appears as a solid form described in naturalistic tones (with the exception of his yellow pupils). Yet perhaps nowhere is the variability of Delaney's portrait practice more evident than in comparing the abstracted 1966 Baldwin bust (plate 17) with a 1966 portrait of a seated Baldwin done in Istanbul that surfaced in an Istanbul collection during the writing of this essay (plate 19). Despite the close proximity of time and place of these two 1966 Baldwin portraits, they appear worlds apart. Unlike the abstracted portrait, the seated composition presents an instantly recognizable Baldwin within a clearly described setting rendered with bright yet relatively naturalistic hues. The seated composition features a somber Baldwin with his back to a steeply sloping landscape, possibly representing the hills above the Bosporus. Clothed in a white dashiki, arms resting casually on a patterned crimson and orange seat, Baldwin's clearly defined figure is set against a pale blue sky and aqua hillside whose slope echoes the contours of his shoulders. Unlike the 1966 bust's hollow structure and bold black outlines, the seated portrait is composed of modulated colors and solid anatomical forms anchored in a compressed pictorial space. Mottled green-brown and red-brown skin tones convey flesh-and-blood qualities entirely absent in the spectral black and yellow bust completed in Paris.

Why, then, does the 1966 yellow and black Baldwin bust look so different than the artist's other Baldwin portraits? A possible explanation for the unusual handling of the 1966 portrait bust can be found among the events that unfolded a few months prior to the artist's trip to Istanbul that year. In January 1966, the international art world reeled at the death of artist Alberto Giacometti after years of his declining health. Delaney had known the Swiss artist since their initial meeting in 1953–54, the American artist's first year in Paris, and for the next twelve years the two lived little more than a half mile apart. From the start, Delaney was struck by his counterpart's art, particularly his expressive adaptation of the abstracted forms found in African sculpture.[6] Archival evidence supports the notion that Giacometti's life and work were in Delaney's thoughts around the time he created the 1966 Baldwin bust. Among items found in the artist's estate was a portrait of the period in which Delaney depicts Giacometti as a disheveled head against a blank paper background (plate 18). Laid down with immediacy and spontaneity, clustered lines of green, yellow, and black define the Swiss artist's cadaverous profile, which is flanked by a pair of Giacometti's signature elongated sculptures. (Delaney's inclusion of such disconnected contextual elements can also be seen in portraits of Marian Anderson, Edna Porter, Jean Genet, and the aforementioned 1968 image of Charlie Parker.) Of Delaney's portrait drawings, the Giacometti likeness is among his most penetrating, animated, and expressive. The handling of the figure effectively maintains a degree of resemblance while incorporating slashing linear patterns reminiscent of those associated with Giacometti's aggressive painting style—and echoed in Delaney's 1966 portrait bust.

Significantly, a letter in the collection of the Schomburg Center for Research in Black Culture offers further support of the notion that Giacometti was on Delaney's mind at the time he painted Baldwin's 1966 portrait bust and that the painting represented a Baldwin likeness altered by what could be termed "the Giacometti Effect." The letter from Delaney, dated April 3, 1966, is addressed to James Lord (1922–2009), an American writer of Baldwin's generation. From the tone, it is evident that Delaney knew Lord well (he apologizes for an "awful" lunch that he had prepared a few years earlier when the writer visited him at his Clamart studio).[7] The main purpose of the letter was to congratulate Lord for his book *A Giacometti Portrait* (1965), which the painter had recently read. Lord's book describes the creation of the portrait *James Lord* (1964) and recounts Giacometti's doubt-wracked process in which he alternately created, destroyed, and reconstructed Lord's figure on a daily basis during the course of a grueling extended sitting (see figure 16.1a–b).

Lord's book had greatly inspired Delaney, who wrote enthusiastically, "Your description of the temperament and of [Giacometti's] dedication of all his forces into one universal source reveals the dominance of the artist over the momentary periods of indecision between patience and haste." Delaney continues by explaining that "this brief note just had to happen as I am so stimulated by your book it's impossible even to pen [only] a few words." In the letter, Delaney judges Lord's book a "splendid statement of the delicate ambiance between two friends."

Delaney's letter firmly establishes the fact that, due in large part to Lord's book, Giacometti's life and painting method were indeed on the artist's mind shortly before he began his 1966 abstracted bust of Baldwin. Delaney's animated response suggests that Lord's book moved him to identify strongly with the bond Lord established with Giacometti, perhaps recognizing its close resemblance to his own relationship with Baldwin. Inwardly, perhaps Delaney also hoped that Baldwin might consider undertaking a similar monograph devoted to *his* studio practice.[8] After all, in many respects, James

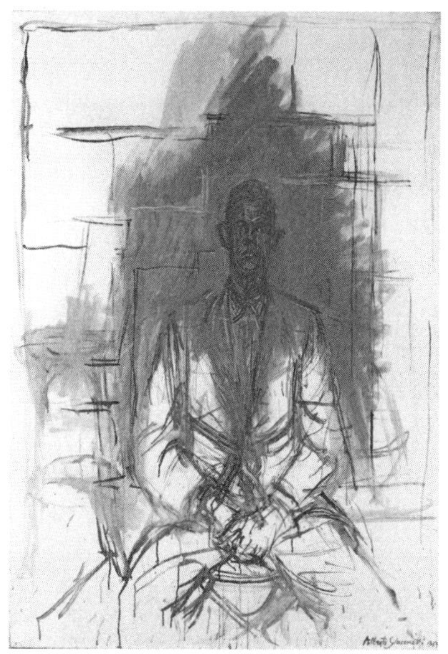
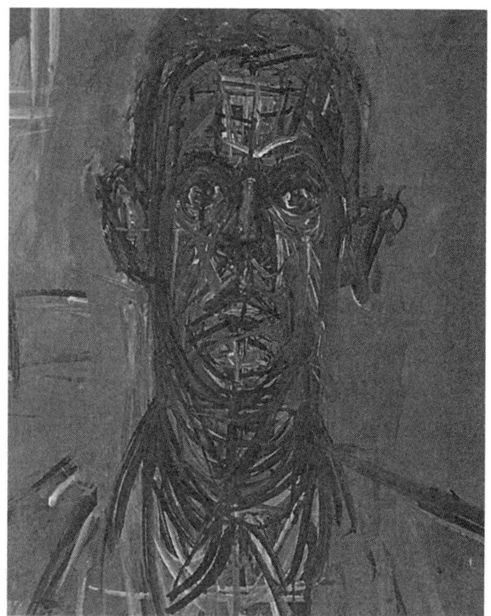

16.1a–b

Alberto Giacometti, *James Lord*, 1964. Oil on canvas, 45¾ × 31¾ in. (116.2 × 80.6 cm), with detail. © Succession Alberto Giacometti/Artists Rights Society (ARS), NY, 2023.

Baldwin was Delaney's James Lord, an insider who witnessed his creative struggles and triumphs from a uniquely intimate vantage point. The "delicate ambiance" Delaney describes, however, is at odds with Lord's colorful account of Giacometti's "nightmarish sense of hopelessness" that fueled the artist's vicious daily cycle of battling with Lord's image on the canvas surface.[9] In the book, Lord's detailed description of Giacometti scraping away the portrait's outer form in order to reveal its enduring internal structure may have reinforced Delaney's ongoing desire to apply his own formidable visual powers in a similar manner in order to present what Baldwin once described as "a new confrontation with reality."[10] Baldwin noted these powers even as a teenager in his initial encounter with Delaney, in which he vividly recalled the artist's "X-ray" eyes and their grasp of the totality of his being at first glance.[11] Perhaps nowhere is Delaney's search for the essence of his subject and desire to penetrate visible reality more evident, in fact, than in the 1966 bust of Baldwin, in which the form of his protégé is pared down to little more than a hollow remnant.

Visual evidence supports the notion that Giacometti's portrait of Lord and photographs of the writer found in Lord's book may have played a role in Delaney's reshaping of the 1966 Baldwin bust after his return to Paris from Istanbul. Although Giacometti enjoyed the luxury of his sitter's continuous presence during the making of Lord's portrait, Delaney, separated from Baldwin, appears to have deferred to his mind's eye for guidance once deprived of access to his sitter. At the forefront of Delaney's thoughts was the book detailing the anguished compositional method through which Giacometti's image of Lord took shape. The Delaney bust's distinctive linear structure and attenuated proportions—absent in the 1965 and 1967 Baldwin portraits—recall none other than those present in Giacometti's *Portrait of James Lord*. Furthermore, despite the distorted contours and eroded surface details in Delaney's 1966 *James Baldwin*—and the work's title—the central figure's features actually bear some resemblance to Lord. Its elongated facial structure, lozenge-shaped eyes, narrow mouth, and pointed chin are reminiscent of Giacometti's painting and period photographs of Lord. (Absent in Giacometti's canvas, and, surprisingly present in Delaney's, is Lord's distinctive bulbous nose.) The result is a conflation of imagery in which Baldwin's visage served as the template for what appears to have evolved into a composite likeness. Like Giacometti, Delaney viewed portraiture as presenting the dual challenge of revealing the eternal through the depiction of the temporal. While Giacometti did so by assaulting the sitter's image through a compilation of violent slashing marks rendered in grayscale tones, Delaney in his 1966 Baldwin bust uses gentle dabs of contrasting hues to construct the emblematic scaffolding of his simplified figure. Giacometti relies on gestural marks as the primary means of conveying emotional content, and Delaney on expressive color passages. The linear patterns and bold contrasts in Delaney's composition serve the artist's objective of sacrificing superficial physical qualities in order to transform even the most familiar figures into transcendent vessels immersed in universes of light.

In its elaborate conception, the portrait bust *James Baldwin* (1966) raises questions regarding Delaney's studio practice that call for a reconsideration of the artist's portraits and the shifting methodology he used to conceive and create them. On the surface, its central image resembles no one in particular. Viewed within the context of the Giacometti-Lord findings, however, it emerges as an enigmatic hybrid representation that fulfills Delaney's lofty portrait agenda on multiple levels: while openly honoring Baldwin, it privately memorializes Giacometti and salutes Lord, and thereby serves as a broad and enduring embodiment of the "delicate ambiance" between friends that Delaney so often sought in all aspects of his life. Stripped of superficial details and physical context, the 1966 portrait bust presents a timeless symbolic portrayal of a towering Baldwin suspended in an infinite universe of Delaney's yellow light. As such, it stands as one of the American master's most inventive and ambitious compositions, one that attests to his awareness of other artists' innovations but also to the remarkable fluidity of his own studio practice and seemingly boundless creative vision.

NOTES

1 David Leeming, *Amazing Grace: A Life of Beauford Delaney* (New York: Oxford University Press, 1998), 170. The author wishes to thank Amy Elias and David Leeming for their invaluable assistance.

2 David Leeming, email message to author, July 23, 2022.

3 David Leeming, email message to author, August 8, 2022.

4 David Butwin, "Booked for Travel: The Cognoscenti Abroad—II, James Jones's Paris," *Saturday Review*, February 1, 1969, 38.

5 James Baldwin, "On the Painter Beauford Delaney," *Transition* 4, no. 18 (1965); reprinted in *James Baldwin: Collected Essays*, ed. Toni Morrison (New York: Library of America, 1998), 720.

6 Leeming, *Amazing Grace*, 122.

7 Beauford Delaney to James Lord, April 3, 1966, Beauford Delaney correspondence, Sc MG 59, Schomburg Center for Research in Black Culture, Manuscripts, Archives and Rare Books Division, New York Public Library.

8 Beauford Delaney to James Lord, April 3, 1966.

9 James Lord, *A Giacometti Portrait* (New York: Farrar, Straus and Giroux, 1965), 36.

10 James Baldwin, "Introduction to Exhibition of Beauford Delaney Opening, December 4, 1964 at the Galerie Lambert," *Tableaux de Beauford Delaney*, exh. cat. (Paris: Galerie Lambert, 1964), n.p.

11 James Baldwin, "The Price of the Ticket," in *The Price of the Ticket: Collected Nonfiction, 1948–1985* (New York: St. Martin's, 1985); reprinted in Morrison, *James Baldwin: Collected Essays*, 830.

PART IV

Continuing Influence

SEVENTEEN

Queer Radiance

Beauford Delaney at the Bathhouse

Tyler T. Schmidt

Beauford Delaney's *Self-Portrait* (1971; plate 30), sometimes titled *Self-Portrait in a Paris Bath House*, is a balm for the color-thirsty traveler.[1] Examining Delaney's depiction of himself as African royalty in this self-portrait, a composition that cites but also subverts European modernists' well-known interest in African sculpture, I roam the bathhouse in order to claim the site as central, rather than incidental, to his Africanist aesthetics and experiments with abstract painting, and to pursue a series of questions about the relationship between aesthetics and eroticism in the late work of Delaney and James Baldwin. This critical conversation converges at Delaney's portraits, Baldwin's comments on public sex, and critiques by queer commentators on the politics of sex with strangers. In thinking about and within public space, particularly sites repurposed for sexual fantasy, how might we theorize the relationship between Africanist aesthetics (and their intersections with modernist reappropriations) and queer sexuality? What lineage of queer Africanist expression might be drawn between Delaney and later artists such Rotimi Fani-Kayode or Michael Armitage? What would it mean, in a parallel act of queering time, to read Delaney's portrait within a later cultural moment that elevated (some would say fetishized) the bathhouse and other public or pseudopublic spaces such as toilets, parks, and movie theaters as ideal spaces for queer sociality and as sites of self-shattering *jouissance*?

My queer sense of Delaney parts ways with a reading of this 1971 self-portrait by art historian Richard J. Powell, whose brilliant scholarship on Delaney and African American portraiture more broadly has been foundational to my own understanding of Delaney's aesthetically sprawling corpus. In his illuminating monograph on Delaney titled *The Color Yellow* (2002), Powell makes this questionable observation about the painting: "While the biographical facts of Delaney's life reduce this painting to a seamy, erotic interlude in a gay bathhouse, the artist's own call for throwing 'light into great darkness' lifts the painted narrative into a less mundane and more spiritual realm."[2] A viewer preoccupied with biography, it's true, risks missing the painting's innovations, but accounts of daily life are rarely banal for queer artists, who make meaning of the mundane with the knowledge that their experiences and their art are too often erased from history. This essay interrogates the prudish claim that the bathhouse is "seamy" and that Delaney's occupation of it requires aesthetic transcendence, a "lift" from its mundane rituals of bathing, emotional restoration, and sexual pleasure. In fact, the opposition of the seamy and spiritual is just the sort of dualism that Delaney's depiction of himself as an African prince, bejeweled and brightly attired, seeks to disrupt.

On this wander in the bathhouse, we have to see what is not there (the implied figures and sexual encounters on the margins of the frame and on the edges of the viewer's imaginary) even as we attend to what is there (a regal portrait whose colors and lines remind me of the work of American modernist painter Marsden Hartley) and what could never be there (Delaney in sexual ecstasy of the sort claimed by later queer theorists writing about the baths). Delaney's transfigurations in the bathhouse—from bather to lecher to lover to prince—also anticipate critical discourses published after his death that explored spaces of public sex including the bathhouse, the movie theater, and public restrooms. His self-portrait is also, if we choose to see it, of a desiring, gay body, a sphere of Delaney's life and art that has been given only surface attention, and largely through the lenses of shame and romantic frustration. Rendered in Powell's analysis as a site of furtive, "dark" pleasures and buried from public view, the bathhouse in Delaney's imagination is, in fact, a site of queer radiance in queer time, in which the bathing Black body is linked to both a past and a future erotic lineage.[3]

Many viewers might argue that Delaney's *Self-Portrait in a Paris Bath House* isn't about sex at all. The painting's arches, the very walls of the bathhouse, wouldn't even be recognizable without their signaling in the title. It is "simply" an image of transfiguration, from aging, demon-plagued man to radiant African prince wrapped in modernist swirls. But I would like to spend some considerable time in the place that critics have been too quick to leave, the place cited in Delaney's title that ostensibly has little to do with the portrait he painted: the bathhouse.

Beginning to cruise, as it were, for public sex, James Baldwin's essay "Here Be Dragons" points us toward the radiance of Delaney's *Self-Portrait in a Paris Bath House*. The original title when it appeared in *Playboy* in January 1985—"Freaks and the American Ideal of Manhood"—is more messy. Like the addition of "in a Paris Bath House" to Delaney's title, it opens up worlds, tilts more audibly toward taboo sexual practices and the spaces occupied by such freaks. With an echo of Powell's disinterest in the bathhouse, Baldwin's writing expresses a markedly different disdain for public sex, particularly as a space for nominally heterosexual men to explore a same-sex desire often depicted as a consuming, unfeeling drive. Discursively taking us into two iconic spaces of queer public sex, public toilets and the movie house, where a young boy "grabbed [his] cock," Baldwin writes:

> These men looked like cops, football players, soldiers, sailors, Marines, or bank presidents, admen, boxers, construction workers; they had wives, mistresses, and children. I sometimes saw them in other settings—in, as it were, the daytime. Sometimes they spoke to me, sometimes not, for anguish has many days and styles. But I had first seen them in the men's room, sometimes on their knees, peering up into the stalls, or standing at the urinal stroking themselves, staring at another man, stroking, and with this miasma in their eyes. Sometimes, eventually, inevitably, I would find myself in bed with one of these men, a despairing and dreadful conjunction, since their need was relentless as quicksand and as impersonal, and sexual rumor concerning blacks had preceded me. As for sexual roles, these were created by the imagination and limited only by one's stamina.[4]

Baldwin's list of men reads today like a casting call sheet of normative masculinity, one that uncannily aligns with the categories one might encounter on gay porn sites, whose algorithms contain our crudely cramped desires. Still, there is beauty in the syntax of Baldwin's accumulative confession of a shame both inevitable and accidental. A Black man in the company of miasma-eyed men, all of them burdened by sexual myths and indifference. Baldwin faults these quick "tricks" for their lack of imagination. He finds magic missing in these communal gropes.

The utopian pleasures of the bathhouse or public toilets would be sung by a different set of queer writers working in the final decade of Baldwin's life and beyond it. Baldwin's stroking men can be read productively alongside another inventory of sexual desire, one by Douglas Crimp that focuses on its social possibility. This assertion of liberation offers another lens for reading Delaney's own occupation of the bathhouse. Crimp argues that an underappreciated result of the gay liberation movement was the "expansion of affectional possibility." He explains: "Coupling was newly seen not as a 'happily ever after' compact, but as an in-the-moment union for sharing pleasure." He goes on a few lines later: "Bathhouses had 'orgy rooms,' steam rooms, and saunas for those who wanted more than one partner at a time and who might also want a little voyeurism and/or exhibitionism in the mix, or the total anonymity of sex in the dark with bodies detached from personhood."[5]

It seems to be just that detachment that Baldwin finds "despairing and dreadful" and critic Leo Bersani finds full of both sexual and social-political potential. But in concert with Baldwin, Bersani punctures utopian sentiments about these public places:

> Anyone who has ever spent one night in a gay bathhouse knows that it is (or was) one of the most ruthlessly ranked, hierarchized, and competitive environments imaginable. Your looks, muscles, hair distribution, size of cock, and shape of ass determined exactly how happy you were going to be during those few hours, and rejection, generally accompanied by two or three words at most, could be swift and brutal, with none of the civilizing hypocrisies with which we get rid of undesirables in the outside world.[6]

Another form of quicksand, this sprawling, scrutinizing desire is mobilized by the racial mythologies that Baldwin, unlike these other writers of public sex, names as burdensome imprints on sexual connections: "Sexual rumor concerning blacks had preceded me."[7]

Bersani famously advocates for creating spaces for sex that are "anti-communal, antiegalitarian, antinurturing, antiloving."[8] Disavowed of nihilistic possibility, Baldwin's tearoom, in contrast, holds despair. Punning, he writes, "At bottom, what I had learned was that the male desire for a male roams everywhere, avid, desperate, unimaginably lonely, culminating often in drugs, piety, madness or death. . . . All of this was very frightening. It was lonely and impersonal and demeaning."[9]

In these queer histories, the bathhouse is microcosm of social exclusion and egalitarian bliss, producing a tension between the solitary and the collective. Historian, theorist, and practitioner of public sex, science fiction writer Samuel R. Delany includes in his account of a visit to the St. Marks Baths an image, which he says filled him with terror, of "an undulating mass of naked male bodies, spread wall to wall" in the bath's upstairs "gym-sized" dorm room.[10] Delany also reminds us of how collectivity took on new meaning there: "In the fifties—and it was a fifties model of homosexuality that controlled all that was done, by both ourselves and the law that persecuted us—homosexuality was a solitary perversion. Before and above all, it isolated you."[11] It is the lack of the communal, the connective, that Baldwin laments in these "despairing and dreadful" encounters. He mentions loneliness twice. But his men's room lament voices the furtive necessity of these public acts and repurposed facilities in a hostile moment (and is it ever not?) of surveillance, discrimination, and violence. It is this very question of detached personhood as promise or anguish within the communal imperative that Baldwin, Bersani, and Crimp press their readers to consider and that Delaney's queer approach to portraiture is poised to explore.

In resituating Delaney's self-portrait in these discourses around public sex, we can read the image of the African king as a challenge to the rumors and myths that circulate about Black gay sexuality. Working in a genre (portraiture) dependent on persona and solitary theatricality, Delaney's *Self-Portrait in a Paris Bath House* reroutes these cultural narratives of shame and disembodied desire. The image also departs from better-known narratives about public sex that many queer theorists have romanticized—as fleeting, communal bliss or home to acts and scenes of self-shattering. The painting's nod to African spirituality also prompts speculation about the relationship between Africanist aesthetics (and their intersections with modernist re-appropriations) and queer sexuality and what lineage of queer Africanist expression might be drawn between Delaney and later artists.

The photography of Rotimi Fani-Kayode is perhaps the most productive site where Africanist iconography and embodied queer desires meet, and it provides a central contact point for repositioning Delaney's *Self-Portrait in a Paris Bath House*. Fani-Kayode's *Adebiyi*, from around 1989, is an exquisite image of ornamented, tender boyhood. A mask floats from the boy's chin in an ambiguous gesture (figure 17.1). Is he covering or uncovering himself? Shedding masks, of course, is a resonant gesture for Black gay men, and masked subjects often appear in Fani-Kayode's work. Delaney's face and body in the Paris bath portrait are similarly wooden and inscrutable. Alive and still, *Adebiyi* also feels as rooted in romanticism as Delaney's modernist portraits. The boy's floral crown recalls Renaissance portraits or medieval tapestry or even the lace and floral veils in a Frida Kahlo self-portrait. In addition, Fani-Kayode's romantic prince can be joined as kin to Delaney's royal figures, including his depiction of a prophet-like Charlie Parker (1968; plate 27) and the powerful still lifes of African sculptures he painted in the 1940s. Fani-Kayode's use of Nigerian/Yoruba objects celebrates ancestry and ritual, but his theatrical details, often indebted to camp humor, also hint toward the queer resonances in such an ancestry. W. Ian Bourland has noted that there are "at least two trajectories through which to read Fani-Kayode's 'gay art': his citation and elaboration of a history of male nude portraiture and his rehearsal and riffing on theatrical and Camp modes."[12]

Although Fani-Kayode's visual exchanges with Robert Mapplethorpe are often noted, if we place his African fetish objects alongside Delaney's art, we can begin to map a lineage of Black gay artists employing African iconography to craft statements about sexual identity. Fani-Kayode's staging and use of tribal statuary can be powerfully homoerotic. In *Bronze Head* (figure 17.2), the fetish object is imagined as a butt plug and performs a kind of doubling—an expression of cultural pride, queer subversion, and embodied pleasure. This statement on Black queer sexuality is also an ironic rejoinder to modernist artists' fetishization of tribal masks and sculptures, a fascination linked to the colonial gaze. In the introduction to *Black Male/White Male*, Fani-Kayode's lover Alex Hirst writes dramatically about modernist empire and the colonial aesthetics that often animate queer desire: "Within megatons of glass and steel, delicate boys on angel dust explore their allergies. Africa occasionally peers into the bathhouse cubicle where Europe lies ready-greased but asleep."[13] In an inversion expected of queer art, Fani-Kayode personifies Africa as the tentative explorer of white gay masculinity. In contrast, Delaney sits in the bathhouse not as a peeping lech but as an adorned figure perhaps receiving guests in an open-arched room. Upending colonial desire for the sexualized fetish, Delaney is not discovering Europe greased-up and receptive in the bathhouse cabin. Holding court, Africa is seated upright and awake.

As Bourland makes clear, the dance club and the bathhouse were important to Fani-Kayode's artistic practice. In both spaces, spirituality and sex merged.[14] Fani-Kayode and Hirst, writing in 1989, offer this explanation of the spiritual crises that shaped the era's public-sex cultures: "HIV has forced us to deal with dark ambiguities. Where better to look for clues than in the secret chambers of African shrines, the sumptuous ruins of Coptic and Eurasian temples, and the boarded-up fuck-rooms of the American dream?"[15] Delaney's seemingly apolitical self-portrait conveys an eroticism less legible but asserts a queer politics of ancestral Africa seated and attentive to these histories. Like Fani-Kayode's *Bronze Head*, greased in worship, Delaney's bathhouse is a temple to restoration and eroticism. The baths are transformed into a shrine where ancestry is queerly imagined and where Delaney's relationship to public-sex cultures later ruptured by AIDS can begin to be explored. Fani-Kayode's objects of ritual, echoed here in Delaney's sculptural pose and his paintings of African figures, contribute to a rich legacy of Black queer artists interested in Africanist spirituality as a space of "dark ambiguities."

The question of Africa for the Black American artist is enduring. From Countee Cullen's query "What is Africa to Me?" in the poem "Heritage" (1925) to Baldwin's "Encounter on the Seine: Black Meets Brown" (1950; originally titled "The Negro in Paris"), there have always been queer considerations to the inquiry. Part of Delaney's answer to that question was sartorial. His interest in "African" style—however geographically vague that term might be—is reflected in several paintings from the early 1970s, informally titled for their focus on African attire. In *Untitled: Man in African Dress* (ca. 1970; plate 29), a rather stoic man, dressed in a brilliantly striped dashiki, sits regally in a peppermint-red chair, autumnal trees in the background.[16]

As a study of the Black male body, Delaney's portrait in a Parisian bathhouse also places him within a Black, queer lineage, one in which the art of Rotimi Fani-Kayode and its explicit erotics is central. As the examples offered earlier illustrate, Fani-Kayode's photographs employ African aesthetics and traditional art forms, including sacred sculptures, textiles, and masks, in ways complementary to Delaney's use of such references. His refusal to limit his approach to portraiture to a single style suited Delaney's practice of blurring the lines between realist portraiture and abstraction, particularly in his approach to rendering the Black male body. As a painter,

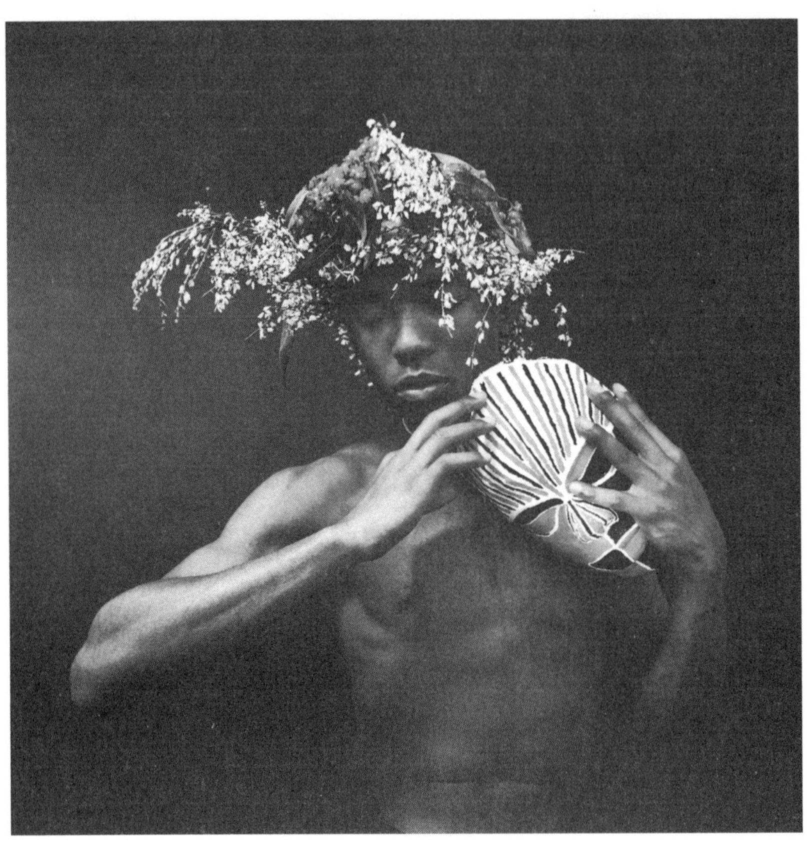

17.1

Rotimi Fani-Kayode, *Adebiyi*, 1989. Chromogenic print, image: 24 3/16 × 23⅞ in. (61.4 × 60.3 cm); sheet: 26¾ × 27 13/16 in. (67.9 × 70.6 cm). Solomon R. Guggenheim Museum, New York. © Rotimi Fani-Kayode. Courtesy of Autograph, London.

Delaney approached blackness as multihued, layered, and energized by his thickly textured lines. To better understand Delaney's experiments with flesh, we might trace his various colorations of Baldwin—from the ochre face and pink eyebrows of his famous nude *Dark Rapture* (1941; plate 1) to the portrait of James Baldwin, from the late 1940s (plate 5), in which the writer's face appears, cheeks tinted a mossy green, a lemony white. In his bathhouse portrait, Delaney's bare torso, a green-tinted blackness, is adorned with epaulets and several necklaces.[17] His flesh, scratched with color, veers to abstraction. Like Baldwin's "sex" (a term the writer favored)

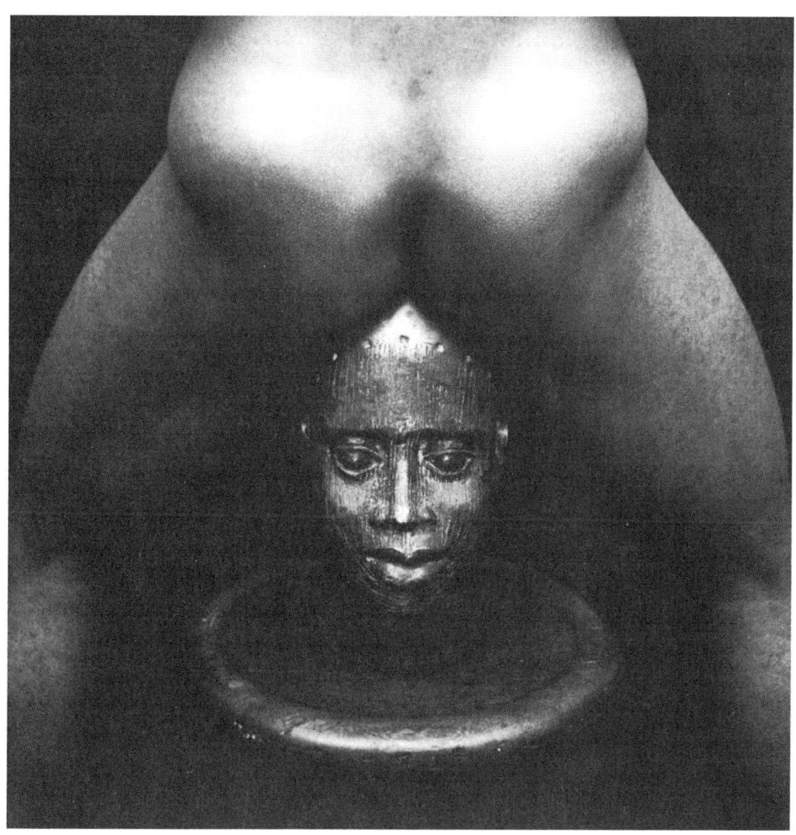

17.2

Rotimi Fani-Kayode, *Bronze Head*, 1987. Gelatin silver print on paper, support: 15⅞ × 15¼ in. (40.3 × 38.8 cm). Tate, London, purchased by the Africa Acquisitions Committee, 2015, P82468. © Rotimi Fani-Kayode. Courtesy of Autograph, London.

hidden in the shadows of *Dark Rapture*, Delaney's pose is one of erotic discretion.

The golden hues that surround Delaney and his sharply etched body are reminiscent of *Charlie Parker* (1968; plate 27), a portrait that imagines the musician as an African deity and that was created in this era when Delaney was making paintings that reflected his interest in African aesthetics, arts, and crafts. In both the Parker portrait and the 1971 self-portrait, the figure holds a wooden pose. Delaney in particular, with his masklike face, resembles an African sculpture.[18] His dress has been said to resemble that of a Masai warrior.[19] Above this ornamented body and his halo of red, as if warmed by the bathing, hieroglyphics hover: serpents and eyes but also modernist swirls that resemble the shapes in the symbolic portrait Delaney made for Baldwin a few years earlier, *Untitled (Yellow, Red, and Black Circles for James Baldwin [Istanbul])* (1966; plate 21).

Baldwin was attuned to Delaney's queer sense of time in his art, a sense that seems imbued in his "African" paintings. In a conversation with Alvin Ailey, Romare Bearden, and Albert Murray in 1978, the writer makes this prescient observation:

> I began to hear that in Beauford's canvases, and I began to see it in your very different journey. It's very difficult to express that; it's a curious process, to use Al's word, which carries you both back, simultaneously back and forward in time. This is to say you learn, yet you're empowered finally by someone else's testimony; to reach back and claim what has always been yours; yet with that same gesture, you're empowered to move forward. So, the chain, in effect, is never broken. You see what I mean?[20]

In these portraits from the early 1970s, Delaney reaches back to an African heritage in a moment of vibrant Black Power movements in the United States and in postcolonial spaces in France and across Africa. His art, too, rushes "forward in time" to inform a moment in Black queer art, unquestionably shaped by the AIDS crisis, that turned to an African past in order to explore eroticism and new histories of the Black male body. In connecting Delaney to a discourse on public sex that arrived after his death and to a queer aesthetic tradition of employing an Africanist past, I have offered an alternative reading of *Self-Portrait in a Paris Bath House*, one that questions Powell's desire to leave "pedestrian interpretations of form, content, and context behind."[21] In linking Delaney's portrait to queer uses of an Africanist presence and to practices of public sex that rethink embodiment and sociality, I embrace the ways both content and contexts matter, particularly for queer people whose pedestrian moments, as I indicated at the start, are often labeled as irrelevant or unseemly and erased.

Delaney's 1971 self-portrait is one of transfiguration and queer embodiment—from aging expat to African royalty to desiring queer body. For all of its symbolic details, however, its sitter speaks to the needs of the flesh. One of the cruel details that emerges from David Leeming's essential biography is how difficult it was for the impoverished Delaney to navigate the brutal cold winters of Paris. In that context, we should take seriously the salve that a bathhouse offers a heat-hungry body. The architecture critic Aaron Betsky reminds us that the bathhouse in American cities at the turn of the twentieth century, modeled after the "Turkish bath," was understood as a public service "that catered to an immigrant, working-class community as places of assignation. They were oases of sensuality where the body could strip itself of all outside appearances to enjoy itself in an environment dissolving into water and steam . . . places of simple hygiene and community-building."[22] The conflation of the bathhouse with the sex clubs of late capitalism (which often forgo the pools and suds altogether) obscures the other forms of social pleasure and inter/intra-class encounters made possible in the cleansing rituals of the public bath. The marks of social status might be less legible on bodies naked and silent, but as Bersani reminded us, exclusions and hierarchies didn't wholly dissipate in the steam. And the bathhouse as a site of social possibility shouldn't be flattened to its libidinal imperatives. We should complicate the utopian promises of such spaces where bodies experience perhaps communal release or democratized desire—or simply, and powerfully, restoration.

In the Paris bath, Beauford Delaney sits alone. As much as I want to bring him back to the seamy collective and bathers' gropes and antics, hidden in steam, the portrait evades both the communal and the pornographic. Such discretion may contribute to the scant attention paid to Delaney's sexuality, particularly in contrast to the robust speculation around Baldwin's—a silence that has always been curious to me. Leeming writes of the importance of Henry Miller to the painter's evolving sense of his sexual self: "It was the reading of Miller that particularly attracted him. Beauford's confrontation with sex had always been secretive and guilt-ridden." Delaney wrote a letter of admiration to Miller praising his exploration of sexualities that challenged "conditioned behavior of humankind."[23] Was some of Delaney's anguish generational? Does a homophobic politics of respectability or simply ageism prevent us from seeing *Dark Rapture*, the painting of a young, nude Baldwin, in the context of Delaney's bathhouse portrait and as part of a larger conversation between the two artists around identity, ancestry, and sex? Baldwin's poetic claim (in response to the unpredictable moods of the men he encountered in public toilets) that "anguish has many days and styles" provides an invitation to think about the various forms of hurt conveyed and transformed in Delaney's abstractions, portraits, and urban scenes. It offers, too, an instructive lens for reading the painter's aesthetic range, one more tidal than linear.[24] Throughout his career, he would return repeatedly to his passions, including music and African sculpture, and alternate between figurative paintings and abstract color studies.

Leeming's biography makes clear that Delaney's art provided him a kind of armor, particularly during moments of social upheaval and his own episodes of mental unease. (He was both agitated and inspired by America's civil rights movement and the student protests in Paris in the 1960s.) But his abstract paintings and numerous portraits (a massive amount of work we are only beginning to contend with) were not mere decorative distraction. His work constructs a space for spectacle, including its understated forms, as a disruptive space of racial-sexual expression that links the Africanist eroticism of Fani-Kayode's work to the unnamed Parisian bath where Delaney, transfigured, sits. His portrait evokes an imaginative space, too, for the men stroking just off to the side of the canvas. The baths and the narratives about them are, to use Aaron Betsky's phrase, "technologies of comfort."[25] They are spectacles, imagined and participated in, that sustain us. The bathhouses, tearooms, and nighttime lots filled with cargo trucks are reminders that critics today haven't adequately accounted for the sexual resonances in Delaney's works and how same-sex cultural spaces and Africanist practices informed his art. The spaces and figures on his canvases enact a "choreography of sensual delights" that we should be more curious to understand.[26]

Delaney's self-portrait in the bath is a visual narrative where sexuality and ancestral reverence meet. His embodied blackness and Africanist elements contest white supremacy, heteronormative pleasure, and the prudery of art criticism that elides the significance of the bathhouse to queer histories (and the racial liberation movements wedded to them). We can't visit *Self-Portrait in Paris Bath House*, done so late in Delaney's life, without seeing it, too, as a memorial. The portrait seems of an earlier time when desire was easier, too. We might say that the painting memorializes the loss of something else, something monumental—the slipping away of a heritage *both* sexual and racial. We mimic Delaney's elegiac gaze in our search for a queer ancestry and within these wanders into the histories of public bathing, sex with strangers, and queer art. "Temples of tomorrow" are much-cited sites of the Harlem Renaissance imaginary, but Delaney's bathhouse portrait invites us to consider other shrines: bathhouses, the underbellies of piers, tearoom stalls, and the tight passages between cargo trucks parked on the darkened edges of a city.[27]

1 On queer *jouissance*, see Leo Bersani, *Homos* (Cambridge, MA: Harvard University Press, 1996).

2 Richard J. Powell, *Beauford Delaney: The Color Yellow* (Atlanta: High Museum of Art, 2002), 28.

3 For foundational work on queer temporalities, see Elizabeth Freeman, *Time Binds: Queer Temporalities, Queer Histories* (Durham, NC: Duke University Press, 2010); Jack Halberstam, *In a Queer Time and Place: Transgender Bodies, Subcultural Lives* (New York: New York University Press, 2005); and José Esteban Muñoz, *Cruising Utopia: The Then and There of Queer Futurity* (New York: New York University Press, 2009).

4 James Baldwin, "Freaks and the American Ideal of Manhood," *Playboy*, January 1985; reprinted as "Here Be Dragons" in *James Balwin: Collected Essays*, ed. Toni Morrison (New York: Library of America, 1989), 821.

5 Douglas Crimp, "DISSS-CO (A FRAGMENT)," in "Before Pictures," *Criticism* 50, no. 1 (2008): 15.

6 Leo Bersani, "Is the Rectum a Grave?," *October* 43 (1987): 206.

7 Baldwin, "Freaks and the American Ideal of Manhood," 821.

8 Bersani, "Is the Rectum a Grave?," 215.

9 Baldwin, "Freaks and the American Ideal of Manhood," 821.

10 Samuel R. Delany, *The Motion of Light in Water: Sex and Science Fiction Writing in the East Village* (Minneapolis: University of Minnesota Press, 2004), 291.

11 Delany, *Motion of Light in Water*, 292.

12 W. Ian Bourland, *Bloodflowers: Rotimi Fani-Kayode, Photography, and the 1980s* (Durham, NC: Duke University Press, 2019), 97.

13 Quoted in Bourland, *Bloodflowers*, 142.

14 Bourland also discusses the importance of "sonic cultures," particularly the house music scene, to Fani-Kayode's artistic-social practices. The club, too, is a temple that connects us to queer ancestors and to the erotic that the music provides. We might remember that the Limelight disco in New York City famously was housed in a church.

15 Bourland, *Bloodflowers*, 145.

16 The other *Man in African Dress* (1972), a watercolor, centers on a young man, sitting, leg draped over the other, in radiant yellow pants and a dashiki and surrounded by pink floorboards. The painting, in a private collection, is reproduced in Powell's *Beauford Delaney: The Color Yellow* (2002). Also relevant is Delaney's portrait *Abdul-Jalilah al-Hakim* (ca. 1971). A handsome man with slightly sad eyes wears a scarf of gold and

sage, the thick-edged squares of his shirt their own tiny canvases of abstraction; the painting is a celebration of color, his style, and tender masculinity. This painting is featured in *Be Your Wonderful Self: The Portraits of Beauford Delaney* (New York: Michael Rosenfeld Gallery, 2021), 110. For further discussion of *Abdul-Jalilah al-Hakim* and Randy Wallace, the subject of the portrait, see "Abdul-Jalil al-Hakim Exemplifies Beauford Delaney's Masterful Portraits: Beauford Delaney (1901–1979) 'Portraitist of the Famous,'" Aaron and Margaret Wallace Foundation, https://amwftrust.org/abdul-jalil-al-hakim-exemplifies-beauford-delaneys-masterful-portraits/.

For a discussion of "Soul style" in the Black Panther Party and 1970s South Africa, see Tanisha C. Ford, *Liberation Threads: Black Women, Style, and the Global Politics of Soul* (Chapel Hill: University of North Carolina Press, 2015).

17 The green lines pulsating through his chest and arms might be read as a shirt, but, matching the color and outline of his bare legs, I read the figure in Delaney's self-portrait as seminude and in conversation with *Dark Rapture* and also with lesser-known works including *Portrait of a Man on Blue*, undated, oil on canvas, 57½ × 44¼ in. (146 × 112.4 cm). In this work a white, pale, brown-mustached man sits either at a beach (blue sky behind him, blue water under his feet) or in an outdoor pool of some sort; he is naked but for white briefs and looks directly at the viewer; his confident pose mirrors Delaney's posture in his bathhouse portrait.

18 Delaney's *Untitled (Fang Sculpture, Crow and Fruit)*, 1945, oil on canvas, 25 × 30 in. (63.5 × 76.2 cm), Brooklyn Museum, Brooklyn Museum Fund for African American Art, A. Augustus Healy Fund, and Ella C. Woodward Memorial Fund, 2014.7, and *Makonde Figure* (1952) are useful references for a study of the painter's sustained examination of African art forms.

19 Stephen C. Wicks, ed., *Beauford Delaney and James Baldwin: Through the Unusual Door* (Knoxville: University of Tennessee Press, 2020), 180.

20 Alvin Ailey, James Baldwin, Romare Bearden, and Albert Murray, "To Hear Another Language," *Callaloo* 24, no. 2 (2001): 676.

21 Powell, *Beauford Delaney*, 29.

22 Aaron Betsky, *Queer Space: Architecture and Same-Sex Desire* (New York: William Morrow, 1997), 162.

23 David Leeming, *Amazing Grace: A Life of Beauford Delaney* (New York: Oxford University Press, 1998), 82.

24 Baldwin, "Freaks and the American Ideal of Manhood," 821.

25 Betsky, *Queer Space*: "By providing a choreography of sensual delights, you can create your own relationship to the physical world. By decorating that world, you can create a technology of comfort that can form a buffer between you and the world, while creating another fantasy-full environment that you can construct within the world" (139).

26 Betsky, *Queer Space*, 139.

27 The phrase comes from Langston Hughes's essay "The Negro Artist and the Racial Mountain," *The Nation*, June 3, 1926, 692–94.

EIGHTEEN

Baldwin, Delaney, and Black Artists' Genealogical Legacies

Shawn Anthony Christian

This essay explores how the friendship and artistic sharing between James Baldwin and Beauford Delaney not only inspired Baldwin's writing but also constituted an instance of Black artistic relation as a kind of genealogical transition, something deeper than "artistic influence" and more historically and culturally *familial* than simply a "transmission of ideas." Just as Baldwin "read" Delaney's paintings and found in them both affirmation and challenge, especially for his own art, subsequent generations of writers have reflected on and documented what it has meant for them to read Baldwin. Rachel Ghansah, Kiese Laymon, and Jesmyn Ward are among a group of contemporary Black writers whose remarks and published writings pointedly declare their readings of Baldwin as an inheritance. Their narratives of the personally transformative effects of reading and rereading Baldwin's life and works reflect the introspection and deep social critique for which Baldwin is known and which he compels us to read as attributable to the perspectives Delaney shared with him. Through attention to a few of Baldwin's public tributes to Delaney and statements by these three contemporary writers, who affirm a relationship with the writer through his words and the life he lived, I argue that what we see in Baldwin's relationship with Delaney is not merely a friendship but an expression of reverence for, and an intimacy with, a Black artist and his legacy. It is an experience of artistic connection that compels consideration of the enduring ways Black artists embrace and then exemplify shared values and aesthetics.

Nearly sixty years after its publication, Baldwin's "On the Painter Beauford Delaney" remains an intimate but public window into the layers of their thirty-eight-year friendship. It is more than just an introduction to Delaney and his art. The brief essay is a poignant reflection on artistry and the life lessons Delaney teaches Baldwin that invites contemplation of its echoes in our own time. As Baldwin notes in the essay, the probing ways that Delaney engages the world he inhabits are central to how Baldwin experiences Delaney as a multidimensional artist. For Baldwin, Delaney's work "leads the inner and the outer eye, directly and inexorably, to a new confrontation with reality."[1] One early instance of this guidance—what their mutual biographer David Leeming describes as "lessons in complex vision"—occurred when Baldwin recognized the colors emerging from the mixture of oil and water on a New York City street.[2] The moment was significant for Baldwin in being catalyzed, as he writes, by Delaney: "I was seeing it with Beauford, [and] because Beauford caused me to see it, the very colours underwent a most disturbing and salutary change."[3] The moment was also a precursor to the many confrontations with reality Baldwin would later experience and probe as a writer. In the years between that early lesson and 1965, when Baldwin published "On the Painter," both he and Delaney struggled, endured challenges, and embraced opportunities that deepened their bond. Against the background of their shared identities as preachers' sons, expatriates, and Black, gay male artists living and working during the middle of the twentieth century, Baldwin developed his voice over the course of their relationship and used it to honor Delaney as a model of complex visioning, the discipline required by that visioning, and the "dogged and splendid journey" such vision could produce.[4]

Alongside "On the Painter Beauford Delaney," Baldwin's other public and private reminisces of his relationship with Delaney convey his responses to the painter's artistry in familial terms. Whether through Delaney's paintings or the Black musical traditions aiding the painter's own artistic development, Baldwin experienced what Delaney shared with him as a younger brother or son. As Baldwin's "father in art," Delaney's life—his art, joys, struggles, and worldview—was part of Baldwin's inheritance.[5] As Baldwin writes in "The Price of the Ticket" (1985), "Beauford was the first walking, living proof, for me, that a black man could be an artist. In a warmer time, a less blasphemous place, he would have been recognized as my Master and I as his Pupil. He became, for me, an example of courage and integrity, humility, and passion. An absolute integrity: I saw him shaken many times and I lived to see him broken but I never saw him bow."[6]

Such reminiscences can be understood as part of a tradition of Black artists' deliberate recognition of other Black artists, which Baldwin was both advancing and personalizing. "On the Painter Beauford Delaney" and Baldwin's other tributes to Delaney are in line with what Marcus Bruce describes as the "epistolary autobiographical manner in which acknowledging the example and the practices of other African American exemplars allows individuals to find and develop their own voice."[7] Baldwin's tributes furthered Delaney's visibility as a living Black exemplar whose presence was active and deeply affecting. Baldwin did more than acknowledge Delaney in these moments. He signaled the depth of their relationship as kinship—as artistic as it was cultural. I contend that this practice of claiming other Black artists as "family" is a central feature of Baldwin's manner and voicing, especially as regards Delaney, a feature which continues, in turn, to inspire others.

Karla Holloway's and Emily Lordi's explorations of influence, intertextuality, and tradition are pertinent here. Lordi develops her notion of "black resonance" through the ways Black writers have consistently figured Black female singers as "inspiring voices, cultural heroes, beloved mothers, imposing icons, and radical stars."[8] Though my focus differs from what she describes as "writer-singer engagements," her attention to how the writers she studies not only align themselves with "masterful artists" but also "perform their own uniquely valuable feats of analysis, expression, and effect" informs how I read the relations between Delaney and Baldwin and between Baldwin, Ghansah, Laymon, and Ward.[9] Additionally, in her study *BookMarks*, Holloway reminds us, "Black writers are certainly not alone in commenting on their literary lineages or in recording the books that have mattered in their adolescence or to their professional lives, but the purpose of such commentary and its pattern . . . seems deliberate in its effect and intent."[10] Whereas for Holloway the pattern is the inclusion of booklists, for me it is the scene of reading, especially of Baldwin's work. As I aim to show, Ghansah, Laymon, and Ward center their readings of Baldwin as stories of race—specifically ones of racial and familial connection and affirmation. Ghansah's, Laymon's, and Ward's accounts of reading Baldwin not only continue a tradition of "marking . . . literate authority," as Holloway suggests; more, through their accounts these writers lay claim to Baldwin as a literary ancestor and position him as a singular inspiration and model for how they read and, by implication, for how they write.[11]

Ghansah's, Laymon's, and Ward's accounts of their artistic indebtedness to Baldwin, like Baldwin's of Delaney, contrast received notions of artistic lineage and tradition, especially Harold Bloom's theories about the anxiety of influence, which Ismail Muhammad invokes when he argues, "We might think of these writers as among a school of black nonfiction writers for which Baldwin is a problem as much as an interlocutor, a specter to which they return cyclically—almost compulsively—to both honor and decline."[12] I read their relation to Baldwin differently precisely because they honor Baldwin's renown by engaging the hard but necessary lessons within his works and rendering them familiar, shareable, and inspiringly useful. In reading Baldwin, these writers come to "read with" Baldwin and report doing so in ways that extend a Black cultural practice of marking nonbiological, familial bonds within their community of artists. Baldwin, then, is not just a pioneering artist. Because of what he teaches and how he nurtures through his words and life, Baldwin becomes (or is already) *family*. Ultimately, Ghansah's, Laymon's, and Ward's recountings of reading Baldwin, like Baldwin's reflections on his experience with Delaney's complex, artistic vision, do not read as narratives of intergenerational anxiety. Rather, their relationship to Baldwin and Baldwin's legacy "issues from receptivity and generosity."[13] As related instances of the genealogical practices of Black artists, their accounts of Baldwin represent, as Brigitte Fielder argues, "what is lived in relation to others. Like familial genealogies, aesthetic genealogies show threads of influence and care—relation."[14]

In Jesmyn Ward's *The Fire This Time* (2016), markers of Baldwin's influence operate beyond the volume's borrowed but adapted title. In her introduction to the volume, Ward recounts how she sought solace and community in the wake of Trayvon Martin's 2012 murder and the rise of the Black Lives Matter movement. Ward relates how social media failed her amid the ensuing desperation and litany of Black death in that time: she declares, "I needed words." More pointedly, she writes, "I couldn't fully satisfy my need for kinship in this struggle, commiserate with others trying to find a way out of that dark closet. In desperation, I sought James Baldwin." Noting her first encounter with Baldwin's words, in *The Fire Next Time* (1963), Ward describes her reading as voracious and relates how she returns to Baldwin "annually, after that first impression-forming reading."[15] As her reaction to rereading *The Fire Next Time*—specifically, Baldwin's urging in "My Dungeon Shook: Letter to My Nephew on the Hundredth Anniversary of the Emancipation Proclamation" that "you can only be destroyed by believing that you really are what the white world calls a nigger" and his professed rationale for his address to his young interlocutor ("I only tell you this because I love you, and please don't ever forget it")—Ward writes about Baldwin in ways similar to how Baldwin reflects on his relationship with Delaney.[16] As Baldwin notes early in "On Painter Beauford Delaney," for example, "Many years ago in poverty and uncertainty, Beauford and I would walk together through the streets of New York City. He was then, and is now, working all the time, or perhaps it would be more accurate to say that he is seeing all the time; and the reality of his seeing caused me to begin to see."[17]

Ward's sense of her figurative relationship with Baldwin casts him as surrogate but chosen family whose bonds foster protection, affirmation, truth, and learning. Ward relates, of reading "My Dungeon Shook": "It was as if I sat on my porch steps with a wise father, a kind, present uncle, who said this to me. Told me I was worthy of love. Told me I was worth something in this world. Told me I was a human being. I saw Trayvon's face, and all the words blurred on the page." What Baldwin does for Ward, as "someone so sharp and gifted and human [who] could acknowledge it all, and speak on it again and again," figuratively honors how Delaney urges Baldwin to confront reality, especially as Baldwin's words give way to the reality that Ward cannot unsee: Trayvon Martin's insisting face.[18] The inspiration Ward derives from this complex vision reverberates in the scenes of reading—her own and those she envisions for the volume—populating her introduction.

In bringing *The Fire This Time* to fruition, Ward builds Baldwin's words into a vision of readers who

> would need a book like this. A book that would reckon with the fire of rage and despair and fierce, protective love currently sweeping through the streets and campuses of America. A book that would gather new voices in one place, in a lasting, physical form, and provide a forum for those writers to dissent, to call to account, to witness, to reckon. A book that a girl in rural Missouri could pick up at

> her local library and, while reading, encounter a voice that hushed her fears. In the pages she would find a wise aunt, a more present mother, who saw her terror and despair threading their fingers through her hair, and would comfort her. We want to tell her this: *You matter. I love you. Please don't forget it.*[19]

The vision of cultural kinship that Ward imparts here and in a later address to her readers is compelling. She notes, "I hope this book makes each one of you, dear readers, feel as if we are sitting together, you and me and Baldwin" and the other writers in the collection; she contends "that we are composing our story together. That we are writing an epic wherein Black lives carry worth."[20] Ward's consideration of the possibilities for solace that *The Fire This Time* could bring is an instance of "genealogical influence" that directly recalls Baldwin's relationship with Delaney.

Kiese Laymon similarly echoes these legacies and familial connections through the different experience of Baldwin-inspired reading and complex witnessing that he recounts in *Heavy: An American Memoir* (2018).[21] Laymon offers this about the writer: "Baldwin's work, definitely *The Fire Next Time* and *Giovanni's Room*, were guides to me." He adds, "I write to these folks in everything I create and I hope they can see and feel their inspiration in my sentences."[22] However, the importance of reading and rereading Baldwin is more a part of his mother's legacy and her (at times difficult and uneven) efforts to compel Laymon to confront reality. Whereas Baldwin's "My Dungeon Shook" in *The Fire Next Time* writes forward, to inscribe for his nephew and other Black youths a Black future and a place for them within it, Laymon writes to and through the past to claim a future for himself different from the one for which his mother, his addressee, rears him. He writes, addressing her: "The presence of all those books, all that laughter, all our lies, and your insistence I read, reread, write, and revise in those books, made it so I would never be intimidated or easily impressed by words, punctuation, sentences, paragraphs, chapter, and white space. You gave me a black southern laboratory to work with words. In that space, I learned how to assemble memory and imagination when I most wanted to die. Your gifts of reading, rereading, writing, and revision are why I started this book."[23]

An account of Laymon's growing up in a ferociously intellectual household, the only child of a single mother and a Black boy who struggles with his weight, *Heavy*, as one reader notes, is about "the jagged, uneven road to becoming a writer and a man; it is a chronicle of daily confrontations with the twin assaults of American racism and America's weight-obsessed culture."[24] *Heavy* is also about confronting lies, bearing witness to the truth, and donning, as Laymon writes, "new lenses and frames to see the world."[25] *Heavy*'s poignancy resides in the fact that Laymon tries to see the world through the eyes of his mother. In the prologue, "Been," he writes, again addressing her: "I am writing a different book to you because books, for better or worse, are how we got here, and I am afraid of speaking any of this to your face."[26] He adds, "I wanted to write a lie. You wanted to read that lie. I wrote this to you instead."[27] Laymon's explanation for why he offers a different book is a recurring element of *Heavy* and a particular form of voicing and confrontation with reality that evokes both Delaney's and Baldwin's legacies. As he writes to his mother, "This is how we are taught to love in America. Our dishonesty, cowardice, and misplaced self-righteousness, far more than how much or how little we weigh, is part of why we are suffering. In this way, and far too many others, we are studious children of this nation. We do not have to be this way."[28] As Baldwin often does in his writings, Laymon writes from personal experience here to provoke familial and national reflection. Such moments position *Heavy* as an echo of what Richard Blint and Douglas Field remind us is Baldwin's "commitment to the unraveling and careful analysis of our inexorable 'familial' ties."[29]

Indeed, Laymon evokes Baldwin's lifelong charge to American citizens that we confront the lies that we tell ourselves and emphasizes his connection to Baldwin, especially *The Fire Next Time*. Reflecting on a difficult and racially charged period of attendance at Millsaps College in Mississippi, Laymon writes, "I listened to The Coup and read everything James Baldwin had written that summer. I learned you haven't read anything if you've only read something once or twice. Reading things more than once was the reader version of revision. I read *The Fire Next Time* over and over again."[30] Like Ward, Laymon finds solace in, and receives an education from, Baldwin's landmark collection of essays. Similarly to how Baldwin learns a "lesson in complex vision" from Delaney's assertion that "the sunset one saw yesterday, the leaf that burned, or the rain that fell, have not really been seen unless one is prepared to see them every day," Laymon comes to understand the discipline of rereading and its benefits for seeing and imagining the world differently.[31] For example, when reflecting on his rereading of Baldwin's essay "Faulkner and Desegregation" in *Nobody Knows My Name* (1961), Laymon sits with Baldwin's idea that "any real change implies the breakup of the world as one has known it, the loss of all that gave [one] an identity, the end of safety" and writes, "I imagined the sentence was written to me. I thought about the safety I found in eating too much, eating too late, eating to run away from memory."[32] The move here and throughout *Heavy* is to honor Baldwin as Laymon aims to "learn from the past without uncritically accepting our ancestors' fears, assumptions, and intellectual legacies."[33]

Similarly, Rachel Ghansah invokes Baldwin's legacy, articulating both her initially conflicted relationship to Baldwin and her new understanding of what it means to die "a Black death." Ghansah's reflection aims to reconcile life and death as a cultural inheritance. A Black death, Ghansah notes, is a "slow death, the accumulation of insults, injuries, neglect, second-rate health care, high blood pressure and stress, no time for self-care, no time to sigh, and in the end, the inevitable, the erasing of memory." It is a process that Ghansah aims to "write against," especially as a means of "writing a history of the people who . . . [she does] not want to forget."[34] Just as Baldwin could not fully appreciate the artist that Delaney was without understanding his struggle as a Black artist—what Baldwin describes as "so dogged and splendid a journey"—Ghansah also understood that bearing witness to Baldwin's living, no matter how well documented, was precarious.[35]

Beauford Delaney often appeared to James Baldwin as a spiritual guide and griot. Ghansah acknowledges initially viewing Baldwin the same way, as the "high priest in charge of [her] prayer of being a black person who wanted to exist on books and words alone," and she notes resenting how he was "praised" as *the* "black authorial exception."[36] That admission gives way to her reflection on the figurative familial bonds she develops with Baldwin through confronting and conflating how her grandfather and Baldwin die. Reflecting on her visit to Baldwin's home in France, Ghansah writes, "Decades after his death in 1987, what I found left behind in Baldwin's house was something like what we experienced when I waded through my grandfather's effects after his house had burned down. Two months later, my grandfather would die from shock and stress caused by the fire. Baldwin's death, too, came at him hard and fast. In both houses, I found . . . that nothing remained. No remembrance of the past." Here, Ghansah images two instances of what it means to die a Black death but also honors what was humane in her grandfather's and Baldwin's lives. She attends to the realness of the living as much as the painful realness that, for many Black people, there is often "not even the sense that a great [person]" lived.[37]

It is a powerful assertion that compels a return to "On the Painter Beauford Delaney," specifically Baldwin's contention that Delaney "is a great painter, among the very greatest."[38] It also recalls how Delaney was forgotten for decades by the art world and as a renowned Black public figure. Delaney's long depression, death in a mental institution, and burial in what became an unmarked grave underscore Ghansah's musings on Black death but are also a forceful reminder of what making art requires of the artist. Baldwin notes that "the darkness of Beauford's beginnings, in Tennessee, many years ago, was a blue-black midnight indeed, opaque, and full of sorrow. And I do not know, nor will any of us ever know, what kind of strength it was that enabled him to make so dogged and splendid a journey."[39] Aligning her grandfather and Baldwin, Ghansah continues the legacy of kinship that Baldwin and Delaney forged.

An important part of Ghansah's reflection is her shift to second-person voice.[40] Ghansah's personal address to her reader furthers Ward's aims for community in *The Fire This Time* and literally disrupts the isolation that she experiences both in her individual memories and at Baldwin's home. We join the immediacy of her reflection just as she confronts the limitations on permanence. Ultimately, in reflecting on how she reads Baldwin's life and death, not simply or even his words, Ghansah inadvertently recalls and answers Laymon's book when she shares the weight of Baldwin's legacy and invites readers to affirm, "He is my brother, he ain't heavy."[41]

Delaney, Baldwin's "principal witness," wrote poignantly of *The Fire Next Time* that Baldwin "reveals for all of us so much that we feel but cannot put into words."[42] Yet Black writers in the twenty-first century read and reference *The Fire Next Time* in ways that bear witness to Baldwin's prescience and seek to sustain and strengthen the vitality of his words and life as intergenerational and culturally familial forces. Throughout Baldwin's essays, creative work, and speeches, in fact, he implored other African Americans to "imagine, invent, write, and fashion a language for themselves that recognizes them and conveys their lived realities."[43] The lineage that Ghansah, Laymon, and Ward share with Baldwin and Delaney is the complementary tradition of honoring the often under- and unacknowledged, the under- and untheorized, and the under- and uncelebrated. For when Black artists reflect publicly on Black artists who precede them, their accounts can reveal the debt that a given generation of artists feels toward previous generations. Their accounts nuance the difficulties of Black artistry, of being a Black artist, and the weight of the oftentimes radical imperatives that such being entails. They also explore and even replicate dynamics of mutual respect, critical visioning, care, and "bonds of love," or what Cheryl Wall describes as a vehicle for achieving "a measure of freedom."[44] These are often the realities drawing Black artists into a legacy of inspiration and regard as cultural and artistic kin.

1 James Baldwin, "On the Painter Beauford Delaney," *Transition* 4, no. 18 (1965); reprinted in *James Baldwin: Collected Essays*, ed. Toni Morrison (New York: Library of America, 1998), 721.

2 David Lemming, *James Baldwin: A Biography* (New York: Arcade, 1994), 91; Baldwin, "On the Painter Beauford Delaney," 721.

3 Baldwin, "On the Painter Beauford Delaney," 720.

4 Baldwin, "On the Painter Beauford Delaney," 720.

5 Lemming, *James Baldwin*, 88; James Baldwin, "The Price of the Ticket," in *The Price of the Ticket: Collected Nonfiction, 1948–1985* (New York: St. Martin's, 1985), x.

6 Baldwin, "Price of the Ticket," xi.

7 Marcus Bruce, "Continuing a Legacy: James Baldwin, Ta-Nehisi Coates, and the African American Witness," in *Of Latitudes Unknown: James Baldwin's Radical Imagination*, ed. Alice Mikal Craven, William Dow, and Yoko Nakamura (New York: Bloomsbury Academic, 2019), 201.

8 Emily J. Lordi, *Black Resonance: Iconic Women Singers and African American Literature* (New Brunswick, NJ: Rutgers University Press, 2013), 2.

9 Lordi, *Black Resonance*, 2, 4.

10 Karla Holloway, *BookMarks: Reading in Black and White, a Memoir* (New Brunswick, NJ: Rutgers University Press, 2006), 9.

11 Holloway, *BookMarks*, 9.

12 Ismail Muhammad, "The Misunderstood Ghost of James Baldwin," *Slate*, February 15, 2017, https://slate.com/culture/2017/02/how-critics-have-misunderstood-james-baldwins-influence-on-todays-great-black-nonfiction-writers.html. See, as well, Harold Bloom's *The Anxiety of Influence: A Theory of Poetry* (New York: Oxford University Press, 1973). Though beyond the scope of this essay, a fuller consideration of Baldwin's genealogical practices regarding other Black artists would surely consider his complex relationship with Richard Wright, which scholars (and Baldwin himself) describe in ways that are evocative of Bloom's notions; see, for example, Baldwin's "Alas, Poor Richard," in *The Price of the Ticket*, 269–88. In addition, an examination of Baldwin's artistic family would include Black women writers and musicians; instructive here is Courtney Thorsson, "James Baldwin and Black Women's Fiction," *African American Review* 46, no. 4 (Winter 2013): 615–31. Ed Pavlić explores Baldwin's indebtedness to Black musicians in *Who Can Afford to Improvise? James Baldwin and Black Music, the Lyric and the Listeners* (New York: Fordham University Press, 2016).

13 Jean-Philippe Marcoux, "Invocations and Evocations: The Griotic Legacy of Margaret Walker and Gwendolyn Brooks on Carolyn Rodgers and Sonia Sanchez," *Journal of American Ethnic Literature* 7 (2017): 64.

14 Brigitte Fielder, "Literary Genealogies and the Kinship of Black Modernity," *American Literary History* 32, no. 4 (Winter 2020): 791.

15 Jesmyn Ward, introduction to *The Fire This Time: A New Generations Speaks about Race*, ed. Jesmyn Ward (New York: Scribner, 2017), 7.

16 James Baldwin, quoted in Ward, *Fire This Time*, 7.

17 Baldwin, "On the Painter Beauford Delaney," 702.

18 Ward, introduction to *Fire This Time*, 7.

19 Ward, introduction to *Fire This Time*, 8.

20 Ward, introduction to *Fire This Time*, 11.

21 I chose to focus on *Heavy* here because it explicitly attends to Baldwin's influence. Laymon also contributes "Da Art of Storytellin' (a Prequel)" to Ward's *The Fire This Time* and writes about the members of the musical group OutKast in ways evocative of Baldwin's reflection on Delaney—especially when Laymon writes, "It was only after listening to *ATLiens* that I realized in order to get where I needed to go as a human being and an artist, in order to release my own spacey stank blues, I had to write fiction. Dre and Big showed me it was possible to create fake worlds wholly concerned with 'what if' and 'maybe' and 'what really was.'"

22 Roxanne Gay, "A Conversation with Kiese Laymon," *The Nation*, September 13, 2013, https://www.thenation.com/article/archive/conversation-kiese-laymon/.

23 Kiese Laymon, *Heavy: An American Memoir* (New York: Scribner, 2018), 9.

24 Martha Anne Toll, "*Heavy* Brilliantly Renders the Struggle to Become Fully Realized," NPR, October 17, 2018, https://www.npr.org/2018/10/17/657824190/heavy-brilliantly-renders-the-struggle-to-become-fully-realized.

25 Laymon, *Heavy*, 141.

26 Laymon, *Heavy*, 9.

27 Laymon, *Heavy*, 10.

28 Laymon, *Heavy*, 10.

29 Rich Blint and Douglas Field, afterword to "James Baldwin," special issue, *African American Review* 46, no. 4 (Winter 2013): 747.

30 Laymon, *Heavy*, 143.

31 Baldwin, "On the Painter Beauford Delaney," 720.

32 Laymon, *Heavy*, 143.

33 Muhammad, "Misunderstood Ghost of James Baldwin."

34 Rachel Kaadzi Ghansah, "The Weight," in Ward, *Fire This Time*, 20.

35 Baldwin, "On the Painter Beauford Delaney," 720.

36 Ghansah, "Weight," 20, 21.

37 Ghansah, "Weight," 29.

38 Baldwin, "On the Painter Beauford Delaney," 721.

39 Baldwin, "On the Painter Beauford Delaney," 720.

40 Ghansah notes, "Because I am telling you this now, writing it all down, I am finding time to regard memory and death differently. I'm holding them up in the light and searching them, inspecting them, as they are not as I want them to be"; "Weight," 31.

41 Ghansah, "Weight," 32.

42 Leeming, *James Baldwin*, 215.

43 Bruce, "Continuing a Legacy," 202.

44 Cheryl Wall, *On Freedom and the Will to Adorn: The Art of the African American Essay* (Chapel Hill: University of North Carolina Press, 2018), 136.

NINETEEN

In a Speculative Light

The Portrait Project

Jered Sprecher

In 2017, the Knoxville Museum of Art (KMA) in Tennessee staged an exhibition of Beauford Delaney's work entitled *Gathering Light: Works by Beauford Delaney from the KMA Collection.*[1] Attendees had the opportunity to see the world through the eyes and spirit of Beauford Delaney. As I wandered through the exhibition, I encountered an arresting portrait of a man. The dark eyes stared back at the viewer, the face tenderly depicted with soft shifts in value and color. This subtle light on the subject's face contrasted with the flat, chromatic shapes of red, violet, magenta, and blue that composed his shirt and robe, as the nearly bald sitter raised a disproportionally small and delicate hand in a Christlike blessing, a subtle halo emanating from behind his head. This pastel drawing was the 1948 portrait by Delaney entitled *Dante Pavone as Christ* (plate 7). The subject, Dante Pavone, was an esteemed vocalist and voice teacher—the son of an Italian opera singer with his own conservatory training in Italy—as well as a friend and frequent muse to Delaney. According to David Leeming, Pavone met Delaney in 1936, when he was singing in Greenwich Village clubs, and he and the painter became fast friends. While they were not lovers, it was clear that Dante did love Beauford, and he was himself for a time Delaney's obsession and principal subject—something remarked upon in print by Delaney's friend Henry Miller.[2]

Seeing that marvelous drawing led me back to *Portrait of James Baldwin* (1944; plate 2), the pastel made by Delaney early in their friendship. In that drawing, Delaney traces the contours of Baldwin's face in an economical but visionary way. Baldwin's full eyes, slight smile, and dynamic intellect are palpable even with the simple materials that Delaney uses to summon his friend's youthful countenance. Elegant strokes of black charcoal work in concert with an array of colors laid in with pastels to bring the ebony lines to life. It is a portrait that pulls the viewer in and instills a desire to know more about the individual, this wonder sitting before the artist. The portrait becomes an embodiment of transactional beauty—the beauty of two humans sitting in a room together, allowing time to slow down for a few generously shared hours while together they record an impression made upon the world.

I was inspired by Delaney's commitment to portraiture and to drawing the "inner light" of his subjects in new ways. During the planning stages for the 2019 Knoxville symposium "In a Speculative Light: The Arts of James Baldwin and Beauford Delaney," I suggested to host Amy Elias and several fellow artists that we pay homage to Delaney's approach by creating a space where attendees could themselves sit for a portrait or watch one being drawn. It was our hope that we could channel some of the magic of that portrait from 1944, when Baldwin sat for Delaney. Baldwin looking to Delaney, Delaney looking to Baldwin. Did they listen to music? Did they have a lively conversation? Were there long periods of silence with only the sound of charcoal and pastel touching the surface of the sheet of paper?

The event thus featured the Portrait Project, held in the symposium space in the University of Tennessee student union, a large, well-lit room outfitted as a portrait studio and open to everyone on campus for the duration of the symposium. The Portrait Project combined an implicit tribute to Delaney with an art studio and what became a warm, friendly communal meeting space. During the run of the symposium, the artists Joshua Bienko, Eleanor Conover, Rubens Ghenov, Mary Laube, Lilly Saywitz, and Jered Sprecher took turns drawing portraits of attendees. Each session lasted around ninety minutes, the artists deftly drawing while conversing with the sitter and learning about their individual connections to Baldwin and Delaney. A symposium attendee—a student, a faculty member, a member of the public—could wander into the studio space to witness an early morning drawing session with Fred Moten as he discussed jazz, drum makers, Delaney, Baldwin, family, and his mother's record collection. Another morning was spent drawing biographer David Leeming as he sat patiently recalling the time decades before when he sat for a portrait by Delaney—a portrait he still owns (ca. 1967; plate 25). The last day of the symposium included an afternoon trying to capture the vitality, grace, and deep wisdom of Sylvia Peters, chair of the Knoxville Gathering Light consortium, which worked with the Knoxville Museum of Art, Monique Wells, from Les Amis de Beauford Delaney in Paris, and other Knoxville cultural organizations to revitalize the memory of Delaney as an internationally important artist. These are just a few of the moments impressed on my memory.

As artists we thank each person who sits for a portrait, allowing us to draw them. Each drawing is a gamble, as not every drawing will succeed in capturing the spirit or likeness of the individual. That is part of the risk that every artist takes when they pick up paper and pencil—what Delaney knew and what is central to the rigor of his drawings. We increased our odds by having two or three artists drawing at a time. Some drawings came together in the last few crucial moments before the sitter had to leave. A final brave line, a smudge to soften a shadow, a flick of the wrist, a tiny pinprick-like touch of color to bring life to the eyes.

The experience for us as artists was deeply rewarding, as we were immersed in the activity of drawing and soaking up the wide-ranging conversations with symposium presenters and supporters as we drew. Each sitting moved from conversation to silence and back again in a natural rhythm. We came away both euphoric and exhausted by the experience and the effort. The drawings register this time together and provide a chance to imagine what Baldwin or Pavone might have thought or felt as they sat and Delaney drew. In particular, as we did portraits of David Leeming, we were reminded of Delaney's own portrait of him and couldn't but wonder what that sitting, and Delaney's remembrance of times together, must have been like (see figures 19.1–19.3; plate 25).

I find myself looking for a metaphor to describe the place of these portrait drawings, these slight objects that tenuously carry a transcribed image of an individual. Perhaps they are like a letter home, a precious note. A machine to slow down time for an hour or two and enjoy the presence of another human. The economy is one of generosity. The sitter learns to trust the artist and gradually relaxes, and the artist in turn relaxes and loosens their hold on the drawing. Alternating lines, smudges, and erasures add up to more than a simple calculus of marks. The artist balances what the drawing continually asks: Does it look like them? Does it feel like them? When we ponder those drawings of Baldwin and Pavone, we find Delaney thinking and speaking in line and color and with a full and longing heart. The drawings that emerged out of the symposium are part of that tradition of thinking and speaking in line and color.

Some of the other artists recall crucial moments in the time spent with those sitting for a portrait. Joshua Bienko, associate professor in the School of Art at the University of Tennessee, where he teaches drawing and painting, has exhibited at NADA (New York), Dallas Contemporary (Texas), Artpace (Texas), and the Guggenheim Museum (New York, in collaboration with YouTube Play Biennial), among other venues, and among his accomplishments is being one of the founding members of the artist-run space Ortega y Gasset Projects in Brooklyn, New York. Of his Portrait Project experience (see figure 19.4), Bienko noted,

> I'm thinking back on the experience of sitting and listening to Fred Moten speak softly while we scribbled. He was relaxed and present and still. I remember feeling a great pressure to find a likeness, I mean to really make sure it looked like him. I've drawn a lot of portraits. This pressure does not typically (for me anyway) bode well. It's like singing when you're nervous; the notes come out flat and your throat is tight. As I listened to Fred talk, I remember easing my body. He giggled as he spoke. Told us some stories about his child. It warmed the space. This drawing is important to me. It's an index of that moment, a slow and purposeful exchange where we observed each other observing each other. Those marks are a record of that moment. It's what it looked like from my seat. I like to think Fred has a snapshot in his head of what we looked like in that moment, too.

Rubens Ghenov was reading Moten's work at the time of the symposium and also worked on a portrait of Moten at the Portrait Project (figure 19.5).

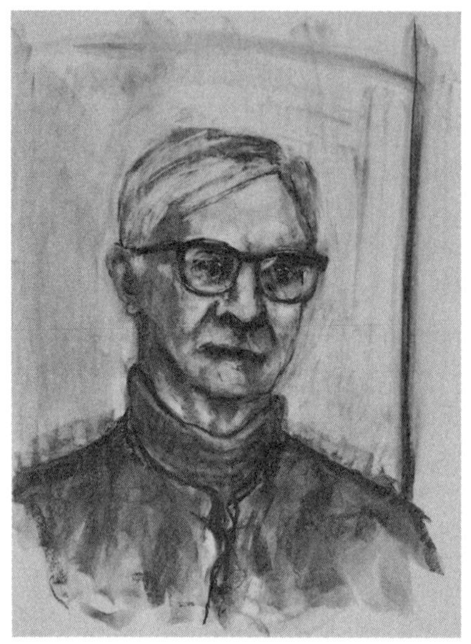

19.1
Jered Sprecher, *Portrait of David Leeming,* 2020. Courtesy of Jered Sprecher.

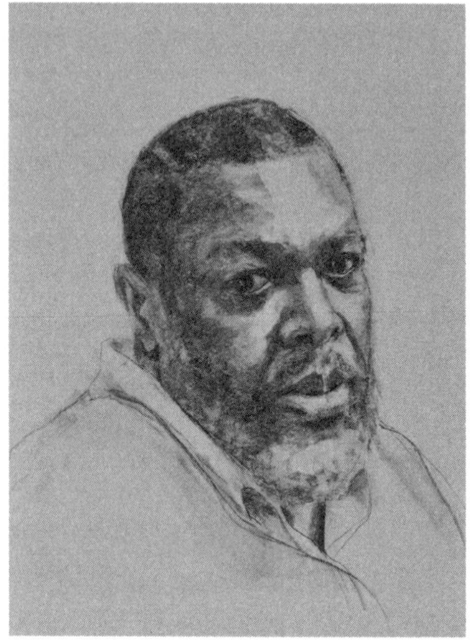

19.2
Jered Sprecher, *Portrait of Hilton Als,* 2020. Courtesy of Jered Sprecher.

An associate professor of painting at the University of Tennessee, Ghenov has shown nationally in both solo and group exhibitions at Morgan Lehman Gallery (New York), Geoffrey Young Gallery (Massachusetts), TSA Brooklyn (New York), and the Philadelphia Museum of Art. In 2013, he cocurated with Dona Nelson the Seventy-Second Annual Juried Exhibition at the Woodmere Art Museum. Philadelphia, and he has been featured in numerous publications, including *Art in America*, the *Village Voice, Bomb*, and the *Philadelphia Inquirer*. Ghenov recalled his symposium experience:

> On the day we drew Fred, I woke up early to prepare. I was rereading *In the Break* and thinking of Fred's writing about Cecil Taylor, specifically his remark that "the poem of construction—geometry of a blue space, geometry of a blue ghost—is the poem that is of the music." My own work is often catalogued under the umbrella of abstraction;

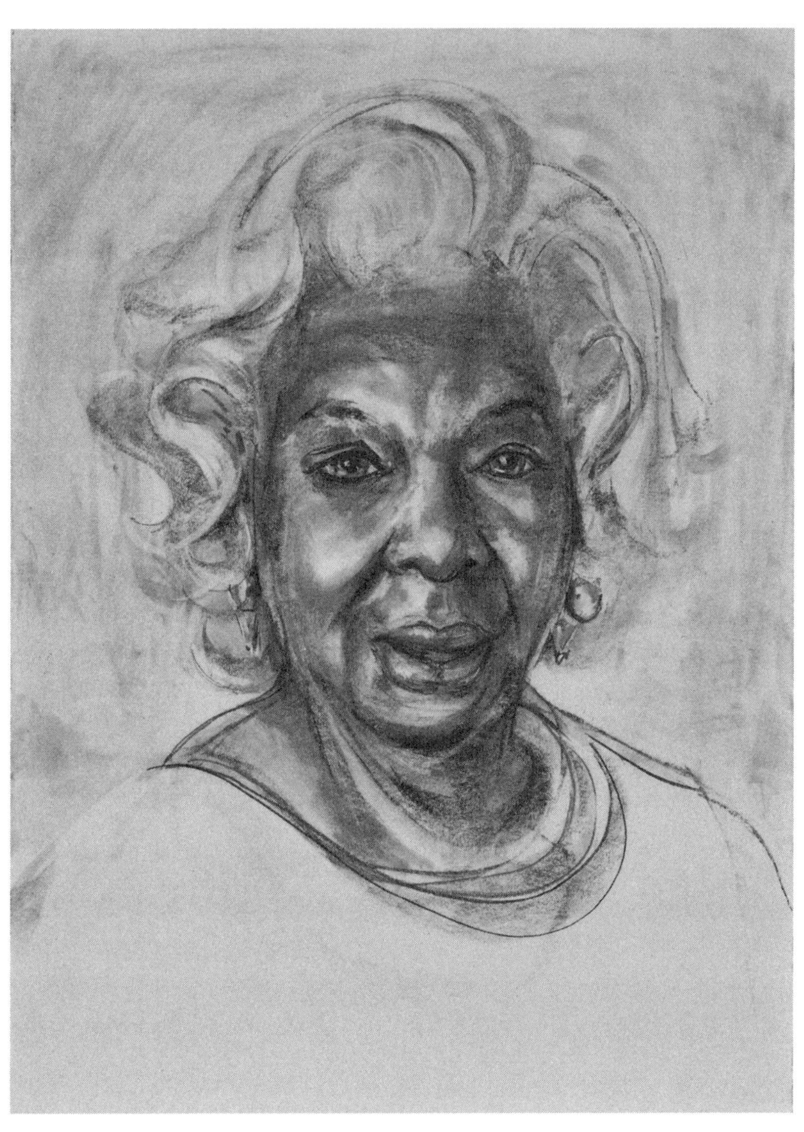

19.3
Jered Sprecher, *Portrait of Sylvia Peters*, 2020. Courtesy of Jered Sprecher.

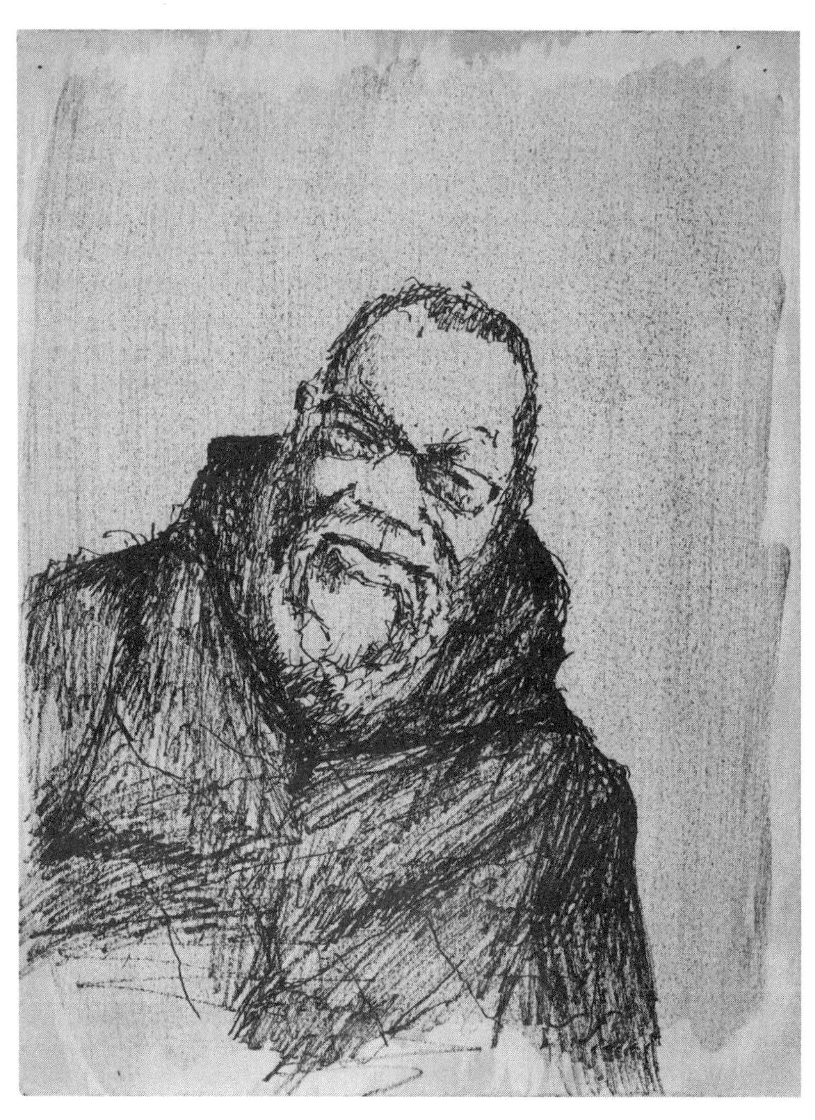

19.4

Joshua Bienko, *Moten in Blue*, 2020. Courtesy of Joshua Bienko.

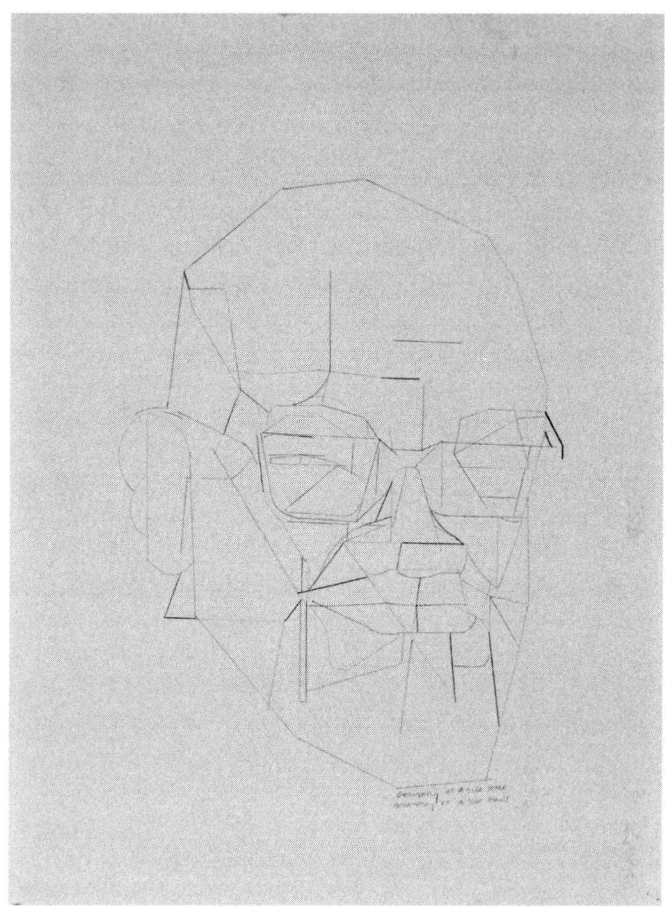

19.5

Rubens Ghenov, *Geometry of a Blue Ghost*, 2020. Courtesy of Rubens Ghenov.

> "abstraction" deals heavily with notions of geometry, while for me, the highest form of any art is when poetry is conjured. This portrait of Fred was the second I made of him that day. While drawing, that line concerning Cecil, improvisation, geometry and a blue ghost loomed large in my thinking. I traveled in a few blues before I reached green or purple and stationed his portrait as a constellation.

Other artists recall how silence entered into the exchange between artist and sitter. Mary Laube recalls scholar Michelle Elam's sitting as embodying this

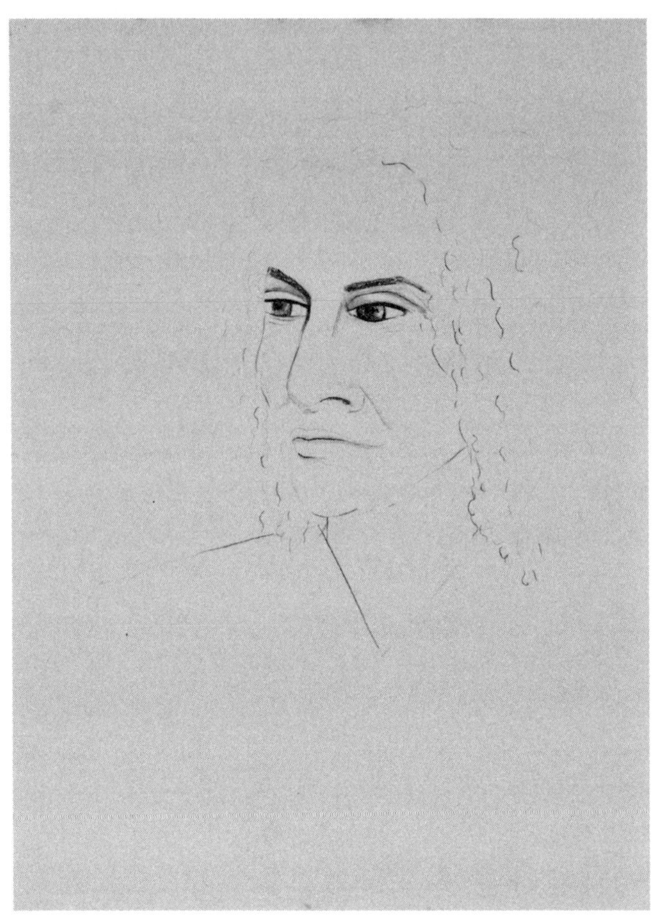

19.6

Mary Laube, *Portrait of Michelle Elam*, 2020. Courtesy of Mary Laube.

exchange (see figure 19.6). Laube is associate professor of art at the University of Tennessee, and her work has been supported by several artist residencies, including at Yaddo, the Virginia Center for the Creative Arts, Stiwdeo Maelor (Wales), and the Fanoon Center for Print Media Research (Qatar). She has been featured in numerous publications, including *Art Maze Mag* and *New American Paintings*, and is a recipient of a Sustainable Arts Foundation Award and an AHL Foundation Visual Art Award; she is a cofounder of the Warp Whistle Project, and she works with composer Paul Schuette to make work that merges kinetic stage sets with music performance. She recalls this of her Portrait Project experience: "Drawing Michelle Elam was a collaborative endeavor. I drew steady, minimal lines informed by the rhythm of her movements and gestures. I described contours and shadows, pausing when she spoke. This interaction between movement and stillness, between Michelle and myself and the room, is all wrapped into her portrait."

The drawings created during the symposium echo a beautiful exchange. The artist asks an individual to sit for a portrait, and in the process the sitter and artist engage each other, occupying the same space, sharing thoughts, exchanging gazes, and ultimately collaborating, as the sitter's appearance, air, words, and presence create a call and response. The artist responds, drawing.

NOTES

1 Knoxville Museum of Art, *Gathering Light: Works by Beauford Delaney from the KMA Collection*, May 5–July 23, 2017, Knoxville, Tennessee, https://knoxart.org/news_articles/the-knoxville-museum-of-art-presents-gathering-light-works-by-beauford-delaney-from-the-kma-collection/.

2 David Leeming, *Amazing Grace: A Life of Beauford Delaney* (New York: Oxford University Press, 1998), 56–58.

BIBLIOGRAPHY

ARCHIVES

Baldwin, James. Papers. Sc MG 936. Schomburg Center for Research in Black Culture, Manuscripts, Archives and Rare Books Division, New York Public Library.

Delaney, Beauford. Correspondence. Sc MG 59. Schomburg Center for Research in Black Culture, Manuscripts, Archives and Rare Books Division, New York Public Library.

Evans, Walter O. The Walter O. Evans Collection of James Baldwin, James Weldon Johnson Collection, Yale Collection of American Literature, Beinecke Rare Book and Manuscript Library, New Haven, CT (JWJ MSS 107, box 2, folder 5).

Galerie Darthea Speyer records. Folder 9: Correspondence, 1969–73. Archives of American Art, Smithsonian Institution, Washington, DC.

Leeming, David. The David Leeming Collection of James Baldwin Research, James Weldon Johnson Collection, Yale Collection of American Literature, Beinecke Rare Book and Manuscript Library, New Haven, CT (JWJ MSS 172, b.1 39900210488627l).

White, Charles. Charles White Papers. Archives of American Art, Smithsonian Institution, Washington, DC.

BOOKS, ARTICLES, AND OTHER SOURCES

Ailey, Alvin, James Baldwin, Romare Bearden, and Albert Murray. "To Hear Another Language." *Callaloo* 24, no. 2 (2001): 656–77.

Als, Hilton. "Strangers in the Village." In *Glenn Ligon: America*, edited by Scott Rothkopf, 211. New York: Whitney Museum of American Art, 2011.

Alter, Alexandra. "A James Baldwin Book, Forgotten and Overlooked for Four Decades, Gets Another Life." Review of *Little Man, Little Man: A Story of Childhood,* by James Baldwin and Yoran Cazac. *New York Times*, August 20, 2018, C11. https://www.nytimes.com/2018/08/20/books/review/james-baldwin-little-man-picture-book.html.

Amin, Kadjj, Amber Jamilla Musser, and Roy Pérez, eds. "Queer Form." Special issue, *ASAP/Journal* 2, no. 2 (May 2017).

Auchincloss, Eve, and Nancy Lynch. "Disturber of the Peace—An Interview with James Baldwin." In *Conversations with James Baldwin*, edited by Fred L. Standley and Louis H. Pratt, 64–82. Jackson: University Press of Mississippi, 1989.

Austin, Cora "Lovie" (music), and Alberta Hunter (lyrics). "Down Hearted Blues." First recorded by Alberta Hunter, 1922, Paramount 12005-A. Recorded by Bessie Smith, 1923, Columbia A3844.

Avedon, Richard, and James Baldwin. *Nothing Personal.* Los Angeles: Taschen America, 2017.

Baker, Houston. *Blues, Ideology, and Afro-American Literature.* Chicago: University of Chicago Press, 1987.

Baldwin, James. *The Amen Corner.* New York: Dial, 1954.

Baldwin, James. "The American Dream and the American Negro." *New York Times*, March 7, 1965. Reprinted in *The Price of the Ticket: Collected Nonfiction 1948–1985*, 403–8. New York: St. Martin's, 1985. Also reprinted in *James Baldwin: Collected Essays*, edited by Toni Morrison, 714–19. New York: Library of America, 1998.

Baldwin, James. *Another Country.* New York: Vintage, 1962.

Baldwin, James. *Blues for Mister Charlie.* New York: Dial, 1964.

Baldwin, James. "Color." *Esquire* , December 1, 1962, 225. Reprinted in *The Price of the Ticket: Collected Nonfiction 1948–1985*, 325–29. New York: St. Martin's, 1985. Also reprinted in *James Baldwin: Collected Essays*, edited by Toni Morrison, 673–77. New York: Library of America, 1998.

Baldwin, James. *The Cross of Redemption: Uncollected Writings.* Edited by Randall Kenan. New York: Pantheon, 2010.

Baldwin, James. *The Devil Finds Work.* New York: Dial, 1976. Reprinted in *James Baldwin: Collected Essays*, edited by Toni Morrison, 477–575. New York: Library of America, 1998.

Baldwin, James. "The Discovery of What It Means to Be an American." In *Nobody Knows My Name: More Notes of a Native Son*, 17–23. New York: Dell, 1961. Reprinted in *James Baldwin: Collected Essays*, edited by Toni Morrison, 137–42. New York: Library of America, 1998.

Baldwin, James. *The Fire Next Time.* New York: Random House, 1963. Reprinted in *James Baldwin: Collected Essays*, edited by Toni Morrison, 287–347. New York: Library of America, 1998.

Baldwin, James. "Freaks and the American Ideal of Manhood." *Playboy*, January 1985, 150–51, 192, 256. Reprinted as "Here Be Dragons" in *The Price of the Ticket: Collected Nonfiction, 1948–1985*, 677–90. New York: St. Martin's, 1985. Also reprinted in *James Baldwin: Collected Essays*, edited by Toni Morrison, 814–29. New York: Library of America, 1998.

Baldwin, James. *Giovanni's Room*. New York: Dial, 1956.

Baldwin, James. *Going to Meet the Man*. New York: Dial, 1965.

Baldwin, James. *Go Tell It on the Mountain*. New York: Dial, 1953.

Baldwin, James. *If Beale Street Could Talk*. New York: Dial, 1974.

Baldwin, James. "In Search of a Majority: An Address." Adapted from an address delivered at Kalamazoo College, February 1960. In *Nobody Knows My Name: More Notes of a Native Son*, 127–40. New York: Dial, 1961. Reprinted in *James Baldwin: Collected Essays*, edited by Toni Morrison, 215–21. New York: Library of America, 1998.

Baldwin, James. "Introduction to Exhibition of Beauford Delaney Opening December 4, 1964 at the Gallery Lambert." In *Tableaux de Beauford Delaney*, unpaginated. Exhibition catalogue. Paris: Galerie Lambert, 1964. Reprinted in *Beauford Delaney: A Retrospective*, edited by Richard A. Long, n.p. New York: Studio Museum in Harlem, 1978.

Baldwin, James. *Just above My Head*. New York: Dial, 1979.

Baldwin, James. "Me and My House." *Harper's Magazine*, November 1955, 54.

Baldwin, James. "The Negro in Paris." *The Reporter*, June 6, 1950. Reprinted as "Encounter on the Seine: Black Meets Brown" in *Notes of a Native Son*, 117–23. Boston: Beacon, 1955. Also reprinted in *James Baldwin: Collected Essays*, edited by Toni Morrison, 85–90. New York: Library of America, 1998.

Baldwin, James. *Nobody Knows My Name: More Notes of a Native Son*. New York: Dial, 1961.

Baldwin, James. *No Name in the Street*. New York: Dial, 1972. Reprinted in *James Baldwin: Collected Essays*, edited by Toni Morrison, 349–476. New York: Library of America, 1998.

Baldwin, James. *Notes of a Native Son*. Boston: Beacon, 1955. Reprinted in *James Baldwin: Collected Essays*, edited by Toni Morrison, 1–127. New York: Library of America, 1998.

Baldwin, James. "On the Painter Beauford Delaney." *Transition* 4, no. 18 (1965): 45. Reprinted in "The Anniversary Issue: Selections from *Transition*, 1961–1976." Special issue, *Transition*, nos. 75/76 (1997): 88–89. Also reprinted in *James Baldwin: Collected Essays*, edited by Toni Morrison, 720–21. New York: Library of America, 1998.

Baldwin, James. "The Price May Be Too High." *New York Times*, February 2, 1969, D9, 148.

Baldwin, James. "The Price of the Ticket." In *The Price of the Ticket: Collected Nonfiction, 1948–1985*, ix–xx. New York: St. Martin's, 1985. Reprinted in *James Baldwin: Collected Essays*, edited by Toni Morrison, 830–42. New York: Library of America, 1998.

Baldwin, James. *The Price of the Ticket: Collected Nonfiction, 1948–1985*. New York: St. Martin's, 1985.

Baldwin, James. "Sonny's Blues." *Partisan Review*, Summer 1957, 327–58. Reprinted in *Going to Meet the Man*, 101–42. New York: Dial, 1965. Also reprinted in *James Baldwin: Early Novels and Stories*, edited by Toni Morrison, 831–64. New York: Library of America, 1998.

Baldwin, James. "Stranger in the Village." *Harper's Magazine*, September 1953, 42–48. Reprinted in *Notes of a Native Son*, 159–75. Boston: Beacon, 1955. Also reprinted in *James Baldwin: Collected Essays*, edited by Toni Morrison, 117–29. New York: Library of America, 1998.

Baldwin, James. *Tell Me How Long the Train's Been Gone*. New York: Dial, 1968.

Baldwin, James. "The Uses of the Blues." *Playboy*, January 1964, 131–32, 240–44. Reprinted in *The Cross of Redemption: Uncollected Writings*, edited by Randall Kenan, 70–81. New York: Pantheon, 2010.

Baldwin, James. "Words of a Native Son." *Playboy*, December 1964, 120, 166, 239. Reprinted in *James Baldwin: Collected Essays*, edited by Toni Morrison, 707–13. New York: Library of America, 1998.

Baldwin, James, et al. "James Baldwin." In *Perspectives: Angles on African Art*, edited by Michael J. Weber, 114–27. New York: Center for African Art, 1987.

Baldwin, James, and Yoran Cazac. *Little Man, Little Man: A Story of Childhood*. London: Michael Joseph; New York: Dial, 1976.

Baldwin, James, and Yoran Cazac. *Little Man, Little Man: A Story of Childhood*. Edited by Nicholas Boggs and Jennifer DeVere Brody. Durham, NC: Duke University Press, 2018.

Baptist, Edward E. *The Half Has Never Been Told: Slavery and the Making of American Capitalism*. New York: Basic Books, 2014.

Barr, Alfred H. *Matisse: His Art and His Public*. New York: Museum of Modern Art, 1951.

Barr, Donald. Review of *Go Tell It on the Mountain*, by James Baldwin. *New York Times*, May 17, 1953. https://archive.nytimes.com/www.nytimes.com/books/98/03/29/specials/baldwin-mountain.html.

Beauford Delaney: Liquid Light, Paris Abstractions, 1954–1970. New York: Michael Rosenfeld Gallery, 1999.

Bechet, Sidney. *Treat It Gentle*. New York: Hill and Wang, 1960.

Berlant, Lauren, and Michael Warner. "Sex in Public." *Critical Inquiry* 24, no. 2 (Winter 1998): 547–66.

Bersani, Leo. *Homos*. Cambridge, MA: Harvard University Press, 1996.

Bersani, Leo. "Is the Rectum a Grave?" *October* 43 (1987): 197–222.

Betsky, Aaron. *Queer Space: Architecture and Same-Sex Desire*. New York: William Morrow, 1997.

Blackman, Lisa. *Immaterial Bodies: Affect, Embodiment, Mediation*. London: Sage, 2012.

"*The Black Scholar* Interviews James Baldwin." In *Conversations with James Baldwin*, edited by Fred R. Standley and Louis H. Pratt, 142–58. Jackson: University Press of Mississippi, 1989.

Blint, Rich, and Douglas Field. Afterword to "James Baldwin." Special issue, *African American Review* 46, no. 4 (Winter 2013): 741–48.

Bloom, Harold. *The Anxiety of Influence: A Theory of Poetry*. New York: Oxford University Press, 1973.

Boggs, Nicholas. "Baldwin and Yoran Cazac's 'Child's Story for Adults.'" In *The Cambridge Companion to James Baldwin*, edited by Michele Elam, 118–33. New York: Cambridge University Press, 2015.

Boggs, Nicholas. "Of Mimicry and (Little Man Little) Man: Towards a Queer-Sighted Theory of Black Childhood." In *James Baldwin Now*, edited by Dwight McBride, 122–60. New York: New York University Press, 1999.

Boggs, Nicholas, and Jennifer DeVere Brody. Introduction to *Little Man, Little Man: A Story of Childhood*, by James Baldwin and Yoran Cazac, edited by Nicholas Boggs and Jennifer DeVere Brody, xv–xxii. Durham, NC: Duke University Press, 2018.

Bois, Yve-Alain. *Matisse and Picasso*. Paris: Flammarion, 1998.

Bois, Yve-Alain. *Painting as Model*. Cambridge, MA: MIT Press, 1990.

Bourland, W. Ian. *Bloodflowers: Rotimi Fani-Kayode, Photography, and the 1980s*. Durham, NC: Duke University Press, 2019.

Bowling, Frank. "Discussion on Black Art." *Arts Magazine*, April 1969, 16–20.

Bowling, Frank. "Discussion on Black Art, II." *Arts Magazine*, May 1969, 20–23.

Bowling, Frank. "Formalist Art and the Black Experience." *Third Text* 2, no. 5 (1988): 78–82.

Bowling, Frank. "Some Notes toward African American Abstraction." In *The Search for Freedom: African American Abstract Painting 1945–1975*, edited by Ann Gibson, 125–28. New York: Kenkeleba Gallery, 1991.

Boyd, Herb. *Baldwin's Harlem*. New York: Atria, 2008.

Bradley, Rizvana, and Denise Ferreira da Silva. "Four Theses on Aesthetics." *e-flux* 120 (September 2021). https://www.e-flux.com/journal/120/416146/four-theses-on-aesthetics/.

Brennan, Maija. "Beauford Delaney: A Study in Portraiture." Wells International Foundation, 2019. https://wellsinternationalfoundation.org/portraiture-exhibition/.

Brennan, Marcia. *Modernism's Masculine Subjects: Matisse, the New York School, and Post-Painterly Abstraction*. Cambridge, MA: MIT Press, 2004.

Briet, Philippe. *Beauford Delaney: A Retrospective, February–March 1991*. Exhibition catalogue. New York: P. Briet, 1991.

Briet, Sylvain. "Chronology of Exhibitions." In *Beauford Delaney: From New York to Paris*, edited by Patricia Sue Canterbury, 125–31. Minneapolis: Minneapolis Institute of Art, 2004.

Brim, Matt. *James Baldwin and the Queer Imagination*. Ann Arbor: University of Michigan Press, 2014.

Bronstein, Michaela. *Out of Context: The Uses of Modernist Fiction*. Oxford: Oxford University Press, 2018.

Brooks, Daphne. *Bodies in Dissent: Spectacular Performances of Race and Freedom, 1850–1910*. Durham, NC: Duke University Press, 2006.

Bruce, Marcus. "Continuing a Legacy: James Baldwin, Ta-Nehisi Coates, and the African American Witness." In *Of Latitudes Unknown: James Baldwin's Radical Imagination*, edited by Alice Mikal Craven, William Dow, and Yoko Nakamura, 197–210. New York: Bloomsbury Academic, 2019.

Buffalo, Audreen, ed. *Explorations in the City of Light: African-American Artists in Paris, 1945–1965*. New York: Studio Museum in Harlem, 1996.

Butorac, Sean Kim. "Hannah Arendt, James Baldwin, and the Politics of Love." *Political Research Quarterly* 71, no. 3 (2018): 710–21.

Butwin, David. "Booked for Travel: The Cognoscenti Abroad—II, James Jones' Paris." *Saturday Review*, February 1, 1969, 38.

Campbell, Adrianna. "Glenn Ligon: Glenn Ligon Speaks about His Curatorial Project 'Encounters and Collisions,'" *Artforum*, June 5, 2015. https://www.artforum.com/interviews/glenn-ligon-speaks-about-his-curatorial-project-encounters-and-collisions-52580.

Campbell, James. *Talking at the Gates: A Life of James Baldwin*. Berkeley: University of California Press, 1991.

Campbell, Mary. "'I Will Not Be Moved': Beauford Delaney's (Self) Portraits of Rosa Parks." In *Beauford Delaney and James Baldwin: Through the Unusual Door*, edited by Stephen C. Wicks, 70–89. Knoxville: Knoxville Museum of Art, 2020.

Campbell, Mary Schmidt. Foreword to *Beauford Delaney: A Retrospective*, edited by Richard A. Long, n.p. New York: Studio Museum in Harlem, 1978.

Campt, Tina M. "How Black Artists Are Shaping a Distinctly Black Gaze." *Hyperallergic*, August 22, 2021. https://hyperallergic.com/671547/how-black-artists-are-shaping-a-distinctly-black-gaze-tina-m-campt/.

Canterbury, Patricia Sue. "Transatlantic Transformations: Beauford Delaney in Paris." In *Beauford Delaney: From New York to Paris*, edited by Patricia Sue Canterbury, 48–75. Minneapolis: Minneapolis Institute of Art, 2004.

Capozzola, Christopher. "Beauford Delaney and the Art of Exile." *Gay and Lesbian Review Worldwide* 10, no. 5 (2003): 10–12.

Charles, Ray (music and lyrics). "Hey Now." 1952. Swing Time 297A+.

Clark, Keith. "Baldwin, *Communitas*, and the Black Masculinist Tradition." In *New Essays on "Go Tell It on the Mountain,"* edited by Trudier Harris, 127–56. Cambridge: Cambridge University Press, 1996. https://doi.org/10.1017/CBO9781139166782.007.

Cleary, Emma. "'Here Be Dragons': The Tyranny of the Cityscape in James Baldwin's Intimate Cartographies." *James Baldwin Review* 1, no. 1 (2015): 91–111.

Clytus, Radiclani. "Paying Dues and Playing the Blues." In *The Cambridge Companion to James Baldwin*, edited by Michele Elam, 70–84. Cambridge: Cambridge University Press, 2015.

Cohen, Rachel. "Beauford Delaney Eyes." *Rachel Cohen* (blog), June 5, 2020. https://rachelecohen.com/blog/The_Frederick_Project/c/1075.

Cohen, Rachel. *A Chance Meeting: Intertwined Lives of American Writers and Artists, 1854–1967*. New York: Random House, 2004.

Cohen, Rachel. "Delaney, Self-Portrait with a Red Hat." *Rachel Cohen* (blog), June 4, 2020. https://rachelecohen.com/blog/The_Frederick_Project/c/1055.

Cohen, Rachel, and Stephen C. Wicks. "Stephen Wicks and Rachel Cohen Discuss Baldwin Portrait: Conversation, Part 2." *Les Amis de Beauford Delaney* (blog), December 11, 2021. http://lesamisdebeauforddelaney.blogspot.com/2021/12/stephen-wicks-and-rachel-cohen-discuss_01943507523.html.

Copeland, Huey. "One-Dimensional Abstraction." *Art Journal* 78 (2019): 111–16.

Corman, Cid. *Tributary: Poems*. Edited by Philippe Briet. New York: Edgewise Press, 1999.

Cowling, Elizabeth, Anne Baldassari, John Elderfield, et al. *Matisse, Picasso*. Exhibition catalogue. London: Tate Publishing, 2002.

Crimp, Douglas. *Before Pictures*. Brooklyn, NY: Dancing Foxes, 2016.

Crimp, Douglas, and Alvin Baltrop. "*Disss*-co (A Fragment): From *Before Pictures*, a Memoir of 1970s New York." *Criticism* 50, no. 1 (2008): 1–17. https://doi.org/10.1353/crt.0.0057.

Crouch, Stanley. *Kansas City Lightning: The Rise and Times of Charlie Parker*. New York: HarperCollins, 2013.

Cullen, Countee. "Heritage." In *Color*, 36–41. New York: Harper, 1925.

Davis, Nicholas K. "Go Tell It on the Stage: *Blues for Mister Charlie* as Dialectical Drama." *Journal of American Drama and Theatre* 17 (Spring 2005): 30–42.

DeCoste, Kyle. "Music All Up and Down the Street: Listening to Childhood in James Baldwin's *Little Man, Little Man*." *Journal of Popular Music Studies* 31, no. 3 (2019): 57–72.

Delany, Samuel R. *The Motion of Light in Water: Sex and Science Fiction Writing in the East Village*. Minneapolis: University of Minnesota Press, 2004.

Dempsey, Joan. "Waiting for You: Beauford Delaney as James Baldwin's Inspiration for the Character Creole in 'Sonny's Blues.'" *Obsidian* 12, no. 1 (Spring/Summer 2011): 60–78.

Diawara, Manthia, dir. *Édouard Glissant: One World in Relation*. K'a Yéléma Productions, 2009. Film, 50 min.

Dickstein, Morris. *Gates of Eden: American Culture in the Sixties*. New York: Basic Books, 1977.

Diggs, Soyica. "Historicizing the Sound of a Ghastly Sight: James Baldwin's *Blues for Mister Charlie*." In *Sonic Interventions*, edited by Marijke de Valck, Sylvia Mieszkowski, and Joy Smith, 193–210. Amsterdam: Rodopi, 2007.

Dixon, Terence, dir. *Meeting the Man: James Baldwin in Paris*. Contemporary Films, 1970. Film, 26 min.

Dove, Rita. *Grace Notes: Poems*. New York: W. W. Norton, 1989.

Doyle, Jennifer, and David Getsy. "Queer Formalisms." *Art Journal* 72, no. 4 (Winter 2014): 58–71.

Dozier, Ayanna. *Rebellious Inventions: Abstraction in the Black Diaspora*. New York: FALSE FLAG, 2020.

Drake, Jamill W. "James Baldwin: Witnessing in Dark Times." *Marginalia*, September 24, 2021. https://themarginaliareview.com/james-baldwin-witnessing-in-dark-times/.

Du Bois, W. E. B. *The Souls of Black Folk*. Greenwich, CT: Fawcett, 1961.

Edwards, Adrienne. "Blackness in Abstraction." *Art in America*, January 2015, 62–69.

Edwards, Brent Hayes. *Epistrophies: Jazz and the Literary Imagination*. Cambridge, MA: Harvard University Press, 2017.

Elam, Michele. "Baldwin's Boys." *CR: The New Centennial Review* 16, no. 2 (2016): 17–30.

Elam, Michele, ed. *The Cambridge Companion to James Baldwin*. New York: Cambridge University Press, 2015.

Elgrably, Jordan. "James Baldwin: The Art of Fiction No. 78." Interview. *Paris Review* 91 (Spring 1984): 48–82. https://www.theparisreview.org/interviews/2994/the-art-of-fiction-no-78-james-baldwin.

Elias, Amy J. "Inappropriate Edges: Beauford Delaney's *Untitled-1969*." *ASAP/J*, May 22, 2023. https://asapjournal.com/hard-soft-lost-the-edges-of-contemporary-culture-inappropriate-edges-beauford-delaneys untitled-1969-amy-j-elias/.

Elias, Amy J. "Yellows and Blues: Delaney, Baldwin, and Synesthetic Expressionism." Paper presented at the annual meeting of the College Art Association, New York, February 15, 2019.

Ellison, Ralph. *The Collected Essays of Ralph Ellison*. Edited by John F. Callahan. New York: Modern Library, 2003.

Ellison, Ralph. *Invisible Man*. 2nd ed. New York: Vintage International, 1995.

Ellison, Ralph. "Richard Wright's Blues." *Antioch Review* 50, nos. 1–2 (Winter–Spring 1992): 61–74.

English, Darby. *1971: A Year in the Life of Color*. Chicago: University of Chicago Press, 2016.

Eshun, Kodwo. *More Brilliant than the Sun: Adventures in Sonic Fiction*. London: Quartet, 1998.

Fanon, Frantz. *Black Skin, White Masks*. Translated by Charles Lam Markmann. New York: Grove, 1968.

Fer, Briony. *On Abstract Art*. New Haven, CT: Yale University Press, 1997.

Ferreira da Silva, Denise. "In the Raw." *e-flux* 93 (2018). https://www.e-flux.com/journal/93/215795/in-the-raw/.

Field, Douglas. *All Those Strangers: The Art and Lives of James Baldwin*. New York: Oxford University Press, 2015.

Field, Douglas. "Pentecostalism and All That Jazz: Tracing James Baldwin's Religion." *Literature and Theology* 22, no. 4 (December 2008): 436–57.

Field, Edward. "With Beauford Delaney." Letter to the Editor. *Gay and Lesbian Review Worldwide* 11, no. 3 (May–June 2004): 4.

Fielder, Brigitte. "Literary Genealogies and the Kinship of Black Modernity." *American Literary History* 32, no. 4 (Winter 2020): 789–96.

Fitzgerald, Ella. *Ella Fitzgerald Sings the Duke Ellington Songbook*. Vols. 1 and 2. 1957. Verve MGV 4008-2 and Verve MGV 4009-2.

Folland, Tom. "Robert Rauschenberg's Queer Modernism: The Early Combines and Decoration." *Art Bulletin* 92, no. 4 (December 2010): 348–65.

Ford, Tanisha C. *Liberation Threads: Black Women, Style, and the Global Politics of Soul*. Chapel Hill: University of North Carolina Press, 2015.

Fraser, C. Gerald. "Beauford Delaney, Painter, Dies; Portraitist of the Famous Was 77." *New York Times*, April 1, 1979, 34. https://www.nytimes.com/1979/04/01/archives/beauford-delaney-painter-dies-portraitist-of-the-famous-was-77.html.

Freeburg, Christopher. "James Baldwin and the Unhistoric Life of Race." *South Atlantic Quarterly* 112, no. 2 (January 2013): 221–39.

Freeman, Elizabeth. *Time Binds: Queer Temporalities, Queer Histories*. Durham, NC: Duke University Press, 2010.

Friedman, Ryan Jay. "'Enough Force to Shatter the Tale to Fragments': Ethics and Textual Analysis in James Baldwin's Film Theory." *ELH* 77, no. 2 (2010): 385–411.

Gaston, Vivien. *The Naked Face: Self-Portraits*. Melbourne: National Gallery of Victoria, 2010.

Gates, Henry Louis, Jr. "Going to Meet the Man." In *Beauford Delaney: From New York to Paris*, edited by Patricia Sue Canterbury, 10–20. Minneapolis: Minneapolis Institute of Art, 2004.

Gay, Roxanne. "A Conversation with Kiese Laymon." *The Nation*, September 12, 2013. https://www.thenation.com/article/archive/conversation-kiese-laymon/.

Gehlawat, Monika. "Baldwin and the Role of the Citizen Artist." *James Baldwin Review* 8, no. 1 (September 27, 2022). https://doi.org/10.7227/JBR.8.6.

Gehlawat, Monika. "Strangers in the Village: James Baldwin, Teju Cole, and Glenn Ligon." *James Baldwin Review* 5 (2019): 48–72.

Getsy, David. *Abstract Bodies: Sixties Sculpture in the Expanded Field of Gender*. New Haven, CT: Yale University Press, 2015.

Getsy, David J., and William J. Simmons. "Appearing Differently: Abstraction's Transgender and Queer Capacities." In *Pink Labour on Golden Streets: Queer Art Practices*, edited by Christiane Erharter, Dietmar Schwärzler, Ruby Sircar, and Hans Scheirl, 38–55. Berlin: Sternberg, 2015.

Ghansah, Rachel Kaadzi. "The Weight." In *The Fire This Time: A New Generation Speaks about Race*, edited by Jesmyn Ward, 19–32. New York: Scribner, 2016.

Gibson, Ann E. *Abstract Expressionism: Other Politics*. New Haven, CT: Yale University Press, 1997.

Gibson, Ann E. "Gay and Black in Greenwich Village: Beauford Delaney's Idylls of Integration." In *Beauford Delaney: From New York to Paris*, edited by Patricia Sue Canterbury, 12–30. Minneapolis: Minneapolis Institute of Art, 2004.

Gibson, Ann E. *The Search for Freedom: African American Abstract Painting, 1945–1975*. New York: Kenkeleba Gallery, 1991.

Glaude, Eddie S., Jr. *Begin Again: James Baldwin's America and Its Urgent Lessons for Our Own*. New York: Crown, 2020.

Godfrey, Mark, and Zoe Whitley, eds. *Soul of a Nation: Art in the Age of Black Power*. London: Tate Publishing, 2017.

Golden, Thelma, ed. *Black Male: Representations of Masculinity in Contemporary American Art*. New York: Whitney Museum of American Art, 1994.

Goldsby, Jacqueline. "The Art of Being Difficult: The Turn to Abstraction in African American Poetry and Painting during the 1940s and 1950s." Presented at the Humanities Lecture Series, Brigham Young University, Provo, Utah, March 7, 2014. https://www.youtube.com/watch?v=pqKe8k4skzs.

Goodyear, Anne Collins, Jonathan Frederick Walz, and Kathleen Merrill Campagnolo. *This Is a Portrait If I Say So: Identity in American Art, 1912–Today*. New Haven, CT: Yale University Press in association with Bowdoin College Museum of Art, 2016.

Graves, Wallace. "The Question of Moral Energy in James Baldwin's *Go Tell It on the Mountain*." CLA *Journal* 7, no. 3 (1964): 215–23.

Gray, Edward, dir. *Different Drummer: Elvin Jones*. 1979. Film, 30 min.

Greenblatt, Stephen, and Peter Platt, eds. *Shakespeare's Montaigne: The Florio Translation of the Essays: A Selection*. Translated by John Florio. New York: NYRB Classics, 2014.

Greene, Nikki A. "Thomas McKeller *sous rature*: John Singer Sargent's Erasure of a Black Model." In *Boston's Apollo: Thomas McKeller and John Singer Sargent*, edited by Nathaniel Silver, 63–82. Boston: Isabella Stewart Gardner Museum, 2020.

Grenier, Jean. "Beauford Delaney." *Preuves*, June 1962, 75–76.

Gresham, Jewel Handy. "James Baldwin Comes Home." *Essence*, June 1976, 54–55, 80, 82, 85–86. Reprinted in *Conversations with James Baldwin*, edited by Fred L. Standley and Louis H. Pratt, 159–67. Jackson: University Press of Mississippi, 1989.

Griffin, Farah Jasmine. *Read until You Understand: The Profound Wisdom of Black Life and Literature*. New York: W. W. Norton, 2021.

Halberstam, Jack. *In a Queer Time and Place: Transgender Bodies, Subcultural Lives*. New York: New York University Press, 2005.

Halberstam, Jack. *The Queer Art of Failure*. Durham, NC: Duke University Press, 2011.

Handy, W. C., ed. *Unsung Americans Sung*. New York: American Society of Composers Authors and Publishers, 1944.

Harper, Philip Brian. *Abstractionist Aesthetics: Artistic Form and Social Critique in African American Culture*. New York: New York University Press, 2015.

Harris, Middleton, Morris Levitt, Roger Furman, and Ernest Smith. *The Black Book*. New York: Random House, 1974.

harrisburg, halley k, and Matthew Newton, eds. *Be Your Wonderful Self: The Portraits of Beauford Delaney*. West Haven, CT: Michael Rosenfeld Gallery and GHP Media, 2022.

Hartman, Saidiya. *Lose Your Mother: A Journey along the Atlantic Slave Route*. New York: Farrar, Straus and Giroux, 2008.

Hartman, Saidiya. *Scenes of Subjection: Terror, Slavery, and Self-Making in Nineteenth-Century America*. Oxford: Oxford University Press, 1997.

Heartney, Eleanor. "Whatever Happened to Beauford Delaney?" *Art in America*, November 1994, 116–19.

Helmholtz, Herman. *On the Sensations of Tone as a Physiological Basis for the Theory of Music*. Translated by Alexander J. Ellis. London: Longman, 1885.

Henry Miller 80. Exhibition catalogue. Paris: Centre Culturel Américain, 1971.

Hentoff, Ned, and Nat Shapiro, eds. *Hear Me Talkin' to Ya*. New York: Rinehart, 1955.

Herbert, John. *Fortune and Men's Eyes*. New York: Grove, 1967.

Hobson, Christopher Z. *James Baldwin and the Heavenly City: Prophecy, Apocalypse, and Doubt*. East Lansing: Michigan State University Press, 2018.

Holloway, Karla F. C. *BookMarks: Reading in Black and White, a Memoir*. New Brunswick, NJ: Rutgers University Press, 2006.

hooks, bell. *Black Looks: Race and Representation*. Boston: South End, 1992.

Huff, Daonne. "On Abstraction: Things You Can't Tell Just by Looking at Us." *Studio Museum in Harlem Magazine*, September 29, 2020. https://studiomuseum.org/article/abstraction-things-you-cant-tell-just-looking-us.

Hughes, Langston. "The Negro Artist and the Racial Mountain." *The Nation*, June 3, 1926, 692–94.

Hurston, Zora Neale. "How It Feels to Be Colored Me." In *I Love Myself When I Am Laughing . . . And Then Again When I Am Looking Mean and Impressive: A Zora Neale Hurston Reader*, rev. electronic ed., edited by Alice Walker, 152–55. New York: Feminist Press, 2020.

Huyghe, René. "Color and the Expression of Interior Time in Western Art." In *Color Symbolism: Six Excerpts from the Eranos Yearbook 1972*, 129–65. Dallas: Spring Publications, 1972.

Huyssen, Andreas. *After the Great Divide: Modernism, Mass Culture, Postmodernism*. Bloomington: Indiana University Press, 1986.

Joans, Ted. "Beauford Delaney." *Black World/Negro Digest* 23, no. 3 (January 1974): 93.

Joans, Ted. *In Thursday Sane*. Edited by Sandra McPherson. Davis, CA: Swan Scythe Press, 2001.

Johnson, Eloise. "Out of the Ashes: Cultural Identity and Marginalization in the Art of Beauford Delaney." Special issue on African American art, *Notes in the History of Art* 24, no. 4 (Summer 2005): 46–55.

Johnson, E. Patrick. Introduction to *No Tea, No Shade: New Writings in Black Queer Studies*, edited by E. Patrick Johnson, 1–26. Durham, NC: Duke University Press, 2016.

Jones, Amelia. "Art History/Art Criticism: Performing Meaning." In *Performing the Body/Performing the Text*, edited by Amelia Jones and Andrew Stephenson, 39–55. London: Routledge, 1999.

Jones, Amelia. *Body Art/Performing the Subject*. Minneapolis: University of Minnesota Press, 1998.

Jones, Caroline A. *Eyesight Alone: Clement Greenberg's Modernism and the Bureaucratization of the Senses*. Chicago: University of Chicago Press, 2005.

Jones, James. *From Here to Eternity*. New York: Scribner's, 1951.

Jones, James. *Go to the Widow-Maker*. New York: Delacorte, 1967.

Jones, LeRoi. *Black Music*. New York: William Morrow, 1967.

Jones, LeRoi. *The LeRoi Jones/Amiri Baraka Reader*. 2nd ed. Edited by William J. Harris. New York: Basic Books, 1999.

Jones, LeRoi. "Return of the Native." In *Black Magic: Poetry 1961–1967*, 147–48. Indianapolis: Bobbs-Merrill, 1969.

Joyce, Justin A., Dwight A. McBride, and Douglas Field. "Baltimore Is Still Burning: The Rising Relevance of James Baldwin." *James Baldwin Review* 1, no. 1 (2015): 1–9.

Judy, R. A. *Sentient Flesh: Thinking in Disorder, Poiesis in Black*. Durham, NC: Duke University Press, 2020.

Kaplan, Cora, and Bill Schwarz, eds. *James Baldwin: America and Beyond*. Ann Arbor: University of Michigan Press, 2011.

Kenan, Randall, ed. *The Cross of Redemption*. New York: Pantheon, 2010.

King, Tiffany Lethabo. *The Black Shoals: Offshore Formations of Black and Native Studies*. Durham, NC: Duke University Press, 2019.

Kirkus Reviews. Review of *Little Man, Little Man: A Story of Childhood*, by James Baldwin and Yoran Cazac. June 15, 2016. https://www.kirkusreviews.com/book-reviews/james-baldwin/little-man-little-man-baldwin/.

Klein, John. "The Mask as Image and Strategy." In *The Mirror and the Mask: Portraiture in the Age of Picasso*, edited by Paloma Alarcó et al., 25–36. New Haven, CT: Yale University Press, 2007.

Klein, John. *Matisse Portraits*. New Haven, CT: Yale University Press, 2001.

Krauss, Rosalind. "The Motivation of the Sign." In *Picasso and Braque: A Symposium*, edited by Lynn Zelevansky, 261–86. New York: Museum of Modern Art, 1992.

Lahelma, Marja. "The Open-Ended Artwork and the Symbolist Self." In *The Symbolist Roots of Modern Art*, edited by Michelle Facos, 59–70. London: Routledge, 2017.

Laymon, Kiese. *Heavy: An American Memoir*. New York: Scribner, 2018.

Leeming, David. *Amazing Grace: A Life of Beauford Delaney*. New York: Oxford University Press, 1998.

Leeming, David. "Beauford, Abstraction, and Light." In *Beauford Delaney: Liquid Light: Paris Abstractions, 1954–1970*, n.p. New York: Michael Rosenfeld Gallery, 1999.

Leeming, David. *James Baldwin: A Biography*. New York: Arcade, 1994.

Leja, Michael. "Jackson Pollock: Representing the Unconscious." *Art History* 13, no. 4 (December 1990): 542–65.

Lester, Julius, "James Baldwin: Reflections of a Maverick." *New York Times Book Review*, May 27, 1984. https://www.nytimes.com/1984/05/27/books/james-baldwinreflections-of-a-maverick.html?searchResultPosition=6.

Lester, Julius. Review of *Little Man, Little Man: A Story of Childhood,* by James Baldwin and Yoran Cazac. *New York Times Book Review*, September 4, 1977, 22. https://archive.nytimes.com/www.nytimes.com/books/98/03/29/specials/baldwin-little.html.

Lewis, Sarah. "African American Abstraction." In *The Routledge Companion to African American Art*, edited by Eddie Chambers, 159–72. London: Routledge, 2019.

Ligon, Glenn. "Artist's Artists: Ligon on Delaney." *Frieze Magazine*, October 10, 2015. https://www.frieze.com/article/artists-artists-2.

Ligon, Glenn. "Glenn Ligon to Beauford Delaney: Two Letters." In *Beauford Delaney and James Baldwin: Through the Unusual Door*, edited by Stephen C. Wicks, xxiii–xiv. Knoxville: University of Tennessee Press, 2020.

Ligon, Glenn, Alex Farquharson, and Francesco Manacorda, eds. *Glenn Ligon: Encounters and Collisions*. London: Nottingham Contemporary and Tate, 2015.

Lomas, David. *The Haunted Self*. New Haven, CT: Yale University Press, 2000.

Long, Richard A., ed. *Beauford Delaney: A Retrospective*. New York: Studio Museum in Harlem, 1978.

Lord, James. *A Giacometti Portrait*. New York: Farrar, Straus and Giroux, 1965.

Lordi, Emily J. *Black Resonance: Iconic Women Singers and African American Literature*. New Brunswick, NJ: Rutgers University Press, 2013.

Lubbock, Percy, ed. *The Letters of Henry James*. Vol. 1. New York: Scribner, 1920.

Mackey, Nathaniel. *Bedouin Hornbook*. Callaloo Fiction Series 2. Lexington: University of Kentucky Press, 1986.

Mackey, Nathaniel. *From a Broken Bottle Traces of Perfume Still Emanate, Vols. 1–3*. New York: New Directions, 2010.

Mackey, Nathaniel. *Paracritical Hinge: Essays, Talks, Notes, Interviews*. Madison: University of Wisconsin Press, 2005.

Malcolm X. *The Autobiography of Malcolm X*. New York: Grove, 1965.

March, Jenny. *Dictionary of Classical Mythology*. Philadelphia: Oxbow, 1998.

Marchand, Jean-José. “Enquête sur la culture noire.” *Preuves*, May 1958, 33–44.

Marcoux, Jean-Philippe. “Invocations and Evocations: The Griotic Legacy of Margaret Walker and Gwendolyn Brooks on Carolyn Rodgers and Sonia Sanchez.” *Journal of American Ethnic Literature* 7 (2017): 63–155.

McBride, Dwight A., ed. *James Baldwin Now*. New York: New York University Press, 1999.

McBride, Dwight A. “Straight Black Studies: On African American Studies, James Baldwin, and Black Queer Studies.” In *Black Queer Studies: A Critical Anthology*, edited by E. Patrick Johnson and Mae G. Henderson, 68–89. Durham, NC: Duke University Press, 2005.

McKittrick, Katherine. *Dear Science and Other Stories*. Durham, NC: Duke University Press, 2021.

Mecklenburg, Virginia M., with Maricia Battle and Mary J. Cleary. “Commentaries on the Artworks: Beauford Delaney.” In *African American Art: Harlem Renaissance, Civil Rights Era, and Beyond*, edited by Richard J. Powell and Virginia M. Mecklenburg, 77–79. Washington, DC: Smithsonian American Art Museum, 2012.

Mercer, Kobena, ed. *Discrepant Abstraction*. London: Institute of International Visual Arts, 2006.

Miller, D. Quentin Miller. *A Criminal Power: James Baldwin and the Law*. Columbus: Ohio State University Press, 2012.

Miller, D. Quentin, ed. *Re-Viewing James Baldwin: Things Not Seen*. Philadelphia: Temple University Press, 2000.

Miller, Henry. *The Amazing and Invariable Beauford DeLaney*. New York: Alicat Book Shop, 1945. Reprinted in *Remember to Remember*, 15–34. New York: New Directions, 1947.

Mitchell, Koritha. “James Baldwin, Performance Theorist, Sings the *Blues for Mister Charlie*.” *American Quarterly* 64, no. 1 (2012): 33–60.

Moore, Jonathan Peter. “Other Than a Citizen: Vernacular Poetics in Postwar America.” PhD diss., Duke University, 2016. https://hdl.handle.net/10161/12192.

Morgan, Benjamin. “Scale, Resonance, Presence.” *Victorian Studies* 59, no. 1 (2017): 109–12.

Morrison, Toni. “Abrupt Stops and Unexpected Liquidity: The Aesthetics of Romare Bearden.” In *The Romare Bearden Reader*, edited by Robert G. O’Meally, 178–84. Durham, NC: Duke University Press, 2019.

Morrison, Toni. *Beloved*. New York: Knopf, 1987.

Morrison, Toni. *The Source of Self-Regard: Selected Speeches, Essays and Meditations*. New York: Vintage, 2020.

Moten, Fred. *Black and Blur*. Durham, NC: Duke University Press, 2017.

Moten, Fred. "The Case of Blackness." *Criticism* 50 (2008): 177–218.

Moten, Fred. *In the Break: The Aesthetics of the Black Radical Tradition*. Minneapolis: University of Minnesota Press, 2003.

Moten, Fred. *Stolen Life*. Durham, NC: Duke University Press, 2018.

Moten, Fred. *The Universal Machine*. Durham, NC: Duke University Press, 2018.

Muhammad, Ismail. "The Misunderstood Ghost of James Baldwin." *Slate*, February 15, 2017. https://slate.com/culture/2017/02/how-critics-have-misunderstood-james-baldwins-influence-on-todays-great-black-nonfiction-writers.html.

Muñoz, José Esteban. *Cruising Utopia: The Then and There of Queer Futurity*. New York: New York University Press, 2009.

Murphy, Michael David. "'Baldwin's Nigger': Transcription of James Baldwin in London, 1968." *Medium*, December 7, 2019. https://whileseated.medium.com/baldwins-nigger-transcription-of-james-baldwin-in-london-1968-358f27723506.

Murray, Albert. *The Blue Devils of Nada: A Contemporary American Approach to Aesthetic Statement*. New York: Pantheon, 1996.

Murray, Albert. *Murray Talks Music*. Minneapolis: University of Minnesota Press, 2016.

Musser, Amber Jamilla. "Architectures of Blue: Race, Representation, and Black and Brown Abstraction." *Brooklyn Rail*, October 5, 2017. https://brooklynrail.org/2017/10/art/Architectures-of-Blue-Race-Representation-and-Black-and-Brown-Abstraction.

Muyumba, Walton. "All Safety Is an Illusion: John Dewey, James Baldwin, and the Democratic Practice of Public Critique." In *Trained Capacities: John Dewey, Rhetoric, and Democratic Practice*, edited by Brian Jackson and Gregory Clark, 159–73. Columbia: University of South Carolina Press, 2014.

Muyumba, Walton. *The Shadow and the Act: Black Intellectual Practice, Jazz Improvisation, and Philosophical Pragmatism*. Chicago: University of Chicago Press, 2009.

Napolin, Julie Beth. "On *Blues Speaker [for James Baldwin]*: A Conversation with Mendi and Keith Obadike." *Social Text Online*, August 21, 2018. https://socialtextjournal.org/on-blues-speaker-for-james-baldwin-a-conversation-with-mendi-and-keith-obadike/.

Nechvatal, Joseph. "Beauford Delaney: Resonance of Form and Vibration of Color." *Brooklyn Rail*, May 1, 2016. https://brooklynrail.org/2016/05/artseen/beauford-delaney-resonance-of-form-and-vibrationnbspofnbspcolor.

O'Meally, Robert G., ed. *The Jazz Cadences of American Culture*. New York: Columbia University Press, 1998.

O'Meally, Robert G., Brent Hayes Edwards, and Farah Jasmine Griffin, eds. *Uptown Conversation: The New Jazz Studies*. New York: Columbia University Press, 2004.

Ové, Horace, dir. *Baldwin's Nigger*. Infilms, 1968. Film, 16mm, 48 min.

Ovid. *Metamorphoses*. Translated by Frank Justus Miller. Cambridge, MA: Harvard University Press, 1916.

Pakay, Sedat, dir. *James Baldwin: From Another Place*. Istanbul: Pakay Productions, 1973. Film, 11 min.

Pavlić, Ed. *Who Can Afford to Improvise? James Baldwin and Black Music, the Lyric and the Listeners*. New York: Fordham University Press, 2016.

Peck, Raoul, dir. *I Am Not Your Negro*. Written by James Baldwin. New York: Magnolia Pictures and Amazon Studios, 2017. Film, 93 min.

Pinckney, Darryl. "Catching Up to James Baldwin." *New York Review of Books*, May 25, 2017. https://www.nybooks.com/articles/2017/05/25/catching-up-to-james-baldwin/.

Piper, Adrian. "Flying." In *Adrian Piper: Reflections, 1967–1987*, edited by Jane Carver, 24–33. New York: Alternative Museum, 1987.

Plante, Michael D. "The Silence of Delaney's French Abstraction." In *Beauford Delaney: From New York to Paris*, edited by Patricia Sue Canterbury, 76–90. Minneapolis: Minneapolis Institute of Art, 2004.

Platt, Susan Noyles. "Modernism, Formalism, and Politics: The 'Cubism and Abstract Art' Exhibition at the Museum of Modern Art." *Art Journal* 47 (1988): 284–95.

Powell, Richard J. *Beauford Delaney: The Color Yellow*. Atlanta: High Museum of Art, 2002.

Prombaum, Levi. "Beauford Delaney's Repetition Creates." In *Beauford Delaney and James Baldwin: Through the Unusual Door*, edited by Stephen C. Wicks, 90–103. Knoxville: Knoxville Museum of Art, 2020.

Raiford, Leah. "'Burning All Illusion': Abstraction, Black Life, and Unmaking White Supremacy." *Art Journal* 79, no. 4 (Winter 2020): 76–91.

Rescher, Nicholas. *Metaphysical Perspectives*. Notre Dame, IN: University of Notre Dame Press, 2017.

Richards, Mary Caroline. *Centering in Pottery, Poetry, and the Person*. Middletown, CT: Wesleyan University Press, 1964.

Roach, Joseph. *Cities of the Dead: Circum-Atlantic Performance*. New York: Columbia University Press, 1996.

Robbins, Christa Noel. "The Sensibility of Michael Fried." *Criticism* 60, no. 4 (Fall 2018): 429–54.

Roberson, Ed. *Voices Cast Out to Talk Us In: Poems by Ed Roberson*. Iowa City: University of Iowa Press, 1995.

Robinson, Cedric J. *Black Marxism: The Making of a Black Radical Tradition*. Chapel Hill: University of North Carolina Press, 2000.

Robinson, Joyce Henri. *An Artistic Friendship: Beauford Delaney and Lawrence Calcagno*. University Park: Palmer Museum of Art, Pennsylvania State University, 2001.

Rodney, Seth. "How to Embed a Shout: A New Generation of Black Artists Contends with Abstraction." *Hyperallergic*, August 23, 2017. https://hyperallergic

.com/389105/how-to-embed-a-shout-a-new-generation-of-black-artists-contends-with-abstraction/.

Savery, Pancho. "Baldwin, Bebop, and 'Sonny's Blues.'" In *Understanding Others: Cultural and Cross-Cultural Studies and the Teaching of Literature*, edited by Joseph Trimmer and Tilly Warnock, 165–76. Urbana, IL: National Council of Teachers of English, 1992.

Schmidt, Tyler. "Lessons in Light: Beauford Delaney's and James Baldwin's 'Unnameable Objects.'" In *Of Latitudes Unknown: James Baldwin's Radical Imagination*, edited by Alice Mikal Craven, 49–68. New York: Bloomsbury Academic, 2019.

Schuessler, Jennifer. "James Baldwin's Archive, Long Hidden, Comes (Mostly) into View." *New York Times*, April 12, 2017. https://www.nytimes.com/2017/04/12/arts/james-baldwins-archive-long-hidden-comes-mostly-into-view.html.

Sharpe, Christina. *In the Wake: On Blackness and Being*. Durham, NC: Duke University Press, 2016.

Sherard, Tracey. "Sonny's Bebop: Baldwin's 'Blues Text' as Intracultural Critique." *African American Review* 32, no. 4 (1998): 691–705.

Sims, Lowery Stokes. "Stroke: Style, Technique, Culture, and Politics." In *Stroke! Beauford Delaney, Norman Lewis, and Alma Thomas*, 5–11. New York: Michael Rosenfeld Gallery, 2005.

Smalls, James. "Picturing Jimmy, Picturing Self: James Baldwin, Beauford Delaney, and the Color of Light." In *Of Latitudes Unknown: James Baldwin's Radical Imagination*, edited by Alice Mikal Craven, 35–48. New York: Bloomsbury Academic, 2019.

Smith, Bessie (lyrics and vocal). "In the House Blues." 1931. Parlophone R2329.

Spillers, Hortense. Introduction to "James Baldwin." Special issue, *African American Review* 46, no. 4 (Winter 2013): 563–72.

Spitzer, Anais N. *Derrida, Myth and the Impossibility of Philosophy*. London: Bloomsbury, 2011.

Standley, Fred R., and Louis H. Pratt, eds. *Conversations with James Baldwin*. Jackson: University Press of Mississippi, 1989.

St. John, Catherine. "A Narrative of Belonging: The Art of Beauford Delaney and Glenn Ligon." In *Proceeding for the School of Visual Arts Eighteenth Annual National Conference on Liberal Arts and the Education of Artists: Art and Story*, edited by Sherry Stone, 43–50. https://www.academia.edu/1411170/INTERPRETATION_NARRATIVE_AND_THE_STUDENTS_SEARCH_FOR_AN_ARTISTS_INTENTIONS.

St. John, Catherine. "Reality and Aesthetics: A Marxist and Crocean Interpretation of the Paintings of Beauford Delaney." In *NAAAS Conference Proceedings*, 397–414. Scarborough, ME: National Association of African American Studies, 2001.

Stroke! Beauford Delaney, Norman Lewis and Alma Thomas. New York: Michael Rosenfeld Gallery, 2005.

Thielemans, Veerle. "Beyond Visuality: Review on Materiality and Affect." *Perspective* 2 (2015). https://journals.openedition.org/perspective/5993.

Thorsen, Karen, dir. *James Baldwin: The Price of the Ticket*. Produced by Karen Thorsen and William Miles. DKDmedia, 1989. Film, 1 hr. 27 min.

Thorsson, Courtney. "James Baldwin and Black Women's Fiction." *African American Review* 46, no. 4 (Winter 2013): 615–31.

Thurman, Howard. *The Luminous Darkness*. New York: Harper and Row, 1965.

Toll, Martha Anne. "'Heavy' Brilliantly Renders the Struggle to Become Fully Realized." Review of *Heavy: An American Memoir*, by Kiese Laymon. *NPR Book Reviews*, October 17, 2018. https://www.npr.org/2018/10/17/657824190/heavy-brilliantly-renders-the-struggle-to-become-fully-realized.

Tomkins, Calvin. "Profiles: 'Putting Something over Something Else.'" *New Yorker*, November 28, 1977, 53–77.

Tompkins, Kyla Wazana. "Crude Matter, Queer Form." *ASAP/Journal* 2, no. 2 (May 2017): 264–68.

Traylor, Eleanor W. *The Humanities and Afro-American Literary Tradition*. Washington, DC: D.C. Community Humanities Council, 1988.

Tutuola, Amos. *The Palm-Wine Drinkard and His Dead Palm-Wine Tapster in the Dead's Town*. London: Faber and Faber, 1952.

van Alphen, E. J. "The Portrait's Dispersal: Concepts of Representation and Subjectivity in Contemporary Portraiture." In *Portraiture: Facing the Subject*, edited by Joanna Woodall, 239–56. Manchester: Manchester University Press, 1997.

Varnedoe, Kirk. "Picasso's Self Portraits." In *Picasso and Portraiture: Representation and Transformation*, edited by William Rubin and Anne Baldassari, 110–79. New York: Museum of Modern Art, 1996.

Vogel, Susan. Introduction to *Perspectives: Angles on African Art*, edited by James Baldwin and Michael John Weber, 10–17. New York: Center for African Art, 1987.

Wagner, Bryan. *The Life and Legend of Bras-Coupé*. Baton Rouge: Louisiana State University Press, 2019.

Wall, Cheryl. *On Freedom and the Will to Adorn: The Art of the African American Essay*. Chapel Hill: University of North Carolina Press, 2018.

Walsh, Melanie. "Tweets of a Native Son: The Quotation and Recirculation of James Baldwin from Black Power to #BlackLivesMatter." *American Quarterly* 70, no. 3 (2018): 531–59.

Ward, Jesmyn. *The Fire This Time: A New Generation Speaks about Race*. New York: Scribner, 2016.

Warner, Malcolm. "Portraits about Portraiture." In *The Mirror and the Mask: Portraiture in the Age of Picasso*, edited by Paloma Alarcó and Malcolm Warner, 11–23. New Haven, CT: Yale University Press, 2007.

Wells, Monique Y. "Beauford and the Michael Rosenfeld Gallery." *Les Amis de Beauford Delaney* (blog), March 2, 2010. http://lesamisdebeauforddelaney.blogspot.com/2010/03/beauford-and-michael-rosenfeld-gallery.html.

Wells, Monique Y. "Beauford Delaney and Paris: Evolution of an Exhibition." In *Beauford Delaney: Resonance of Form and Vibration of Color*, 42. Paris: Columbia Global Centers, 2016.

Wells, Monique Y. "Brief Musings on Beauford and James Baldwin." *Les Amis de Beauford Delaney* (blog), December 1, 2010. http://lesamisdebeauforddelaney.blogspot.com/2010/12/brief-musings-on-beauford-and-james.html.

Wells, Monique Y. "Welcome." *Les Amis de Beauford Delaney* (blog), December 14, 2009. http://lesamisdebeauforddelaney.blogspot.com/2009/12/welcome.html.

Wicks, Stephen C. "Beauford Delaney and James Baldwin: A Selected Timeline." In *Beauford Delaney and James Baldwin: Through the Unusual Door*, edited by Stephen C. Wicks, xv–xxi. Knoxville: University of Tennessee Press, 2020. https://knoxart.org/wp-content/uploads/2021/09/delany-baldwin-timeline.pdf.

Wicks, Stephen C., ed. *Beauford Delaney and James Baldwin: Through the Unusual Door*. Knoxville: University of Tennessee Press, 2020.

Wicks, Stephen C. "Beauford Delaney's 'Metamorphosis into Freedom.'" In *Beauford Delaney and James Baldwin: Through the Unusual Door*, edited by Stephen C. Wicks, 7–42. Knoxville: University of Tennessee Press, 2020.

Wilmerding, John. *Signs of the Artist: Signatures and Self-Expression in American Paintings*. New Haven, CT: Yale University Press, 2003.

Wood, Yolanda. "Beauford Delaney: Resonance of Form and Vibration of Color." In *Beauford Delaney: Resonance of Form and Vibration of Color*, n.p. Paris: Columbia Global Centers, Paris, 2016.

Wye, Pamela. "Beauford Delaney." *Arts Magazine*, Summer 1991, 71.

Wynter, Sylvia. "No Humans Involved: An Open Letter to My Colleagues." *Forum NHI* 1, no. 1 (1994): 42–71.

Wynter, Sylvia, and Katherine McKittrick. "Unparalleled Catastrophe for Our Species? Or, To Give Humanness a Different Future: Conversations." In *Sylvia Wynter: On Being Human as Praxis*, edited by Katherine McKittrick, 9–89. Durham, NC: Duke University Press, 2015.

Zaborowska, Magdalena J. *James Baldwin's Turkish Decade: Erotics of Exile*. Durham, NC: Duke University Press, 2009.

Zaborowska, Magdalena J. *Me and My House: James Baldwin's Last Decade in France*. Durham, NC: Duke University Press, 2018.

Zaborowska, Magdalena J., and David Leeming. "Remembering Sedat Pakay, 1945–2016." *James Baldwin Review* 3 (2017): 173–85.

CONTRIBUTORS

Hilton Als is an award-winning journalist, critic, and curator. He has been a staff writer at the *New Yorker* since 1994. Previously, Als was a staff writer at the *Village Voice* and an editor-at-large at *Vibe*. He has received numerous awards for his work, including the Pulitzer Prize for Criticism (2017), Yale's Windham-Campbell Literature Prize (2016), the George Jean Nathan Award for Dramatic Criticism (2002–3), and a Guggenheim Fellowship (2000). His first book, *The Women*, was published in 1996. His next book, *White Girls* (2013), was a finalist for the National Book Critics Circle Award and the winner of the Lambda Literary Award in 2014. His most recent book is *My Pinup* (2022). Als is a teaching professor at the University of California, Berkeley, and has taught at Columbia University's School of the Arts, Princeton University, Wesleyan University, and the Yale School of Drama.

Nicholas Boggs is the author of *Baldwin: A Love Story*, forthcoming from Farrar, Straus and Giroux, which has been supported by fellowships and grants from the National Endowment for the Humanities, the Leon Levy Center for Biography, the Whiting Foundation, the Scholars-in-Residence Program at the Schomburg Center, as well as the Gilder Lehrman Center and Beinecke Library at Yale. He is also the coeditor, with Jennifer DeVere Brody, of James Baldwin's collaboration with French artist Yoran Cazac, *Little Man, Little Man: A Story of Childhood* (2018), and he has published in *The Cambridge Companion to James Baldwin* (2015), *James Baldwin Now* (1999), *Callaloo*, and the *James Baldwin Review*. He is a 2024–25 Fellow at the National Humanities Center.

Indie A. Choudhury is Lecturer in Modern and Contemporary Art in Black Diasporas at the Courtauld Institute of Art, London. She is working on her first book project, a monograph on Frank Bowling's White Paintings, a body of work that spans six decades of his practice. She has published in *Nka: Journal of Contemporary African Art*, *Panorama: Journal of the Association of Historians of American Art*, and *caa.reviews*. She curated the exhibition *In Praise of Black Errantry* with Unit London at the Sixtieth Venice Biennale and co-edited the related exhibition catalogue.

Shawn Anthony Christian is Associate Professor of English and African American Studies and Chairperson of the Department of English at Florida International University. He is the author of *The Harlem Renaissance and the Idea of a New Negro Reader* (2016). His writings on James Baldwin, the Harlem Renaissance, and African American literature and print cultures also appear in the volumes *The Harlem Renaissance Revisited* (2010), *Reading African American Experiences in the Obama Era* (2012), *Editing the Harlem Renaissance* (2021), *African American Literature in Transition, 1930–1940* (2022), and *The Cambridge History of the American Essay* (2023); and in the journals *American Periodicals*, *College Language Association Journal*, and *Legacy: A Journal of American Women Writers*.

Rachel Cohen is Professor of Practice in the Arts, University of Chicago. She is the author of *Austen Years* (2020), *Bernard Berenson: A Life in the Picture Trade* (2013), and *A Chance Meeting: Intertwined Lives of American Writers and Artists* (2004), which won the 2003 PEN/Jerard Fund Award and was reissued for its twentieth anniversary by New York Review of Books Classics. She has been awarded a Guggenheim Fellowship, has written essays for the *New Yorker*, the *Guardian*, *London Review of Books*, *Apollo*, the *New York Times*, *The Nation*, *Threepenny Review*, *The Believer*, *McSweeney's*, and other publications, and her essays have been anthologized in *Best American Essays* and the Pushcart Prize anthology.

Amy J. Elias is Chancellor's Professor and Distinguished Professor of English at the University of Tennessee, Knoxville, where, since 2017, she has served as Director of the Denbo Center for Humanities and the Arts. She is the author of *Sublime Desire: History and Post-1960s Fiction* (2001), winner of the George and Barbara Perkins Book Prize from the International Society for the Study of Narrative; coeditor of *The Planetary Turn: Relationality and Geoaesthetics in the Twenty-First Century* (2015); coeditor of *Time: A Vocabulary of the Present* (2016); and author of more than forty articles and book chapters. She was principal founder of ASAP: The Association for the Study of the Arts of the Present and the founding coeditor-in-chief of *ASAP/Journal*.

Monika Gehlawat is Professor of English and Associate Director of the School of Humanities at the University of Southern Mississippi. She is the recipient of the Charles W. Moorman Distinguished Alumni Professor of the Humanities for 2023–25 and Series Editor for *Literary Conversations*. She is the author of *In Defense of Dialogue: Reading Habermas and Postwar American Literature* (2020) as well as numerous essays in such journals as *Post45: Peer-Reviewed*, *Contemporary Literature*, *James Baldwin Review*, *Word and Image*, *Literature, Interpretation, Theory*, and *Soundings*.

David Leeming is Professor Emeritus of English and Comparative Literature at the University of Connecticut in Storrs. He served as James Baldwin's assistant for many years and is the author of an authorized biography of Baldwin, *James Baldwin: A Biography* (1994), and the to-date foundational biography of Beauford Delaney, *Amazing Grace: The Life of Beauford Delaney* (1998). He is coauthor of *Gods, Heroes, and Kings: The Battle for Mythic Britain* (2001) and the author of numerous books on mythology, including *The Oxford Companion to World Mythology* (2005).

D. Quentin Miller is Professor of English at Suffolk University in Boston and the author or editor of three books on James Baldwin: *Re-Viewing James Baldwin: Things Not Seen* (2000), *"A Criminal Power": James Baldwin and the Law* (2012), and *James Baldwin in Context* (2019). He has also published more than two dozen articles or reference-volume entries on Baldwin and organized two conferences on the writer (Boston, 2009; Montpellier, France, 2013). He is coeditor of the anthologies *The Compact Bedford Introduction to Literature*, 13th edition, and *Literature to Go*, 5th edition (2024). His most recent book is *The Routledge Introduction to the American Novel* (2024).

Fred Moten is Professor in the Departments of Performance Studies and Comparative Literature at New York University. His recent projects include a poetry collection, *Perennial Fashion Presence Falling* (2023); a music album, *Fred Moten | Brandon López | Gerald Cleaver* (2023); an appearance in Wu Tsang's film *MOBY DICK; or, The Whale* (2022); and an essay collection, *All Incomplete* (2021), written with Stefano Harney.

Walton Muyumba is Ruth N. Halls Associate Professor in the Department of English at Indiana University–Bloomington. He is the author of *The Shadow and the Act: Black Intellectual Practice, Jazz Improvisation, and Philosophical Pragmatism* (2009). His scholarship has appeared in *Film Quarterly, Journal of Popular Music Studies, liquid blackness: journal of aesthetics and black studies, The Cambridge History of the American Essay, The Cambridge History of American Poetry, The Oxford Handbook of Critical Improvisation Studies,* and *Trained Capacities: John Dewey, Rhetoric, and Democratic Practice.* He has published personal essays and criticism in *Virginia Quarterly Review, Oxford American, New York Review of Books, The Nation, Los Angeles Times, The Atlantic,* and other outlets.

Robert G. O'Meally is Zora Neale Hurston Professor of English, Columbia University. He is the founder and director of Columbia's Center for Jazz Studies and the author of *Antagonistic Cooperation: Collage, Jazz, and American Fiction*; *The Craft of Ralph Ellison*; *Lady Day: The Many Faces of Billie Holiday*; *The Jazz Singers*; and *Romare Bearden: A Black Odyssey*. His edited volumes include *The Romare Bearden Reader*; *The Jazz Cadence of American Culture; Living with Music: Ralph Ellison's Essays on Jazz*; *The Norton Anthology of African American Literature* (coeditor); and the Barnes and Noble editions of Mark Twain, Herman Melville, and Frederick Douglass. For his production of a Smithsonian record set called *The Jazz Singers*, he was nominated for a Grammy Award.

Ed Pavlić is Distinguished Research Professor of English and African American Studies at the University of Georgia and author of thirteen books and pieces in seventy magazines, including *Who Can Afford to Improvise?: James Baldwin and Black Music*; *Crossroads Modernism: Descent and Emergence in African American Literary Culture* (2015); and the book-in-progress "No Time to Rest: James Baldwin's Several Lives." His awards include the Darwin Turner Memorial Award from *African American Review* (1997), the *American Poetry Review*/Honickman First Book Award (2001), the National Poetry Series Open Competition (2012, 2014), the Author of the Year award from the Georgia Writer's Association (2009, 2023), and the Staige D. Blackford Nonfiction Prize from *Virginia Quarterly Review* (2023).

Levi Prombaum is a Fulbright Postdoctoral Fellow in Tel Aviv studying the knotted histories of Israeli and Palestinian art. He has worked as a curator at Colby College Museum of Art and the Solomon R. Guggenheim Museum.

He served as an American Council of Learned Societies Leading Edge Fellow at Mass MoCA, where he directed the project Care Syllabus. He holds a PhD in History of Art from University College London, where he completed the dissertation "Disagreeable Mirror Though One May Be: Portraits of James Baldwin, 1945–1965." Prombaum has contributed art criticism to journals and collections, including the exhibition catalogue *Beauford Delaney: Through the Unusual Door.*

Robert F. Reid-Pharr is Professor of Social and Cultural Analysis at New York University. A specialist in African American culture and a prominent scholar in the field of race and sexuality studies, he has published four books: *Archives of Flesh: African America, Spain, and Post-Humanist Critique* (2016); *Conjugal Union: The Body, the House, and the Black American* (1999); *Black, Gay, Man: Essays* (2001); and *Once You Go Black: Choice, Desire, and the Black American Intellectual* (2007). His essays have appeared in, among other outlets, *American Literature, American Literary History, Callaloo, Afterimage,* *Small Axe, Chronicle of Higher Education, Women and Performance, Social Text, Transition, Studies in the Novel, African American Review, Feminist Formations, Art in America,* and *Radical America.* He was the recipient of a 2016 John Simon Guggenheim Memorial Foundation Fellowship.

Tyler T. Schmidt is Associate Professor of English at Lehman College, City University of New York. He is the author of *Desegregating Desire: Race and Sexuality in Cold War American Literature* (2013), and his critical work has appeared in *African American Review, Women Studies Quarterly, Radical Teacher, Postmodern Culture,* and *Of Latitudes Unknown: James Baldwin's Radical Imagination.* A Black Metropolis Research Consortium Summer Fellow in 2019, he is completing a manuscript centered on a group of queer writers and visual artists active in the Midwest in the 1950s and 1960s.

Abbe Schriber is Assistant Professor of Art History and African American Studies at University of South Carolina. Her writing has appeared in journals such as *Arts, Women and Performance,* and *Archives of American Art Journal,* and in catalogues for institutions such as the Solomon R. Guggenheim Museum, the Museum of Modern Art, and the Studio Museum in Harlem. She is currently finalizing her first book project, a study of David Hammons amid a network of interdisciplinary African American and Afro-Caribbean artists and legacies of the Black Arts Movement in 1970s–1980s New York.

Jered Sprecher is a practicing visual artist and Professor of Art at the University of Tennessee. He has had solo exhibitions at Jeff Bailey Gallery, New York; Wendy Cooper Gallery, Chicago; Steven Zevitas Gallery, Boston; Kinkead Contemporary, Los Angeles; Whitespace, Atlanta; Ferrara Showman Gallery, New Orleans; and Gallery 16, San Francisco. His work has been included in exhibitions at the Drawing Center, Brooklyn Academy of Music, Irish Museum of Modern Art, the Chinati Foundation, Espai d'Art Contemporani de Castelló, Weatherspoon Art Museum, Hunter Museum, and the Knoxville Museum of Art. Sprecher has been artist-in-residence at the Irish Museum of Modern Art, the Chinati Foundation, and the Marie Walsh Sharpe Space Program in New York. In 2009 he was the recipient of a John Simon Guggenheim Memorial Foundation Fellowship.

Stephen C. Wicks is the Barbara W. and Bernard E. Bernstein Curator at the Knoxville Museum of Art. He organized the museum's 2020 exhibition *Beauford Delaney and James Baldwin: Through the Unusual Door* and edited the related exhibition catalogue. This exhibition coordinated with University of Tennessee symposium "In a Speculative Light: The Arts of James Baldwin and Beauford Delaney," and he has since worked closely with the editor of the present volume as an arts adviser. He has served as curator of collections and exhibitions at the Columbus Museum (Georgia) between 2003 and 2006, and in a similar capacity at the Knoxville Museum of Art between 1993 and 2003. Wicks has organized dozens of exhibitions devoted to contemporary art, including *Forest of Visions* (1993), *Awakening the Spirits: Art by Bessie Harvey* (1998), *Richard Jolley: Sculptor of Glass* (2000), and *New Directions in American Drawing* (2006).

Magdalena J. Zaborowska is Professor in the Departments of American Culture and Afroamerican and African Studies at the University of Michigan. Her books include *Me and My House: James Baldwin's Last Decade in France* (2018); *James Baldwin's Turkish Decade: Erotics of Exile* (2009; MLA Prize winner); and *How We Found America: Reading Gender through East European Immigrant Narratives* (1995); as well as the edited and coedited collections *Other Americans, Other Americas: The Politics and Poetics of Multiculturalism* (1998); *The Puritan Origins of American Sex: Religion, Sexuality, and National Identity in American Literature* (2001); and *Over the Wall/After the Fall: Post-Communist Cultures in the East-West Gaze* (2004).

INDEX

Page references in italics indicate figures. JB stands for James Baldwin; BD for Beauford Delaney.

PLATE CREDITS

Plates 1, 4, 5, 12, 23, 24, 28, 29. Courtesy of Michael Rosenfeld Gallery LLC, New York, NY.

Plate 2. Knoxville Museum of Art, 2017 acquisition with funds provided by the Rachel Patterson Young Art Acquisition Reserve. Image courtesy of Knoxville Museum of Art.

Plate 3. Art Institute of Chicago, purchased with funds provided by Alexander C. and Tillie S. Speyer Foundation; Samuel A. Marx Endowment, 1991.27.

Plate 6. Terra Foundation for American Art, Chicago, Daniel J. Terra Art Acquisition Endowment Fund, 2018.2.

Plate 7. Knoxville Museum of Art, 2016 acquisition with funds provided by the KMA Collectors Circle with additional gifts from Barbara Apking, June and Rob Heller, Donna Kerr, Alexandra Rosen and Donald Cooney, Ted Smith and David Butler, Mimi and Milton Turner, John Cotham, Jan and Pete Crawford, Cathy and Mark Hill, Florence and Russell Johnston, John Z. C. Thomas, Donna and Terry Wertz, Jayne and Myron Ely, Sarah Stowers, Robin and Joe Ben Turner, and Jacqueline Wilson. Image courtesy of, and reproduced by permission of, Knoxville Museum of Art.

Plate 8. Museum of Modern Art, New York, Committee on Painting and Sculpture Funds. Reproduced by permission of Museum of Modern Art.

Plates 9, 13, 14a–b, 15, 20, 21, 30. Knoxville Museum of Art, 2018 acquisition with funds provided by the Rachael Patterson Young Art Acquisition Reserve, Ann and Steve Bailey in honor of Rachael Patterson Young, Natalie and Jim Haslam in honor of Lindsay Young, Molly and Bob Joy, the KMA Collectors Circle, The Knoxville (TN) Chapter of the Links Incorporated, Daniel McGehee, Marty Begalla, Nancy and

Charles Wagner III, June and Rob Heller, Sandi Burdick and Tom Boyd, the Guild of the Knoxville Museum of Art, Debbie and Ron Watkins, Emerson Automation Solutions, John Z. C. Thomas, Richard Jansen, John Cotham, Monica Crane and Luke Madigan, Susan and Kent Farris, Lane Hays, Sylvia and Jan Peters, Patricia and Alan Rutenberg, Barbara and Steve Apking, Pam and Jeff Peters, Ebbie and Ronald Sandberg, Barbara and Bernie Bernstein, Mardel Fehrenbach, Karen and Reinhold Mann, Penny Lynch and Kimbro McGuire, David Butler and Ted Smith, Home Federal Bank, Knoxville Airport Authority, Avice and Gary Reid, Jonida and Theotis Robinson, Mimi and Milton Turner, Kitsy and Lou Hartley, Diane Humphreys-Barlow and Jack Barlow, Debbie and Jimmy Jones, Merikay Waldvogel and Jerry Ledbetter, Meredith and Mark Overholt, Chris Powell, Alexandra Rosen and Donald Cooney, Sandy and Frank Steer, Donna and Terry Wertz, Jackie Wilson, Pat and Geoff Wolpert, Marie and Bob Alcorn, Susan and Jeff Arbital, Ursula Bailey, Janda and Adolphus Brown, Linda and John Haines, Alane and Jan Houston Hickman, Sandy and John Lucas, Venice Peeke, Dorothy and Caesar Stair, Brenda and Larry Thompson, Twuanna and Derick Ward, Gwen and Sam McKenzie, Wokie Massaquoi-Wicks and Stephen Wicks, Elnora and Erven Williams, Brenda Anderson, Evelyn Davidson, Gloria Deathridge, Kathy and Jack Gotcher, Denise DuBose and Francis Lloyd, Falen and Clark Gillespie, DeLena Feliciano, Anna Fraser and Douglas Goode, and Georgia and William Pace. Image courtesy of, and reproduced by permission of, Knoxville Museum of Art.

Plate 10. Smithsonian American Art Museum, Gift of the James F. Dicke Family.

Plate 11. Knoxville Museum of Art, 2014 acquisition with funds provided by Brenda and Larry Thompson. Image courtesy of Knoxville Museum of Art.

Plate 16. Chrysler Museum of Art, Norfolk, VA, museum purchase 2015.28.

Plate 17. Courtesy of The Hutchins Center for African and African American Research, Harvard University.

Plate 19. Courtesy of Christie's.

Plate 26. SCAD Museum of Art, Savannah, GA, permanent collection, gift of Dr. Walter O. Evans and Linda J. Evans.

Plate 27. Memorial Art Gallery of the University of Rochester, 2015.9, purchased with the Maurice R. and Maxine B. Forman Fund, Herdle Fund, Lyman K. and Eleanore B. Stuart Endowment Fund, Marion Stratton Gould Fund, and the Estate of Susan Eisenhart Schilling.

Plates 31, 32. Clark Atlanta University Art Museum, bequest of James Baldwin, 1995.005.011 and 1995.005.014.